Additional Praise For
The New Polymath

"Don't know what a Polymath is? If you learn and become one before your competitors do, you can eat rather than be eaten. Mirchandani's thoroughly insightful work will become 21st Century Acumen."
—Don Tapscott, Author of 14 books, including (with Anthony Williams) *MacroWikinomics: Rebooting Business and the World*

"*The New Polymath* brings to life the powerful idea of innovating by bringing the right mix of people together, regardless of function or geography. It's must reading for anyone leading multi-disciplinary teams or looking to drive innovation."
—Chris Curran, CTO, Diamond Management & Technology Consultants

"Every 10 to 15 years the technology industry reinvents itself, taking all the achievements and knowledge from the prior generation and turning them into a platform for new innovation. That regular cycle of rebirth has transformed the way we work, live and play—around the world. Mirchandani has done a fabulous job shining a light on examples of people and organizations that take what exists around us and turn it into what is possible. These are the innovators that inspire us."
—Dave Duffield, Co-CEO and Chief Customer Advocate, Workday; Former Chairman and CEO, PeopleSoft, Inc.

"Mirchandani has long been not only one of the leading enterprise software analysts, but someone who has always understood the value of innovation and ideas in the marketplace. *The New Polymath* is both a key discussion on how to innovate and who is innovating but also an appreciation of how we innovate. This isn't just a useful book, it's a must read."
—Paul Greenberg, Author of *CRM at the Speed of Light*

"Mirchandani describes a future of possibilities—'fortunate accidents of innovation'—enabled by the convergence of technologies with a dose of ideas from 'left field.' As the founder of Rural Sourcing, we believed in the untapped potential of our young people in Rural America. The possibilities are limitless when there are no geographic boundaries to our workforce and we can truly move the work to the worker rather than the worker to the work."

—Kathy Brittain-White, Former EVP and CIO, Cardinal Health; Founder, Rural Sourcing, Inc.

"*The New Polymath* takes a close look at the rate of innovation, not just in the U.S. but around the world, chronicling the rapid evolution of technologies and business. If you are wondering about the future, then find time to read this book."

—Om Malik, Author of *Broadbandits: Inside the $750 Billion Telecom Heist* & Founder, GigaOM.

"Mirchandani has done a great job tying together many of the multi-dimensional forces which are fueling a new generation of technological innovations aimed at addressing some of our most important business and social challenges."

—Jeffrey M. Kaplan, Managing Director of THINKstrategies and Founder of the SaaS Showplace

"Mirchandani produces the ultimate journey through the world of information technology innovation and its impact on today's globally integrated society. Not many evangelists have lived through IT/business innovation with the unique proximity of Mirchandani—his case discussions, interviews and perspectives are a truly enlightening experience to enjoy."

—Phil Fersht, Founder & CEO, Horses for Sources

"At *Science Debate*, we focus the attention of Presidential candidates on the *Top 14 Science Questions Facing America*. Solving them requires collaboration between technologists, economists, industrialists and governments. *The New Polymath* profiles numerous examples of this cross-silo innovation."

—Shawn Lawrence Otto, CEO and Cofounder, Science Debate, Inc

"As I watch Meg Whitman, my boss at eBay for seven years, pursuing one of the toughest jobs in the country—the Governor of California—and I am now focused on changing the world of work the same way we changed the world of ecommerce, I am inspired by this book. As you'll see when we all aim higher, and embrace the power of 'AND,' we are all capable of contributing far more than we imagined!"

—Maynard Webb, Chairman and CEO, LiveOps; Former COO, eBay

The New Polymath

The New Polymath

Profiles in Compound-Technology Innovations

VINNIE MIRCHANDANI

WILEY

John Wiley & Sons, Inc.

Library of Congress Cataloging-in-Publication Data

Mirchandani, Vinnie.
   The new polymath : profiles in compound-technology innovation / Vinnie Mirchandani.
      p. cm.
   Includes bibliographical references and index.
   ISBN 978-0-470-61830-1 (cloth)
1. Technological innovations.   I. Title.
   HC79.T4.M55 2010
   658.4′063—dc22   2010005944

ISBN 978-0-470-61830-1

Printed in the United States of America.

10 9 8 7 6 5 4 3 2 1

To Margaret, Rita, Tommy, and Peanuts—thanks for letting the book monopolize my time, which rightfully is yours.

Contents

Foreword

Vinnie Mirchandani aptly describes today's "dark ages" of information technology. Let me tell you how much darker it was eleven years ago when I started salesforce.com. Companies were paying hundreds of thousands to buy enterprise software, and then they were blowing millions to install it. The worst part? It didn't even work very well. A change was necessary, but the change we were advocating—delivering services through the Internet—wasn't readily accepted, or even understood.

The industry was suffering from "The Innovators Dilemma," a concept popularly attributed to mature technology companies. There were too many defenders of the status quo (analysts, media, investors) who were financially integrated into the current model and too self-interested to consider the potential for a better future.

But innovation was far from dead; it was just emanating from a different place than we were expecting. And, in fact, a revolution was underway. The rapid evolution of the Internet sparked an industrywide transformation. Innovative companies such as Amazon.com, eBay, and Yahoo! changed everything for consumers and changed the business landscape as well.

Inspired by the consumer Web, we developed a better way to serve enterprise customers. We knew we could deliver business applications cheaply through a Web site that was easy to use. The skeptics didn't think much of it (history always repeats; there's always persecution with some new ideas), but in just a few years we were able to transform the enterprise software industry. The old model of how people bought and built software was disrupted and the packaged services that companies used to buy separately from software vendors, systems integrators, hosting providers, and offshore application management firms were compounded into a single contract and service agreement.

The idea—and the rapid adoption of the cloud computing model—addressed the challenge of massive waste in most IT budgets. A recent Galorath study showed that our model led to a five-year cost savings of

78 percent and a development and time savings of 75 percent. Recycled-countertop maker Vetrazzo built a custom ERP suite at half the cost associated with a traditional software implementation; Japan Post Network created a custom app for 40,000 users in only two months; and Haagen-Dazs Shoppe built a franchise management app with no capital expense. We can look back and see that the last decade was the end of the dark ages and, in fact, the start of a period of enlightenment.

Now, in this new decade, the Renaissance continues—and matures. There has been massive innovation in mobile and social technologies that, when brought to the enterprise, will create more value for users, customers, and vendors by an order of magnitude over what we saw in the last wave. And while information technology continues to massively evolve, newer sectors of biotechnology and green technology have also been growing exponentially. This sets us up for the next revolution.

The best companies—from established corporations to pioneering start-ups—are creating incredible value by succeeding in a new way: amalgamating distinct strands of technology (infotech, cleantech, healthtech, nanotech, biotech) to create compound new products, services, and processes that address the big and small problems in this world. These are what Mirchandani calls the New Polymaths (Greek for the Renaissance men and women who excelled at multiple disciplines) and nothing captures this powerful, emerging pattern in the marketplace like this book.

I am honored that salesforce.com which amalgamates the consumer Web, social, and mobile technologies—as well as philanthropy to effect change—is profiled as a New Polymath. I am also humbled.

These pages are filled with incredible examples of passionate entrepreneurs, established leaders, and multinational companies innovatively leveraging technology to tackle big problems, "grand challenges," related to health, hunger, and natural disasters—and, of course, information technology. You'll meet individuals like Elizabeth Horn, the mother of a child with autism, who has created ChARMtracker, a Web-based treatment management software to get children, parents, and the medical community the important cause/effect data they need to identify biomarkers that may help guide treatments in the future. You'll be inspired by the "refugees" from information technology, like Ray Lane, who fled Oracle and now, as a VC, is investing in a new generation of cleantech companies addressing various energy and environmental challenges. You'll travel the halls of General Electric's Global Research Center and see how it brought together multiple technologies to respond to problems in healthtech with access to clean water supply.

The book shows us that the future can be brighter because people and companies are doing more by leveraging various technologies to make it so.

In what we can expect from someone as knowledgeable, prescient, and committed to industry disruption as Mirchandani, the most pivotal trends a company needs to know are illuminated. Through his R-E-N-A-I-S-S-A-N-C-E framework (each letter is a chapter that discusses a building block for the New Polymath), we learn about 11 key ideas: Residence; Exotics; Networks (Bluetooth to broadband); Arsonists; Interfaces; Sustainability; Singularity; Analytics; Networks (social); Cloud Computing; and Ethics. This is the first book to reveal why these changes are important and how to take full advantage of them for your business.

Mirchandani not only explores thought-provoking topics, but he walks us through compelling case studies and high-impact examples, such as how the Schumacher Group, through its aggressive deployment of cloud computing and MAXroam, will make the entire world one area code with no mobile roaming charges. We also learn where innovation is coming from (and where it's not), especially in telecom, where we see the biggest breakthroughs from Apple and Skype and Google and Ericsson, and less from the telcos themselves—an important theme, which we see mirrored in other industries (e.g., IT, publishing, music).

One of the best parts about this book is its courage to take a stand. Mirchandani is never afraid of saying what is required of us (he was known as a "growling tiger" at Gartner) and he closes his RENAISSANCE framework with a focus on ethics with conviction and compassion. This deftly harkens back to the historical polymath like Plato and Socrates, who were also philosophers—and is an idea that is timeless. Ethics must not be an afterthought, but woven into the culture of innovation.

We live in a time of great change and with that comes great responsibility. In today's business world, Milton Friedman's famous mantra "the business of business is business" is dated. The business of business is not only business. The business of business is to do good while doing well.

There is a way to combine creativity, ingenuity, and business acumen to address social issues—from substandard health care or schools in developing nations to problems with homelessness or illiteracy. We combined philanthropy into our business model. Our 1-1-1 model (1 percent employees' time; 1 percent equity; 1 percent product donation) has allowed us to donate more than $19 million in grants, deliver our service to over 8,000 nonprofits for no charge, and give more than 178,000 hours of community service. This charge also changed our company. It established us as a meaningful place to work and made us more committed to the success of our employees and our customers. And it was easy. Being a polymath isn't that difficult—and it always yields multidimensional rewards.

The New Polymath—a book about how to unlock innovation—is told through the perspective of a true innovation seeker who is dedicated to implementing productive and disruptive change. And what better guide to walk us through examples of a modern-day polymath than a true polymath himself? Mirchandani's varied career as a technology advisor, outsourcing executive, industry analyst, entrepreneur, and implementation consultant makes him one of the industry's most provocative thought leaders. Most important, his fresh insights and wise counsel prepares us for how to best navigate, compete, and flourish in this Renaissance.

The well-researched examples in this book will inspire you. But the people who are going to change the world aren't only in this book. They are reading this book. Join them—as entrepreneurs, as executives, as leaders. You are in a position to make a contribution to people's lives in a meaningful way. No large enterprise was ever built by addressing only a small market. And the world's problems are not a small market.

We are now in a time of extraordinary opportunity. People always ask me: What's in store for the future? Where is technology going? Where is philanthropy going? Predicting the future is simple. The future is whatever we imagine. What's ahead of us is whatever we innovate.

What do you see in the future? I see less disease. I see less poverty. I see new sources of energy, amazing advances in healthtech, and a planet on which the next generation can still breathe. I see hope because I know there's a generation of talented people out there combining a renaissance of new technologies to help us make pivotal changes.

You have the power to create or join organizations that address society's issues. You do not have to decide between making a social contribution or building a successful company or career. You can do many things. You can be a polymath. As Mirchandani says, "It's time for AND not OR."

Read on; be inspired. I'm looking forward to enjoying the future that we create.

Aloha,
MARC BENIOFF
Chairman and CEO of salesforce.com

Preface

Mick Jones of the band Foreigner says a fan who stood in the rain for hours to get a glimpse of the band inspired their hit "Juke Box Hero." Impressed with his dedication, the band rewarded him with a backstage tour and, of course, the song.

Substitute innovation for rock concert, and that describes this fan.

Over the last five years, I have cataloged close to 2,000 technologies, companies, and projects on my innovation blog. They cover more than 40 technology categories, from cloud computing to nanotechnology.[1] The innovation blog is my antidote from the day job, where I don't see enough innovation but plenty of greed and waste. For the last 15 years, at the research firm Gartner and in my own businesses since, I have helped clients navigate technology scenarios. I also write another blog on the economics of technology.[2] Based on a back-of-napkin calculation, my fingerprints are on $10 billion of technology contracts. Don't be too impressed—as a race, we spend more than $3 trillion *a year* on information technology. Much of it, unfortunately, is fat. When I first started at Gartner, if I saved a client 10 to 15 percent, I would feel we had justified our fees. In the last couple of years, I have renegotiated some contract renewals at 75 percent of the incumbent price. It is waste that makes the much-maligned $600 military commode look like chump change. Printer ink for $5,000-plus a gallon— yes, more than *1,000 times* what you pay for gasoline. Twenty-minute calls to software help desks, which amortize to over $10,000 each. Even more painful is when I see clients take savings that I and others deliver and apply them to compliance and control projects, not toward innovation. You can see why I don't mind standing in the rain for hours to catch glimpses of innovation.

Not all my innovation posts are business-related—several are about innovations that apply more to life and play. One was about the most-planned Space Shuttle mission, which fortunately never flew. Mission

STS-400 required two shuttles simultaneously at launch pads, ready to go, in May 2009 in case *Atlantis* needed rescuing. *Atlantis* was on a severely delayed trip to the Hubble Space Telescope, which unlike the International Space Station could not provide it shelter for weeks. The planning called for multiple rescue spacewalks and crash-landing sequences. Another post was about technology used in the Haitian earthquake relief and how it benefited from software written to coordinate Asian tsunami relief in 2004 and sensitive microphones and heat-seeking sensors developed after the 9/11 rescue experience.

One of my inspirations to start the blog was a visit to the Marriott Marquis in New York a few years ago. On previous stays, I had noticed long—sometimes seemed like 30 minutes long—waits for the elevator. You often had to also change elevators at the "hub"—the eighth-floor lobby level.

How do you add new or bigger elevators in a hotel without causing months of chaos? Particularly in a hotel that is bang in the middle of bustling Times Square—and that is a tourist attraction by itself. Innovatively, the hotel found a way out without adding any new elevators. A relatively simple solution of kiosks helped optimize the use of elevators. Users punch their destination floors in the kiosks, and algorithms group the users and direct them to specific elevators. Software and some electronics on the elevators had obviated months of likely chaos.

Nice, but hardly a complex problem compared to the some of the grand challenges the National Academy of Engineering has laid out, including ensuring plenty of clean water around the world and reverse engineering the brain.

Fortunately, as the database of posts grew year after year, I started to notice two patterns. I was seeing ever-more complex products and services that blended a variety of technologies. An example was General Electric's plans for the Net Zero Home (as in zero annual energy costs), which plans to bring together solar, wind, next-gen battery, smart grid interface technology, and energy management software to efficient appliances, water heaters, and other devices at home. Or the BP CTO group, which effortlessly weaves sensory networks, predictive analytics, and other technologies to bring innovation to a variety of refineries, exploration sites, and other aspects of its global reach.

I was also seeing refugees from information technology increasingly move into cleantech and healthtech. Ray Lane, ex Oracle, and Bill Joy, ex Sun, are key leaders at Kleiner Perkins, which has made 50-plus investments in cleantech. Little in Kleiner's past success as a venture capitalist in information technology (including blockbuster investments in Netscape, Amazon, eBay, and others) prepared it for a world of methane and selenium. Yet here the company is reinventing itself utilizing new sciences. Similarly, Shai Agassi left the German software giant SAP to found Better

Place, focused on services that electric cars increasingly call for. Likewise, Google, Microsoft, and others are increasingly offering products in the healthtech market.

Those are modern-day polymaths, I thought. Polymath, as in Greek for someone who excels in many disciplines, like Isaac Newton, the English physicist, astronomer, and philosopher, and Hypatia of Alexandria, who was a mathematician, astronomer, philosopher, and teacher.

We call them Renaissance men and women these days. They exemplify an AND not OR mind-set. Put many of them together and we have a fighting chance at solving some of our grand (and day-to-day) challenges.

I have had an interest, going back to 1993, in polymaths. How can I be so precise? That was the year a few Americans like me qualified for a green passport, instead of the usual blue-colored ones that had become standard in 1976. No, there was nothing special about us, and it did not recognize us as members of the Green Party. Celebrating 200 years of U.S. Consular Service, the Passport Office decided to issue green Benjamin Franklin commemorative passports that year.

Besides making me an owner of a collector's item, the green passport reacquainted me with Franklin. The last page in that passport described him as someone with "distinguished parallel careers as author, journalist, scientist, inventor, political philosopher and statesman."

That led me to read more about Franklin and to research other polymaths, including the ultimate polymath, Leonardo da Vinci, who was an artist, sculptor, architect, and so much more. Look up the term "Renaissance man" in an encyclopedia and Leonardo should be on prominent display.

So now I am fascinated when I meet someone like Andrea Olivieri, who is *direttore di crociera* in the Costa family of cruise ships. His job is to play master of ceremonies for the ship's varied entertainment. He introduces them in rapid-fire Italian, Spanish, German, French, and English. Then my wife pointed out that he is himself the star of many an event on the ship. He leads a lecture with PowerPoint slides and video clips that touch on the Fibonacci sequence, quantum physics, fractal geometry, and lots more. He leads another session that elaborates on his ship's technology—its azipod, its thrusters, and its satellite communications.

His job requires him to be charming and alert at all hours. But he is a chemical engineer by training and he has an MBA from the University of Southern California. He leads star-gazers at night on the ship's deck and points to "Taurus, the Bull defending the Seven Sisters from Orion the Hunter." He keeps switching between Taurus and *il Toro,* Italian for "bull," during that session. I later found out he also speaks Portuguese and is an avid sailor. He would have set Christopher Columbus straight. Leonardo would be proud of the modern-day Renaissance man from his country, hailing as he does from the city of Genoa.

Invoking the Spirit of the Renaissance

This book asks, What would Leonardo do today in the midst of our technology bounty? How wide would his vision of AND not OR be today?
Which disciplines would he choose to focus on: Nanotechnology?
Biochemistry? Would he work on architecture of next-generation green
cities? Prepare for the Mars shot? Or would he be told to quit dabbling and
be good at one thing—like plastics, à la Dustin Hoffman in *The Graduate*?
Given that the grand challenges have grown exponentially in the five centuries since Leonardo lived, the new polymath can no longer be just one
person but a collection of many. How would Leonardo leverage other
Leonardos and Olivieris?

Of course, the Renaissance was not just about Leonardo. It was also
about Michelangelo and tens of other polymaths. This book brings out the
diversity of today's Renaissance. There are hundreds of innovator companies and their products profiled, including large companies, such as Best
Buy and Starbucks. There are plenty of smaller companies, such as
Schumacher Group with its aggressive deployment of cloud computing.
I profile start-ups, such as Altimeter Group and also profile individuals,
such as Karin Morton and Dennis Howlett, and technologies that are allowing them to be extremely productive and connected with the world for a
pittance. The book covers many aspects of infotech, but it also touches on
healthtech and cleantech. There are plenty of examples from manufacturing
and financial services industries. But we also profile education companies
like DeVry and dairies run by farmers like Tony McCormack. There are
several examples from the larger countries, such as Germany, Japan, and
China. In addition, we also profile examples from Estonia, Rwanda, and
the United Arab Emirates, and innovative cities like San Francisco. There
are examples from larger technology vendors like Microsoft, IBM, and HP,
but many more from start-ups and mid-caps. I cover customer, human
resource, finance, and other business processes, not just research and
development. CIOs and vendor executives, venture capitalists, and industry
analysts; various journalists and bloggers are cited. The spirit of Leonardo
and Franklin—AND not OR—pervades this book.

The bulk of the book is organized around eight polymath enterprises
and 11 chapters around the acronym R-E-N-A-I-S-S-A-N-C-E. Each letter
explores a certain group of technologies and the problems they are
solving—or, in some cases, new issues and challenges they are raising. So,
the first *S* covers Sustainability and cleantech components. The second
S is for Singularity and covers healthtech. Each of those chapters profiles
5, 10, or 15 of the innovators just described, most speaking in the first
person. GE and BP CTO cut across a wide range of the R-E-N-A-I-S-S-A-

N-C-E building blocks. The other six polymaths—Cognizant, Plantronics, Hambrecht, Kleiner Perkins cleantech, the National Hurricane Center, and salesforce.com are associated with specific R-E-N-A-I-S-S-A-N-C-E building blocks—so salesforce.com is associated with the chapter covering *C* for cloud computing.

Polygons, as we may remember from high school geometry, can be three-sided triangles or five-sided pentagons or eight-sided octagons. They can be convex or concave. Their sides need not be equal. In other words, they can be virtually millions of shapes.

The polymaths I profile in this book represent similar diversity. So comparing number of products, locations, and the like, if salesforce. com is a triangle, the units of GE profiled would be an eight-sided octagon or a 10-sided decagon. If we profiled the whole global organization, it could be a 20-sided icosagon. Given the breadth of challenges China is tackling at the same time, that country would be a 50-sided pentacontagon.

The "more-sided" polymaths are trying to solve the really big, hairy problems. The "fewer-sided" ones are a bit less ambitious, but they are helping us run our enterprises and lives much better. We need all kinds. Given their diversity, there is no single "cookbook" for innovation, but in Chapter 22 we do summarize ten common themes.

Flow of the Book

The book is organized in three parts:

- Part I sets the stage for the challenges of today and opportunities for polymaths of today and profiles GE, a new polymath.
- Part II is organized around an acronym—R-E-N-A-I-S-S-A-N-C-E—each letter of which discusses a building block for the new polymath to leverage. *I*, for example, stands for interfaces. This part also profiles another six polymaths associated with one of the specific building blocks: salesforce.com with cloud computing.
- Part III is focused on how helping you groom your own new polymath. It profiles the BP CTO group, its tools and processes, and its vast ecosystem of innovation ideas. We also bring together common threads from the seven other polymath profiles and the 11 building blocks in Part II.

Let's go through each individually.

Part I: Sprezzatura: The Art of Making the Complex Look Easy

This part is made up of two setup chapters and one polymath profile:

Chapter 1, "The New Polymath: In an Age of 'Wicked Problems' and Technology Abundance." This chapter provides a historical perspective of polymaths like Leonardo and contrasts them to modern ones like Apple and its CEO, Steve Jobs. But the Renaissance was so called because there were plenty of Leonardos. Similarly, in our New Renaissance, even though most of attention seems to go to innovation in mobile and social technologies, there is plenty of complex industrial innovation going on.

Chapter 2, "Modern-Day Dark Ages: So Much Stagnation." *Renaissance*, by definition is "rebirth." The European Renaissance was an escape from the Black Death—the plague that decimated Europe—and the Dark Ages, a time of little intellectual progress. We describe the modern dark ages—massive waste in infotech, the rancor around sustainability and cleantech, and the wildly inconsistent availability of healthtech around the globe.

Chapter 3, "Polymath Profile #1: General Electric." Here we present the first of our eight polymath profiles and explore four aspects of innovation at GE at its Global Research Center: its "Magic Factory," at corporate IT, how it brought together multiple technologies in its Net Zero Home concept and with an agile—a rapid deployment—project in the highly regulated environment at GE Healthcare. It showcases how GE is rising to help respond to some of the challenges we discussed in Chapter 2.

Part II: The R-E-N-A-I-S-S-A-N-C-E Framework: Building Blocks for the New Polymath

This part is the bulk of the book with 11 chapters depicting the R-E-N-A-I-S-S-A-N-C-E framework—each of which discusses a building block for the new polymath to leverage. *C*, for example, stands for cloud computing. This part also interweaves another six polymaths associated with one of the specific building blocks—for example, Plantronics with Networks:

Chapter 4, "Residence: Better Technologically Equipped Than the Office." This chapter explores consumerization of technology and how in industry after industry customers are becoming technologically more savvy than employees. And the economics in the consumer world are dramatically lower even at their bite-size procurement units. The consumerization trend has been accelerating for the last decade, yet in many enterprises, the prime response has been a sexier graphical user interface around their business applications to make them more alluring to younger staff.

Chapter 5, "Exotics: Innovation from Left Field." "Not invented here" used to be a defense mechanism. When former communist countries have some of the best telecom infrastructure in the world, something has really changed. When public utilities are hotbeds of innovation, you know the changes are tectonic. There are few barriers to entry—other than closed minds—and innovation is coming from all kinds of new geographies, verticals, and business processes. The next polymath profile for Cognizant is associated with this chapter.

Chapter 6, "Polymath Profile #2: Cognizant." Francisco D'Souza, the CEO of Cognizant, seeks out "innovation from left field." Over the last few years, he has grown 50 technology service delivery centers in India, Argentina, Hungary, the Philippines, China, and elsewhere. That's something far more mature companies have not done as successfully.

Chapter 7, "Networks: Bluetooth to Broadband." The radio spectrum is sliced thinly into land mobile, land mobile satellite, maritime mobile, maritime mobile satellite, and many more. These divisions reflect the proliferation of gadgets, the number of phone numbers and sign-on IDs and passwords we possess. Most telecommunications innovation is not coming from telcos; it is coming from the likes of Apple, Skype, Google and Ericsson. That in itself is a sea change. The polymath profile for Plantronics is associated with this chapter.

Chapter 8, "Polymath Profile #3: Plantronics." Neil Armstrong used a Plantronics headset when he spoke his famous words from the moon in 1969. Since then, Plantronics has navigated call centers spawned by toll-free calling, the growth of small and home offices, and now mobile communications. Its devices are polymaths that "unify" communications: They converge landline, VoIP (Voice over Internet Protocol), and mobile calls with audio streaming and software telephony while bringing a keen sense of consumer tastes in their design.

Chapter 9, "Arsonists (and Other Disruptors)." In technology, we have long benefited from Moore's Law—where the next generation of technology disrupts the previous one. Well, at least we like to think so. In fact, the majority of technology spend is in software, services, and telecom, which has little to do with transistor economies. So we need external disruptors like Rimini Street, Zoho, and Cartridge

World, and HP disrupting Cisco in networking, or SAP disrupting Oracle in analytical tools. These rebels are helping innovate economics in technology. The profile on Bill Hambrecht that follows is associated with this chapter.

Chapter 10, "Polymath Profile #4: W. R. Hambrecht." Bill Hambrecht had a successful investment bank that took public a number of disruptive technology vendors. Instead of retiring after that successful three-decade career, he launched a new firm to disrupt the established Wall Street method of pricing initial public offerings. Recently he has launched the United Football League in a market long dominated by the NFL.

Chapter 11, "Interfaces: For All Our Senses." How we interact with computers is undergoing a radical shift. The keyboard and the mouse are still around, but auto companies, in particular, are innovating with new approaches involving haptics, voice, and location. There are all kinds of exotic bar codes and scanners, even brain–machine interfaces. As consumer and work generational differences become more pronounced, organizations will need to leverage an even wider range of interfaces.

Chapter 12, "Sustainability: Delivering to Both the Green and Gold Agendas." Sustainability is about reducing demand for fossil fuels and increasing supplies of renewable fuels, such as solar and wind. It is also about local, organic produce, and other lifestyle changes people are making. In this chapter, we explore how individuals, enterprises, cities, and countries—often with competing agendas—actually make technology one of the least complex areas to navigate. The profile in Chapter 13 is associated with this chapter.

Chapter 13, "Polymath Profile #5: Kleiner Perkins Cleantech." Kleiner, the storied venture capitalist—which made whopping investments in infotech, from Netscape to Amazon to Google—has moved into cleantech. It has a portfolio of 50-plus companies doing work with smart grids, next-generation batteries, and wind technology. To do so, it has had to learn, polymath style, new sciences and disciplines far removed from its historical roots.

Chapter 14, "Singularity: Human–Machine Convergence." There is a convergence coming. Human beings are gradually leveraging personalized medicine, replacement body parts, and other technological advances to live better and become much more productive. In many enterprises, over 75 percent of messaging today is between nonhumans—it is called the "Internet of things." Sensors, motes, devices, servers, and robots are doing so much that humans did before. Smart enterprises are leveraging this convergence of humans and things.

Chapter 15, "Analytics: Spreadsheets, Search, and Semantics." If you think you are drowning in data, this chapter will depress you. Think of a quadrant with internal/external as the x-axis and structured/unstructured as the y-axis. So far, most enterprises primarily have tackled the internal/structured quadrant. That's why most business forecasts failed so miserably in the last economic meltdown. Opportunities to better visualize that growing mountain of data and the need to store it more efficiently lead to innovation in deduplication and optimized tiering of storage devices. The profile in Chapter 16 is associated with this chapter.

Chapter 16, "Polymath Profile #6: National Hurricane Center." The NHC mines a wide range of data sources: satellites, dropsondes, "Hurricane Hunters" and water based sensors. That's not data you can Google or get from Bloomberg. It then crunches multiple models on supercomputers and presents them in a wide range of reports and graphs. Of course, what matters is that it reduces, year after year, the "false positives" that cause unnecessary and expensive evacuations. That is why we present the NHC as the polymath when it comes to analytics.

Chapter 17, "Networks Again: Communities, Crowds, Contracts, and Collaboration." The networks this time are about people or, as Cisco calls it, it's about the human network. Love it or ban it, you have to admire the massive scale at Facebook. More than 400 million members and a billion chat messages each day. At peak times, it serves more than 1.2 million photos every second. It is teaching us about communities. An even more interesting development concerns the use of crowds as a talent source. Of course, employees and contractors continue to be the major talent source for companies. Technology is helping manage that talent in a number of recruiting, training, and administrative areas. No wonder the term "human resources management" is considered so 1990s. It is now about talent management in its various forms.

Chapter 18, "Clouds: Technology-as-a-Service." Cloud computing is an exciting new paradigm where you can buy applications, development platforms, and IT infrastructure "by the drink." This market is spawning a new generation of vendors, tools, and metrics. It is also forcing vendors to become polymaths and understand many new disciplines around operations, data centers, networks, and more. The salesforce.com profile in the next chapter is associated with this chapter.

Chapter 19, "Polymath Profile #7: salesforce.com." salesforce.com is a cloud computing pioneer that combines services that enterprises used to buy separately from software vendors, systems integrators, hosting providers, and offshore application management firms. Marc Benioff, the colorful leader of the company, has launched a new religion with its own set of passionate supporters and detractors.

Chapter 20, "Ethics: In an Age of Cyberwar and Cloning." Look back at historical polymaths and you see many were also philosophers. This chapter, different from the preceding ones, is not so much about innovative companies or products but includes perspectives from several industry observers on the ethical issues being spawned by technology. These include issues around privacy, the biofuel/ food trade-off, "God powers" around genetics and nanotechnology, tech/life balance, government surveillance, and censorship. Ethics cannot be an afterthought as we innovate.

Part III: Grooming Your Own New Polymath

This part has one polymath profile and two other chapters that focus on tools to help develop and nurture your own polymath enterprise.

Chapter 21, "Polymath Profile #8: BP CTO." See the tools and vast innovation sources this small group leverages as it rolls out sensory networks, predictive analytics, 3-D virtualization—years ahead of mainstream market adoption—to the vast BP energy family across the globe.

Chapter 22, "Moon Shots for Budding Polymaths." This chapter weaves together learning from the eight polymath profiles and the hundreds of other innovators whose voices were presented in the R-E-N-A-I-S-S-A-N-C-E chapters. It does so in the form of conferences that develop challenges to the enterprise that wants to become a polymath. We bring to life 10 polymaths from history to host this event and help guide the discussions.

"Epilogue." Markets continue to evolve, technologies continue to converge, and new disruptive players continue to emerge. This chapter presents a Zen Buddhist concept that refers to wide openness when studying a subject. It is a good approach to finding innovation even in the midst of constant change and turmoil.

What Got Left Out?

What about space exploration? What about new converging markets like bioinformatics? Why not open source in the chapter on arsonists? What about new contracting and intellectual property issues in the world of massively shared, multitenancy clouds? What about peers and competitors of companies profiled in this book—are they sitting still, or innovating on their own? These are all fair questions.

As I wrote the book, I felt like Francis Ford Coppola editing *The Godfather.* Plenty was originally left behind in the director's cut. In fact, the studio made him add almost 50 minutes back to the movie when it was released. In my case, some of those "50 minutes" can be found in online materials at www.thenewpolymath.com and on my two blogs. These are living, breathing documents—compared to a printed book that can be only a snapshot.

Of course, I would welcome reader comments and conversations. Regarding ethics in Chapter 20, for example, I would be delighted to hear that some of you had a brown-bag lunch where you discussed (or argued) with your peers or friends the various sides of each scenario. Your attorneys probably will have guidelines on how and where you can discuss ethical topics around your own products, but the key is to get comfortable discussing the tough, often emotional, topics.

The goal of the book, of course, is not to make you uncomfortable. We know the ratio of "oh no" to "aha" is off kilter. This book's goal is to help you reverse that ratio in big and small innovation opportunities.

Join me in the rain—fellow Juke Box Heroes!

Acknowledgments

I profile hundreds of innovators in this book. Many more helped coordinate those conversations. To each, a heartfelt thank-you. In this section, I want to acknowledge those who went out of their way to be generous, such as Mark Mastrianni at GE. I cold-called him. He could have ignored me. He's not naive either. He told me he did his homework on me, and then called me back. On weekends and nights he shared time around his busy schedule and made other introductions in the GE family. When I told him I owed him a nice dinner, he said, "Now you know I am not a big fan of SG&A in technology. Don't go increasing yours. Besides, GE policy would not let me." Wow!

Many people opened up their Rolodexes and said you should also talk to so and so. The winner in this category is Zach Nelson. Not only did he spend time talking about NetSuite (in Chapter 18), he also introduced me to his wife, Elizabeth Horn, who discusses ChARM (in Chapter 14). Autism is not easy on parents, so I particularly appreciated their openness. Zach also introduced me to the legendary Bill Hambrecht, profiled in Chapter 10, and to Steve Yeffa of Cartridge World, a customer of his, profiled in Chapter 9.

Ray Lane at Kleiner offered me introductions to several more of his cleantech portfolio companies than I have profiled. Carol Comeaux allowed me to pick from a wide portfolio of BP CTO group innovation projects. Karen Auby kept showcasing product after product at Plantronics. Carlye Adler offered episode after episode of Marc Benioff's exhilarating decade at salesforce.com and along with Jane Hynes details of Benioff's own experience writing a bestselling book. Balakrishna Narasimhan (Nara) and others at Appirio showcased their own operations and their projects at Avon and Starbucks, among others. Troy Angrignon, who shared his personal guiding principles (in Chapter 20), was full of other introductions and ideas. Peggy Taylor at B Cubed Ventures offered several introductions beyond FICO I profile in Chapter 15. My entire list of blogger colleagues offered input, and you hear many of their voices in the chapters that follow.

Judith Rothrock of JRocket Marketing introduced me to Agresso, which is profiled in Chapter 9, and whose Swedish customer, Offentliga Dokument, is profiled in Chapter 11 and to Corefino, profiled in Chapter 17. She also inspired me to bring the 10 polymaths from history back to life in Chapter 22. She had invited me to her annual Grape Escape Analyst Event, which was held at the historic Old State House in Boston. There was President John Adams, circa 1809, in his traditional costume mingling with an audience two centuries later talking about his peer founding fathers and his uncomfortable time as the first U.S. ambassador to England.

Paul Greenberg, author of a very successful book on CRM and with a brutal travel schedule, somehow found hours to coach me. Jeffrey Word, David Axson, Howard Dresner, Nenshad Bardoliwalla, Jon Reed, and Phil Simon—each a seasoned author—usually responded within minutes to my queries about the mysteries of the publishing process. Jim Spath, Charlotte Otter, Kimberly Baker, Gretchen Lindquist, Dennis Howlett, Sean Mirchandani and Debbie Brown unselfishly proofed and critiqued various drafts. May every author have such a supportive ecosystem.

Everyone I interviewed has shared personal details or proprietary business nuances some would say they were stupid to share. Innovation, after all, brings competitive advantage. The reality is that they are big believers in sharing and learning from others. Most of them spent hours patiently explaining things to me. As far as competitive advantage: Trust me, they have moved on to newer innovations.

Brian Sommer, my cofounder in a prior start-up, and Charlie Bess of EDS, now part of HP, deserve credit for inspiring some of my thinking. At various points I had discussed coauthoring a book with each. The style we had discussed would have been more in our voices, less that of the polymaths and innovators I ended up profiling. In the future, perhaps I can still collaborate with them—as I mentioned, there is plenty more to cover. Brian does contribute a perspective in Chapter 20 as he asks: "Where are the 10 Commandments for Technology?"

How do you express enough gratitude to those who review books? It takes passion for technology and a love of reading to take time out of busy schedules and pore through hours of proofs. So many executives, successful authors and industry observers (listed on the back cover and in the front pages) took time out to review this book—it is testament to their commitment to helping technology make work, life, and play better.

Of course, I owe a debt of gratitude to Benioff—for the foreword. He is a colorful, passionate technology leader who you will read about in Chapter 19—but what I admire is how he treats his people and how responsive he is even to casual acquaintances. While he is clearly a technology pioneer, he is also a philanthropy pioneer. His 1-1-1 model—1 percent of equity to a foundation, 1 percent of the company's product to nonprofits, and 1 percent of employee time to community service is a generous and innovative way to help society.

Finally, I want to thank John DeRemigis, Emilie Herman, and Andy Wheeler at John Wiley & Sons, Inc.—of course, for their editing and marketing efforts on the book, but just as important, for continuing to encourage me to stick with the title. I loved it to start with but got increasingly nervous as I presented at various conferences and polled audiences. Very few had heard the term "polymath."

Here we are with new polymaths throughout the book, and many of them from the past, like Thomas Jefferson and Shen Kuo, brought back to life. We need all the help we can get with the grand and not-so-grand challenges we all face today.

Prologue

The Field of
Polymath Dreams

It had been a glorious few days. This Tuscan evening promised to be the icing on the cake. The rows of long tables had been laid out in a field with a stunning view of rolling mustard fields and grapevines. In the distance was the walled medieval town of Sam Gimignano, whose castles and towers had been home for many of the guests. Crisp linen, Italian lace, and Murano crystal decorated the tables.

Christine Virsunen, who arranged all the conference logistics, had lived up to her promise with the meals: Little of the food had seen the inside of a fridge. As she had planned the meals, for a moment she had wished she could have had her Bay-area suppliers, Riverdog Farms and Driscoll's, do the catering. Then she chided herself—how can you go wrong with the local pecorino cheese, the Panzanella bread salad, and the bistecca alla fiorentina?

Of course, she had panicked when *they* had arrived. Not just her, the whole conference was thrown into a tizzy. There had been no voice announcing they might come. They had shown up from the past, nonetheless like Shoeless Jackson and the others in the movie.

Karin Morton tried to text "OMG" to her mother on her iPod Touch and forgot there was no Wi-Fi in that conference room. After years of fattening her Brazilian telephone carriers, she had weaned herself off voice or data plans on any carrier. She did fine with Skype wherever she could find Wi-Fi. So she did the next best thing without Wi-Fi—just kept whispering "wow!" to herself as *they* walked in one by one.

They—as in Michelangelo and Plato. And Leonardo da Vinci, Thomas Jefferson, Isaac Newton, Socrates, Hypatia of Alexandria, Shen Kuo, Nasir al-Din al-Tusi, and Benjamin Franklin. Yes, 10 polymaths from history. They said they had heard about this gathering of modern-day technology polymaths and decided to partake.

So the conference agenda had been redone so each of these historic giants could lead sessions and impart their wisdom. Frankly, the polymaths from the past seemed more fascinated with today's technologies. Leonardo insisted on sitting next to the GE Aircraft Engines team—and hearing about how aviation has evolved since his vision of Flying Machines. Shen Kuo acknowledged he was mightily impressed—and terrified—by the pace of change in modern China. Newton was fascinated to hear about the Hubble Space Telescope.

There were awkward moments. Google had to rush to the conference a still-experimental contraption that brought its Voice and Translate features together so the Masters could communicate with the group. Leonardo and Michelangelo still hated each other after six centuries. Someone asked Ben Franklin to reconcile his views on chastity with his many mistresses. Everyone worried if the Italian Polizia would come knocking for these visa-less visitors.

It was mostly magical, though. The group had chuckled at how different the old and new "earth is flat" arguments are and yet how the arguers continue to be so passionate. There were back-to-the-future conversations. Would Google Maps have changed the course of the spread of the Black Plague and European history? How would GPS have affected Columbus's travels and world history?

Then Karin started whispering to herself again. Michelangelo had stood up and called everyone to attention.

He toasted the *uomo universale*, the Italian term for polymath. He invoked the *zeitgeist* his Renaissance-era contemporary Leon Battista Alberti summarized as:

"A man can do all things if he but wills them."

PART I

Sprezzatura

The Art of Making the Complex Look Easy

Sprezzatura is a term from the Italian Renaissance that would translate to what we would today call "being cool"—a certain nonchalance even when tackling complex assignments. It is a good way to describe this lead-in part, which consists of three chapters:

- Chapter 1 defines the new polymath and explains how many of them are coming together to solve many of our "grand challenges."
- Chapter 2 lays out the modern-day version of the Dark Ages. In spite of huge budgets for infotech, cleantech, and healthtech, there is plenty of "nothingness" and stagnation.
- Chapter 3 looks at our first polymath profile—General Electric—and showcases how its research and development and information technology units are tackling some of the challenges in infotech, cleantech, and healthtech.

CHAPTER 1

The New Polymath: In an Age of "Wicked Problems" and Technology Abundance

The dying curator at the Louvre assumes the position of the *Vitruvian Man*. An ultraviolet light reveals an anagram scribbled in invisible ink next to him, pointing to the *Mona Lisa*. The bulletproof glass case around the *Mona Lisa* shows another puzzle, which decodes to *Madonna of the Rocks*. Behind that painting is a key, a clue to a whole new set of adventures, including speculation about who really sat with Jesus at *The Last Supper*.

Contrived? Blasphemous?

Whatever you may think of Dan Brown's book *The Da Vinci Code*[1] or Tom Hanks's acting in the movie, they introduced the work of Leonardo da Vinci to a new set of fans. The book and movie, however, only scratched the surface of Leonardo's body of work.

Martin Kemp has spent a lifetime studying Leonardo. He helped design the parachute based on a drawing of Leonardo's that was used in a successful 3,000-foot jump. He collaborated on a contraption that mimicked Leonardo's flying machine. More substantively, the Oxford University professor has written several books on Leonardo's works. He also organized "Universal Leonardo," a European tour of the artist's work. Long after the exhibits ended, a Web site keeps their visuals alive, showing Leonardo's portfolio: 25 paintings, 22 manuscripts, 10 inventions, and 50 drawings.[2]

Even that doesn't cover Leonardo's work as an architect for bridges and even entire cities, his talent as a musician especially on the lyre, the fables he wrote for children, his unfinished sculptures of horses, his work on botany and on human anatomy.

President John F. Kennedy said, when honoring Nobel Prize winners at a White House dinner in 1962, "I think this is the most extraordinary collection of talent, of human knowledge, that has ever been gathered

3

together in the White House—with the possible exception of when Thomas Jefferson dined alone."[3]

Kennedy was describing a polymath—which is Greek for someone of learning in many fields of study. In modern times, we call polymaths Renaissance men and women.

Over the centuries, around the world, we have seen polymaths such as Cicero, the Roman orator, philosopher, statesman, and lawyer; Hypatia of Alexandria, a mathematician, astronomer, and philosopher; Akbar "the Great," the Mughal Indian emperor gifted in many skills; Isaac Newton, the English physicist, astronomer, and philosopher; and Mary Somerville, from Scotland, who wrote on a wide range of subjects, including astronomy, geology, and physics. We met some of these polymaths in the prologue and will meet others in Chapter 22.

Even among these giants, Leonardo set a high-water mark. Mention Renaissance man, and most people will immediately think of Leonardo.

The Modern-Day Technology Polymath

Fast-forward six centuries and travel six thousand miles west from the small town of Cupertino in the heel of the boot of Italy, Leonardo's birth country, to a modern-day Leonardo, who is holding court in the namesake town in California.

Steve Jobs is explaining one major reason for the iPhone's success—Apple's ability to integrate hardware *and* software engineering: "We realized that almost all—maybe all—of future consumer electronics, the primary technology was going to be software. And we were pretty good at software. . . . None of the handset manufacturers really are strong in software."[4]

That is a modern polymath at work—integrating multiple modern disciplines. An AND versus an OR mind-set.

Tear down an iPhone 3GS and it shows Bluetooth AND Wi-Fi AND GPS transceivers AND lenses AND chips AND circuits AND batteries—a marvel of miniaturization. It functions as a Web access device, a camera, a music player, a navigation device, a compass, a voice recorder, a modem, and more—and, of course, it is also a phone.

That is a polymath as devices go.

Historically, the telecommunications device market has been fragmented. Nokia, successful in many parts of the world, is a small player in the U.S. market. Japan, which is the gadget exporter to the world, spectacularly failed with its mobile devices outside its shores.

Then along came Apple and launched the 3G version of the iPhone in 22 countries in 2008, with another 50-plus countries following over the next few months. Among the carriers it coordinated the rollout with were

VimpelCom in Russia, three companies in Hong Kong, Etisalat in Dubai, and Telia in Sweden. Most readers would not call them household names.

That is a Renaissance enterprise as global citizenship goes.

If there is one negative in the iPhone's huge success, it concerns problems with AT&T's cellular network—the company with which Apple signed an exclusive agreement for the U.S. market. Can you imagine if Apple had also taken on the task of integrating the network piece? The idea isn't far-fetched for a company that had tackled music with iTunes and is now poised to focus on TV shows and publishing with the iPad and for an executive who also made movies at Pixar.

Okay, so we have unrealistic expectations. And why not? Like Leonardo, Steve Jobs and Apple have raised the bar for modern polymaths.

Yes, but . . .

Apple is impressive, but surely music and mobile apps pale when we look at the complex challenges the world faces. So it is good to see what companies like BASF are doing to help with the world's food supply chain.

BASF brands itself "The Chemical Company." That moniker is too narrow when you look at the technologies it deploys in its quest for better strains of rice. Its Metanomics unit in Berlin, Germany, studies the changes that occur when an individual gene in a plant's genetic code is modified. A few hundred miles away, the Ghent, Belgium greenhouse of its CropDesign unit, uses robots, conveyor belts, radio-frequency identification chips, high-resolution cameras, and software algorithms to find the best rice seedlings.

The metabolite research from Berlin and the phenotype research from Ghent are combined into "bio-informatics" knowledge base, one of the largest gene-function databases in the world. What's impressive is the wide range of infotech and biotech components it leverages. That is the New Polymath—comfortable with a wide range of technologies.

Comfortable, of course, means deeply specialized. Modern cars now run on tens of millions of lines of code of software. As showcased in Chapter 11, you could argue the auto industry is miles ahead of the average software vendor when it comes to innovation in user interfaces. Modern polymaths don't just dabble in multiple technologies; they often lead the specialists in many of them.

The emergence of such polymaths is timely. We face many "grand challenges."

Our "Grand Challenges"

John Kao, a former Harvard Business School professor and entrepreneur, says we face "wicked problems" of global concern—around climate, disease, and financial meltdowns. Kao founded the Institute of Large Scale

Innovation, where he convenes innovation-savvy officials from around the world so they can explore models for collaboration and stewardship.[5]

Others call these hairy issues the world's "grand challenges."

The tradition of grand challenges dates back to David Hilbert, the mathematician. Preparing for a conference in 1900, he asked a colleague what a compelling presentation topic would be and was recommended the following: "Most alluring would be the attempt to look into the future and compile a list of problems on which mathematicians should test themselves during the coming century."[6]

The end result was Hilbert's list of 23 (he dropped 1 from an original list of 24 in his final paper) problems that continue to challenge us, even into the twenty-first century.

Hilbert's challenges have led to many lists of grand challenges over the last few years across many disciplines. One of the better-known lists is one developed by the National Academy of Engineering in 2008, which challenges:

- Make solar energy economical
- Provide energy from fusion
- Develop carbon sequestration methods
- Manage the nitrogen cycle
- Provide access to clean water
- Restore and improve urban infrastructure
- Advance health informatics
- Engineer better medicines
- Reverse-engineer the brain
- Prevent nuclear terror
- Secure cyberspace
- Enhance virtual reality
- Advance personalized learning
- Engineer the tools of scientific discovery[7]

In 2000, the United Nations (UN) adopted eight millennium development goals to be achieved by 2015. They are:

1. Eradicate extreme poverty and hunger
2. Achieve universal primary education
3. Promote gender equality and empower women
4. Reduce child mortality
5. Improve maternal health
6. Combat HIV/AIDS, malaria, and other diseases
7. Ensure environmental sustainability
8. Develop a Global Partnership for Development[8]

While cynics will say the UN missed "boil oceans," it is tracking these goals along 21 quantifiable targets that are measured by 60 indicators. There is a lot to be accomplished in the five years left—which should motivate plenty of innovation.

Compared to those challenges, a list of seven IT challenges that Gartner, the research firm, issued in 2008 sounds downright mundane:[9]

1. Never having to manually recharge devices
2. Improve parallel programming
3. Develop nontactile, natural computing interfaces
4. Improve automated speech translation
5. Develop persistent and reliable long-term storage
6. Increase programmer productivity 100-fold
7. Improve financial models for IT investing

"Challenge" has entered the lexicon of many innovation shops. In the BP CTO profile in Chapter 21, you hear the challenges their business unit customers invite them to help solve. In turn, they throw out challenges to their "seeker" network.

Why just look at the big, hairy UN challenges? Frank Scavo, president of Computer Economics, an IT research and advisory firm that provides metrics for IT management, also sees "grand challenges" in small to midsize enterprises. Scavo elaborates:

These growing organizations need plenty of IT support. And today's small organization is often multinational from day one. So, Quickbooks used to be fine for many companies till they crossed a certain revenue threshold. Often that's not true anymore. They are also dealing with more tech-savvy consumers than a small company did a few years ago. But with limited IT budgets, they have to seek resources that can wear many hats.

An Extinct Species in Our Complex World?

As Yogi Berra quipped, "The future ain't what it used to be." Ray Kurzweil, famous for his vision of _singularity_ (described more in Chapter 14), is a bit more precise: "We won't experience 100 years of progress in the 21st century—it will be more like 20,000 years of progress (at today's rate)."[10]

With that explosion in knowledge, we survive by specializing. Sometimes organizations encourage it to mitigate risk. Scavo again: "I have seen several instances where small and midsize businesses are effectively held hostage by one or two key IT staff members, who are the only ones who understand critical systems. So, they need to take advantage of local IT services firms that can supplement internal staff with less than full-time resources."

Polymaths are a dying species as Edward Carr, the editorial director of the *Economist*, wrote in his essay "The Last Days of the Polymath": "Isaiah Berlin once divided thinkers into two types. Foxes, he wrote, know many things; whereas hedgehogs know one big thing. The foxes used to roam free across the hills. Today the hedgehogs rule."[11]

Carr calls the hedgehogs "monomaths." He may be right to talk about the end of individuals as polymaths. But he does not explore a new generation of technology polymaths, such as Nathan Myhrvold and Bill Joy, who make Leonardo look like a mental midget. Carr certainly does not factor in the new polymath enterprise where many "monomaths" with a variety of technical disciplines and technologies create an Apple or a Google or a BASF.

Leonardo 2.0

"Penguins, it turns out, have amazing sphincter muscles. And they are able to project like there is no tomorrow," says Nathan Myhrvold in an interview with CNN's Fareed Zakaria.[12] Nathan is also said to be fascinated with fossilized dinosaur vomit.

Don't let that put you off.

Myhrvold was CTO at Microsoft before he left to start Intellectual Ventures (IV). The company is less than a decade old, but it already has thousands of patents in a wide range of interests. Along with Bill Gates, his former boss at Microsoft, one of its entities filed for patents that would slow hurricanes by pumping in the paths of the storms cold, deep-ocean water.[13] IV's Web site shows less exotic areas of interest, such as "computer software and hardware, user interface design," but also shows ambitious ones, including "advanced medical procedures, digital imaging, nanotechnology, nuclear energy and advanced particle physics."[14]

The organization reflects Myhrvold's personal diversity. He has a doctorate in theoretical and mathematical physics with a master's degree in mathematical economics from Princeton University. He also has a master's degree in geophysics and space physics plus a bachelor's degree in mathematics from UCLA.[15] He started college when he was just 14 and worked as a postdoctoral fellow under the famous Stephen Hawking.

Malcolm Gladwell, of *The Tipping Point* fame, describes the kind of talent Myhrvold has access to at IV: "You know how musicians will say, 'My teacher was So-and-So, and his teacher was So-and-So,' right back to Beethoven? So Lowell Wood was the great protégé of Edward Teller. He was at Lawrence Livermore. He was the technical director of Star Wars (the defense initiative)."[16]

Recently, Myhrvold stirred up another radical idea: Pump sulfur dioxide into the stratosphere to accomplish global cooling, as happens when active volcanoes explode. He thinks that most current global warming blame on carbon is bunk and has told the authors of *SuperFreakonomics* the current anticarbon thinking hurts billions of poor people around the world.[17]

Less controversially, Myhrvold:

- Is an accomplished cook, winning several world barbecue championships. He is also an assistant chef at a French restaurant.
- Is working on a book on molecular gastronomy, which explores physical and chemical changes to food in the cooking process.
- Has been involved in major archeological finds (several *T. Rex* skeletons).
- Has studied penguins and their "projectiles."
- Is a prize-winning wildlife photographer.
- Has built a section of Babbage's Difference Engine #2, the predecessor of the modern computer.
- Has funded Search for Extraterrestrial Intelligence (SETI) projects, such as the Alien Telescope Array.
- Has explored active volcanoes—he got the sulfur dioxide ideas above by studying weather impact after volcanoes blow.

Yes, he is definitely a polymath for our times.

Unlike what Carr would predict, Myhrvold is not being targeted by "monomaths." He has been accused of being a "patent troll."[18] Large incumbent companies with patents of their own are worried that either IV or a company it transfers patents to may come after them. Of course, those who accuse Myhrvold conveniently stay quiet about how they themselves take advantage of an overwhelmed U.S. Patent Office and a system where patent litigation is often more lucrative than revenues from patents: "Our patent system for most innovations has become patently absurd," wrote a *Wall Street Journal* editorial.[19] Indeed, by itself the patent gridlock is a grand challenge, which the U.S. Congress has tried multiple times to reform over the last decade.

Bill Joy, like Myhrvold, has roots in software. In fact, he is quite a legend in that sector. His fingerprints are all over the UNIX operating system, the Java language, and the Sun SPARC processor, earning him the moniker "Edison of the Internet" from *Fortune* magazine.[20] His personal interests are more mainstream—no culinary or dinosaur razzle-dazzle: an art gallery in San Francisco, on the board of the Oregon Shakespeare Festival, and work with some architects.

Joy, by the way, is no fan of Microsoft—the run-ins between Sun, the company he cofounded with Scott McNealy and others, and Microsoft were legendary. One of his gentle jabs included: "I've often wondered why they [Microsoft] can't, for once, do something new. I mean really, really new?"

Not surprisingly, even after leaving Sun, Joy continues on the other bank of the river from Myhrvold. For the last several years, as we show in Chapter 13, he has been helping the firm of Kleiner Perkins, a more traditional venture capitalist than IV's model, make cleantech investments. He is in the business of reducing our dependence on carbon-based energy.

Unlike Myhrvold, who is having to defend his patent strategies, Joy spent a couple of years defending an article he wrote in *Wired* magazine in 2000 that raised significant ethical issues regarding nanotechnology, genetics, and robotics. We discuss those issues in Chapter 20.

Two modern polymaths, very different in style and approach—but we should all be grateful because both are helping us look at the wicked problems we face. They embody AND not OR. But just as important, they are building a version of the new polymath: the IV and Kleiner talent ecosystem and product portfolio.

Even more assuring, while they may not be as visible as Jobs, Joy, or Myhrvold, there are plenty more big thinkers around building other new polymath enterprises, leveraging a breathtaking variety of technical disciplines and technologies.

Don't Forget Michelangelo, Raphael, and . . .

Baldesar Castiglione's *Book of the Courtier* is considered one of the most comprehensive perspectives of life during the Renaissance in Europe. Born into the nobility in 1478, Castiglione held court in Urbino, considered one of the most refined cities in Italy, and later he was the papal nuncio to Spain.[21]

The book describes conversations between members of a court over the course of four evenings about what makes a "perfect gentlemen" (and to a lesser extent, a perfect lady). The breadth of expectations is wide:

> *In volleying, in running bulls ... he should be outstanding among the Spaniards.*
> *Painting, since it is a worthy and beneficial art*
> *The man who does not enjoy music can be sure there is no harmony in his soul.*
> *He should have knowledge of Greek as well as Latin.*

Well-equipped as to horses, weapons and dress ...
Swim, jump, run, cast the stone ...
Attractive manners, wisdom, speech, gestures ...

It sounds like Castiglione's characters were describing someone as gifted as Leonardo. Amazingly, the group discusses Leonardo only once in those evenings, and then only as a painter. Why? Because there were so many other multidisciplinary people to talk about, such as Michelangelo and Raphael.

If the characters in Castiglione's book were having their conversation today and discussing technology innovation, they would surely mention Apple. And Google. And Kleiner. And IV. They would, however, only mention them once or twice as they stepped back and looked at the emerging innovation at companies like CME and Redbeacon.

In September 2009, CME—the Chicago Mercantile Exchange, which is the world's largest derivatives exchange—was honored at an *InformationWeek 500* awards ceremony in southern California. The magazine described why: "The trading volume grew more than 300% a year. In that same time, the average time for a quote or order to come into and back from CME's data center was collapsed from 180 milliseconds to less than 6 ... and cut maintenance and capital expenses 90%."[22]

A few hundred miles to the north and a few hours apart, Mike Arrington was handing a $50,000 check to Redbeacon at his TechCrunch50 event. Founded by ex-Google employees, Redbeacon, a consumer shopping site, does not just return local business listings, leaving users to sort through dozens of entries. Instead, it manages the quote process and allows users to book appointments with qualified suppliers.[23]

Arrington was an attorney at Wilson Sonsini, a Silicon Valley law firm that has helped countless start-ups get founded, funded, and go public. He is now one of the most influential players in the technology start-up world, with product reviews and commentary on his TechCrunch site. Redbeacon was one of 50 finalists that got to present for six minutes—yes, just six minutes—to five judges, including Arrington and an audience of two thousand.

That day, 499 other established companies were honored in the *InformationWeek* 500. More than 1,000 start-ups competed to show at the TechCrunch event. Many more chose not to be or were not considered for either honor.

The speed of processing at the CME and the rate at which start-ups are forming is breathtaking, but neither can compete with what is happening in China.

The general thinking was that once China showed off its progress at the 2008 Beijing Olympics, things would slow down in the country. The country, however, is redefining scope and time to market over and over again. A bullet-train system will cover 16,000 miles at an investment of $300 billion by 2020. The nation will have 244 airports by then—almost 100 more than it had in 2006. In the West, we take years to get approvals just to extend existing airports. In Chapter 12, on sustainability, we talk more about China's cleantech investments and ambitions.

A *National Geographic* article titled "China's Instant Cities" shows the hurry the whole country is in:

> *In 23 minutes, they designed an office, a hallway, and three living rooms for factory managers. On the top floor, the workers' dormitories required another 14 minutes. All told, they had mapped out a 21,500-square-foot (2,000 square meters) factory, from bottom to top, in one hour and four minutes. Boss Gao handed the scrap of paper to the contractor. The man asked when they wanted the estimate.*
> *"How about this afternoon?"*
> *The contractor looked at his watch. It was 3:48 p.m.*
> *"I can't do it that fast!"*
> *"Well, then tell me early in the morning."*[24]

You can argue about China's autocratic approach to solutions, its ethics, and even the quality of its construction, but few could disagree that it is redefining time to market.

Yes, Castiglione's characters would only mention Apple or Kleiner once or twice, just like they barely touched on Leonardo. They would also talk about "faux" innovators.

"Spray Painters" in the New Renaissance

The CIO is presenting about the exciting opportunity for his public utility with the coming trend of "smart grids" and other industry innovations. Unfortunately, his back-office system was designed for manual meter reading every 30 to 60 days. In the new world of smart meters, communications with customers would become much more real time. The meters would facilitate consumers selling surplus energy from their solar panels and wind turbines back to the grid, as is already common in Germany. That is a good reason to upgrade your customer systems. The CIO has done the numbers, and the cost of custom modifications to his old "house" would have been expensive on its own. The packaged solution from SAP is a less-risky decision.

He then presents a slide that draws attention. It shows Accenture would need 40,000 person-days to implement the system. Some back-of-napkin numbers show the project would cost $150 million to $200 million over the next few years, considering what the company would pay SAP, Accenture, its infrastructure provider, and its internal staff.

The expensive back-office investment would likely smother the benefits offered by the smart grid. Over the last couple of decades, companies around the world have spent more than $2 trillion on similarly well-intentioned SAP projects that would not meet most definitions of "innovation."

Can you imagine what China could deliver for $2 trillion as it redefines time and economics in its rush to develop bullet trains and wind farms while we have been investing it in back-office systems?

We are not just picking on SAP and Accenture—later in the book, we show ways in which both are also innovating.

Or consider the opportunistic behavior around sustainability. Terrachoice has been surveying brands for several years and concluded, in its 2009 report, that 98 percent of "green" products are committing at least one of what it calls its "Seven Sins of Greenwashing."[25]

Those sins range from false claims to irrelevant statements on product labels. It defines "greenwashing" as "the act of misleading consumers regarding the environmental practices of a company or the environmental benefits of a product or service."

Let us note that there is innovation and then there is innovation by association—"spray-painted" innovation. Fortunately, as we describe next, there is also plenty of unheralded innovation going on.

Less Visible Signs of Our New Renaissance

Most people have heard of the iPhone. Many of us have seen a DIAD but probably cannot recall what it is. It is the device that helps UPS drivers in their brown trucks deliver 22 million packages a day during the peak holiday season. It was introduced back in 1990, way before the iPhone. Now in its fourth generation, it does many of the things an iPhone does. And its battery lasts much longer than the iPhone's.[26]

A delivery information acquisition device (DIAD) allows the driver to scan the package bar code, collect the receiver's signature electronically, type in the receiver's last name, and push a single key to complete the transaction via the mobile network or by Wi-Fi—no need to activate a cell phone or return to the vehicle. It supports a Bluetooth wireless personal area network and an infrared port to communicate with peripheral devices and customer PCs/printers. It also has a GPS chip to allow UPS to track the whereabouts of its trucks.

Every UPS driver logs into a central ODS (On-Demand Services) system first thing in the morning. This allows dispatchers to access the driver via the DIAD throughout the day via text messages. Virtually all drivers start their day with a list of predefined customer pickup locations. ODS allows the addition of a one-time pickup to a driver's work list on the fly, depending on which driver is nearest.

The 100,000 DIADs are only a small part of the technology landscape at UPS, which uses 15 mainframes, more than 11,000 servers, and 150,000 workstations. UPS says its package tracking is done by the world's largest DB2 site (the IBM database software). It is the largest user of mobile minutes in the world. UPS.com, available in 32 languages, handles 35 million tracking requests on a peak day during holiday season.

Its technology helps optimize truck routes and minimize left turns. It is investing in a variety of fuel-efficient trucks and techniques, such as continuous descent approach, to glide its planes for fuel efficiency and noise reduction.

Yet most of us do not marvel when Mr. Brown—the UPS delivery person—stops by. We similarly do not realize how broadly talented are colleagues like Gretchen Lindquist and Edgar Moore.

Lindquist works in IT security for a large multinational in Houston, Texas. She is also a soprano soloist at her local church. Her husband, Moore, is professor of music at a local college and a conductor of a men's chorus. Lindquist is also his recording engineer.

Their music has made her a linguist of sorts: "Having learned Latin by rote repetition at Mass as a small child before I could even read, learning to sing works in Latin such as the Verdi Requiem was not too difficult. However, learning to sing in new-to-me languages such as Catalan, Polish, and Russian was a matter of a lot of listening and repetition, and that was how I did it."

Lindquist's master's thesis was focused on a Renaissance-era bishop, Marco Girolamo Vida, and his work *De Dignitatae Republicae* ("On the dignity of the republic"), which is about the timeless question of the value of civic life and government. The thesis contrasted the bishop's views on statecraft with those of Machiavelli and Erasmus.

The couple spends as much time on the road as they can. Lindquist says: "We both enjoy combining cultural/artistic activities and active recreation when we travel. I have taken a pair of inline skates along and gone skating in various U.S. and international cities including New York, Denver, Santa Fe, Buenos Aires, Rio de Janeiro, London, Aberdeen, Dubai, and Singapore."

There is more to Lindquist, including "gardening, three dogs, animal activism and environmentalism, and healthy gourmet cooking." In his spare time, Moore rebuilds classic British cars and is a Hollywood movie buff, and he almost became a baseball umpire.

Their varied talents, travels, and experiences probably do not show in her company's or his college's skills database. But they should. Put several Lindquists and Moores together, and we can create polymaths of innovative enterprises.

Or how about the Amish?

Hold on now.

The Amish, with their straw hats and horse buggies, did not adopt two of the most impactful technologies of the twentieth century: electricity and the automobile. Why would they care about the technology of the twenty-first?

"The Amish are not Luddites—though their view of technology veers sharply from the mainstream," says Dr. Donald Kraybill, senior fellow at the Young Center for Anabaptist & Pietist Studies at Elizabethtown College in Elizabethtown, Pennsylvania. He is leader of a research project with a working title of "From the Buggy to the Byte: How the Amish Tame Technology."[27] He continues:

> *Amish engineers are expert at stripping electric motors from shop equipment and replacing them with air or hydraulic ones powered by diesel engines, which are common in change-minded settlements. This so-called Amish electricity [air and hydraulic power] is widely used to operate state-of-the-art machinery—table saws, sanders, grinders, drill presses, and large metal presses.*
>
> *In some Amish settlements, battery-powered word processors are accepted, but not computers. One Old Order inventor, assisted by non-Amish technicians, developed a classic word processor, essentially a basic computer with a Microsoft operating system. With a small monitor, it supports word processing and spreadsheet software, but it has been neutered to disable the use of email, Internet access, video games, and other interactive media.*
>
> *An Amish shop developed an alternator that mounts on the axle of a buggy and uses the wheel rotation to recharge the battery which powers lights and signals. And get this—the manufacturing is contracted to a factory in China.*

It certainly sounds like we can learn from the Amish as we look for sustainable technologies.

The UPS DIAD, Lindquist and Moore, the Amish—no, they will never be written about in the same vein as Leonardo or Apple, but they are also signs of our New Renaissance.

Recap

For the most part today, most of us seem to specialize: We are monomaths in a world of exploding knowledge. Of course, there are exceptions, such as Jobs and Joy. And, importantly, well-designed enterprises are taking individual monomaths, leveraging a wide array of technologies and becoming the new polymaths. And as during the European Renaissance, there are plenty of polymaths.

Though a lot of attention these days seems to go to innovation in mobile and social technologies, plenty of complex, hairy "industrial innovation" is also going on.

This is encouraging because we face a daunting series of challenges at the global, enterprise, and individual level. We need polymaths to help with those grand challenges and our more routine ones.

CHAPTER 2

Modern-Day Dark Ages: So Much Stagnation

Renaissance, or rebirth, by definition follows something terminal. The European Renaissance followed its Dark Ages. While today's historians use more politically correct terms and don't call them Dark Ages, most agree there were decades, if not centuries, of "nothingness." Life went on, but there was little enlightenment. The establishment—the clergy and the nobility—seemed okay with the stagnation.

Similarly, there is so much "nothingness" today. In IT, it's about lack of nutrition and much of the spending is wasted. In sustainability and cleantech, it's about lack of agreement—there's rancor in spite of so many global concerns. In health care, it's about lack of availability—much of the world does not have access to advances, some even after decades of progress. It's fine to throw out grand challenges like reverse-engineering the brain, but in many ways, would it not be easier to just bring light to our Dark Ages?

Let's explain—starting with information technology.

"Empty Calories" in Infotech

The research firm Gartner expected global IT and telecom spending to be $3.3 trillion in 2010. Robert Mahowald, a director at IDC, another IT research firm that collects market data by sector—software, telecom, and so on—says there is some cross-selling between sectors, but, in total, it is safe to say that the global spend is in excess of $3 trillion a year. Neither IDC nor Gartner, however, tabulates internal corporate IT costs: salaries, benefits, and internal burdened charges.

If they did, it would reveal that most enterprises spend 80 percent to 90 percent of their IT and telecom budget with outside vendors. That is a dangerously high dependence on a supply chain. Many enterprises don't even realize this because only a fraction shows up in the budget of the CIO. Research and development (R&D) technology is charged to product development, telecom to call centers and business intelligence to the corporate planning group. Mobile charges come via expense reports and Amazon Web Services via corporate cards and are charged to even more budgets.

Even in automobile and aerospace, which have much more mature supply chain management, companies such as Ford and Boeing get around 70 percent of components from suppliers. In those industries, supplier consolidation and tiering makes sense because Ford and Boeing are dominant customers and can dictate design standards and justifiable economics.

In technology, by contrast, buyers have little leverage—even companies as big as Ford and Boeing make up less than 0.5 percent of an IBM's or Oracle's revenue. The top 25 global technology vendors, such as HP and AT&T, now make up more than 50 percent of the volume of the IT amount spent externally. The top 25 global technology buyers (dominated by large banks and government entities), however, barely make up 5 percent of the total spend.[1] As a result, buyers have little control over vendor product design and innovation strategy when they individually control so little of a vendor's revenue.

With a few exceptions, such as Apple, Intel, and Google, the bigger technology vendors have not been innovating much. The three biggest chunks of external technology spend are in telecommunications, outsourcing, and software. Telecommunications vendors invest in capital expenditures (capex), outsourcing vendors in training their people, and software vendors in tweaking older versions. Not much is spent on breakthrough R&D or real innovation. Would you believe Verizon does not use the word "research" anywhere in its 10-K? Why should it invest in R&D when it can just leverage all the cool stuff that Apple and Google are delivering? Even those companies spend only 10 percent or so of revenues on R&D. Outsourcing vendors—by the way, over half of IBM's revenues are from outsourcing—typically spend less than 2 percent of revenues on R&D, and much of that is on "solution centers," which are more about marketing than research. They, in turn, conveniently leverage innovation coming out of salesforce.com and Dell. Software vendors invest somewhat more in R&D than do telecom and outsourcing vendors—but parse that spend and you find much of it is going toward version 7, 8, or 12 of their products, some first introduced 10 to 20 years ago. So it is not really impactful innovation. Also, many of the software R&D dollars go toward porting products to new hardware platforms and devices or in "localization" to newer countries. Here's the irony: Some technology vendors spend more on internal IT than they do on R&D. The attitude toward real innovation is that "It's somebody else's job." When pushed, the stock answer from most technology vendors is that too much R&D spending offers only diminishing returns.

In contrast, they do not believe they get diminishing returns from their sales and general and administrative (SG&A) costs, which make up 25 percent to 60 percent of their revenues—five to ten times what they spend on R&D. Indeed, Paul Melchiorre, who did very well as an "elephant hunter" selling mega-dollar contracts at software vendors like SAP and Ariba over the last two decades now says, "The next generation of software winners will not just re-architect their products for cloud computing. They will also drastically reengineer their own sales style and operations." Take a look at SG&A roles at technology vendors, and you see opportunities to "deduplicate" many of the roles—or, to use our term, turn them into polymaths that could handle multiple roles:

- Sales operations manager
- Inside sales manager
- Analyst relations director
- Public relations manager
- Revenue accountant
- Pricing analyst
- Customer contracts attorney
- Investor relations manager
- CIO
- Controller
- Alliance manager
- Business development manager
- Channel manager
- Channel marketing manager
- Competitive intelligence manager
- Events coordinator
- Advertising manager
- Industry/vertical sales manager
- Marketing coordinator
- Web leads marketing manager
- Pre-sales lead support
- Database marketing manager
- Inbound/outbound sales support
- CFO

By the way, often that's not just one employee per role. In addition, many roles are supplemented with consultants who, for example, coach vendors how to deal with industry analysts.

But let's not just blame IT vendors. What Ford and Boeing keep in house in their manufacturing are strategic areas—for example, design of the aircraft or manufacture of the engine. In many IT shops, the thin sliver that stays in house is often not strategic: Many are technicians such as desktop support staff, database administrators, and network managers. They are important, but they mostly provide infrastructure—not innovation—support. Some CIOs keep such staff members in-house because they are the most visible to users and so they give the perception of "better customer care."

In a *CIO Magazine* Executive Council survey of 600 CIOs, 34 percent were classified as "function heads": Only 4 percent of this group were focused on "driving business innovation" whereas 79 percent of them reported they supported "improving IT operations/systems performance." This is at the highest level; further down in the IT organization, there is even less of a focus on innovation. Yet these companies still spent 5.1 percent of their revenues on IT. Another group—45 percent of the CIOs were classified as "transformational"—and 40 percent of this group reported that they were "driving business innovation" while spending a bit more— 5.5 percent—of their revenues on IT. Finally, the third group—another 21 percent—were classified as "business strategist"; 70 percent of this group reported they were "driving business innovation," and they spent 7.2 percent of revenues on IT.[2]

So, across all groups, a bedrock of about 5 percent of revenues is going toward "keeping the lights on", not innovation, IT. Traditionally, IT has been conservative—the old adage used to be "No one got fired for buying from IBM." Today, that saying has become a little broader—to include IBM, Verizon, Oracle, Accenture and other large vendors. Too many IT executives live in fear of one of their smaller vendors going out of business. And since many CIOs report to the CFO, their mandate is often focused on control and compliance, not on innovation.

Two grand challenges for most IT groups should be:

1. Spend 25 percent of IT budgets with start-up vendors less than 5 years old
2. Dramatically reduce the "empty calories" in the five IT budget areas we discuss in the next section.

Let's start with software.

Software

Every year, software vendors send customers a bill for 15 to 25 percent of the "licensed value" of their software. This payment is supposed to cover support (bug fixes, help desk) and maintenance (periodic regulatory updates, enhancements). During implementation, few customers tax the software vendor's support lines. In fact, most customers additionally pay a systems integrator (SI) or the software vendor's consultants to provide on-site implementation help. Yet they are charged the full software support and maintenance fee. Typically, after a year of going "live" on the software, support needs drop off again. Yet companies continue to be charged full support and maintenance fees. Since the support fees are on the licensed value, users are also charged on the "shelfware"—software licenses the company originally bought but has not deployed. If you were to amortize the cost of annual software vendor's support and maintenance charge over the number of calls made to its support desk, a price of $10,000 per call would not be unusual. Makes the much ridiculed $600 military commode look downright affordable, right?

In the meantime, software vendors have been automating much of the support into knowledge bases so customers can self-service. They are moving support for stable, older releases to their offices in low-cost locations (or using offshore firms to support them). They are increasingly letting user communities handle routine queries. If users resist migrating to newer releases, software vendors often charge them a premium to stay on a stable older release that costs little to support. No wonder software maintenance gross margins are often at the 90 percent-plus level, and is attracting third-party maintenance from the likes of Rimini Street described in Chapter 9.

Even at that huge premium, software quality and warranties are weak. The torrent of patches from Microsoft is just one proof point. A common joke in the industry is that if Microsoft made a car, it would crash twice a day, and it would require you to retrain every time you traded in an older model—and ask you if you were sure if you wanted the airbag to deploy.

The American Law Institute issued the final draft of the *Principles of the Law of Software Contracts* in 2009. The introduction says, "Law governing the transfer of hard goods is inadequate to govern software transactions because, unlike hard goods, software is characterized by novel speed, copying, and storage capabilities, and new inspection, monitoring, and quality challenges."[3]

In many software negotiations, buyer enterprises assign a general counsel who finished a real-estate transaction the day before and will work the day after on a labor issue. Counsel is hopelessly outgunned compared to the battery of intellectual property attorneys available to software vendors.

IT Infrastructure

The average corporate data center is shockingly inefficient compared to the next-generation centers being built by Google, Amazon, and Yahoo! Some of the centers being built for Wall Street buck this trend, but it is not uncommon to see power usage effectiveness (PUE)—the ratio of power entering a data center divided by the power used to run the computer infrastructure within it—at 2.0, when a world-class benchmark approaches

1.2. Additionally, as we describe further in Chapter 18, new world-class data centers are being located by the Googles and Amazons in places that deliver significant tax breaks and attractive energy rates.

So why can enterprises not walk away from their internal boat anchors? Many are locked into multiyear outsourcing contracts and face stiff early-termination penalties. Meanwhile, there is little in the legal language to force outsourcers to move to more efficient data centers.

In the traditional hardware sourcing model, companies bought servers and routers that were grossly underutilized. As enterprises start to deploy "virtualization" software, they are finding their baseline usage is often lower than 20 percent.

You and I can buy a terabyte of storage for less than $100 and it's a one-time payment. Yet many enterprises are paying $100 or more per gigabyte over a three-year useful life, when you amortize the cost of storage and support for it. Granted that is high-availability, enterprise-grade storage, but is it worth 1,000 times as much? Then, when you look at duplication of storage—multiple backups to meet compliance needs, archived e-mails sent to multiple addresses with the same attachment, and the like—the waste is numbing.

Most companies sign up for multiyear outsourcing contracts to support their PCs and other office equipment. These contracts are priced on assumptions of likely incidents based on employee counts. If most companies kept a small reserve of loaner units and bought support "by the drink"—say, from Best Buy's Geek Squad or from a local PC support shop—they could spend 20, 40, perhaps 60 percent less. Even more efficient would be a move to dumber but cheaper net terminals and to perform more computing "in the cloud."

Technology Services

As companies implement technology projects, they tend to hire SIs like BearingPoint. Even though many SI proposals proudly state they have done hundreds of SAP or Java development projects, typically these SIs do not pass along much in the way of productivity or automation gains. In fact, since they are more "experienced," they expect to be paid a premium. But even after companies pay premiums for specialized talent, IT projects still fail at unacceptably high rates. Time-to-completion metrics coming out of newer "agile" development methods , as described in Chapter 3, often show a two to three times improvement opportunity compared to traditional SI delivery models.

Another problem in the SI world is consultant travel. That often adds another 15 to 25 percent to base fees, which are already high to begin with. The common reasoning is "We are bringing the best talent to the project." Often, the reality is those consultants are available, and on the bench. The traveling consultants usually have a Monday–Thursday on-site policy, which forces the entire project to adjust to a four-day workweek. There is a reason why it is nearly impossible to get an upgrade on most U.S. airlines on a Thursday night. Consultants who fly weekly qualify for elite levels, which get upgrade priority. Over the longer term, some clients also report health and other productivity issues with consultants who travel that frequently. SIs implement constraint-based solutions for their clients all the time, so implementing a staffing model that constrains their own travel would not be difficult. Many SIs are implementing telepresence for internal communications but have not shown much initiative in using it on client projects and cutting back on project travel.

SIs are engaged on a project basis, but outsourcers, in contrast, get multiyear support contracts and bring their own issues. Typical productivity gains they agree to pale compared to what disruptive vendors like Amazon are showing is possible. Their service levels are deceptively generous—they may say 99.99 percent system availability—but there are plenty of exceptions for planned and unplanned downtime. Compared to cloud computing vendors, which are supporting hundreds and thousands of customers simultaneously at the 99.99 percent level and are frequently reported in the media for unscheduled downtime, the average outsourcer leads the life of Riley and rarely gets negative press or much of a punitive penalty for missing a service level.

Offshore vendors, particularly those from India, won plenty of kudos (and plenty of hostility from the Lou Dobbses of the world) in the last decade not just for their affordable rates but also for their commitment to quality and productivity improvements. Just as the Japanese auto manufacturers took good lessons from teachers like W. Edwards Deming in the 1960s and 1970s, Indian vendors took Capability Maturity Models and Six Sigma seriously in the 1990s. In recent years, however, that intensity has worn off. Toyota's recent issues with its brakes, in particular, have affected the Japanese quality image, and something similar has been happening with India's image around services. Much of the Indian staff—60 to 80 percent of their employee bases—are recent college graduates. In fact, they are called "freshers" in most Indian firms. They are technically sound but, typically, have little understanding of the client's business processes. Also, as is common in many young employee bases, they tend to have high staff-turnover issues. In contrast, cloud computing vendors we discuss in Chapter 18 are showing massively (often across thousands of customers) shared-service application support models, which offshore firms are having a hard time matching as they mostly support customers on an individual contract, siloed basis.

Telecommunications

Most companies pay a bewildering range of landline, conference calling, calling card, employee Wi-Fi, mobile, and other messaging fees. Phone companies are also creative with their monthly plans, with shortfall charges, early-termination, and other fees.

In most companies, the spend on telecommunications typically exceeds the cost of all other IT costs—hardware, software, technology services, internal staff—put together. Not surprisingly, there is plenty of waste.

International mobile roaming is an example of significant "empty calories" in this sector. A study by Harris Interactive showed that the average U.S. employee spends $693 in international roaming calls on an overseas trip.[4] Although that may sound exaggerated, it buys only 200 to 500 minutes on many U.S. mobile plans, depending on the country you are visiting. It seems like everyone is in cahoots. Providers such as AT&T charge $3 to $4 a minute for a call to the United States from some countries. The European Union has capped roaming costs of its telcos but has no such caps for U.S. providers from its jurisdiction. United States regulators have largely ignored the issue. In fact, they exacerbate the problem since telco bills attract heavy taxes—15 percent to 25 percent of base charges, as we show below. Device manufacturers sometimes have a locked subscriber identity module (SIM) card like Apple does on the iPhone. You cannot swap (without "jailbreaking" the phone and potentially invalidating the warranty) in a SIM card of a local provider or that of MAXroam described in Chapter 9, which would allow you to make the same calls for pennies, not dollars, a minute.

Multinational companies are reporting increased competition in carrier-provided multiprotocol label switching (MPLS) services for their global wide-area-network (WAN) deployments. The major North American providers—AT&T, Verizon, Sprint, and Global Crossing—are having to compete with European providers, such as BT, Cable & Wireless, Orange, and T-Systems and Asian ones such as NTT. As Chinese, Korean, Brazilian, and Indian vendors mature, expect even more competition; but for now the cost of that networking is sizable.

Then there is the waste around telecom taxes—like tobacco, telcos are a favorite target for all kinds of taxes. Here are some taxes listed on the Web site of Eatel, a local telecom serving portions of the U.S. state of Louisiana:[5]

- E-911 Emergency Service Fee
- End User Charge (End User Common Line Charge)
- FCC Local Number Portability Charge
- Federal Universal Service Charge (FUSC) Federal Subscriber Fee
- Franchise Fee (Municipal Fee)

- Line Recovery Charge (LRC)
- Local Access Charge
- Mississippi Emergency Telecommunication Training Charge
- Network Access Charge (NAC)
- State Subscriber Line Charge
- Regulatory Cost Recovery
- Telecommunications for the Deaf Fund
- Universal Service Fee (USF) or Federal Universal Service Charge (FUSC)

Other IT Spend

What if gas cost $5,000 a gallon and you had a leaky gas tank? That describes the situation with printer ink.[6] Many enterprises are starting to look at options such as Cartridge World described in Chapter 9. They also have guidelines (driven by cost and a desire to be more "green") for their employees to avoid much printing. Still others are reevaluting the volume of their printed advertising and other marketing material—since much of that seems to go straight into the recipient's garbage.

Another area of spend coming under scrutiny is that on IT strategy consultants and IT research firms. An expression has been been making the rounds the last few years:

In the '70s, buyers turned to IBM for advice.
In the '80s, to Andersen.
In the '90s, to Gartner.
Today, they turn to each other.

Peer benchmarking opportunities and market intelligence via boutique research firms like Altimeter Group (discussed in Chapter 17), Redmonk, Horses for Sources, and decent quality but free blogs, such as ZDNet (featured in Chapter 9), GigaOm, TechCrunch, and other sites, are helping companies lower costs of IT market intelligence.

Everywhere you turn, there is waste in infotech. Let's now look at some of the issues around sustainability and cleantech.

Lack of Agreement around Cleantech

In 1987, the United Nations laid out a simple, uncontroversial definition for sustainable development: It is development that meets "the needs of the present without compromising the ability of future generations to meet their own needs."[7]

Sustainable development has turned out to be anything but simple and uncontroversial. Remember the story of the blind men who tried to describe the elephant—by its tail, by its trunk, and so on? If they were to try to describe sustainability, we would get similar, wide-ranging feedback:

- It's a massive opportunity for a new generation of technology.
- It's a new revenue source for governments via carbon-based taxes.
- It's about energy independence and national security.
- It's about climate change—we are running out of time.
- It's the next generation of good jobs, as Germany's Solar Valley has shown.
- It's about back to basics. As Chapter 1 described, the Amish now look progressive.
- It's a move by businesses to "guilt" us into paying more for "green" products.
- It's about our kids and future generations.

As he left Copenhagen in December 2009, President Obama softened the criticism around what was widely called a disaster of a summit on climate change: "This is hard within countries. This is going to be even harder between countries."[8]

Obama was not kidding about it being "hard within countries." Reader comments on the U.S. Chamber of Commerce site reveal a very wide range of disagreements about climate change:[9]

I'm an avid environmentalist and make a living practicing environmental engineering. We are against cap and trade. It is just another excuse for the government to collect money based on the bogus argument that global warming is largely the result of industrial activities.
                                                                    Reader in Florida

Someday we're all going to pay for our energy usage and its waste, one way or another, so we better start dealing with it sensibly now, rather than wait until things get even worse. It's time to put ideology aside and become excited about the possibilities!
                                                                 Reader in California

Our business has a high cost of energy, and if cap and trade passes and our electrical costs go up any more, we are going to be driven out of business and over 100 people will lose their jobs.
                                                                Reader in Wisconsin

The Chamber supposedly believes in measures to address climate change but opposes any [legislation] it sees ... despite the indisputable fact that every National Academy of Science of the entire industrialized world has stated unequivocally that we need to do something about carbon buildup.

Reader in Montana

Even savvy investors like Vinod Khosla, the legendary venture capitalist and now a major cleantech investor, point to the difficulty in building consensus across varying viewpoints, when he writes, "There are many, many solutions in the 'green' space that will make a good return, but will not move the needle on carbon emissions."[10]

Don't get us wrong. As in infotech, there is already plenty of waste in cleantech, but the biggest issues seem to be around the emotion and disagreement on how to even get started. The doomsday ecological and energy scenarios should be unifying consensus—instead, the scenarios themselves are spawning debates.

Inconsistent Coverage in Healthtech

Total U.S. spending on health care was $7,290 a person in 2007, nearly two and a half times the Organization for Economic Cooperation and Development average of $2,984.[11] Yet the number of medically uninsured in the United States grew from 39.8 million in 2001 to 46.3 million in 2008.[12] That's almost 15 percent of the country uncovered. We are starting to see scenarios like these at health camps: "The sea of tents and pilgrims wasn't in Haiti or Guatemala. It was in Virginia, where uninsured Americans turned up in such big numbers [for health checks] that hundreds had to be turned away."[13]

What about coverage for the mainstream, insured population?

Margaret Newman (the author's wife) has spent 20 years in nursing, doing her training in the United Kingdom and working at various health facilities in the United States. She qualifies her comments by saying they reflect "my narrow perspective working in the bowels of a hospital" as she lists various areas for improvement:

- Insufficient conversations with patient:

Studies have shown that a doctor who sits at the level of the patient—on the side of the bed and spends even three to five minutes talking with the patient is sued less frequently. Patients feel the doctor really heard them and that the doctor had related to them as a person and picked up information this way that impacted the patient's care and successful recovery. Instead, we rely mostly on tests to provide that "conversation."

- Incomplete patient records:

I'm looking forward to the day when a person comes to a hospital and their medical records from any part of the world can be accessed instantly. This would provide a complete medical record for the doctor, avoid possible delays in diagnosis and treatment, avoid repeat testing and so save money, and of course, add to the patient's comfort and confidence in the doctor and the medical system.

- Overdependence on hospital care:

Doctors in the spirit of not taking away hope continue to offer/encourage costly treatments for a terminal patient that often does not add much to their quality of life. Hospice can provide excellent medical, emotional, and spiritual support for the patient and family, and doctors need to get over their "death is a failure" attitude and refer patients in a timelier manner.

- Overworked medical staff:

Some doctors work very long hours, and I'd say one of the most important questions to ask a doctor in the ER is "How long is it since you came on duty and when did you last sleep?" Many mistakes can be made because the caregiver is simply tired.

Of course, things are much worse in the developing world. Some sub-Saharan countries report life expectancy at less than 40 years. Infant mortality is unconscionably high in the developing world, where the Bill and Melinda Gates Foundation has been giving out grants for health care research. HIV/AIDS, malaria, and other insect-borne diseases; respiratory ailments like pneumonia and tuberculosis; and poor-water-driven diarrhea and hepatitis are prominent areas of research.[14] Some of these diseases were supposed to have been cured long ago—another case of inconsistent availability.

The World Health Organization provides other sobering statistics in its 2009 summary:

- 112 million underweight children
- 9 million child deaths
- 99 percent of maternal mortality is in the developing world[15]

Of course, as in infotech, there is plenty of waste in healthtech—in some ways, it's worse. As in cleantech, there are rancorous disagreements—especially around the beginning and ending of life. The major failure in healthtech, however, is that a large percentage of the world still does not benefit from significant medical breakthroughs.

Turning the Tide

As Camus famously said, "In the midst of winter, I finally learned that there was in me an invincible summer." Funding for innovation projects is right there in the trillions of dollars wasted each year in technology. Just go chisel off this baseline—you don't need to get out a begging bowl for new funding.

Over the next 21 chapters, we show how innovators and disruptors are addressing some of the grand challenges and some of the more mundane ones we discussed in this chapter. Several innovators showcased in Chapter 7 are challenging traditional telco mentality. Chapter 9 showcases disruptors who are influencing technology economics in a major way. Chapter 12 and the profile on Kleiner Perkins show how cleantech is evolving. Chapter 14 shows how healthtech is changing.

Recap

There was plenty of living during the Dark Ages, but there was little forward movement. It was defined by its relative "nothingness." Similarly, in many ways, we are living in our own Dark Ages. In information technology, there is lack of nutrition—much of the spending is wasted. In sustainability, there is lack of agreement—there is rancor in spite of so many global concerns. In health care, it is about lack of availability—much of the world does not have access to all the advances in technology—or even basic health care.

Enough of the focus on problems. Let's move to solutions that enable us to escape these Dark Ages. Let's start with General Electric in the next chapter to see how its product R&D and IT groups are addressing many of the opportunities in infotech, cleantech, and healthtech.

CHAPTER 3

Polymath Profile #1: General Electric

G eneral Electric (GE) is a polymath when it comes to industry coverage. Its products include aircraft engines, power generation, water processing, security technology, medical imaging, business and consumer financing, media content, and countless others. It has customers in more than 100 countries and it employs more than 300,000 people worldwide.

GE stays young through innovation. Indeed, it is the oldest remaining company in the Dow Jones Industrial Average. In 2008, GE ranked number four on *BusinessWeek*'s "World's Most Innovative Companies" list for the second year in a row. It was included in the 2008 and 2007 Dow Jones Sustainability Index.

In this profile, we look at four aspects of GE innovation:

1. GE Global Research
2. Its corporate IT
3. R&D at one of its business units
4. IT at one of its business units

GE Global Research

The Last of the Mohicans—the James Fenimore Cooper classic set in 1757— the movies it spawned, and the critical discussion it encouraged paint a vivid picture of the birthing motions of a New World.

In the valley in Niskayuna, New York, where the Mohicans, the Mohawk, and the Huron roamed and schemed with the Dutch, the French, and the English, a new tribe has emerged at GE Global Research. There are no scalps to show off these days, but there are plenty of patents, Nobel Prizes, and other recognitions. The 1,700 technologists, a majority of them PhDs in a variety of science and engineering disciplines, are at the crossroads of a New World. It is a world of grand challenges laid out by the National Academy of Engineering and the United Nations Millennium Development Goals. These are goals that call for new medicine, new energy, and new algorithms.

GE Business Units take a challenge and weave it into their mission statements. The big market opportunity for the water business is to go from "scarcity threatening" to "abundant and cleaner sources"; for aviation and transportation, it is to go from "steady progress" to "breakthroughs in efficiency, emissions, and noise."

Jeff Immelt, the CEO of GE, is a modern-day polymath. He has to be to run a company with such a wide portfolio of products and geographic locations. He is, additionally, an ambassador who knows most world leaders on a first-name basis. He is also a salesman who has met every major CEO around the world. At the core, though, he is a geek. The helipad at GE Global Research, a short flight from corporate headquarters in Fairfield, Connecticut, is a favorite destination.

His predecessor, Jack Welch, earned the nickname "Neutron Jack" for his focus on efficiency; Immelt will likely go down in history as "Proton Jeff," as he encourages positive vibes toward all kinds of technology. GE Global Research is organized into 10 technology competencies: energy and propulsion, chemical technologies and materials characterization, material systems, biosciences, power conversion systems, electronic systems and controls, computing/decision sciences, imaging, micro and nano structures, and ceramics and metallurgy.

GE Global Research, of course, was born long before Immelt became CEO. This is, after all, the company that Thomas Edison started. (The GE Global Research blog is called Edison's Desk. The antique desk itself is still on display in the main lobby at Niskayuna. So are pictures of the most prolific GE scientists—members of the exclusive club must have 25 patents or more.)

Immelt is gradually and indelibly leaving his mark on the company with a refocus on complex, industrial technologies. In his annual letter to shareholders in 2009, he wrote: "I believe that a popular, thirty-year notion that the U.S. can evolve from being a technology and manufacturing leader to a service leader is just wrong."[1]

So, Immelt's tribe is marching to a different tune as the company diversifies from its finance operations after the recent market turmoil and as it sells a majority interest in NBC Universal to the cable operator Comcast.

Not that these PhDs just write esoteric papers or wear tweed jackets. They have Immelt's DNA. They are the company's ambassadors to the 14,000-plus visitors who annually visit the 550-acre campus: customers, collaborators, chiefs of state, and even curious media folk willing to look beyond the latest mobile device or social network for innovation.

They are a secret weapon of the sales team—they help close deals. A cynical prospect wondering what a health care presentation during his visit had to do with his interest in telematics finally had his "aha" moment: "Jeez, if they can track proteins which attach themselves to cancer cells, I am reasonably sure they can track the trucks in our supply chain."

Edison once said: "I find my greatest pleasure, and so my reward, in the work that precedes what the world calls success."

To make sure the technologists are focused on delivering usable technology that helps GE businesses grow, not just their pet projects, GE has honed a series of tools and methods.

Broadly, we can classify them into five categories:

1. Core innovation processes
2. Adjacencies and game changers
3. "Compounds" and collaborations
4. Global extensions
5. "Serendipities"

Core Innovation Processes

Not surprisingly, an organization with a long history of innovation has core processes in place. Roland Sedziol explains some of them. He is "Business Program Manager, Transportation"—that translates to his being the Global Research interface to GE's locomotive and other transportation businesses.

Sedziol starts with funding:

> *Global Research funding is roughly 55% from businesses, 25% from corporate, and 20% from outside sources. The 55% keeps us focused on business needs, the 25% allows us to think longer term and not just on the short-term business focus. The 20% is to make sure we collaborate with governments, universities and other business partners to advance technology for the benefit of many.*
>
> *Global Research funding by itself is only $550 million out of the total GE R&D annual budget of $4.3 billion. So, there is plenty of shorter-term product, industry-centric development also happening at the businesses. And of course, we need governance to make sure GE Global Research focuses on the R in R&D, and the businesses the D. There are surprisingly few turf battles.*

Patrick Jarvis, communications and public affairs manager at GE Global Research, expands on the lack of turf battles: "At Global Research, we don't focus on building a new aircraft engine. We work on new alloys and combustion technologies for the engine. We don't focus on a new scanner but on new materials for the scintillator."

Sedziol's presence at GE Global Research—like those of peers who interface with other business units—is a statement in itself. There are plenty of tours of duty from the business to GE Global Research. The year-round planning and budgeting processes are anchored around such concepts as the "Growth Playbook Process" and "Imagination Breakthroughs," which are part of the GE vernacular. There are the famous "Session T" formats, where business marketing and Global Research technology teams come together. There are internal "vendor fairs," similar to going to a technology conference and having vendors display their products in booths.

One of the competencies GE has honed is what Sedziol calls "traversing the Valley of Death." It happens all the time, where R&D hands off a product but a business cannot find a market for it or cannot grow it to sufficient manufacturing scale. According to Sedziol, deciding when to continue funding and when to pull the plug is an art form.

Art form is not good enough, though, so at the Pilot Development Center at the edge of GE Global Research campus, Paul Myers and Jonathan Janssen, both mechanical engineers, talk about the GE Manufacturing Readiness Levels methodology. It is an adaptation of the Technology Readiness Level maturity model the U.S. Department of Defense has been propagating. Says Myers: "Stages 1 to 2 deal with concept development, stages 8 to 9 with scaling of production. Stages 3 through 7 relate to prototypes and proof-of-concepts—where many new products typically fail. For each stage, we have maturity measures for components, packaging, etc., that make up the solution."

In the nondescript 10,000-square-foot Pilot Development Center facility, they test the maturing of a manufacturing process for flexible organic LEDs (OLEDs). The concept involves using printing-press-type concepts to mass-produce sheets of the next-generation lighting. The flexible OLEDs will soon become part of home furnishings and garments. Myers salivates at the thought of a similar facility 10 times its size being planned for an Advanced Manufacturing Center in Michigan to test out even more complex processes.

Sedziol, in the meantime, talks about GE Global Research "entrepreneurs" and other ways in which innovation flows:

We encourage our technologists to come in and ask for seed investments for ideas they are passionate about. Ideas flow in every direction.

At the base level we have plenty of "core improvements" to existing products like the electronic fuel engine injection for locomotives and the GEnx aircraft engine, which improves fuel efficiency by 15% and reduces emissions by 50%.

Adjacencies and Game Changers

GE has also become better over time at extensions into new markets and disruptive leapfrogs. Sedziol continues: "'Adjacencies' are new markets for innovations to the core, like a new gearbox for locomotives which we found an application for in mining. And across all our business units, we have been increasingly getting into services of all kinds."

The services are not run-of-the-mill—they generally involve complex intellectual property. The Booz & Co. *Strategy+Business* journal describes how GE reengineered the sales and support of one of its line of turbines:

> It developed a proprietary remote monitoring and calibration system that did away with the need to dispatch technicians. But retaining ownership of the remote tuning technology and simply deploying it as-a-service enhancement was not a high-value solution either. It devised an entirely new business model for its remote technology, one that leased it to customers while simultaneously licensing to them the associated IP and service procedures. One utility, Florida Power & Light, saved more than $18 million within just the first few weeks of the new agreement. Over the last three years, this strategy has enabled GE to generate $300 million in new, high-margin revenue.[2]

Sedziol continues: "Then there are 'game changers,' like a hybrid locomotive to reduce dependence on diesel fuel."

Jarvis points to game changers in other GE areas: "Our integrated gasification combined cycle system converts coal into a cleaner burning fuel. Our Economic Simplified Boiling Water Reactor makes nuclear energy safer. We are looking to harness the power of pulse detonation of fuel and the resulting pressure increase—more efficient than combustion engines."

The hybrid locomotive concept, in turn, drove an investment in next-generation batteries. Across the campus, Glen Merfield, manager of the Chemical Energy Systems Lab, and with a PhD in chemical engineering, shows off a square-inch, 10-inch-long sodium-nickel cell, with a beta-alumina conductor optimized for sodium ions:

> Twenty batteries, each with 500 of these cells, could power a locomotive. The cells can be packaged in smaller batches for other applications such as supporting telecom towers or backup energy for data centers. The core—basically salt—is pretty cheap to produce. They do not have leaking issues like today's lead acid batteries do and each cell is independent—so individual failures do not degrade the whole battery.
>
> GE is building a manufacturing facility to come on-line in 2011 with a capacity of 10 million of those cells. Through an investment in A123 systems, we also continue to advance the technology in lithium-ion batteries more common for smaller devices.

GE has not been that focused on infotech markets, but Dr. Joseph Salvo, director at the Telematics group at Global Research has been talking about the "end of the Information Age." When it comes to sensory networks, he believes that "while the 20th century was the era of 'commoditization' of most physical assets, the 21st will change the perceived value of pure data in all its forms—because having data is far less important than connecting it."[3]

So instead of storing data at multiple locations, connect to it and access it only as needed. That could be a game changer.

Of course, the reality is that in other areas, storage is likely to explode. Indeed, the digital pathological image discussed below is 18 gigabytes (GB) in size. That opens up an opportunity for a holographic disc GE has developed, which can hold up to 500 GB of data—the equivalent of 100 DVDs. Blu-ray discs today go up to 50 GB. The big challenge was to find a way to allow these holograms to reflect enough light. GE achieved a quantum increase in the reflective power, which allows the new discs to be readable by current or slightly modified Blu-ray players. GE expects the cost to be around 10 cents a GB and is working on a format that would hold up to 1 terabyte. This size would be enough for many household and small businesses not to need external storage for archiving needs. Additionally, in previous generations of discs, the plastic acted as an inert carrier for the data that sits in a thin layer of metal, such as aluminum; in the new GE version, the plastic becomes the storage medium itself. The all-plastic disc could last a century. That could change long-term archival markets, where today's magnetic tape is good for only up to 20 years. That could be a game changer for the storage market.

There is a sidebar to the disc story, as is so common when discussing anything at Global Research. GE's interest in discs originally related to its GE Plastics division, which has since been sold to SABIC, a Saudi chemical company. GE often keeps rights to promising technologies and nurtures them even after it exits a business.

"Compounds" and Collaboration

In recent years, one of the biggest changes has been the evolution of "compound" solutions that leverage innovation, polymath fashion, across many technology disciplines.

Over the 2009 holiday season, the Global Research Web site displayed a new sleigh for Santa using a wide range of its innovations:

- Hydrophobic coating to keep ice off the sleigh
- Self-powered OLED lighting to help guide Santa
- Ultralight and durable sleigh blades made from ceramic composites

- Sleigh frame made from carbon composites
- Sodium batteries to store energy
- Cruise control via the Trip Optimizer
- Wearable radio-frequency identification sensor to check airborne particles and warn if the milk and cookies left out have gone bad
- The 500 GB holographic disc to hold the entire list of gifts he is carrying
- Wireless medical sensor to track Santa's heartbeat
- Asset Intelligence Tracking tech so his elves can keep track of Santa's whereabouts

While that was in fun, such compounds are increasingly common in GE products. Sedziol points to one compound—the Trip Optimizer for the locomotive:

It leverages concepts from multiple businesses like telematics—sensors and GPS—and advanced software algorithms to optimize performance on locomotives. It is "cruise control" for the locomotive—smoothes out the typical start and stop and slowdown common with a human operator. It is far more sophisticated, of course, and can optimize the velocity based on time, fuel efficiency and other constraints.

Jarvis points to another:

Engineers from the Imaging Technologies group were looking at a system that would allow someone to see into the near infrared. At the same time, biologists in our Biosciences organization, who had joined Global Research following the GE acquisition of Amersham Biosciences, were working with imaging agents that had the potential to fluoresce in the near infrared. The two groups connected and the optical imaging program was born. The biologists immediately saw the opportunity to design agents to be used in a surgical setting, letting doctors see into the body like never before. Last year, the team transitioned an imaging agent to GE's Healthcare business that can identify tumor margins. These agents will one day allow surgeons to improve patient outcomes for cancer surgery.

Jarvis also points to growing collaboration with other enterprises:

A decade ago, the GRC campus was pretty secretive and not that open to many outside visitors. Today, we are working with Eli Lilly on cancer diagnostics and therapies, with Schlumberger on carbon sequestering, Chevron on subsea electrification, Konica Minolta on organic LEDs, and many more.

We do joint research with leading universities like MIT and UC Berkeley. Our Munich location is on the campus of the Technische Universtät München. We are working with government research groups like the National Institute of Health. We are constantly talking to VCs [venture capitalists] about collaboration with their portfolio companies.

An example of such collaboration is Omnyx, a joint venture of GE Healthcare and University of Pittsburgh Medical Center.

Robert Filkins is an electrical engineer by training, but he is showing off GE's digital pathology product. It digitizes the process that lab technicians use to look at tissue on the traditional format of a glass slide under a microscope. Filkins is using an Xbox controller to twist, turn, and magnify the image on a computer screen and explains that "Not only is it easy to store the digital results in an Electronic Medical Records database; it can be reviewed by peers halfway across the world if need be. It also cuts into expensive FedEx charges for sending those slides to labs."

Global Extensions

Software competencies such as those needed in the locomotive Trip Optimizer led GE to open its first international branch of Global Research in Bangalore, India, in 1999. Now with 400 technologists, it helps beyond software on research on applied fluids and electromagnetics. Later centers, such as one in Shanghai, China, with competency in water desalination, and another in Munich, Germany, with a focus on renewables, bring other unique specialties. Like Bangalore, though, they are leveraged across multiple areas. A fifth center is planned for Brazil. Satellite offices in Japan, Russia, and Israel draw on other local competencies.

These centers also position GE better for local opportunities as these markets grow rapidly. As we will discuss in Chapter 5, there is the opportunity for "trickle-up" innovation, as with the MAC 800 ECG, which was introduced in the United States after being designed (and priced) for Chinese and Indian markets.

Immelt was quoted saying, "Globalization is in its fourth stage. It started out importing high-end products from the United States to India, then turned to local joint ventures, followed by moves to build factories in China and India, its current focus. The next stage is designing technologies in India for the rest of the world."[4]

In 2009, the U.S. Congress saw the introduction of an immigration bill titled STAPLE (Stopping Trained in America PhDs from Leaving the Economy). It would fast-track the immigration process for foreign students doing their doctoral studies in technical sciences at U.S. institutions of higher education. Given the current U.S. mood on immigration, it will likely meander for a while, but GE Global Research is the poster child for supporting the bill. Walk the halls of GE in Niskayuna and you see last names like Liu, Krishnan, and Potyrailo—talented immigrants from everywhere. The tradition of Charles Proteus Steinmetz, the founder of the original GE research lab and an immigrant from Germany, is alive and well.

"Serendipities"

GE Global Research has not been called the "Magic Factory" for nothing. There is a secret sauce that even a Six Sigma, documentation-intense organization cannot completely codify. Conversations in the cafeteria, in the hallways, and at the 40-room lodge attached to the center effortlessly drift from pathology to holography, from one "aha" to another.

The Global Research ethos is "Innovation occurs at the intersection of disciplines." So, put chemists, mathematicians, engineers of all stripes, and biologists in close proximity and who knows where the conversations will lead. It is a great setting for what the Kate Beckinsale character in the movie *Serendipity* calls "fortunate accidents."

Todd Alhart, a colleague of Jarvis's in Communications and Public Affairs, has a couple of examples:

> *GE had developed composites for aviation uses, now as we explore much longer wind turbine blades (increased from 40 to 55 meters) and increased yield (from 1.5 to 2.5 megawatt) the composites of carbon and fiberglass are delivering higher efficiency and lowering noise.*
>
> *The lotus leaf repels water and is self-cleaning. Our research on nano-hairs is showing up in hydrophobic [water-resistant] coatings to reduce wind turbine blade drag and antifreeze applications. It has significant safety and fuel efficiency implications.*

Biomimetics—a term Mark Little, senior vice president of GE Global Research, used in a presentation to financial analysts in 2006[5]—refers to the discipline of science mimicking nature, as in drawing innovative inspiration from the lotus leaf.

How many financial analysts would have heard that term? Hey, if you have communications folks like Alhart and Jarvis who are tech savvy, why should Wall Street analysts not keep up? Jarvis humbly jokes about it: "Our general assumption is when we walk into a room with all the PhDs, here we are the dumbest people in the room."

What keeps the technologists themselves humble and focused? The grand challenges. Two-thirds of the way through to 2015 the UN Millennium Development Goals are far from accomplished. That fact spurs the GE technologists. Also, let's face it, many of the technologies discussed in this profile have been announced and showcased by GE for years as it commercializes them. Its PhDs are toiling away at plenty more in the labs that GE is not ready to discuss.

And then there is the short-term deliverable for the technologists: the 2010 model sleigh for Santa.

Let's now turn attention to how corporate IT at GE is innovating.

Corporate IT

"We have an initiative we call turning IT inside-out," says Mark Mastrianni, Manager, GE Global Technology Acquisition and Licensing. He is an attorney with a law degree from Syracuse who also studied Computer Science at Union College, legal economics at the London School of Economics and did an entrepreneurial stint prior to joining GE. As such, he has a broad charter at corporate IT in GE—he is into IT strategy, negotiations with technology suppliers, and even some marketing and licensing of GE-developed IT capabilities and technologies to third parties. Mastrianni continues, "It's about support of growing digital opportunities across our businesses—in software, systems integration, etc."

It would be easy to dismiss that statement as coming from yet another IT group struggling to transition from an internal cost center to an external, results-focused mentality. This is, however, a company whose sophistication in IT and other internal technology usage is typified by three industry episodes from the past decade:

- In 2000, a dot-com entrepreneur found a prime piece of real estate at an affordable price. Excited about the move into the facility, his attorney pointed out that the lessor wanted share warrants in his company. "Warrants? Is this a private equity firm?" the entrepreneur asked. No, but it was a unit of GE, which is savvy enough to understand the risks and potential upside from such warrants in a technology start-up.
- In 2003, a Siemens executive was both impressed and annoyed. As he visited several vendors on a due diligence trip to India, he noticed that he was not allowed to enter any GE-designated areas. Siemens competes with GE in many markets, and the executive took it as a good sign, since his company's interests would be similarly protected. He was bothered, though, with the number of GE units he saw at each vendor. His advisor explained: "GE has a mature global IT delivery program that is embedded in most of their units. Across all of GE, it gives them at least an annual $1 billion advantage over Siemens."
- In 2007, Genpact, the leading business process outsourcing (BPO) firm, went public after a decade of explosive growth, most as a captive unit of GE. Says a customer:

Pretty impressive that GE was so ahead of the curve. Back then (1997), few of us had even heard of BPO. We were trying to grapple with the basic concept of internal shared services, and our version of low cost was Florida or, at a stretch, Ireland. GE was thinking of consolidating all our shared services for even more scale. And applying Six Sigma concepts and doing it in Hungary, India, or China for even better process quality and economics.

As Mastrianni discusses various GE corporate IT initiatives, you can see how the company is innovating based on savvy understanding of global technology economics and astute leverage of licensing and intellectual property rights. It shows in two big areas: IT as a profit center and vertical opportunities.

IT as a "Profit Center"

Mastrianni talks about several GE projects, aimed first at internal needs but then getting ready to springboard to market through licensing arrangements with external technology vendors. They include:

- *SupportCentral.* This "professional networking platform," launched with former GE global CIO Gary Reiner's vision and support in 2000, has more than 50,000 communities with over 100,000 experts across almost 20,000 business process flows signed up to answer questions and manage information. It gets a mind-boggling 25 million hits a day in 20 languages from GE employees around the world. SupportCentral is the biggest business-focused social network you have never heard of in a market dominated by fawning media coverage of Facebook and Twitter. And with workflow, mashups, and connectivity to more than 2,000 enterprise systems, it has evolved to a "self-service cloud," helping people manage processes and projects and solve business problems.
- *Mobile application framework.* While the iPhone App Store has seen explosive growth—more than 175,000 active applications as of April 2010 and billions of downloads—the majority of the applications are aimed at consumers. GE has built a framework to allow it to rapidly develop business applications on BlackBerry and iPhone platforms.
- *Advanced collaboration lab.* Mastrianni says: "Team productivity—we have barely squeezed that lemon in terms of opportunities." GE has been leveraging telepresence, shared whiteboards, and other emerging technologies to enable widely dispersed teams to collaborate better in product design.
- *PR insight.* GE has made a multiyear investment in a platform to visually aggregate snapshots of the company's social media activity and

signals from Twitter, YouTube, blogs, and the like. PR insight gives GE business intelligence on external perceptions and market acceptance of a given campaign.

Go to Market with Vertical Technology Opportunities

Below, Mastrianni talks about a number of the technologies we heard about in the previous section on GE Global Research:

In sector after sector, we find that technology suppliers sometimes lack deep domain knowledge when it comes to vertical technology solutions. That has opened the door for GE Healthcare, GE Transportation and other units to become technology leaders in their markets. We are a multi-billion dollar software and technology company in our own right.

When we say aligning IT with business, it also means making these units smarter about what we have learned over the years in IT procurement and contracting. Part of my role is to coach these business units on the unique nuances of technology sales compensation, revenue recognition, IP issues, and other technology industry opportunities and challenges.

It also means IT getting close to businesses in other ways:

In our planned Michigan Advanced Manufacturing and Software Technology Center, we will have experts in software development, data architecture, networking, business intelligence, and program management—right next to those from next-generation manufacturing technologies in areas such as renewable energy, jet engines, gas turbines, and other high-technology products. In fact, it will be the only GE Center where every one of our many business units is represented and core IT skills will be right there with all of them.

Asked about GE's guiding technology acquisition principles, Mastrianni outlines a few, as described next.

Objectively Evaluate All Options: Buy, Build, Lease, Rent, Whatever

Many IT groups face an interesting dilemma. Their CFOs frown on any staff hiring—spend on contractors is far easier to get approved. It's the same thing with custom development versus a packaged software acquisition. Often, it is more convenient for IT to buy than to build new technology. That explains the 90 percent spend with outside vendors we talked about in Chapter 2.

Mastrianni has a refreshingly different perspective:

At GE, we are becoming really good at agile development methodologies. And we are pretty good at technology talent pool identification and sourcing around the world. So we are not afraid to build captive units that compete with what we also buy from external suppliers. Buy, build, rent—we are agnostic.

Clearly in the new business climate, conserving cash is key. So capex [capital expenditures] versus opex [operating expenditures] gets more scrutiny. But we go with whatever the business case justifies.

Often, a vendor decision has more to do with domain knowledge and time-to-market issues:

You think we would be market leaders in adopting the new trend of cloud computing. In some ways perhaps we are—for example, we have developed a portal to normalize the offerings across cloud infrastructure providers. That way each user does not have to make that supplier decision every time they need to provision new capacity.

We have one of the largest current deployments of Aravo—a supply chain management SaaS [Software-as-a-Service] software to help with our half a million indirect suppliers. It was a domain knowledge decision more than a SaaS decision. Same thing with a security SaaS offering. In many other business processes and IT areas, we have not made the shift to SaaS. It's got to make business sense.

Start-Ups Can Be Vibrant Sources of Innovation

While many companies have consolidated much of their IT spend with larger vendors (over 50 percent of technology and telecom spend is with the top 25 global vendors, as shown in Chapter 2), thousands of innovative vendors fight for scraps, and many are shut out of an opportunity at too many large IT shops. Mastrianni says:

We have always tried to keep an open mind about opportunities with start-ups and mid-caps—they can be a good a source of technology innovation. In fact, we have demanding due diligence standards before smaller suppliers can become part of the GE ecosystem. Our culture of root cause analysis and Six Sigma means we push our smaller suppliers as much as our larger ones. [Former CIO Gary Reiner also led their company-wide quality initiatives.] But most suppliers tell us we are very constructive in our feedback and that their products grow with our enhancement requests.

Many suppliers use the GE experience to go on to bigger things. Talk to many GE and Infosys executives, and emotions flow about the Infosys decision in 1994 to exit a technology services relationship with GE. Risky as the decision was—GE accounted for a third of its revenues—Infosys did not want to reduce its rates any farther. It has not done too badly since—annual global revenues are now more than $5 billion, and the company was celebrated in the Thomas Friedman bestseller *The World Is Flat.* In turn, GE has gone on to find many newer vendors in India, Mexico, Eastern Europe, and China to diversify far beyond what Infosys would likely have provided it.

Mastrianni jokes about other benefits that sometimes accrue to smaller tech suppliers at GE:

> *From time to time after we have completed and implemented technologies with an emerging firm, they became an acquisition target. Perhaps coincidental, perhaps not. We signed a broad licensing deal with Mercury Interactive. HP eventually acquired them. We did a deal with Opsware. HP acquired them.*
>
> *Both sides owe us broker fees!*

Economics Are Not Just about Lowest Price per Unit

Over his career, Mastrianni has seen every conceivable trick in the technology vendor playbook. Although he finds some irritating, he looks at the bigger picture:

> *We value compelling economics, to be sure, but low prices have to be viewed against the filter of a framework of long-term procurement volumes, quality, service levels—and frankly, overall competitive advantage.*

As companies search for innovation, few look at IT economics and licensing as a source. Mastrianni and GE provide compelling reasons to turn IT "inside out" for more innovation, for better alignment with core business growth, and for opportunities to monetize the value that IT brings to the business.

R&D at a Business Unit

In Chapter 12, we discuss how Silver Spring Networks is helping in the rollout of smart utility grids, how many German consumers today sell surplus solar energy from their homes back to the grid, and other cleantech innovations.

In July 2009, the GE Consumer & Industrial business unit announced plans to make the Net Zero (as in annual energy bills) home a reality by 2015. The concept blends appliances it already offers with cleantech products it plans to introduce. The newer products include "small" wind products. GE has an investment in Southwest Windpower, which makes 3-kilowatt-rated Skystream turbines, ideal for homes. Other new products include the software that will be the "brains" of home energy management, hybrid home heaters, LED lighting, and next-generation batteries. As we saw earlier in this chapter, the Global Research Center has initiatives around many of those technologies in such products.

Figure 3.1 describes the components GE showcased.

Much will need to evolve between now and 2015. Will smart grids be available in many markets? Do we expect nighttime energy costs to be low enough to change consumption patterns? Will the economics of solar panels—which can cost as much as $10,000 per kilowatt to install—and wind turbines get much better with manufacturing scale and global

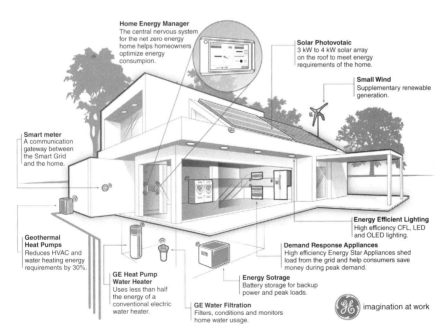

FIGURE 3.1 GE Targets Net Zero Homes by 2015
Source: GE.

competition? What tax credits will governments offer for home improvements around home cleantech? Will homeowners wait to replace current appliances at the end of their useful lives, or will they replace them earlier with smarter ones given proper incentives?

There are lots of questions, but it is interesting to see the polymath-style unified vision that GE has pulled together across its product lines.

Business Unit IT

Trying to implement an agile project with its emphasis on iterative design-development and minimal planning in the regulation-heavy health care industry sounds like an oxymoron, but GE's Healthcare (GEHC) division did just that successfully. Striving for constant improvement, the team used agile methods to reduce the project timeline by 25 percent while maintaining quality and scope. These techniques provide another perspective on how GE innovates.

In 2007, GEHC began an initiative to streamline its international sales and marketing processes through an improved customer relationship management (CRM) solution and seamless integration of the supporting processes. Chad Dodd, GEHC IT leader, Damon Auer of Tribridge, Inc., and Bob Glynn of Affinity Inc. led the program office. Auer and Glynn represented two boutique systems integration firms that assisted on the implementation. Using Tribridge and Affinity, even though the companies had little experience with GE and its rigorous implementation processes, was the first of many innovations for the project team, which ultimately paid off for GE.

The initial plan was to use a sequential "waterfall" implementation and testing methodology (common in many traditional IT projects) to develop, validate, and deploy a Siebel (now part of Oracle) solution to more than 2,500 users in a 36-month period. The methodology was deeply integrated into GEHC's quality processes and ensured compliance with Food and Drug Administration (FDA) regulations and quality standards. It was a good plan, but three months in, business needs changed. Now, the team was under pressure to deliver the same scope solution but in 25 percent less time. If the solution was not deployed in that shortened time frame, the business was at risk of losing millions of dollars. Due to this risk, the team began to rethink its implementation strategy and plan. Team members quickly came to the harsh realization that the waterfall methodology, while tried and tested, would never get them successfully across the goal line in time.

To meet this challenge, the team considered another innovative but risky suggestion: "Let's change gears and try an agile methodology."

Agile is a relatively new religion in software development that has grown over the last few years and emphasizes iterative design-development, collaboration, process adaptability, and continuous improvement. The Manifesto for Agile Software Development emphasizes four elements by stating:

> *We are uncovering better ways of developing software by doing it and helping others do it. Through this work we have come to value:*
>
> - *Individuals and interactions over processes and tools*
> - *Working software over comprehensive documentation*
> - *Customer collaboration over contract negotiation*
> - *Responding to change over following a plan*
>
> *That is, while there is value in the items on the right, we value the items on the left more.*[6]

Even though other GE units had experience with agile IT projects, the GEHC organization raised many questions and concerns—particularly the manifesto's deemphasis of processes and documentation.
Other questions came up:

- How do you execute an agile project while dependent on 26 other teams?
- How can you collaborate effectively when the team is located across seven countries and three continents?
- How does a custom development methodology such as agile work for a packaged application such as Siebel?
- In a short cycle, how can you document the design, test scripts, and test results with sufficient detail and traceability to satisfy FDA regulations?
- How does this methodology work with the current IT and documentation standards required within the waterfall methodology?
- How does this methodology affect the system integrators' fixed-fee contract?
- And what exactly are agile terms like "scrum," "sprint," and "backlog"?

After getting support from GEHC's leadership, the GE program office made another innovative—but again risky—change to the project. It introduced a third boutique consulting firm, ThoughtWorks, to an already large and complex project team. ThoughtWorks, led by Glenn Kapetansky, brought a unique view and expertise around agile, which was desperately needed. The team was broken into five small "scrums" with no more than six people in each. Each was tasked to complete requirements analysis, design, development, unit testing, and document creation in a two-week cycle: a sprint.

ThoughtWorks wisely proposed a "garden wall" around the project team. This concept protected the team members from the barrage of questions and concerns raised by other stakeholders in the organization. Dodd took on the thankless job of establishing this garden wall and protecting the team from external distractions.

Auer looks back at the scribbles in his notebook and says that if there had been a team Twitter message stream, it would have shown the skepticism and chaos the team navigated:

> *05/14/08: New challenge to deliver 9 mos early—evaluating plan*
> *05/28/08: Mtg w/ Infrastructure—says we'll never make it*
> *06/04/08: Validation and Quality team says we'll never make it*
> *06/10/08: Reorganized Program Team into 5 Scrums—working out Sprint schedule*
> *07/18/08: Sprint 1 complete—shortening subsequent Sprints to 2 weeks*
> *08/01/08: Product Backlog is a mess—need Product Owner help to clean up*
> *08/12/08: Scope change—adding Korea to 1st deploy plan*
> *09/16/08: Falling behind—adding more capacity to Pricing Scrum*
> *09/24/08: Chicken or a pig? Scrum of Scrums mtg at 8AM CT*
> *10/18/08: Adding 3 more Sprints to handle new reqmts*
> *11/04/08: Release mgmt says we won't make our first go-live in July*
> *01/06/09: Crunch is on to hit user acceptance—pls prioritize*
> *01/18/09: Final Sprint 13 complete—thanks everyone!*
> *02/02/09: Scrums dissolved—Validation and migration focus for next 4 months*
> *07/08/09: Application in Prod now—great job all!!*

The new CRM system was migrated to production just 14 months after the decision to use agile to speed product development. While not lightning fast, this was an incredible delivery pace for a program of this scale in GEHC's highly regulated environment. Many of the program skeptics became vocal supporters, and the agile method is now in use in numerous programs across GEHC. The international CRM system is now being enhanced on a regular release schedule, and dozens of additional country deployments are in the works.

After celebrating, Dodd summarizes:

> *It's been said that constraints drive innovation. This project certainly forced the team to innovate. From the selection of boutique system integrators to the decision to adopt agile for a packaged application to the implementation of the "garden wall," the team was continually pushing*

the envelope and redefining its own comfort zone. Just like the GEHC product teams who are constantly pushing the envelope of new medical technologies, IT can also innovate and change how solutions are delivered. With the right team members, a strong methodology, and good tools, anything is possible.

Recap

Take any of the grand challenges we listed in Chapter 2, and GE appears to relish signing up for them. In a world focused on light innovation around social networks and mobile devices, GE is making industrial innovation fashionable again.

The thousands of PhDs in its labs are converging technologies to come up with complex new solutions. Its solutions seamlessly bring products together from multiple business units. Its internal IT innovates on its own and coaches its business unit on intellectual property and technology contracting issues as the businesses increasingly embed technology into their products. Looked at from multiple dimensions, GE is clearly a polymath that many others should emulate.

The R-E-N-A-I-S-S-A-N-C-E Framework

Building Blocks for the New Polymath

Part II brings together 11 building blocks—representing the letters in the word "renaissance" and each representing a group of innovative technologies, vendors, and practices. Associated with six of the building blocks are profiles of polymaths which showcase how they have exploited that grouping of technologies, vendors, and practices.

- Residence: Better Technologically Equipped than the Office
- Exotics: Innovation from Left Field
  Polymath Profile #2: Cognizant
- Networks: Bluetooth to Broadband
  Polymath Profile #3: Plantronics
- Arsonists: And Other Disruptors
  Polymath Profile #4: W. R. Hambrecht
- Interfaces: For All Our Senses
- Sustainability: Delivering to Both the Green and Gold Agendas
  Polymath Profile #5: Kleiner Perkins Cleantech
- Singularity: The Human–Machine Convergence
- Analytics: Spreadsheets, Search, and Semantics
  Polymath Profile #6: National Hurricane Center
- Networks Again: Communities, Crowds, Contracts, and Collaboration
- Clouds: Technology-as-a-Service
  Polymath Profile #7: salesforce.com
- Ethics: In an Age of Cyberwar and Cloning

CHAPTER 4

Residence:
Better Technologically
Equipped Than the Office

The year 2001 was a milestone for both Apple and Southwest Airlines. Apple launched the iPod, and Southwest, like most in the global aviation industry, changed after the 9/11 tragedy. The year 2001 also marked the beginning of a trend the research firm Gartner recognized a few years later as "consumerization of technology." It called it "the growing practice of introducing new technologies into consumer markets prior to industrial markets."[1]

Why are we talking about Apple and Southwest Airlines in the same breath? One competes on its superbly designed products, the other on operations that are highly efficient but detractors continue to mock as "cattle cars."

Bear with us and join us on a Southwest flight over Florida.

Southwest Airlines and Consumerization

"No popcorn on board, but would you like Cokes to go with that movie?" asked Mike, the Southwest flight attendant as he came to a row with all three passengers peering down intently at a laptop.

"Not a movie—GPS maps," responded the passenger in the middle seat.

Mike then noticed the tether coming out of the laptop and disappearing under the window shade. He could not see it, but the passenger's laptop showed the GPS-derived bearings as *29.00058 N/ 81.48425 W/ 25466.86 ft.*

"I bet you have more detailed maps than our pilots do up front," Mike continued.

He was right about that. A few minutes earlier, the passengers had laughed at how quickly McDonald's were zipping by as they flew the length of the Sunshine State at 500 miles an hour.

"Of locations on the ground, yes. But I hope the pilots have better information of what is around us in the air," the passenger responded, and everyone around nervously chuckled.

Walking away, Mike could have been thinking that, the way things are going, even the last statement would not hold true for too long. As Southwest installs Wi-Fi radomes (humps that shield the antennas) near the tails of its 737s, passengers would have even more real-time information about the flight on their laptops or PDAs—with somewhat delayed information, one hopes, so as not to compromise air security. Passengers would definitely have far more choices in live news and sports and other Web fare—far beyond what its competitor JetBlue pioneered with satellite TV a few years ago. That technology had stolen a number of Southwest's faithful, and another upstart, Virgin America, was starting to do again by equipping 100 percent of its fleet with Wi-Fi.

It would have only mildly surprised Mike to find he was the first Southwest employee the passenger had talked to on this trip. The passenger had booked his flight online and had printed his boarding pass at home. He had no bags to check so he did not need to interact with any Southwest ground employees. Southwest's accountants must love such low-touch customers!

Mike would have been a bit more surprised to find that the passenger had tracked the in-bound flight on a Web site called FlightAware and noticed the flight was running a bit late, so he had stayed home and had that extra cup of coffee. When he got to the airport, he had jumped on the free Wi-Fi the airport offered and checked on the in-bound flight again. In prior years, gate agents would often "stretch the truth" about flight status. Now, passengers can double-check on their own. While at it, the passenger had checked for likely thunder clouds on the route via Weather.com. It looked like a fine day to fly.

It would have impressed Mike that, for around $100, the passenger had bought Microsoft Streets and Trips, which was up on his laptop. It had come with a postage-stamp-sized GPS chip from Pharos, which he had tucked under the plane window shade and had tethered it via a USB cable to his laptop. It wasn't what the manufacturer had intended the device for, but who can imagine what intrepid consumers use stuff for these days? The Microsoft software allowed him access to all kinds of useful—and not so useful—information, including the street address of every McDonald's the plane was zipping by. The GPS signals were free—compliments of U.S. military–funded satellites.

Things sure had changed in the last few years, Mike thought.

Changed so much that Southwest had tested various GPS units and had the confidence to allow passengers to use them in-flight while most airlines banned them. Authorities, such as the U.S. FAA, leave the decision to airline discretion.

For three decades, Southwest had successfully navigated the turbulent aviation industry, making money as competitors bled by being conservative about everything, including technology. Southwest actually had reusable, plastic boarding passes that were collected as passengers boarded. In fact, the airline made a virtue of being low tech. New security after 9/11 forced the airline, kicking and screaming, to rethink ticketing and other automation. That was fortuitous because it allowed Southwest to align with a trend that started to accelerate around that time: the increasingly tech-savvy customer, the one around whom Apple had built its phoenix-like renewal.

Apple and Consumerization

In the 1990s, Apple almost went out of business as it struggled to sell technology to enterprises competing against the Microsoft juggernaut and its PC partners in IBM, HP, Dell, and others. Then Apple spectacularly turned its fortunes around by selling its Macs and iPods directly to consumers through its retail stores, through partners like AT&T and on the Web.

As Steve Jobs told *Time* magazine in 2002, "I would rather compete with Sony than compete in another product category with Microsoft."[2]

Rich Karlgaard of *Forbes* blogged, "The genius of Steve Jobs has always been to marry his good-enough layman's understanding of technology with his world-class design eye and his preternatural understanding of cultural moods."[3]

Apple's attitude during the turnaround almost seemed to be "Who cares about the corporate buyer? Sure, we'll take his money, but we don't need to chase after him. In fact, we'll run humorous ads mocking the PC and the enterprise." You can afford to do so when some of the most diehard consumers—"fanboys" in Apple lingo—willingly pay you premium prices.

Of course, it was not just Apple.

Microsoft introduced the Xbox in 2001; HP announced more of a focus on entertainment with its Media Center PC in 2002; Skype arrived in 2003 and would change calling habits for millions around the world; the massively multiplayer game World of Warcraft disrupted our lives in 2004; and in 2005, with the Sony Rootkit issue, consumers started to hear about intellectual property issues previously limited to corporate corridors.

Since 2005, Google's growing Web and mobile presence has introduced consumers to analytical power that big companies paid bucket loads of money for. The Apple iPhone—considered one of the most successful product launches ever—and all kinds of GPS, gaming, entertainment, and other gadgets have only accelerated the consumerization trend. The Wii reshaped our expectations of computer interfaces; the Kindle, our expectations of books. *Electronic House* magazine has celebrated houses with all kinds of home theaters and elaborate security systems. eBay has built a cottage industry of individuals doing business from home. JetBlue has moved call reservations to agents working from home. SOHO is no longer just a Manhattan neighborhood but a growing revenue category for technology companies as the acronym for small office, home office.

The Southwest story has its own innovation sidebar. When the airline introduced online check-in, the first passengers to do so precisely 24 hours before the departure time got "A group" boarding passes. They got to board first and sit where they wanted on an airline that has always had open seating. A company called BoardFirst went into business in 2005 to help passengers get those coveted A passes. For $5, you told them your electronic reservation code, and they would check you in. It saved you from missing out on an A pass if you were too busy, asleep, or just plain forgetful 24 hours prior to the flight. Southwest drove BoardFirst out of business in 2007 by persuading a court that BoardFirst's Web site could be used only for "personal, noncommercial purposes."[4]

In 2009, realizing that the service had indeed been valuable, Southwest introduced in own EarlyBird check-in—this time for $10 per flight! Seeing how far Southwest has come since 2001, few would dare call it a technology Luddite any more.

Rise of the Tech-Savvy Consumer

Josh Snowhorn works for a data-center outsourcing firm and gets animated when discussing fluid dynamics and CAT-6 cable:

> *One of the first things I discussed with the architect was thermodynamics and fluid dynamics. Structural insulated panels (SIPS) are polystyrene foam core panels with a very high R-value that effectively keep in cold/ warm air and keep out the contrasting warm/cold air from the outside. Once I knew we had a tight envelope, I chose geothermal cooling for the HVAC [heating, air conditioning, and ventilation] system using multiple 300-foot deep bores connected to a closed loop liquid manifold system.*

Snowhorn is not discussing a new data center. He is describing the building plans for his new dream house in Austin, Texas!

Snowhorn was one of more than 75 acquaintances the author invited to guest blog about how technology was influencing their weekend hobby or passion. In Snowhorn's case, the construction of his house has been his passion the last couple of years.

Others who wrote in the series had more mainstream interests but showed just as keen an eye for all kinds of technology that has influenced their interests:

- Mike Prosceno, in software, described braided "Spectra Filter" and newfangled polymers that make his fishing line stronger and the "billet 6061-T6 aluminum stock" in fishing reels he covets.
- Joy Wald at ADT Security described her hobby as being "supermom." Having just returned to work with a young baby, she talked about how technology was allowing her to manage the most intense work/life balancing phase in a modern woman's life.
- Jim Rafferty, an executive recruiter, described how GPS had supplanted laser technology on the golf course and said with a sigh, "Most of us do not score better, but we are having more fun trying."
- Naomi Bloom, a human resource consultant, talked about how she stays in touch with friends around the world with a Skype Web cam and via SmugMug, a photo-sharing site.
- Harish Malani, an entrepreneur, described how technology has influenced his travels over the last five decades. He is in rarefied company as someone who has been to over 100 countries. He described missing bags and lost hotel reservations that technology is increasingly making an exception.
- Joe Thornton of Lawson Software described how technology allows him to sync up with members of the River City Jazz Orchestra in Minneapolis/St. Paul, where he plays sax. He joked: "I tried living close to Bob Dylan's birth home—he is a Minnesota boy—and this is where it got me."
- Kimberly Baker, who works for an Oracle implementation partner, described how much safer she feels on her side trips across Michigan in a car equipped with GPS and other sensors.
- Dr. Michael Lamoureux wrote about how Google Earth allows him to be an archaeologist from his armchair as he also juggles life with young kids, a wife in university, volunteer commitments, and a consulting business.
- Will Scott described how technology allows him to perform community service for his birthplace in Zambia while running a business in Chicago. He talks with pride about the changes in Zambia: "An enduring memory is young people using their cell phones from an ox cart in the African bush, an hour from the nearest road."

Consumerization Impact—Not Just on the High-Tech Industry

Snowhorn, Wald, and Scott are increasingly the new consumer, and they are changing expectations of the technology they expect from every industry, not just from the high-tech industry.

Take hospitality: "Somewhere along the way ... the hotel industry fell behind with regards [sic] to the in-room technology. Even in high end luxury or resort level hotels, the average guest settles for an in-room technology package that was far less than what he or she had available at home."[5]

Consider the clubby, agent-driven world of residential real estate: "[In] a perfect market, where the true value of a home is crystal clear to all parties and the fairy-tale note on a napkin comes in the form of an anonymized e-mail, 6 percent begins to look an awful lot like a luxury."[6]

Take the impact of "citizen journalism" on traditional media, as ordinary Joes take videos with mobile phones and Flip camcorders and then blog and Twitter about them at lightning speed in obscure places: "You can learn more about how Americans live just by looking at the backgrounds of YouTube videos—those rumpled bedrooms and toy-strewn basement rec rooms—than you could from 1,000 hours of network television."[7]

Or look at sporting arenas—no slouches when it comes to adopting technology—having to react to home theaters with HD and 3-D TV and surround sound: "That has forced sports officials to rethink the game experience and desperately attempt to bring the living room to the game, not the other way around."[8]

Indeed, bring the living room to the game, not the other way around. And increasingly, you don't even need Snowhorn's high-powered data center of a house to stake a claim for such a living room.

If Cardinal Richelieu were alive today, he would surely be tempted to write, "The Den Pen is Mightier than the Board Sword."

Wait until You See the Next-Generation Consumer

Now imagine when the next consumer generation comes along. Look at the high school student who goes to a Microsoft-sponsored school of the future near Philadelphia. Students there use smart cards to register attendance, open their digital lockers, and track calories they consume. They carry laptops, not books; their teachers use interactive "smart boards," and the entire campus has Wi-Fi access. This is the "You mean there's no app for that?" generation, which suspects you have not looked hard enough in the 175,000-plus and exponentially growing base of applications in the iPhone App Store for solutions to any of life's challenges.

Some companies are trying the superficial "let's put lipstick on the pig": change the user interface to look more "cool" and use language and graphics in manuals younger employees can relate to.

That will not help with Mia Lindheimer, who knows treasure hunts are not just for pirates. Since she was six, she has been geocaching. In this game, people set up caches all over the world and share their locations on the Internet. GPS users can then use the location coordinates to find the caches. How do you find more about the game? "Oh, just Google it," she says to the annoyance of her father, who works at Microsoft and would rather she say "Bing it."

Even younger Mias are growing up with Nabaztag, the cuddly name for "rabbit" in Armenian. It's also the brand of a toy that entertains kids with its flashing colors and dancing ears. What's the big deal? Such toys have been around for a while. Not the kind wired with Wi-Fi, MP3, a radio-frequency identity (RFID) reader, USB, and other technology that allows the toy to listen, talk, tell you the weather and when you have e-mail and read you books (at least those with an RFID tag that it can scan). By the way, these also are part of the entertainment for the grand-parents who are baby-sitting virtually on Skype Web cams from hundreds of miles away.

Why wait for those young consumers to grow? Consumerization repre-sents huge opportunities and risks today for the polymath enterprise:

The opportunities:

- Can we embed technology in our products and services to competitive advantage?
- How can we use technology to delight existing customers of more traditional products?
- Can we leverage new consumers for new product ideas?
- Can we take advantage of consumer technologies for our own internal use?

The risks:

- Do our culture, our channel, and our other characteristics allow us to successfully embed technology into our products—to ourselves become, in a sense, technology vendors?
- How will these new consumers react to corporate IT and business processes as they enter our workforces?
- Are we letting a focus on the tech-savvy customer distort our view of the rest of our customer base?

Technology, Finally, Can Be about Revenue Generation

The tech-savvy consumer is allowing even nontech companies—auto, appliance, shoe makers—to embed all kinds of technology in their prod-ucts. Historically, enterprise technology has been mostly about efficiency and productivity. Now it is showing up as product revenue:

- Nike embeds sensors in its shoes that can send to iPods information such as run time, distance, pace, and calories burned. It also has a social network, Nike+, with a legion of fans. Last year, 800,000 runners logged on and signed up to run a 10K race sponsored by Nike simultaneously in 25 cities, from Chicago to São Paulo.
- Companies like Moen are replacing faucet handles in tubs and showers with touch screens and other electronic controls that remember preferences for water temperature and flow patterns and even sing for you in the shower.
- Ford ran a campaign, "MPGs meets MP3s," around its Focus car. The campaign reflects the growing range of consumer electronics for entertainment, telephony, navigation, toll payment, and other features in the modern auto.
- Starbucks has become synonymous with Wi-Fi on the road—Java applets with your cup of java. It is also a significant channel for digitized music, and its paid-value cards are allowing it to play in other consumer markets.
- LED lighting beads in many costumes and carpets stole the show at the spectacular opening ceremony at the Beijing Olympics. The beads are now being embedded in many home furnishings, including rugs.

Technology as a Competitive Advantage or Disadvantage

Every generation of enterprises underestimates its consumers, as David Ogilvy, the legendary advertising executive, reminded us when he quipped, "The customer is not a moron. She's your wife." Too many companies dismiss customer ideas with "the suggestion box is over there."

Today's generation of enterprises smugly counts its data centers and satellites but forgets that its customers, in many cases, have better technology than front-line employees. In addition, other companies—some competitors, some in other industries—are raising customer expectations regarding pricing, service, and delivery through their innovative use of technology. Here are some examples:

- Ochsner Medical Center in New Orleans posts wait times for its emergency rooms so that patients can calculate which of its locations to head toward. That's a huge step up in the seemingly disorganized nature of doctor visits around the world, where 30-, 45-, 60-minute waits seem routine in spite of a specific appointment. Rarely is there even an apology for the wasted patient time.

- Delta Airline's Red Coats used to be an exemplary form of customer service. If you had a problem, you easily found a person in the distinctive jacket among the thousands of passengers at an airport. After an absence of several years, Delta is bringing them back, this time equipped with new Motorola handhelds that will allow them to scan tickets, rebook passengers, remotely assist a gate agent, and do plenty of other things at the point of need. In contrast, many airlines make their passengers walk and walk to get to service counters.
- Steve Ballmer, CEO of Microsoft, routinely gives out his e-mail address when he speaks at events. Then he personally responds to many e-mails or forwards them to others for further attention. In contrast, most corporations refuse to give out executives' e-mail addresses. "Too much spam" is the usual reason.
- As we see in Chapter 7, telephone and cable companies have the image of being big and uncaring—indeed, they score only slightly better than tobacco on reputation scores. Comcast monitors Twitter for disgruntled customers and reaches out (with its handle of ComcastCares) to offer assistance. In contrast, the majority of companies ignore the one-to-one customer relationship management opportunity. And many ban their employees from commenting on blogs, forcing many into even worse scenarios where they post anonymously or behind pseudonyms.

Consumer Sourcing

Most companies have learned to use focus groups, consumer surveys, and other customer input as they design new products. But in the last couple of years, there has been a marked increase in using "crowds" for ideas:

- David Pogue, the *New York Times* journalist who writes about electronics, ran a poll on Twitter about product enhancements people would like to see in cell phones, home theaters, cameras, laptops, and music players. Within hours, he had hundreds of suggestions.
- Google has a Product Ideas site that invites users to submit ideas for its mobile products. Then other users score the ideas. In Chapter 17, we note how a similar concept, MyStarbucksIdea, has improved customer loyalty at that chain.
- While they are not exactly "consumers," Netflix Inc. awarded a seven-member group of researchers, scientists, and engineers from around the world $1 million in a contest to improve its movie recommendation

engine. The publicity around the three-year contest paid off in its own way, though it was dampened as Netflix was hit with a privacy lawsuit that said the improvements made to the recommendation engine made it easier to identify people even via anonymous information.

Consumer Technology Economics Are Not Just for Consumers

Enterprises are gradually waking up to the fact there is no law precluding them from using products aimed at consumers themselves, sometimes at startling savings. Here are some examples:

- William Mougayar, CEO of Eqentia, a "knowledge-tracking" company, says, "We are seeing individual enterprise users and small businesses set up competitive intelligence environments that previously required expensive subscription services and plenty of IT support."
- EMC is a leading storage provider to most large companies. It is not uncommon for companies to pay $3 per gigabyte per month in the total cost of high-end EMC storage arrays. EMC also offers consumers its Mozy service at $4.95 a month—*unlimited*. The high-end EMC products are designed for enterprise-grade scale and reliability, but you can see how customers also lust for better economics.
- At any given time, 10-million-plus users around the world use Skype to talk to each other or watch each other live via video—most of them for free. Enterprises are waking up to the fact that their mobile carriers are actually charging their employees $1 to $4 *a minute* when they call back from an overseas trip.

Looking favorably at consumer technologies often means accepting what *Wired* calls "good enough" technology: "We get our breaking news from blogs, we make spotty long-distance calls on Skype, we watch video on small computer screens rather than TVs, and more and more of us are carrying around dinky, low-power netbook computers that are just good enough to meet our surfing and emailing needs."[9]

The CIO of JetStar, an offshoot of the Australian carrier Qantas, explained in an interview his "good enough" philosophy as what he calls the "97.5% enterprise": "That [final] 2.5 percent—you'd be surprised at how much that locks you in, and how much that costs. That last 2.5 percent is really where the big dollars are, where the big resourcing requirements are, and it's like a ball and chain."[10]

If You Embed Technology into Your Products, Think Like a Technology Company

As companies embed technology into their products, they are learning they have to behave like technology companies themselves:

- It means thinking of service engineers, spare parts, and contact centers. That requires getting used to working with specialized service providers for product engineering and with chip and sensor manufacturers. Let's face it, enterprise track records with technology are poor— there is plenty of waste and overruns. Just because there is an opportunity to embed technology does not mean companies will do it well.

- It means understanding nuances of technology licensing, warranties, and other legalities. Nike+ has four pages of terms of use on its Web site. Many car navigation systems warn you each time you turn them on not to take your eyes off the road. Smart coffee shops have a sign releasing them from any of your risks with their insecure Wi-Fi offerings.

- It means getting used to Moore's Law–type steep price declines. Not every industry adjusts to that easily. Take auto dealers. Initial versions of DVD players, navigation systems, and Bluetooth speakers all cost thousands of dollars. Dealers continue to expect those prices even as handheld Garmin GPS units and BlueAnt speakerphones are available at a fraction of the cost. Importantly, these devices are portable, so customers can take them when they travel or switch from one family car to another. Indeed, there is a cottage industry of FM transmitters, power inverters, backup cameras, portable satellite radios, coolers, and other gadgets you can buy for your car, many for less than $20.

- It means not just "digitizing" old cow paths. In a world where no training is needed to navigate Amazon.com and any "live" help is a keystroke away, companies still ship products with clumsy product manuals. Sure they feel good they have digitized the manuals into Adobe PDF files. That's missing the point. There should be little need for a manual even for complex products. Try using a CD that contains your previously paper-based auto safety manual when you are on the side of a highway with a misbehaving car.

Your Employees Are Tech-Savvy Consumers at Home

Each of us might be a muckety-muck at work, but when we go home and become individual consumers, we compare what we get at home versus what our IT department allows us to have. Consumerization is also affecting internal workforce expectations as they benefit at home from consumer technologies as described below:

- Google, Yahoo!, and other e-mail providers give you multiple gigabytes of personal storage—for free. Many companies barely allow mailbox sizes of 100 megabytes. In many cases, employees forward official mail to their personal accounts, which have greater online storage, exposing companies to loss of privacy protection.
- We can buy computing and storage cycles with our credit cards, and it can be provisioned in minutes over the Web. At work, we wait weeks for IT to order servers and then we get hit with the full brunt of bills for assets that IT tells us we use barely 20 percent of the time.
- The newer generation of workers comes in expecting to have their own team wikis and the company directory all populated in Facebook. They also want to develop Flash interfaces and move files around with tiny Zip drives. They do not understand why IT frowns on all this.

Tech-Savvy Consumer = Smartass Consumer?

Back to Southwest Airlines. A small army of its employees had to spend days handling massive Web traffic set off by Hollywood director Kevin Smith and his more than 1.5 million Twitter followers. He was bumped from one of Southwest's flights earlier in 2010 and took his grievance to his community. The new "social customer" (discussed further in Chapter 17) shares positive—and negative—commentary with lightning speed and incredible reach.

But does he or she represent the average customer?

One of the biggest risks with the consumerization trend is that a focus on the tech-savvy customer may distract from other, more mainstream customers. Customers come in bell curves, and the key is to segment and have different product mixes and strategies for customers who vary in their "affinity" for technology:

- *USA Today* reports what it calls "Tech-Nos": "Some tech-no's shun e-mail. Others don't use the Web or … don't even have a computer. Many avoid cell phones. In a few rare cases, people say no to just about all of it."[11]
- Then you have customers who are cynical—with good reason. Banks sold automated teller machines (ATMs) as customer self-service, and then tacked on fees for that self-service. Companies are now selling electronic invoices as "green" and progressive but then trying to tack

on fees for that "privilege." Hollywood has made money on the same content in VHS, DVD, and now Blu-ray formats. Customers feel that their privacy is not protected and their lives are subject to surveillance as technology increases in products. These customers are not Luddites, just wary.

- Of course, once you cross borders, customer bases are even more diverse. In the United States, a Hertz frequent customer can get away with as few as two 30-second human interactions with its employees. The car is preassigned to a specific slot and highlighted on an electronic board. The contract is preprinted. All the renter has to do is show a driver's license leaving the garage. Coming back, the return process is expedited by an employee with a handheld device. That same Hertz #1 Club customer visiting from the United States is likely to have a far longer conversation with Hertz employees in Greece. Of course, there are more variations—manual versus automatic shift car choices, different insurance requirements, and need for local directions. More likely, though, it is because local customers expect more personalized service.

To accentuate the point about the limits of tech-savvy consumers, take a look at the GPS altitude on our passenger's screen on the Southwest flight at the start of this chapter. It shows 25466.86 feet. Airplanes cruise at altitudes in multiples of 1,000, so 25,466 may seem strange. The pilot would report the altitude as 25,000 feet—in airline lingo, FL250. Is the disparity of 466 feet an accident waiting to happen?

Above 18,000 feet, pilots in the United States and Canada make what is called the 29.92 adjustment (in other parts of the world, this transitional altitude varies). They adjust their altimeter setting to 29.92 inches of mercury, the barometric pressure corresponding to sea-level pressure in a standard atmosphere. This setting is used regardless of the true barometric pressure. As a result, the altimeter no longer reads actual height above sea level but "pressure altitude."

Even tech-savvy customers cannot be expected to know or understand unique operational nuances of the products they are using. They are likely to still stubbornly argue their point because that's what their technology tells them. Imagine that argument with a pilot at 25,000 feet!

Recap

If there were a contest for a mega-trend in technology in this decade, consumerization would be a heavy favorite to win it. It has reshaped customer expectations of technology and how mainstream companies use it to service customers. Companies can develop new products with embedded technology for their tech-savvy customers and can seek direct customer input on features and enhancements. Consumerization has ushered in an era in many enterprises where, for the first time, IT can help enhance revenue and provide competitive advantage, not just be used as an efficiency enhancer. It is also allowing for savings as companies leverage "good-enough" consumer technologies and their much more reasonable economics.

Enterprises have a poor track record with technology projects. Embedding technology in products, in some ways, jeopardizes more than an IT project. It could tarnish brands and lead to product liability. The tech-savvy consumer is also an employee and is increasingly restless with internal IT. Finally, the tech-savvy customer may be too demanding and not representative of the wider customer base. Enterprises need to be careful not to hitch their wagon completely to this consumer.

CHAPTER 5

Exotics:
Innovation from Left Field

Tom Peters, the management philosopher, has long advocated getting innovation ideas from what he calls "saviors-in-waiting": disgruntled customers, off-the-scope competitors, rogue employees and fringe suppliers.[1]

And yet there is safety in numbers and in previous experiences. So when you think financial innovation, you automatically think New York. For fashion, you cannot ignore Milan. For robotics, Japan. For pharmaceuticals, Switzerland.

Of course, these locations are also some of the most expensive in the world. In Chapter 6, we will see how Cognizant, led by its CEO, Francisco D'Souza, handles clients with unique needs from around the world and delivers high-quality services from a wide network of locations in the United States, India, Hungary, Argentina, and elsewhere. His team clearly understands innovation from left field when it comes to leveraging global talent pools.

People are Cognizant's product, and it invests heavily to get a competitive advantage for talent in promising markets. But exotic locations are only one place to look for innovation.

Doblin, a Chicago-based innovation strategy firm, has long advocated that there are plenty of other business areas to innovate. It suggests looking at such areas as the following:

- *Business models.* Dell revolutionized the PC business model by collecting money before the consumer's PC was even assembled and shipped.
- *Service.* Singapore Airlines offers the most attentive, respectful, and pampering preflight, in-flight, and postflight services you can imagine.
- *Channel.* Martha Stewart has developed such a deep understanding of her customers that she knows just where to be: stores, TV shows, magazines, online, and so on.

- *Brand.* Absolut conquered the vodka category with advertising and packaging innovations.
- *Customer experience.* "Being a Harley Davidson owner" is a part of how Harley Davidson customers fundamentally see, think, and feel about themselves.

Using Doblin's broader brush, we have identified other left-field sources of innovation. These underexplored sources include better leverage of women in technology, turning your IT department into a profit center, reinvigorating back-office processes, unconsolidating vendor bases and several from newer business models.

Then we go back to geography and explore the long, successful Silicon Valley model of attracting talent. We also explore innovation from specialized talent pools around the world and ones right in our backyards.

Let's start with women in technology.

Women in Technology

"Your question has me stumped," responds Gerlinde Gniewosz to a question the author posed to several women in technology fields: Which women in tech do you consider innovative? Not powerful or successful, but innovative?

Gniewosz has experience at Yahoo! (the Web company), Orange (the telecommunications company), and McKinsey & Co. (the strategy firm). She has an MBA from Harvard Business School and is now an entrepreneur developing learning products on mobile devices. She was born and educated in Australia, went to business school in the United States, has worked in Germany and the United Kingdom, and has traveled the world. It is a telling comment if someone that "global" and aware of technology trends is stumped by the question above.

Depressingly, a couple more women also long in the technology industry respond the same way. They point to the fact that science and technology are not attracting enough women.

Mary Hayes Weier provides the breakthrough. She used to be editor-at-large at *InformationWeek* and points to WITI—Women in Technology International, a trade association for tech-savvy women.[2] It honors innovative women each year, and Weier was one of the judges for the 2008 awards. She has several candidates for innovative women in tech, including Mary Lou Jepsen, the cofounder and CTO of One Laptop per Child.

Julia King, executive editor for events at Computerworld, mentions Cora Carmody, former CIO at SAIC and now at Jacobs Engineering, for founding Technology Goddesses, an organization to attract girls into science and math at a very early age.[3]

Marilyn Pratt, who works at SAP, points to inventive women from history, including Marie Curie, the first female recipient of a Nobel Prize for the discovery of radioactive elements; and Stephanie Kwolek, the inventor of Kevlar.

Karen Beaman, who runs a consulting firm appropriately named Jeitosa (Portuguese for "innovation"), names Linda Avey, who brought genetic testing to the masses with 23andMe. Avey has since left to start a foundation focused on neurological conditions.

Other recommendations start flowing in. They include Lily Allen, who pioneered music distribution via social networks like MySpace, and the astronaut Sally Ride, for her work encouraging young girls to take a bigger interest in science and engineering. Esther Dyson is mentioned—she has been a investor and industry influencer in infotech and healthtech and is preparing to be a space tourist. Others point to Ada Lovelace Day in March, when bloggers post about women they admire in technology. Gniewosz thinks some more and comes back to the author's question with a similar, wider-reaching body: GWIIN—Global Women Inventors & Innovators Network.[4]

But even if these role models and recognitions do not drive women to science and technology in droves, there is a significant opportunity to leverage women in product design as technology enters so many consumer products.

Take the *New York Times* story about Alison Lewis, who is part of a wave of young product designers embedding electronics into "soft" areas, such as fashion or home furnishings:[5] "In Alison Lewis's girlish, pale-blue living room here, pillows light up when you sit on them and the sofa fabric has a dimmer switch."

Lewis may seem out of left field—but not for too long. Women like her will influence our design and deployment of technology-led-innovation much more going forward.

Turn Your Internal Technology into an Asset

"You can fire us at a moment's notice."

"They are in the business of removing complexity."

The two quotes would be magic to any CIO saddled with multiyear, underperforming vendor contracts while still stuck with the spaghetti that most of today's IT resembles. But they don't expect to hear it from Amazon. Buy technology services from the retailer?

The first quote is from Adam Selipsky, Amazon's vice president of product management and developer relations. The second one is from John Doerr, the Kleiner Perkins venture capitalist who is on Amazon's board.

They are describing Amazon Web Services, which, out of left field, has become one of the hottest products in cloud computing. If you had asked IBM or Accenture five years ago neither in its wildest dreams would have thought of Amazon as a potential competitor.

Actually, IBM may have had a clue. It had sold Amazon a mainframe that could not scale to its fast-expanding retail volumes. Amazon's CTO, Werner Vogels, chuckled in a presentation when he said, "This is an Internet company in 1999 and we bought a mainframe." That debacle pushed Amazon into the world of what, in the industry, is called service-oriented architecture (SOA). "We were doing SOA before it was a buzzword," said Vogels. Each Web page calls specific services designed to do specific tasks. Some of the pages call as many as 150 Web services.[6]

Having invested in these services and found a much cheaper and scalable Linux-based infrastructure, Amazon decided to "externalize" the Web services starting in 2002. While Amazon Web Services focuses primarily on small to midsize enterprises, plenty of developers in Fortune 500 companies buy storage and processing services from the entity using their corporate cards. It's tough to ignore economics that are 10 times cheaper than what traditional outsourcers have been charging for years.

Clients, of course, love the "fire at a moment's notice" and "they remove complexity" parts.

In the GE profile in Chapter 3, Mark Mastrianni described "turning IT inside-out" and how GE has leveraged its IT competence to increasingly build intellectual property it can then license to technology vendors for broader distribution. Both Amazon and GE provide another left-field source of innovation: treating internal IT as a profit center. In most organizations, IT is treated as a cost center and not thought of as a source of potential product or service ideas.

Innovation from Back-Office Processes Like Human Resources

Remember the scene in the movie *Dirty Harry* where the Clint Eastwood character is grounded and assigned to personnel? His incredulous reaction is "Personnel is for "ass@!*$s.""

Personnel has since morphed to HR and increasingly to a new moniker, talent management. Yet most executives still consider HR an innovation backwater—it is expected to have more of a control and compliance role.

Actually, HR is seeing plenty of innovation:

- The department is being called a "corporate X-ray"—mapping "hot spots" and conversation flows around employees to measure their impact on their workgroups or organizations. Cataphora, based in Redwood City, California, started as a data mining company to help companies with fraud analysis and other sleuthing. It has since expanded to do statistical studies of employee performance and individuals' positions in companies' internal social networks.
- A New Zealand–based vendor, Sonar6, is making performance reviews a pleasure with a striking graphical representation of scores. It is also making talent management and succession planning a lot easier to visualize.
- Would you consider using TiVo for a job interview? A company called HireVue from Salt Lake City, Utah, is facilitating TiVo-like capabilities in recruiting. Recruiters can fast-forward candidates who do not appeal or rewind and review responses or mannerisms. It's ideal for first interviews. HireVue estimates it saves between 50 and 75 percent of costs to have people fly or drive in. The process allows candidates from Chile and China to be reviewed by employers in France and New Zealand.
- Two-thirds of Washington's government workforce is estimated to be eligible to retire between now and 2015. Most large companies have smaller but similar challenges. To allow aging workers to continue to be productive, "boomer-friendly" gadgets like tremor-monitoring mice and features from magnified text to speech recognition have emerged. Web sites and wikis keep alumni connected to previous employers. Former employees will continue to represent a useful part-time workforce for many companies. Documenting and transitioning knowledge—capturing nuggets of best practices and industry knowledge to train next-generation staff—is another significant opportunity.

So, HR could be another place to find innovation where you don't expect much.

Innovation from "Game Scores"

Jesse Schell, who used to be creative director at Disney Virtual Reality Studio, has a comprehensive book on game design (and teaches on the topic at Carnegie Mellon).[7] One of the aspects he goes into is "mechanics," which includes scoring. Interesting scoring paradigms motivate players while very complex ones turn many of them off. Of course, as we know in some sports, such as baseball, scoring by fans is an art form unto itself.

What's fascinating about technology is that we love to talk in game win/loss paradigms but we don't focus too much on scoring as a feature in our products. That opens up other opportunities for innovation, such as:

- In Chapter 19, Marc Benioff of salesforce.com describes how the company reluctantly started showcasing performance metrics, such as system availability, to quell competitive rumors. Today, that transparent set of metrics on its "trust site" has raised the bar for the industry and has given salesforce.com a competitive advantage. In the same chapter, Zach Nelson talks about opportunities for benchmarking and forecasting based on real-time, real business data from thousands of NetSuite customers.
- In Chapter 12 on sustainability, we see a new world of measurements opening up around energy efficiency and "natural capital": carbon, natural ecosystems, and the like. In Chapter 15 on analytics, we see new forms of data visualization becoming prevalent.
- Emerson Electric may run commercials that say "It's never been done before," but Charlie Peters, its former CIO and now its innovation officer, is not that easily impressed. He tallies results where Emerson managers divide new-product sales into one of four categories: minor improvements, major improvements, products that are new lines for the business, and ones that are completely new to the world. The quadrant replaced a previous metric that measured Emerson's 60 business units against a much higher-level goal: Make a third of sales from products released in the past five years.[8]

More "exotic" scorekeeping—especially that which can present succinctly complex and new forms of data—is increasingly another form of innovation.

Innovation from "Unconsolidating" Vendor Bases

Most companies have consolidated vendor bases. As justification, they cite concerns about viability of smaller vendors and the administrative hassles of managing many vendors. As we discuss in Chapter 2, we have consolidated dangerously in IT and given many larger suppliers "lock-in" margins even as those suppliers have delivered little innovation.

John Hagel III, of the Deloitte Center for Edge Innovation, likes to cite Li & Fung, the Chinese conglomerate that leverages 10,000 suppliers spread across 50 countries. Not every supplier is involved in every transaction, but the collective wisdom benefits the whole supply chain. Some of Li & Fung's reasoning for vendor diversity includes:

- *Less bureaucracy in smaller vendors.* "The person on the other side is not a lawyer or a procurement executive—it's someone who has run a plant like mine."
- *An interesting twist to intellectual property protection issues.* "I need to continually innovate . . . so I can stay a step ahead . . . even though I know I am being copied."

That, most of you will agree, qualifies as innovation from left field.

Now let's look at three innovations in business models—one from deemphasizing your core product, one from taking advantage of the age of your customer, and finally one from the "freemium" pricing model.

Business Model Innovation: Demarketing Your Core Product

A business model based on "demarketing" your core product would seem heretical. Some public utilities are betting, however, that it is better to invest in technologies that encourage customers to consume less power rather than invest in new power generation. They call it their "virtual power plant." Of course, they are not altruistic—they do it because regulators allow them to make money on their investments in those consumer efficiencies.

Ask most venture capitalists to name innovative companies and, of course, they will name some in their portfolios. But several will likely also name Pacific Gas and Electric (PG&E) in that group. *Newsweek* named it the "greenest utility" for its "strong efforts to control demand" and "because renewable energy makes up 12% of its electricity," with a mandate to get to 20 percent by 2010.[9]

For managing consumer demand, PG&E has had one of the widest deployments of smart meters—close to three million so far (more in Chapter 12 on sustainability). These meters can be monitored remotely and provide customers real-time information on their power usage. On the business side, PG&E has had one of the more aggressive programs to incent efficiencies in data centers and electronic equipment, some of the largest power consumers in corporations.

On the supply side, PG&E is being goaded by a State of California goal requiring it get 33 percent of its electricity from renewable sources, such as solar and wind power, by 2020. It is doing so by expanding its supply chain through a series of innovative relationships with independent power generators.

The new technologies in meters and alternative fuels are by themselves examples of innovation, but the real innovation from left field here is the proactive cannibalization of the core product. You expect that from Intel, which thrives on "eating its children"—each generation of chips obsolescing the previous one—not from traditionally slow-moving public utilities.

Business Model Innovation: "Make It Up in Years"

Historically, a successful business model has focused on "making it up in volume." Scale your operations, lower your unit cost. Newer telcos around the world are discovering that to get to that scale, they also have to target younger consumers. The average age in India and Mexico is 25 years. In Pakistan, it is 20!

Interestingly, because these younger consumers also are targeted as labor prospects, they are increasingly affluent and mobile—as India's outsourcing success has shown. In other words, this customer demographic is much more attractive than it appears on the surface. To attract this market, however, telcos have to package services very differently. They have to provide more prepaid cards, offer plenty more text-based services, and provide add-ons to Facebook and Twitter.

Microsoft is trying something similar as it rolls out its cloud computing offerings. It's aiming not at young consumers but at young businesses: Firms less than three years old and under $1 million in revenues get software for free under Microsoft's BizSpark program.[10] Microsoft is betting these companies will continue with its software—on a paid basis—as they get older and bigger.

Business Model Innovation: Beyond "Freemium"

In the freemium model, entry-level services to consumers are free, with the expectation that enterprise advertisers will pay for those eyeballs. The expectation is also that consumers will ratchet up to higher-paid tiers of service once they experience the solution.

Chris Anderson, editor of *Wired*, summarized the thinking behind freemium in a column in the *Wall Street Journal*: "The Web has become the biggest store in history and everything is 100% off ... 'attention' and 'reputation' are the currencies most in demand, with the expectation that a sufficient amount of either would turn into money someday, somehow."[11]

The "100% off" model has stoked massive traffic to YouTube, Facebook, Twitter, and others. The advertising revenues have, however, been slow to materialize, especially during the recent economic slowdown, and the conversion of free customers to paid tiers has been even slower.

Nonetheless, there is growing recognition at enterprises that these large customer bases, nonpaying as they may be today, are a largely unmined asset. We see examples at Starbucks and Avon in Chapter 17 and how they have coaxed dollars out of their Facebook communities—one for charities, another for products.

The end result for the Web companies may be a different revenue stream than advertising (though they will certainly keep focusing on advertising revenues as Twitter did with its "Promoted Tweets" it announced in April 2010). It will more likely be a community-service fee from companies like Avon, as they make revenues from those channels. It may also mean that Web companies continue to be free to consumers and give up on their own attempts at tiered consumer pricing.

If companies continue with tiered consumer pricing, they need to be careful to not go the way of Ryanair. A few years ago, Ryanair looked innovative as it brought low-fare competition à la Southwest Airlines to Europe. It has increasingly tacked on a variety of baggage, check-in, and other fees to the annoyance of its customers. It is tough to tell whether the CEO, Michael O'Leary, is jesting or serious when he says, "Our ideal passenger is someone with a pulse and a credit card, who will follow the simple instructions to lower our costs to the maximum."[12]

Once an entity loses sight of the fact that its base pricing is at market equilibrium, there is an organizational sense of entitlement that incremental fees are justified. The company starts to build compensation plans to incent salespeople to sell beyond the basic pricing.

The research firm Gartner has traditionally compensated its sales force on a metric called net contract value increase (NCVI). This model creates a potential risk that paying customers actually are resented for not increasing their annual revenue volume. As Carter Lusher, a former Gartner analyst, says on his blog, "That is why Gartner sales reps start getting desperate when it looks like contract renewals are going to be less than the previous contract."[13]

Now let's go back and explore some other geography-based innovations.

The Silicon Valley Model: Move West, Young Man

In March 2009, McKinsey published its "Innovation Heat Map," the result of research with the World Economic Forum. As part of this effort, McKinsey examined the evolution of hundreds of "innovation hubs" around the world and analyzed more than 700 variables, including those driving innovation (business environment, government and regulation, human capital, infrastructure, and local demand) along with proxies for innovation output (e.g., economic value added, journal publications, patent applications) to identify trends among the success stories.[14]

Silicon Valley was head and shoulders above other centers. The McKinsey report covered wide ground but did not home in on the fact that the Valley has done very well by welcoming immigrants from around the world. According to the *New York Times*, "The foreign-born elite dating back even further includes Andrew S. Grove of Hungary, who helped found Intel; Jerry Yang, the Taiwanese-born cofounder of Yahoo; Vinod Khosla of India and Andreas von Bechtolsheim of Germany, the cofounders of Sun Microsystems; and Google's Russian-born cofounder, Sergey Brin."[15]

Many mainstream U.S. companies, in contrast to Silicon Valley, have tended to use outsourcing firms to bring them this diversity while shielding them from "adminis-trivia" around H1-B and other visas. India-centric firms have seen a disproportionate number of such visas, which tempers the "diversity" of the employee base.

Europe has, of course, seen significant technology-employee migration due to the European Union integration of the last two decades.

Still, Siemens, the German high-tech giant, with more than 400,000 employees in 190-plus countries, announced in 2009 that Jill Lee, a Chinese national, had been appointed as Chief Diversity Officer. The company employs some two-thirds of its workforce outside Germany. At the same time, only 30 percent of the positions in its senior management team are currently filled by international executives. Lee's role, among other things, is to correct that imbalance.

Munich, where Siemens is headquartered, has several other innovative companies, such as BMW and the MAN Group, and there are plenty of software start-ups in the Bavaria region, of which Munich is the capital. Nevertheless, in the McKinsey report and other measures of innovation, it pales in comparison to the innovation hot spot that is Silicon Valley.

So it could innovate by borrowing a leaf from Silicon Valley and try to attract talented immigrants. The pushback often is that between German reunification and EU-spawned labor mobility, Munich has already absorbed plenty of "immigrants" over the last couple of decades—immigrants who have provided local companies with its version of innovation from left field.

"Trickle-Up" Innovation

In 2009, *BusinessWeek* noted a trend it called "trickle-up" innovation: "[The electrocardiograph machine] will retail [in the United States] for a mere $2,500, an 80% markdown from products with similar capabilities. But what really distinguishes the MAC 800 is its lineage. The machine is basically the same field model that GE Healthcare developed for doctors in India and China in 2008."[16]

Innovation in many ways has moved to the "BRICK" nations: Brazil, Russia, India, China, and South Korea. (Note: Goldman Sachs coined the term "BRIC" in 2001. The author extended the term on his technology blog to also include South Korea. More recently, derivatives like "BASIC" to include Brazil, South Africa, India, and China, have also gained prominence.) Each one of the five countries stands out, as we showcase below and in other chapters in the book:

- *Fortune* magazine calls Brazil the "Saudi Arabia of biofuels." Brazil's experience with ethanol production from sugarcane goes back three decades. More recently, the country has risen to the forefront of research and experience with soybeans and renewable-fuel innovations.
- In a hurry to return to its pre-1949 "Paris of the East" status, Shanghai has become famous for stunning modern infrastructure with the construction of some of the world's tallest buildings and fastest trains. Although many say the soul of Shanghai has died with the modernization, few argue that some of the best innovations in city planning and construction technologies are being pioneered there.
- India is known the world over for software outsourcing and IT support, but it has a wide range of boutiques that provide specialized services. These services support market research, animation, product design, and "medical tourism" we discuss in Chapter 14. Wipro, one of the larger Indian IT services firms, has a vibrant R&D business around chip design and product engineering. It is gradually building up a sizable intellectual property base, including a large set of patents around wireless local area networks and Bluetooth technologies.
- Novosibirsk, the capital of Siberia in Russia, is not the easiest place to attract talent to, yet it has become an innovation hive for software and metallurgy. The ultimate compliment comes from an Intel executive—the company has facilities in the city—in a *Fortune* magazine article: "If you have something tough, give it to the Americans. If you have something difficult, give it to the Indians. If you have something impossible, give it to the Russians."[17]
- Competing against gadget-crazy Japan and Taiwan, the device manufacturer to the world, South Korea (as we elaborate in Chapter 7) is blazing a trail with next-generation mobile products and providing its own citizens high-speed networks that provide them the ability to view streaming video on trains—years ahead of the West.

Don't Forget Your Backyard

Monty Hamilton calls it the "Monty Misery Meter." He asks anyone doing business overseas to honestly factor in the human cost: the fatigue from red-eye flights and jet lag, endless days with phone calls at ungodly hours with teams many time zones away, and the lost-in-translation factor.

Hamilton is on a crusade to replace offshoring with backyard sourcing. He is convinced that just as auto jobs were created by European and Asian car manufacturers in Alabama and Tennessee and not Detroit, technology jobs are ripe to be created and brought back, but not to New York and Silicon Valley and not to firms like IBM and Accenture.

Rather, Hamilton aims to get these firms to locations such as Jonesboro, Arkansas. That is where his company, appropriately named Rural Sourcing Inc., has a team that services technology needs of clients such as Stiefel Laboratories and Blue Cross Blue Shield. Rural Sourcing takes advantage of a community nurtured by the nearby Arkansas State University campus.

It's ideal, he says, "particularly for higher-touch, higher-collaboration work that requires more cognitive interaction."

He lays out his differentiators crisply:

- *Ease of collaboration.* Overlap between your working day and ours.
- *Ease of communication.* American English, served with Southern hospitality.
- *Distance compatibility.* Quick access to our facility and our people.
- *Business continuity.* Geopolitical stability.
- *Business practice familiarity.* Deeper understanding of say, Food and Drug Administration (FDA) regulations and local business practices.

Unlike Cognizant's 50 centers around the world (to be described in Chapter 6), Hamilton's plans call for growth into 30 other "rural" U.S. locations. He is concentrating his search on towns two to three hours from major metropolitan areas, with "plenty of highly skilled and loyal professionals" who do not want to relocate or commute from their "high quality of life and low cost of living" locations.

Rural Sourcing was the brain child of Kathy Brittain-White, former CIO of Cardinal Health and now on the board of Mattel and Novell. Brittain-White was driven to start Rural Sourcing partly by Hamilton's "Misery Meter" in her role as CIO and partly by altruism to give back to the region where she was born—the town of nearby Oxford, Arkansas, with a population of just 650. More recently, Brittain-White has moved her rural sourcing focus to one of the most depressed areas in the United States—Pocahontas County, West Virginia. And she has become involved with the nearby High Rocks Academy, which focuses on creating positive role models for young women in that state.

Oxford, Arkansas, not Oxford, England? That's more innovation from left field.

Beyond BRICK

BRICK, as described earlier, represents a group of larger, fast-developing countries, but there are similar innovation stories from around the world:

- Estonia, in a hurry to escape its communist detour, is one of the most "wired" countries in the world. Its "Tiigrihüppe" ("tiger leap") initiative provides a prototype of the digital life citizens in most other countries will achieve in a decade. More than 90 percent of bank transactions are conducted online. The citizens of Tallinn (the capital) pay for their parking tickets and their bus passes by sending text messages from their mobile phones. They elect their representatives from their home computers. Parliamentary and town hall debates are now recorded without producing any paper trail.
- Israel continues to be an "overachiever," with innovation way beyond its small size. The Organization for Economic Cooperation and Development ranks Israel highest in R&D intensity—4.65 percent, twice as much as the average of other countries at 2.26 percent. This innovation shows in Israeli software, sustainability, and many other disciplines.
- In decades past, the city-state of Singapore attracted a number of regional operations of many multinationals. Now it has positioned itself as an R&D and intellectual property base for many pharmaceutical, medical device, and technology companies.
- Denmark is winning kudos for its aggressive use of wind energy and other sustainability initiatives.
- Australia's major telecom company Telstra is rolling out its next-generation mobile network, which allows the country to pioneer connectivity over its very wide distances.

Recap

We expect most technology innovation to originate in Silicon Valley. But talent pools around the world are diamonds in the rough waiting to be explored. Some are in the rural United States; some are in far-flung countries. Women are not a scarce resource by any means, but in technology we have not leveraged their creativity enough. Beyond talent pools, innovative results can come from rethinking business processes and revisiting even so-called laggard industries. Innovation can come from rethinking business models and most certainly from supplier bases.

"Not invented here" is a defense mechanism for many, but the polymath enterprise keeps its eyes and ears open for all kinds of "left-field" inspirations. After all, when former communist countries can boast some of the best telecom infrastructure in the world, something has really changed. When public utilities can become hotbeds of innovation, you know the changes are tectonic.

CHAPTER 6

Polymath Profile #2: Cognizant

*O*rganizations today will only achieve real business advantage through labor arbitrage if they augment the initial cost-savings with business transformation.

That's Francisco D'Souza, CEO of Cognizant Technology, speaking. Cognizant is a $3.4 billion company (at end of 2009)—one that continued to grow spectacularly, even during the steep recession of 2008–09. D'Souza explains some of the drivers of that success:

> While organizations in the past, have made some fast cost savings moving work to lower-cost locations, many have seen them quickly eroded as they failed to improve the quality of their processes. Smart organizations have enjoyed more significant business benefits over the longer term when they reinvested some of the initial savings by incorporating technology and process improvements.
>
> Take Sanofi-Pasteur. They were one of a handful of pharmaceutical companies chosen to develop the swine flu vaccine. That's a very high-profile product to develop, given all the media attention. It also reflects real-time pressure, given you have to wait to produce the vaccine based on the latest mutation of the virus. Using a core team located in France, the United States, and India, we helped them conduct over 30 large clinical studies. However, Sanofi-Pasteur did not partner with Cognizant simply to find affordable talent—they needed the ability to meet stringent deadlines and our proficiency in life sciences processes. If Sanofi-Pasteur had focused solely on removing labor cost, they might easily have ended up losing more than they had gained by missing their deadlines. Not only has Sanofi-Pasteur benefited through cost savings, it has achieved new operational efficiencies and enhanced its reputation in the life sciences market.

Also, when you're building a global platform to service multiple industries, you need to embrace talent across the world to source a diverse mix of skills, language, process, and technical abilities. For Kimberly-Clark, our Argentina-based services made sense as part of the delivery footprint. For AstraZeneca, it was Hungary. For Molina Healthcare, it was Phoenix, Arizona. Our clients are multinational, and expect us to give them plenty of choices.

The Early Years

To get a better view into the global journey on which D'Souza has been guiding Cognizant, you need to understand his own globally diverse upbringing. The first chapter begins in Kenya where he was born.

"Placido is definitely a Renaissance Man. I wish I was that well rounded."

D'Souza is describing his father, a career diplomat. Placido used his stints around the world to bond with and sketch 400-plus heads of state (including Nelson Mandela), which he now exhibits at galleries at the United Nations in New York and around the world. Placido also made time to socialize with local artists everywhere he went and to publish a magazine in his "spare time."

D'Souza describes his observations growing up:

I grew up when the world was siloed. I would observe the differences as our family moved from one capital city to another with my dad's diplomatic assignments and his extracurricular activities. I was fascinated with why India had an engineering culture, why New York City attracted artists, why Eastern Europe had so many mathematicians. Is it the education system? Is it local culture? Is it genetics? I would ask myself as we moved around. I was also acutely aware that people migrated to where the work was, but there were many barriers to that flow.

The second chapter started with a career with Dun & Bradstreet (D&B). In 1994, years ahead of most other companies, D&B encouraged a small team to set up a technology services unit in India. The internal unit was spun off as Cognizant a couple of years later. D'Souza continues:

That [move to India] allowed us to take advantage of telecommunications and aviation advances to go around the barriers I saw growing up. Now we could move work to where the talent was, rather than the move people to work.

When I first got to India, I was in awe of the TATAs, Infosyses, and the Wipros. They had done a remarkable job building brands in the

West considering how long their odds were. India had gone through a socialist phase in the '70s and '80s. They had thrown out IBM and Coca-Cola, so Indian IT firms did not have an easy path selling in the West back then.

We knew we had to be very differentiated from the Indian firms. The D&B brand helped us win American and European clients who wanted to do global business. In our recruiting, we focused on Indians in the United States and Europe who wanted to go back home—and, in so doing, built a team that leveraged the best of both worlds: experience dealing with client situations in the United States and Europe and a cultural affinity for India.

That differentiation, however, was skin deep. The real differentiation came from what Cognizant calls "Two-in-a-Box," or TIB for short. In contrast to the prevailing logic at the time, which dictated that projects should be managed from offshore delivery centers, Cognizant offered a twofer: It tasked a senior leader within Cognizant to manage customer relationships in the United States or Europe while assigning another senior manager to oversee services delivery from Cognizant's facilities in India. The U.S.-based CEO and India-based COO were the first TIB designates, and they propagated this model and mantra throughout the organization for every engagement and every client.

The customer manager and the delivery manager were jointly responsible for all project metrics, including top and bottom lines. The customer managers typically were individuals with consulting or industry backgrounds and experience handling IT service relationships. The delivery managers tended to have engineering backgrounds and experience delivering complex software and managing technical teams.

D'Souza describes the impact of that approach:

Differently from Infosys run from Bangalore, or TCS from Mumbai, we became known as a U.S.-headquartered, Nasdaq-listed company which offered clients a unique blend of Western and Indian talent.

The combined TIB business and technical skill sets also helped as clients started trusting us beyond basic IT project work. We were winning multiyear application maintenance contracts with demanding service levels and productivity improvement expectations. And each was unique—around financial services and other vertical processes, or around global SAP and Oracle environments—so the business and technical combination was critical.

The other early decision we made was not to compete with Infosys and Wipro for talent in Bangalore. We went with a location in Chennai.

It was a couple of hundred miles away, but with just as big an IT talent pool, and we soon became one of the largest employers there.

And another differentiator: We stayed away from building massive campuses. We have 40 development centers now spread over 9 Indian cities and another 13 [as of late 2009] scattered all over the globe. Tom Friedman may never write a book about our facilities like he did about Infosys's gorgeous campus, but to me this geographic diversity is key for business continuity and also to be able to tap specialized regional talent pools across the globe.

While I was in awe of the bigger Indian firms, I am glad they were not that impressed with our brand. In fact, for our first decade I think we stayed under their radar.

The larger Indian firms did notice, in late 2005, when the author coined the term "SWITCH" on his blog to include the then-top-six India-centric vendors: Satyam, Wipro, Infosys, TCS, Cognizant, and HCL. The acronym also conveyed a dramatic shift in the outsourcing market, where larger Western service providers were finally waking up to the threat from this new breed of firm. By then, of course, Cognizant was well on its way to becoming a billion-dollar company and being listed on the Nasdaq 100 Index.

The larger Western firms had plenty of their own opportunities to develop a global delivery model like Cognizant did in its first decade. Accenture (back then, part of the Arthur Andersen family) had helped SGV, an affiliated firm in the Philippines, set up a software development center as far back as 1986. That could easily have been leveraged and expanded as a link in Accenture's global delivery supply chain. That talent base was used primarily to service its Asian clients. EDS set up a subsidiary in India in 1996 and did business with local branches of Western companies, such as GM. It eventually bought a majority stake in MphasiS, another Indian outsourcer, in 2006. Through that decade, the storied firm that Ross Perot had built stagnated in revenue growth and eventually was sold to HP in 2008. IBM had reentered the Indian market in the early 1990s but did not start to bulk up local hiring until a decade later. Also, none of these firms could come anywhere close to Cognizant's TIB model. In general, their Western staff looked at their global colleagues as "commoditizing" their brand.

The Structure for Growth

The third chapter has seen D'Souza take over the reins, in 2007, as CEO of the company. At 38 years old, that made him of one of the youngest public company CEOs around. It has been a trial by fire, as the world economy tanked soon after. Cognizant maintained its growth in spite of the turbulent climate, staying focused on its reputation for operational excellence and distinctive industry acumen. The continued growth also qualified Cognizant for *Fortune's* 2009 list of "supercharged performers."

The last few years have given D'Souza even more appreciation for the modern-day version of Ricardo's "comparative advantage of nations":

> *There are specialized pools of talent—some are regional, some are industry based, some language based—you learn to harness. Take voice-based services. Philippines is grabbing the global leadership from India. Hungary is doing that around many European languages.*
>
> *But such competitive advantage is fleeting. Bangalore can no longer be as competitive around application management services as other Indian cities, so it is diversifying by attracting entrepreneurs in a number of other areas. You see that with Silicon Valley—different genre of start-ups every few years.*
>
> *Egypt is a good example of leap-frog. Its ITIDA [Information Technology Investment Development Agency] is tasked with emulating the Indian outsourcing success story. They hired McKinsey, which was a consultant to NASSCOM, the Indian services trade body which is credited with helping build its successful outsourcing model. In addition, ITIDA has hired staff from NASSCOM. These resources are helping them rapidly climb the learning curve. The new talent has, in turn, brought in firms like Infosys, Hewitt, Firstsource, and IBM Daksh [its Indian business process outsourcing [BPO] unit] to help train Egyptian talent. Egypt is well positioned to be a significant IT and BPO services provider in the traditional outsourcing markets of USA and UK and has a unique multilingual talent pool (consisting of Arabic, English, French, German, Italian, Spanish speakers) to serve the fast-growing continental European market and the large Arabic-speaking market in the Middle East and North Africa. There are early signs of success of ITIDA's initiatives across supply enhancement and investment promotion with over 15,000 export FTEs serving international customers out of Cairo and Alexandria.*
>
> *Personally, growing up in Africa, it is exciting for me to now see so much hope there. Just a few years ago it looked so bleak. The competitive talent landscape is changing so rapidly that their turn will come far sooner than I would have thought.*

Cognizant's recruiting machine has been hyperactive to keep up with this global diversification—the company now has employees in more than 30 countries. The company systematically assesses the talent pool in targeted locations, probing for experienced project managers or team leaders as well as the stream of new graduates to fuel a ramp-up. The diversification feeds on itself, as local clients in new countries also seek out the talent they know Cognizant is fussy about recruiting.

Despite its brisk global expansion, Cognizant cannot be omnipresent. So D'Souza's 30 key executives around the world use telepresence to communicate regularly between their quarterly in-person meetings.

The real glue comes from its "Cognizant 2.0" knowledge-sharing and project management environment, which has empowered Cognizant's globally diverse talent to be uniquely integrated. To offer clients a follow-the-sun model, where teams can hand off from one location to another and expedite time to market, it is critical to have consistent talent and processes everywhere.

Essentially, Cognizant 2.0 leverages Web 2.0 technologies, such as blogs, wikis, instant messaging, and search engines, that can comb both structured data (e.g., information in formatted databases) and unstructured data (e.g., words used in e-mails and audio and video clips). This enables an associate anywhere in the growing family to tap into the firm's best thinking on how to handle a specific aspect of a project to leverage pre-existing IT and business process artifacts as well as domain experts across the globe.

An embedded workflow management system actively coordinates complex global projects by automatically presenting standardized process templates and workflows that must be followed across Cognizant's integrated IT and BPO services portfolio. With Cognizant 2.0, the company's globally dispersed teams work more collaboratively, and with dramatically less effort and time. D'Souza elaborates:

> *With over 10,000 internal bloggers (and growing), it represents a Cognizant "virtual town square" that receives 2 million page views a month, and with a repository of over 1,750 reusable software assets (with over 100 added every month), shared knowledge is available to Cognizant associates, select business partners, and clients in a constant knowledge-sharing stream and dialogue.*
>
> *These tools reflect technology and transparency new recruits take for granted. Additionally, by allowing clients and business partners to participate in this "Intelligent Delivery Ecosystem," the content is richer. And it differentiates us from many others who keep their communities closed.*
>
> *Cognizant 2.0 has helped knit our organization together, essentially making distance and geography a nonissue.*

In a Harvard Business School case study on Cognizant 2.0, Robert G. Eccles and Thomas H. Davenport described how Cognizant employees who blogged and were otherwise active in the community reported "higher levels of satisfaction and engagement with their jobs."[1] According to research house International Data Corp., Cognizant 2.0 is "a 'game changer'" for Cognizant, helping to shift the competitive field from labor arbitrage to intellectual arbitrage. "This greatly benefits Cognizant's position in the global services space," IDC wrote in a November 2009 profile.[2]

The Future "Future of Work"

What does the future hold?

> *I see even more mobility in workers. I mean, my kids have three passports—United States, Brazilian, and Indian Overseas Citizen [D'Souza's wife is Brazilian]. Ten years from now, dual or more citizenship will not be unusual. Of course, the next generation of worker will also have "millennial" expectations—a much more "consumery," untethered view of technology. Distance and geography will be even less of an issue than we are seeing today. I can see a talented employee from, say, Botswana as part of our team even though we don't have an office there.*
>
> *But we will have cross-currents. Some of the talent will want to travel the world. Some of it will want to work from home. To help us work through all these conflicting trends, we have been partnering with Carnegie Mellon University to help define the future "future of work."*
>
> *In the end, it's not about us. We need to help our clients create new revenue streams by doing things differently—help them innovate. In doing so, they will lead us into new markets, point us to new avenues for sourcing growth and productivity, and keep us at the forefront of leveraging emerging new technologies, such as cloud computing and virtualization, into their business environments.*

That is spoken in typical D'Souza modesty. D'Souza's clients, of course, expect him to be their tour guide. Born in Kenya, he is intimately familiar with the Serengeti, where guides take you in hot-air balloons to watch the spectacular annual migration.

D'Souza provides his clients a much wider "balloon"—and the view is even more spectacular. It allows you to see pockets of innovation around the world—especially those coming out of left field.

Recap

Anyone can open an office anywhere around the world. It requires, however, sophisticated analysis of shifting talent pools around the world to build a global network. It also takes seamless solutions and concepts like Two-in-a-Box and tools like Cognizant 2.0 to bind these talent pools together.

For their ability to identify and harness talent pools from left field, D'Souza and his team have earned the right to be called polymaths when it comes to leveraging "exotic" sources of innovation.

CHAPTER 7

Networks:
Bluetooth to Broadband

How can a single industry present two such contrasting images? One is of iPhone owners leaping for joy when they get handed the device. The other is the sickening parade of more than 40 employee suicides since 2008 at France Telecom.

This chapter explores six areas in which the telecommunications industry has been changing rapidly in the last few years. We first look at the wide range of new applications, especially those enabled by mobile telephony. Then we look at a trend being played out in country after country. Traditional telcos like France Telecom are under siege even as the markets around them rapidly evolve. We look at a perspective on how traditional telcos can reshape themselves and examine three case studies where consumers have minimized roles for traditional telcos in their lives. We evaluate how global markets are emerging. Finally, we touch on the global supply chain that drives the telecom industry.

The Plantronics profile, in Chapter 8, shows how the company has navigated the morphing telecommunications market over the last few decades. Its audio devices benefited from the call centers, which grew as toll-free calling became available. Then the company grew along with work-at-home employees. As the volume of mobile phones exploded, Plantronics benefited from Bluetooth devices. Now as unified communications takes off, it is prepared for software-based telephony.

Alexander Bell Is Looking Down in Awe

Yes, Alexander Bell, the beneficiary of U.S. Patent 174465, would drool at a text messages like this one: "Welcome to town! We are 2 blocks away and would love to offer you 25% off this item if you come in within 30 minutes."

Location-based applications that take advantage of the GPS on your phone are growing rapidly. Other applications take advantage of the cameras, accelerometers, and other technology packaged in today's cell phones. You can scan business cards using the phone's camera. NTT DoCoMo of Japan has developed "augmented reality" applications, including an "Intuitive Search." Point your phone at a store, and its icon and other details show up. Click to trigger a Web search about the store. PopCatcher from Sweden can capture an FM signal, filter out commercials, and save the music as an MP3 file that can be used on the cell phone. The CellScope project at the University of California at Berkeley focuses on the development of a modular, high-magnification microscope attachment for cell phones for health care applications.

Oh, did we mention the applications in the iPhone App Store? More than 175,000 applications created in a couple of years.

BusinessWeek provides a convincing perspective: "Two-year-old Zynga, which makes popular game apps, is already profitable, with more than $100 million in revenues. By comparison, Google didn't start making money until its third year—and still had less revenue."[1]

Mobile applications are actually just hitting their stride. Most so far have been consumer-oriented. Wait until enterprises like General Electric start cranking out applications using the mobile framework described in Chapter 3. The apps are also putting new demands on telco networks. One iPhone user is estimated to generate as much data traffic as 30 basic-feature phone users and is exposing significant gaps in infrastructure investments the industry has been making. We'll provide more on that in a bit.

Although we may be impressed at what mobile applications are delivering, they represent only a thin sliver of the radio spectrum. Portable phones, garage door openers, microwaves, TVs, home Wi-Fi, the Plantronics Bluetooth headset, toll transponders, ham radios, AM radio, FM radio, XM radio, and more coexist without interference.

Now take that to a higher level, where marine mobile, meteorological, aeronautic, and other uses have specific frequencies, and you see a growing list of scenarios like the following:

- ■ "Careful if you use it during negotiations. The beads of sweat actually seem to get magnified," says a veteran user of Cisco telepresence as he describes the experience of sitting across the table with a vendor who is thousands of miles away. Each side watches the other in 1080p-resolution video on three 65-inch screens on a low-jitter line. It is not cheap to build a telepresence infrastructure around the world and to pay telcos for bandwidth 150 times as much as a voice call requires. Contrast that to the saved business-class airfares and the wear and tear from jet lag, however, and companies are lining up for the product. Hotel chains such as Marriott and Starwood are betting on telepresence "by the drink" in cities around the world. It's a lot easier to drive to their facilities than to fly around the world. Not to mention there's no capital expenditure for the Cisco infrastructure and the monthly AT&T bills.

- Sign in any time of the day or night and you can see 15 to 20 million people are on Skype. It has been dubbed "Cisco telepresence for the poor," since many people use the free Skype-to-Skype video capabilities. Skype is particularly popular with immigrants and international travelers calling home; 25 billion minutes in 2008 on its VoIP network were of the free Skype-to-Skype variety. Skype has become the bane of most telcos around the world as it eats into their lucrative global and roaming rates. Because of Skype's huge success, VoIP has become an unpopular acronym for telcos. Some have been accused of tampering with blocks of data that Skype transmits on their data networks.

- "The broadcast business of the future is all digital—high-def radio, satellite radio, HDTV, audio and video on your mobile phone, Wi-Fi, Wi-Max, iPods, iPhones, iTunes, podcasts, the list goes on," says Conrad Trautmann, former senior vice president of operations and engineering at Westwood One, the largest provider of audio content in the United States. "So we have had to upgrade to IP-based broadcast infrastructure, satellites and related modulation, and things like 'spring sun outages,' 'cartchunks' (to attach metadata to .wav files), 'copy splitting' (to allow advertisers to target specific markets in their national campaigns). In the last couple of years, Westwood has been investing in Media Access Xchange (MAX). We shipped MAX receivers to 2,000 radio stations across the country. This allowed content delivery direct to the affiliate's automation system—no more ripping CDs or downloading from an FTP site. And authentication to make sure only authorized, in-good-standing affiliates can access the content."

- Virgin America, in business just a couple of years (the affiliated airline, Virgin Atlantic, has been flying international flights much longer), has won a loyal following for its cool décor and other perks. But what is really distinguishing is its "Wi-fly" fleet. Passengers can get on the GoGo network and be productive or entertained through the flight.

- Take a cruise in the Caribbean, and your ship will likely have Sea Tel satellite calling. Passengers will be coordinating on DECT™ 6.0 walkie-talkies with their families who could be anywhere on those monster ships. You see microwave towers in the islands you visit. It is quite likely that as your ship passes some of these islands, their cell towers will try to tempt your mobile phone to roam at their "reasonable" rates.

- Pilots fly Predator drones via satellite over Afghanistan while sitting at Creech Air Force Base about an hour outside Las Vegas, Nevada.

Sensors and a GPS chip on dropsondes (weather reconnaissance devices parachuted down from planes) help relay location, wind, pressure, temperature, and humidity data as they descend through hurricanes. Sensory networks with devices and radio-frequency identification chips communicate with each other. Today, communications are not just people-to-people; in fact, in many enterprises, traffic to and from non-humans increasingly exceeds that between humans.

While Alexander Bell would be marveling at the applications, he would also be shaking his head in disappointment at how the descendants of his company and many other traditional telcos have evolved.

Bell Is Also Looking Down in Consternation

"Mah pihpes."

Bloggers cruelly mocked Ed Whitcare's Southern accent in 2005 as Whitcare, then CEO of SBC (which later acquired and renamed itself AT&T, old Ma Bell), talked about VoIP providers like Skype.

"Why should they be allowed to use my pipes?"

Ever since Lily Tomlin started making fun of the phone company in the late 1960s with her telephone operator character Ernestine and the "One ringy dingy, two ringy dingy" line, the big, bad phone company has been a butt of jokes. But it has gotten worse—much worse. This is not just about AT&T but about most major phone companies around the world.

The 2009 survey of consumers in 32 countries by the Reputation Institute put telecoms as fourth lowest rated of the 25 industries surveyed—scoring just slightly above tobacco, which was ranked, not surprisingly, the lowest.[2]

While most consumers are shocked by the suicides at France Telecom, the low ratings reflect displeasure with telcos as they cling to older revenue models and sneak in ever-creative "shortfall," roaming, early-termination, and countless other charges that keep them in constant battles with their customers and in court disputes with the communities they serve.

In response, Verizon president and COO Denny Strigl is on record as saying that the U.S. telco industry is "unfairly maligned."[3] He does have a point. To be able to convert millions of homes from copper to fiber, to handle the rapid transition away from voice to data traffic, to efficiently handle orders and billings of a growing number of products—Web, TV, etc.—telcos have had to dramatically automate and reshape their field service logistics, their problem diagnosis, and their billing and dispute resolution processes.

Fairly or unfairly, though consumers do not see enough progress. *Consumer Reports'* annual surveys of customer satisfaction show some of their lowest ratings across all products for mobile and other telecom services.

Here is an industry sitting bang in the middle of four major trends we cover in other chapters: globalization, cloud computing, collaboration, and sensory networks. Its companies are going to be selling billions of mobile phones in emerging markets and roaming minutes and hot-spot coverage to all of us as we travel globally. They will be hosting and connecting massive cloud grids. They will facilitate collaboration via telepresence and Web conferencing and Twitter messages. They will relay messages across billions of sensors.

Yet they continue with rate plans that should have been retired long ago. Stories circulate of elderly consumers who are still being billed a rental fee for their home phone. The AT&T monopoly on home phone equipment ended in 1982. Over the years, these consumers have paid amounts with which they could have bought hundreds of phones.

Someone in his marketing group should have coached Whitacre never to use the term "pipes." Too many telco executives use that term, and it subliminally reinforces the perception that they are just a "dumb pipe."

In fact, telcos should learn to talk like their customers, not the other way around.

Ted Thonus of Cottonwood Communications jokingly asks his readers on his blog, "How good are you at speaking *our language?*"

And the quiz that follows has language few of us understand:

- *Why would a company implement a WAN using MPLS when they want to install an IP/PBX at all of their branches?*
- *How would SIP trunking (SIP service) help me expand my business?*
- *Is wireless Internet better than a land-based MOE Internet connection?*
- *What is the difference between a /30 and a /24?*[4]

It is a statement of some irony that the industry calls its own legacy products by yet another acronym: POTS, plain old telephone service.

The telecom industry also has a stodgy, quasi-government image that is reinforced by the mind-numbing list of taxes telecom bills are subject to. A cottage industry of thousands of telecom audit consultants has arisen to review these taxes and myriad charges that telecom companies themselves dream up on their bills.

It's gotten to the point that family budgets around telecommunications and media—home line, cable, multiple cell phones, Internet access, and others—now exceed those of all other utilities—electricity, gas, heating, lawn care, and the like. The telephone has clobbered the thermostat. In most companies, the spend on telecommunications typically exceeds the cost of hardware, software, and technology services put together.

Yet even as telcos sit in the midst of widely respected innovators such as Apple and Google, their own innovation track record is poor. It does not help that Verizon's 2009 10-K filing does not contain the word "research" anywhere. Most telcos have outsourced the proud tradition of Bell Labs (which gave the world the touch-tone telephone and the UNIX operating system) to the Ciscos and Plantronics of the world.

Worse, like tobacco, telcos spend way too much on attorneys. Alexander Bell probably wondered why he had bothered to invent the telephone. He is said to have considered his invention a nuisance and would not have one in his study. But worse, over its first two decades, the Bell Telephone Company faced more than 500 lawsuits about the telephone.

That litigious trait has unfortunately become part of the telecommunications industry DNA. Some examples:

- Verizon, Sprint, AT&T, and Nortel serially filed lawsuits against the VoIP provider Vonage in 2006 and 2007.
- The European Union had to intervene to cap mobile roaming rates in its geography.
- The Federal Communications Commission had to mediate between AT&T, Apple, and Google on Apple's rejection of the Google Voice application for the iPhone.

Verizon's SEC 10-K filing for 2009 shows that just about every aspect of its operation had to spend plenty of time and money on attorneys:

Our business faces a substantial amount of litigation, including, from time to time, patent infringement lawsuits, antitrust class actions, wage and hour class actions, personal injury claims and lawsuits relating to our advertising, sales, billing and collection practices. In addition, our wireless business also faces personal injury and consumer class action lawsuits relating to alleged health effects of wireless phones or radio frequency transmitters, and class action lawsuits that challenge marketing practices and disclosures relating to alleged adverse health effects of handheld wireless phones. We may incur significant expenses in defending these lawsuits. In addition, we may be required to pay significant awards or settlements.[5]

The telecommunications market also faces thorny ethical issues. It has been accused of aiding Web censorship in China, of surveillance in the

United States, and of assisting "deep packet inspection" of citizen e-mail traffic by the Iranian government. All this time, money, and attention could be going toward innovation, not attorneys.

It is an industry changing at blazing speed on the one hand and stuck in a time warp on the other.

Someone in his finance department should have also warned Whitacre that he should not be talking about Skype using its infrastructure. There was no reason to bring attention to the fact that AT&T itself may not have been investing enough in its mobile network infrastructure.

Whitacre's successor, Randall Stephenson, has had to face the embarrassing scenario of diluting the huge success around the iPhone. In fact, AT&T will likely become a poster child for the adage "If you are too innovative in your marketing but cannot deliver, you may have in fact under-marketed because you have tarnished your brand."

AT&T had branded itself the "fastest 3G network in the nation," and it had ads showing Amelia Earhart, snowmen, and leprechauns suggesting wide coverage everywhere: in the oceans, in mountains, even at the end of the rainbow. In the meantime, even in major cities, such as New York and San Francisco, consumers were reporting inadequate coverage as iPhone data traffic was exploding and taxing its network.

Then AT&T started to promote its 3G data cards for netbooks to add even more to the traffic. Sensing a major weakness, Verizon started to mock AT&T in ads for having just a fraction of its mobile network coverage. Both companies had started a 3G network rollout a decade ago. The slow AT&T deployment around its fastest-growing market seemed incomprehensible. Instead of accelerating its investment, AT&T started making noises about how iPhone data users were taxing the network and how the company would "incentivize" heavy users to use less of the network.

It led to a widely read, sarcastic rant by the blogger "The Fake Steve Jobs" that included "Do you think the guys who were running Capital Records said, 'Gee whiz, the kids are buying up this record ["Meet the Beatles" in 1964] at such a crazy pace that our printing plant can't keep up—we'd better find a way to slow things down.'"[6]

As a result, the AT&T brand is under stress. A survey by CFI Group, which measures customer satisfaction metrics, said, "AT&T's exclusive iPhone arrangement with Apple has been a double-edged sword. While it acquired millions of new customers, half of iPhone respondents said they would like to defect to another provider."[7]

AT&T has had to innovate in its delivery to try to match its marketing "innovations." It has done so in a number of ways:

- It encourages consumers to use more Wi-Fi, which routes traffic through the home broadband pipe.

- It is attempting to market its MicroCell, which acts like a mini-cellular tower in your home or small-business environment but also routes traffic through the home broadband pipe.
- It has made it easier and cheaper (free under many plans) for consumers to get on its Wi-Fi hotspot network at Starbucks and elsewhere when they travel.
- It is significantly increasing its "backhaul" capacity (i.e., the choke point in many networks is the pipe from the cell towers to the network's spine).

But when the real Steve Jobs's epitaph is written, one asterisk will mar his otherwise amazing career—that of the AT&T performance around the iPhone. Of course, the issue is not just with AT&T. Most large, traditional telcos have a major morphing challenge—and opportunity. Let's hear from Martin Geddes.

Reinventing the Traditional Telco

"Replace minutes with moments."

Martin Geddes was strategy director at BT Innovate & Design division and now runs an independent consultancy business. He has major makeover ideas for the telcos. Geddes is somewhat unusual for a telco executive in that he thinks in terms of applications, not just network infrastructure. After all, it has taken an Apple to build a vibrant mobile application community and a Cisco to popularize telepresence. Geddes explains:

> *Telcos face turmoil. On the consumer side we see declining landlines, vigorous price competition for mobile voice and data, and difficulty squeezing money from old and new media industries. On the enterprise side, growth opportunities such as cloud computing and unified communications are more tightly associated with IT enterprise players than with telcos.*

He is afraid, though, that telcos are clinging to older models and focusing on short-term threats from Google and Skype: "The Internet is still so young. I am more worried about the next generation of Googles and Skypes, which will be far more terrifying."

Geddes does not even mention global competition, which is cutting its teeth with consumers who deliver low average revenue per user (a metric the industry calls ARPU) of between $5 and $20 annually. The bigger Western telcos are spoiled by ARPUs in the hundreds.

Geddes likes to draw parallels to how containers revolutionized global shipping a few decades ago:

As containers were being adopted, some ports doubled down on the old business model and built better breakbulk facilities—and lost. Manhattan's quays are gone; Newark has replaced it. Others waited to become "fast followers," and lost too. London went from being one of the world's busiest ports to zero activity. Dubai did the reverse by investing exclusively in the new model, with a low-cost base and high volume. The winners were those who staked out the key nodes of the new value chain.

The other interesting trend was [that] containers shifted the balance of profit away from the shipping lines and towards the ports. But even more profitable than the ports are the agents who arrange the end-to-end logistics and supply chains for their customers.

In telecoms we need to think similarly—it's the operator who can assemble a multitude of fixed and mobile networks, content delivery systems, and partnerships with the application providers that wins.

The era of minute-based telephony is going away; however, there is a huge opportunity to replace it with something different. Global communications platforms need to make communication between enterprises and their customers more efficient and more effective. This flips the business model on its head. Make money from enterprises who want to interact and transact with telecoms users, not directly from the users themselves. Think of it as the "Googleization" of telecoms, where users pay in privacy and attention, not cash.

Geddes discusses how a core telecom product, such as voice mail, could be reimagined:

There's so much inefficiency surrounding the voicemail product. In our example, an enterprise—such as a mail order retailer—leaves a customer a voicemail message reminding them to pay a late bill. They had to pay somebody for that one-minute voicemail: to sit there, listen to the user's phone ring, wait out the voicemail greeting, and then hand-craft the message. It's like the hand-weaving of the twenty-first century, totally lacking in automation, and prone to simple error from both parties, such as mishearing the message.

It is down to chance whether the user is in the right context to receive the message and make the call back. It's so easy to forget the message once heard. There's no option in the voicemail system to "press # to schedule a call with Acme Corp." That uncollected cash sucks up more operational cost for the retailer.

Then if the user does call back, they must navigate through call center process, which fails to recognize that the call is a response to the original voicemail. Thus the user has to (manually) identify and reauthenticate themselves to a customer service agent. More wasted money.

> *Even worse, before listening to the voicemail message, say the recipient goes to the enterprise Web site and pays their bill. The enterprise should be able to expire that voicemail message, since it is no longer relevant. However, we cannot do this today. The recipient may unhappily call back to say they have paid their bill and don't understand why they got the voicemail, just to hear an apology that the whole call was unnecessary. Even more wasted money, and a terrible customer experience.*
>
> *Also, it's an insecure process. We can't really for sure know it's the right person you are calling so you do not leave many details. The recipient does not know it is a legitimate call. That's not a minor problem because even at BT we had a problem with people phoning up BT customers, pretending to be BT, and trying to defraud them in various ways.*
>
> *And for all that, the mobile telco made about seven euro cents worth of termination fee out of that one message, and that's a declining figure that's being regulated downward.*

Geddes believes the real opportunity lies in the space between enterprises and consumers, in at least three ways:

1. Reinvent existing products. Voice mail is just one example. The biggest innovation in recent years is visual voice mail:

   > *But we could put IVR features inside the voice message, the recipient could complete voice processes inside the voice message; no calling back to a call center. Or we could leverage voice-to-text capability as BT could do with its Ribbit acquisition.*

2. Around newer social media, telecoms could build capabilities enterprises need, such as federated identity:

   > *If you recycle a Twitter account and it's assigned to someone different, they need to know. If all their employees use a single Twitter ID, how can they federate employee IDs with the Twitter IDs? Security and authorization features are needed so that certain types of data that they send to customers doesn't become publicly searchable or get automatically re-tweeted.*

3. Telecoms need to offer newer services:

   > *Every day in call centers around the world, call center operators are paid to transcribe names, addresses and credit card numbers of people for whom the telco they're placing the call from already knows. Trucks deliver parcels to homes where the telco knows you're already out.*

Utilities send out paper bills and reminders when the telco already knows the email address, the Twitter ID and the mobile phone number associated with that home.

Who Is Willing to Wait for Telcos to Morph Themselves?

Three examples—one of an internationally mobile consumer, another of a small business, and one of a local community in Louisiana—show how consumers have learned to trivialize the role of the traditional telcos. Let's start with Karin Morton.

As Rio de Janeiro prepares for the 2016 Summer Olympics, the city will see massive change. But according to Karin Morton, a technology consultant, that will pale compared to the changes the city has seen in telecommunications in the last couple of decades. Morton lives in that beautiful city, but her work and family take her out of Brazil frequently.

Before the advent of cell phones in Brazil, landline telephone numbers were bought and sold like commodities. The price to purchase a landline from Embratel [the local phone company] fluctuated from expensive to outrageously expensive. There was a long waiting list, and brokers controlled the "gray" market. Of course, once you had a line, you still had to pay monthly fees and per-call usage fees. For international calls, I remember it was close to $5 a minute. My father had minor heart attacks every time we called relatives on birthdays or holidays.

Cell phones and competition changed all that. Cell phones eliminated the parallel landline market, and the brokers are gone. Competition lowered rates, and my dad no longer meters calls. Still, with international calls and my travel, my monthly bill was often $250 to $300.

Then Internet technology, such as Skype, arrived and my bill dropped to $25 a month. However, Skype, via a computer, was limiting. Even if you used a laptop to walk around, you had to carry it with the top open so that it would not hibernate and lose the connection.

Now I think I am at an optimal place. I make calls using an Apple iPod Touch with the iPhone Stereo Headset (which has a microphone and costs about $30). Most people do not realize the iTouch does most things the iPhone does and you do not need to sign up for mobile voice and data plans. If you can get on Wi-Fi, the free Skype application allows you to call and SMS anywhere. I have friends who use JaJah, Truphone, and other VoIP calling services—so there are alternatives to Skype also. For someone who travels frequently, that also means no surprise roaming or usage costs. You need a backup phone *for emergency services, incoming calls, or for when there is no Wi-Fi signal, but for the savings, that hassle is worth it.*

Needless to say, I now look for airports and hotels that offer free Wi-Fi. Staying with friends who have Wi-Fi is also a plus!

It is amazing how far we have come in the last decade. The way things are going, by the time the Olympics get here, maybe the phone companies will pay us to call on their network!

Actually, Martin Geddes would agree with her: Give her services for free so telcos can get access to her vast global network.

Now let's look at how Charlie Wood runs his business on the Web: "For me, it's just like a country club. If that's where your customers, partners, and competitors hang out, you should too."

Charlie Wood spends his life on the Web and he makes a fine living at it, but the phone company for him is just a pipe—the value comes from applications from Google and Apple.

Wood and his partner, Larry Hendricks, and some contracted help run Spanning Sync, a Web service that bridges content on Apple devices to Google's Calendar and Contacts. The service, which has been rated "5 Stars" on the Google Solution Marketplace, keeps over 40,000 worldwide customers on the right bank of the right river at the right time.

But what is impressive is how various tools at Google, many of which are free, allow Wood to pretty much run his business and his life:

- *Google Calendar.* He uses this application for personal, work, and school and to coordinate calendars with his wife, Hendricks, and contractors. His own technology allows using the iPhone's calendar app and, voila, it is in sync with Google Calendar.
- *Gmail/Google Contacts.* Wood uses Gmail for personal e-mail and Google Apps (Premier Edition) e-mail for work. Again, his technology keeps contacts synced across machines and devices. He has a 25-gigabyte e-mail account—everything is archived there—searchable in seconds.
- *Google Docs.* His contractors keep their timesheets in shared Google Docs spreadsheets. Anything they need to collaborate on—design documents, lists of feature requests, legal stuff, basically all of the docs for the company—are in Google Docs.
- *Picasa Web Albums.* "We used to make custom Web pages to show screenshots of products. Now we just create a Picasa Web Album and link to the slideshow view."
- *YouTube.* Sales are 100 percent online, and screen casts are their "demos." Spanning Sync uploads a high-definition version to YouTube— free bandwidth, multiple resolutions (high and standard definition), and a nice iPhone version, all for free.

- *Google Groups.* The company uses it for customer discussion forums. Again, it's free—plus it has good spam-filtering features.
- *Google Analytics.* Spanning Sync does all its own Web site analytics, including funnel tracking from visit to download to sign-up to purchase, using Google Analytics.
- *Google Blog Search.* The company monitors online reputation using Google Blog Search (and Twitter search). "People are astounded when they write a post about us even on a low-traffic blog and we post a comment 5 minutes later."

A huge benefit from hanging out at the country club sponsored by Google and Apple!

Now let's look at the Lafayette Utilities System. After five years of bruising court battles with AT&T and Cox (the local cable company), which went all the way to the Louisiana Supreme Court, the community can now take advantage of broadband download speeds approaching 50 megabytes per second (mbps) for $58 a month.[8]

The maximum AT&T offered the community was 6 mbps; Cox did somewhat better with 15 mbps (although in 2010, Cox finally started to increase speeds—it started offering the Cisco DOCSIS 3.0-based "Ultimate Internet" service with up to 50 mbps). Of course, both companies wanted customers to sign up for bundles that included local/long-distance calling and TV services. And they wanted long-term contracts and installation fees. The Lafayette community clearly decided—and fought—to get choices beyond the local telco/cable.

A more activist Obama-administration Federal Communications Commission (FCC) has told Congress it wants to see dramatically improved speeds throughout the country—setting a goal of 100 million U.S. homes with 50 mbps Internet speeds by 2015.

If the telco and cable companies don't step in to deliver to the FCC vision, Google might. Google has announced plans to test ultra-high-speed broadband networks—with speeds of 1 gbps—in a small number of trial locations across the country. Communities such as Lafayette would be ideal candidates.

Scenarios involving alternatives to traditional telcos are being repeated around the world. In fact, some real innovation is happening in emerging markets that were either not burdened by traditional telcos or have chosen to allow a newer generation of telcos to emerge.

Global Telecom Race

Remember the wake-up call the U.S. Olympic men's basketball team got in the 2004 Olympics? Losses to Puerto Rico, Lithuania, and Argentina were embarrassing after decades of global domination.

Something similar has been happening to the United States, United Kingdom, Germany, and France. Study after study suggests they are not in the top 10 telecom infrastructures in the world anymore. A joint study by Oxford University's Saïd Business School and the University of Oviedo's Department of Applied Economics in Spain showed that those four countries were not "ready for tomorrow's broadband" (to facilitate, as an example, watching high-definition video). Only nine countries in the review of 66 were so ready: South Korea, Japan, Sweden, Lithuania, Bulgaria, Latvia, Netherlands, Romania, and Denmark. In the study, the researchers looked at broadband penetration across the country and measured actual upload/download speeds rather than advertised speeds.[9]

Unlike basketball, broadband penetration can have a significant trade impact. South Korea has consistently been ranked as having one of the best consumer telecom infrastructures in the world; its mobile and broadband speeds are many times faster than those in most Western countries. That infrastructure, while clearly helping the quality of life of its citizens, has allowed South Korea to become a world leader in animation and gaming development. That, in turn, has propelled the local device manufacturers Samsung and LG to become viable competitors in fiercely competitive mobile markets around the world.

Like basketball, though, the opportunity exists for the United Kingdom or Germany to come back with a "Dream Team," as the United States did in the 2008 Olympics. Unfortunately, when the issue is discussed, most of their telcos get defensive, exclaiming, "How can you compare us to a small country like South Korea with its high population density?"

We can do that because the West has its own pockets of high density; they are called large cities. Why are we not competitive at least in those pockets? After years of 3G and fiber rollouts, why are rural communities not similarly supported? How is the Lafayette Utilities System able to deliver?

In the meantime, the impact is dramatic when it comes to emerging markets such as India. Consider the new local expression "I gave you a missed call."

It's not bad grammar but something that Rajagopal Sukumar repeatedly heard when he moved back from the United States to India.

Most subscribers in India do not sign up for voice mail on their mobile phone service. The tacit expectation is that you will check your list of missed calls and call them back. This way you save on the monthly voice mail charge and callers do not use up minutes leaving a message.

Consumer ingenuity and provider flexibility through prepaid calling cards versus monthly charges has led to almost 400 million mobile subscribers in India. It's been a remarkable turnaround led by new-age mobile carriers such as Reliance and Bharti in a country famous for decades of wait time to get landlines from state-run telecom companies. (Morton talked about her experience in Brazil; India was far worse.)

And Bharti has been innovating how it runs its operations. It has outsourced most of its back office to IBM and other services firms. It has even has outsourced the "crown jewels": The network is being managed by the equipment providers Ericsson and Nokia-Siemens Networks, so they can manage peaks and valleys in demand and Bharti can focus on customer acquisition and service.

While they may not come close to South Korea's telecom leadership, country after country is being transformed economically and politically by the explosion in high-speed broadband and mobile communications. Here are a few examples:

- Fifteen years after genocide left a million dead and tore the country apart, Rwanda has invested in buses with laptops and satellite dishes. These buses travel around to provide the countryside—despite the lack of paved roads or electricity—a taste of the Web.
- The Qinghai-Tibet railway is the highest in the world and goes through some of the harshest terrains. It already has 80 percent mobile coverage and keeps expanding. The Chinese may be wary of Tibetan strife, but it has not stopped the development of a Tibetan-language user interface. (Few of the locals speak or write Mandarin, the official language.)
- The whole country of Macedonia—one of the poorest in Europe—is a "hotspot" with equipment funded by the Chinese and U.S. Agency for International Development. Broadband pricing dropped dramatically, according to Kiro Velkovski, a manager on the project. Its landlocked children can now easily revisit, over the Web, the path of its famous king, Alexander the Great as he took his armies all the way to India.
- Alexander was also famous for having annexed Persia (modern-day Iran), which made headlines last year with its "Twitter revolution." The *Washington Times* reported:

  Tehran's authoritarian leaders clearly were caught off-guard. . . . As open defiance of the election results broke out, citizen journalists used new media to spread the word. And the whole Web was watching.[10]

Karl Marx must be turning in his grave: Telecommunications, not competing political ideologies, are changing the world.

Innovating the Telecom Supply Chain

AT&T's issues around iPhone bandwidth are a symptom of frequent supply roadblocks in the telecommunications industry. Few industries have seen this much turmoil in so short a time. It would be the equivalent to the United States saying we are convinced traffic circles do a better job regulating traffic than red lights, then making the switch in a few years and letting the private marketplace deliver the infrastructure changes. We would have chaos.

Behind the scenes, there is severe chaos in the telecom supply chain. Capacity via undersea trunk cables, "dark fiber" (built but unused fiber optic capacity), backhaul (from cell towers to the backbone), and fiber in the last mile to the home varies dramatically across time and region. The big telcos clearly understand the supply chain well but they try to optimize against their own capital expenditure budgets.

Sometimes they guess right; at other times they don't—spectacularly.

One area of consistent innovation they have come to rely on comes from equipment manufacturers, such as Nokia-Siemens Networks (NSN).

Siemens can trace its roots back to telegraphic systems in Berlin, Germany, in 1847. Over the last century and a half, it has been on the forefront of most communication industry innovations. Nokia has pioneered many mobile communication trends in the last few decades. The two launched a joint venture in 2007 to provide telecom equipment to a seemingly insatiable global demand.

NSN's forecast then was:

> *Within less than a decade, we predict that most of the world's population—some five billion people—will be connected to mobile, wireless broadband or fixed broadband communication services. This means that today's global customer base will approximately double, with over two billion new customers making phone calls for the first time and worldwide data usage soaring to at least 100 times today's levels.*[11]

NSN is innovating beyond just product performance to offering plenty of services—in effect, outsourcing the operations of equipment (as in the Bharti example above) and increasingly making those boxes more energy efficient.

NSN needs to as Chinese providers Huawei and ZTE increasingly compete globally on economics. They also benefit from burgeoning demand at home as China speeds to build out the biggest single telecom market in the world. They can also leverage that experience to emerging, high-growth countries all over the world. As we see in Chapter 12, China Inc. has been making significant strides in building bridges with a number of African and other developing economies. That level of government support and their price points could give Huawei and ZTE an unfair advantage in these emerging markets.

Recap

The innovation is breathtaking: Apple and the thousands of applications around the iPhone, Cisco around telepresence, Skype around international calling, Plantronics around telephone devices, and GoGo around airplane Wi-Fi. Even more innovation is happening in GPS applications, digital radio, network management tools, undersea fiber, and many areas of the radio spectrum. In the middle of all this innovation, traditional telcos are slow and unpopular with their customers.

These conflicting trends are opening up opportunities as policy makers ask, "How do we become like South Korea? Can we compete with devices, applications, and/or bandwidth with other countries?"

Policy makers look at their country's capacity needs and ask, "Should we provide a shared, public backhaul pipe? Should we encourage a new generation of telcos to emerge, not just depend on the older legacy vendors to transition to the new world?"

Similarly, CIOs are asking, "Should we look at providers from around the world, not just domestic ones? Should we buy our own dark fiber? What bandwidth issues will we hit if we move our employees from BlackBerries to iPhones? What telecommunication-enabled applications can we build or leverage?"

Telcos are asking, "How can we change quicker and not turn into 'dumb pipes'? Where do we focus and innovate: broadband or mobile? Sensor to sensor, nonhuman communications? Global markets? What about newer business models, as Martin Geddes suggests?" All these telecom opportunities should be salivating to any aspiring polymath.

CHAPTER 8

Polymath Profile #3: Plantronics

*S*ea *of Tranquility, the Moon:* "Good luck, Mr. Gorsky!"
In the run-up in 2009, to the fortieth anniversary of the moon shot, it was inevitable that all the fascination and intrigue and rumors around the *Apollo 11* mission would be replayed. So the debate started anew about why Neil Armstrong had invoked Mr. Gorsky during that poignant moment. Was Gorsky someone influential in Armstrong's life? Was Armstrong taking a swipe at the Soviet competition?

Wait!

NASA transcripts show Armstrong never spoke those words. The Plantronics headset he wore faithfully recorded everything historic he said. No Gorsky.

Yet the Web insisted Armstrong did. The rumor supposedly started in 1995 and refuses to die. As in so many things on the Web, if anything it has since grown in color.

How Plantronics and the Web have evolved over the last few decades provides a glimpse into the evolution of modern telecommunications and networks.

Five Decades of Telecommunications

Gunjan Bhow, a vice president at Plantronics, recounts the company's history: "We spent much of its early life making specialized headsets for aviation and space, including the one Neil Armstrong used. We also found a niche in mission-critical communications in the air traffic control system and emergency services."

Then came the growth in toll-free numbers in the 1980s (even though AT&T had first offered what it called "inward WATS" in the late 1960s) fueled by the declining prices as the "Baby Bells" divested from AT&T competed vigorously for long-distance calling. That opened up a vast new market in contact centers. PCs started to proliferate, and the need for headsets to stay productive while typing on keyboards opened up another market.

The 1990s saw the company move into the emerging SOHO (small office, home office) market, which had mushroomed as companies allowed employees to work from home or at satellite offices and as corporations shrank and used smaller contract firms more.

The last few years have seen Plantronics products get untethered. Bluetooth headset use has grown rapidly with the explosion in mobile phones and with an increasing number of laws mandating hands-free calling while driving. By the end of 2009, Plantronics had grabbed almost a third of the retail market for Bluetooth headsets.

Services such as VoIP also make the computer into the telephone and Plantronics is happy to provide the device to talk with it.

Says Bhow, "UC [Unified Communications] is what is driving our next stage of growth."

He was recruited to help Plantronics with its UC strategy. It is an industry term for software that coordinates the broad range of ways we communicate—chat, text, fax, voice mail, video conferencing, and more. The UC market is expected to grow to 50 million voice seats by 2014, about half of which will need headsets. Plantronics estimates that could add $350 million to its revenue base. Various corporate customers are piloting rollouts, with the largest deployment in excess of 60,000 seats.

UC has also brought convergence to the traditionally separate technology and telecommunications markets. Bhow continues:

> We are selling much more to the CIO. In the past we sold to a specialist focused on PBXes, routers, and switches.
>
> Actually, the CIO primarily provides the due diligence and approvals. We are marketing more to end users with their rapidly changing expectations. Think of how little the office phone has really changed compared to the form/factor of mobile devices that consumers are now much more attuned to.

As the next generation of workers moves in, Plantronics' surveys show they find untethered communications more private than those based at their desks. And to meet increasingly mobile lifestyles, the company offers rugged products, such as the Explorer 370, which is water, dust, and shock resistant and features its WindSmart technology to ensure users experience clear calls no matter what the ambient noise.

Plantronics says every one of the Fortune 100 companies uses its products. Of the 25 companies named in *BusinessWeek*'s 2009 customer service report, 24 of them use Plantronics headsets in their contact centers. Given its traditional range of call center products and its more recent Bluetooth and VoIP products, Plantronics' enterprise success is understandable.

Consumerization Effect

Until it sold its Altec Lansing unit in 2009, Plantronics was also in the entertainment market with digital-powered audio systems for personal computers and portable audio devices. It is still in the gaming market, where Web comments say, "With its surround sound, I could easily distinguish between friendly suppression fire from my right and enemy shouts of terror directly ahead as I led the ambush."

The consumer mind-set keeps Plantronics focused on the marriage of sound innovation and personal fashion and comfort. So it is not uncommon to see product reviews calling them "cool" and "sexy." The gaming headset just mentioned was developed in collaboration with Dolby. The Plantronics Discovery 975 wireless Bluetooth earpiece comes with a protective and stylish case that doubles as a charging station, which allows the mobile professional to recharge the headset while on an airplane, on the street, or anywhere that power is not accessible. The case can recharge twice—in effect, tripling call and standby time on the road.

Darrin Caddes, vice president of corporate design, spent more than 20 years designing products for some of the world's best automotive and motorcycle brands, including BMW, Fiat, and Indian Motorcycle. His unique design philosophy at Plantronics is summarized in these comments:

> *Each member of the Plantronics Design team brings a specialty expertise from human behavior and anatomy to color and complex surface development.*
>
> *Headsets will continue to evolve as fashion accessories as we have seen with both watches and eyewear . . . we make decisions on which ones to wear based on how we feel or choose to express ourselves at that moment. I believe headsets are destined for the same cultural evolution.*

Pushing Form/Function Boundaries

One of Plantronics' most innovative products is the Calisto Pro—a polymath of a device. Calisto Pro allows you to make landline, VoIP, and mobile calls and listen to a music player. The product comes with a compact phone and a headset that share a common charging base station. The phone is built on digitally encrypted DECT™ 6.0 technology, which frees it from interference with other home appliances, such as microwaves. It provides up to 300 feet of roaming range, a built-in speaker and flip-up waist clip for walkabout dialing, and caller ID viewing. It has its own voice mail system with multilingual menus.

Or users can don the headset that plugs into the ear and is lightweight (0.65 ounce). It does not need a headband, making for less fatigue during lengthy calls. A successor product, the Savi Office, added a headband option. The headset combines a noise-canceling microphone and an extended boom to reduce background noise.

Work-at-home professionals can also pair the headset with their Bluetooth mobile phone while on the road, and a call can automatically reconnect with the Calisto Pro phone upon their return.

Hold on, there's more!

The product is enhanced with its PerSono Suite software. A series of icons available in the software allow users to interact with their music player, IP phone, PC, and headset with simple button presses on a graphical user interface. Users can tell the media player to pause or mute when a call is received or ended.

Plantronics' Outlook Utility allows users to transfer up to 200 Outlook contacts with three numbers each (work/mobile/home) from their PC into the Calisto Pro Series handset and then dial any of those numbers from the handset. It also allows users to dial from the PC, transfer the call to the headset/handset/speakerphone, and then walk around.

The Calisto Pro qualified as a finalist for the 2008 International Design Excellence Award and is offered in a bundle with voice recognition software Dragon Natural Speaking. The software benefits from the sound quality with the extended boom closer to the mouth and because the built-in noise-canceling microphone also improves the sound quality.

More advances in audio quality come with the Plantronics Voyager PRO Bluetooth headset, which has a dual-microphone boom to accurately isolate voice signals: One microphone captures voice while the second microphone identifies and removes background noise. It also incorporates the company's WindSmart technology, which filters and reduces wind distortion. The end result is the cancellation of ambient noise in a crowded restaurant or car without overprocessing audio, so voices sound natural during conversations.

Looking ahead, the company has qualified for a patent for a "movement-powered headset." Wireless headsets are convenient but having to charge them regularly is not fun. The patent seeks to use kinetic energy from the user's body movements to charge the headset.[1] The patent filing says:

The human head moves a large amount during normal daily activities, such as subtle nods, turns, shaking, etc., as well as when the whole body is experiencing movement such as walking, running, climbing stairs, riding in a vehicle, riding a horse, riding a bicycle, scooter, skateboard, skiing, climbing a mountain, and virtually any physical activity. Additionally, movement and vibration of the headset when not being worn, such as when stowed in the user's pocket, briefcase, purse, or a vehicle, would also contribute to the headset's charging ability.

"Is voice dead?" Bhow recently asked that provocative question on the Plantronics blog. He also provided the answer: "In a culture drowning in text, the power of emotion and the role of voice are more important than ever before." In other words, we may use voice less, but we use it for more impact. Plantronics plans to continue to make sure you can put your best voice forward.

Recap

Each decade or so Plantronics has successfully transitioned with major swings in the telecommunications industry—from call centers to the small/home office, to the explosion in mobile devices to increasing IP-based telephony.

In addition, its devices are allowing for the convergence of the growing number of voice channels, including landline, VoIP, and mobile. The company also is blending streaming audio and consumer fashion trends. For all this, Plantronics qualifies as a polymath in the telecommunications market.

CHAPTER 9

Arsonists:
And Other Disruptors

As we saw in Chapter 2, we express shock at the $600 military commode, but for technology we pay over $5,000 a gallon for printer ink, we amortize over $10,000 a support call for our enterprise software, and we pay several dollars a minute to call home on our mobile phones when traveling overseas. The price of specialty drugs can run to tens of thousands of dollars per patient per year. While many industries scrape by with less than 5 percent operating margins, we continue to pay so-called cheap offshore services vendors 30 percent operating margins.

The standard technology vendor response is "We have to invest so much in expensive research and development." But look closely at their income statements and often only 2, 5, or at most 15 percent goes toward R&D. The vendor tune then turns to "Well, we don't put a gun to our customers. They write us checks voluntarily."

Customers do keep writing those checks when they should be turning to disruptors like Bill Hambrecht with his mantra of "80% value for 20% of the price," as we see in Chapter 10.

Hold on, you say. Don't technology and pharmaceutical vendors constantly reinvent themselves and thus themselves provide the disruption? What about Moore's Law, which has driven our expectations of technology economics? Version 1.0 may be pricey, but later versions keep delivering significantly better price/performance.

Yes, let's first look at Moore's Law.

Myth of Moore's Law

Moore's Law predicates that the number of transistors on an integrated circuit will double every couple of years. The Intel 4004, introduced in 1971, contained 2,300 transistors. Intel is now introducing its next-generation

Itanium processors (code-named Tukwila) with two billion transistors. And the industry has passed the savings along in constantly improving price/performance around servers, PCs, and devices.

The reality is that while the technology industry proudly talks about Moore's Law, the majority of the industry has not been subject to it for decades. Most technology investment these days is not in hardware but in software and services—costs that are more closely tied to labor economics, not trends in transistor design and scale manufacturing. In telcos, pricing has often been driven by regulatory influence and, in many countries, monopolistic positioning.

Even in chips, Moore's Law may be hitting a wall. Gordon Moore, who first enunciated the principle, says, "It can't continue forever. The nature of exponentials is that you push them out and eventually disaster happens."[1]

Moore has repeated that cautionary mantra since 2005. But we ignore it, as we did the boy who cried wolf. Oh, there will be other breakthroughs from Intel or from nanotechnology. Should we ignore, though, Intel's direction, the company Moore cofounded? As *Fast Company* observed, "[Intel itself has been] pushing the Atom mobile chip, in a dogleg pivot from Moore's Law, the founding axiom behind Intel, that chips get exponentially faster; and embracing new territory, new markets, and new ways of playing with others."[2]

At least Intel benefited us all by "killing its own children" and unleashing generation after generation of chips. Most other tech companies pay lip service to new products—managers of their incumbent products undermine the new ones. The industry has validated over and over the "Innovator's Dilemma" that Clayton Christensen made famous. He pointed out the phenomenon where many large, successful companies are turned off by the initially poor economics of disruptive technologies (even those from their own labs) and so they fight them. They pamper their older children, and allow them to kill their younger siblings.[3]

The technology industry is replete with examples:

- IBM announced "On-Demand" services in 2001 in response to growing customer clamor that IT had become too fixed an expense. But it isn't IBM but cloud computing vendors, which we discuss in Chapter 18, that are delivering small, bite-size, variable units of technology procurement and provisioning.
- Major telcos such as Verizon, AT&T, and Sprint sued Vonage, claiming prior art around VoIP dating back to the 1990s. But in spite of claiming prior art, they were not very interested in, and then not very successful at, offering VoIP to their customers. In fact, many have fought providers like Skype from offering VoIP on their mobile networks.

- Accenture (in a predecessor entity, Arthur Andersen) pioneered a software development center in the Philippines in the mid-1980s. It did not scale that low-cost pool for years and did so years later only in response to the global delivery model that firms from India and younger U.S. companies, such as Cognizant (see Chapter 6), showcased to Western customers.
- SAP and Oracle are both years late in offering their own version of Software-as-a-Service (SaaS). In fact, it could be said that Larry Ellison, CEO of Oracle, smartly invested in two SaaS start-ups—salesforce.com and NetSuite—because he realized starting them as projects within Oracle would not generate much success. This is confirmed by Timothy Chou, who helped start Oracle's version of online services in 1999: "While the business grew to nearly $200M in four years, the biggest impediment to growth was educating Oracle people. Never underestimate the power of the white corpuscles."[4]

So if incumbents have no incentive to deliver the 80 percent for 20 percent improvements, shouldn't we be looking elsewhere for disruptions? And shouldn't we insist on choices, so there is no single-vendor lock-in?

We should be insisting on the J1962.

Learning from the Automobile Service Model

Ask most mechanics and at-home auto tinkerers what the J1962 is and they will tell you it is their bridge to auto diagnostics. What started off as an interface to monitor car emissions that the Environmental Protection Agency (EPA) and various governments around the world mandated has provided transparency to what's under the hood. Even as cars became more and more complex, it allowed independent garages to survive and thrive. This occurred even as auto manufacturers packaged "free" 3-year/60,000-mile warranties that overwhelmingly drove repair business to their dealers.

Edmunds, *Consumer Reports*, and several other auto industry watchers report that, in many cases, independent garages provide much better prices and service than authorized dealers. To quote an article on Edmunds' Web site: "Truth is, some dealerships are truly more concerned with keeping 'corporate' happy than their customers, and it shows. Local repair shops, on the other hand, report to no one but *you*. And since they're smaller, corner garages depend on repeat business and word of mouth to keep a steady stream of customers."[5]

Whether you prefer going to the dealer or have your independent mechanic or you do your oil changes, it is about customer choice.

Of course, the relatively unregulated technology industry does not have things like the J1962. And absent government mandates, it takes flame-throwers and their pioneering customers to keep the industry from too much lock-in. The industry does have a fine tradition of rebels like Gene Amdahl, who left IBM in 1970 and developed "plug compatibles." Over a weekend, a data center could literally remove its IBM 360 mainframe, attach peripherals and channel interfaces to the Amdahl 470, and be back in business.

Most rebels tend to be start-ups, but often larger, established vendors will go after one another, especially when they are trailing in a market or introducing a new product. Let's first look at how some start-ups are disrupting technology markets, and then how some bigger vendors target each other.

We look at MAXroam, which is disrupting the international mobile roaming market; Zoho, focused on the Microsoft Office market; Cartridge World, focused on printer ink from HP and others; Rimini Street, focused on maintenance charges from Oracle and SAP; and ZDNet, which is disrupting traditional industry analysts and media coverage. Next we look at Agresso, whose value proposition is that it helps its customers adapt rapidly to disruptions in their own sectors. Finally, we look at larger vendors disrupting each other—HP and Cisco, pharmaceuticals and generics, SAP and Oracle and Verizon versus other telcos and cable companies.

MAXroam: Disrupting the International Mobile Roaming Market

Penrose Quay in Cork celebrates the tens of thousands of Irish emigrants who left its shores and enriched the world. In the 1800s, vendors walked the quay offering passengers the last clean water and cooked meals they would find for a while. Cork's modern-day son Pat Phelan offers today's global nomads something as elusive: reasonable mobile roaming service. Phelan wants to create the first "global mobile company." In his vision, the world would become one giant area code with no roaming charges. Says Phelan:

> *Roaming is 4% of mobile revenue but 35% of mobile margins for larger telcos [such as AT&T and BT]. I am counting on telcos remaining addicted to those margins while we offer rates which are 60 to 80% lower. With my MAXroam, you don't need a fancy $500 phone, you don't need flaky Wi-Fi, and you don't need to download any software. All you need is an unlocked GSM phone and to replace your SIM card with ours and you are good to go in most of the world.*

That definition of "world" enables voice services in over 210 countries and data coverage in over 140. Oh, and you can avail of 50 numbers associated with the MAXroam service—so you can give out a local number in the country you are at and also save your callers an international toll. You can also receive text messages for free. AT&T, in contrast, charges 20 cents a message on some international plans.

Phelan then points to a sweet irony:

Several of our customers are large manufacturers of mobile networks— so they build the equipment for the tier 1 operators but route all their roaming through MAXroam. One company, in particular, had spent almost $50,000 a month on their roaming bill. Their staff was going overseas to build networks for their customers—the mobile operators. We now look after all their roaming and they have reduced their bill by 40%.

Zoho: Disrupting the Microsoft Office Market

"Overkill," Sridhar Venbu, CEO of Zoho, says about Microsoft Office. Zoho offers a competing spreadsheet product called Sheet (and a word processor, Write, and several other applications) "as-a-Service" (see Chapter 18 on cloud computing for more on as-a-Service):

The majority of Microsoft Office users are not power users. They do not use—or if they do it is very occasional—advanced features such as pivot tables in their Excel spreadsheets or watermarks in their Word documents or animations in their PowerPoint presentations. Twenty percent of the enterprise could use Microsoft Office, the rest of the users could move to ours at a quarter of the cost.

I estimate the amortized cost of Microsoft Office and Exchange (e-mail), after volume discounts, works out to $200 a user a year in many companies. Zoho charges $50 per user. And we include 25 gigabytes of storage per user—far more generous than email storage most companies give their users. And there are substantial cost savings in terms of drastically simplified desktops, much lower cost of administration (Exchange administration alone is a nightmare), higher user productivity resulting from browser-based services, etc.

How does he deliver so much cheaper?

The open secret of enterprise software is the amount of sales, general, and administration [SG&A] compared to research and development [R&D] that vendors spend; specifically, on the sales and marketing *header. It varies from $3 in SG&A spend for every dollar of R&D to as much $8 in SG&A for every dollar of R&D.*

Given this, it would be possible to charge lower prices to customers while increasing the R&D spend that actually delivers increased customer value, by cutting down SG&A. Lower prices, by themselves, act as a magnet, which is a key driver of reduced SG&A. Second, both download software model and SaaS leverage the Internet for distribution, which reduces costs. Last but not the least, we leverage the Internet for both pre- and post-sales support—from Web meetings to instant messaging to online discussion forums to serve the customers faster and cheaper: increased productivity at lower cost.

The increased velocity of R&D is also allowing Zoho to expand into a number of other SaaS markets. So the target is not just Microsoft but also other SaaS vendors, such as salesforce.com. Venbu's economics may just allow him to disrupt even the disruptors:

Feature parity to Microsoft Office (and other software) will come sooner than you may think. We provide new updates every month. Cloud software has an intrinsic advantage in terms of speed of evolution. In fact, the comparison I make is between mobile phones versus wired phones. Mobile phones started out bulky and only had voice capabilities. Today, even cheap mobile phones beat expensive corporate PBX phones in terms of features, with mobility a huge added bonus.

Cartridge World: Disrupting the Printer Ink Market

What if gas cost $5,000 a gallon and you always had a leaky fuel tank? That pretty much describes the situation around printer ink. Ink is far more expensive, ounce for ounce, than the most expensive perfumes or rare spirits. Worse, the ink gauges can be inaccurate and force consumers to discard cartridges before they should have to.

Steve Yeffa, president of Cartridge World USA, says some of the gauges are just "page counters": "Print just one word per page and they will warn you are out of ink once you reach their rated page capacity, when in fact you may still have 80% ink left."

Cartridge World operates more than 1,600 retail stores around the world to provide refilled inkjet cartridges or remanufactured laser toner cartridges. It also has a business program where it delivers the cartridges. Its pricing can be 25 to 50 percent lower than cartridges from the OEMs such as HP and Canon.

Yeffa argues: "We have been reporting double-digit increases in same-store sales for the several months now. In contrast, HP, for example, has been reporting declining revenues in its printer unit. It highlights that consumers are fundamentally shifting to value."

The OEMs counter the original cartridges are better from three perspectives:

1. *Page yield.* The original yields more than remanufactured ones.
2. *Cartridge reliability.* Remanufactured ones fail more often or just don't work with their machines.
3. *Refill time.* You can spend 30 minutes to hours getting the cartridges refilled.

Yeffa counters with:

Refilling is a scientific process and involves sophisticated micromanufacturing and . engineering. We use cartridge-specific OEM-like ink, toner, parts, and refilling processes to ensure that our customers get OEM-like output, both in print quality as well as yield. At the same time we respect the OEMs' patents and ensure that we do not in any way impinge them. That makes us very different from shoddy suppliers who just "drill and fill" cartridges.

We have a money-back guarantee. And, even better, since OEMs have been known to scare customers that third-party products damage their equipment, we provide warranties in those unlikely situations.

So the war continues.

In the meantime, many consumers are learning to become more cautious about printing costs. Some companies are reducing printers and instead adding high-end copiers, which allow for easier scanning and distribution to multiple users in digital format. Some companies encourage their employees to use, for internal-use printing, the printer's draft mode (most printers offer monochrome, and other lower-resolution print options). Also, two-sided copies and two printed pages on one can bring more savings for internal-use copies. "Best practice" forums are growing by leaps and bounds to provide other tips on printing efficiencies.

In addition to all this, though, customers do even better with recycled cartridges. Steve Yeffa summarizes: "And, don't forget, you can also feel good about our products. Each year, through our recycling, we prevent more than 9 million cartridges from going into landfills."

Rimini Street: Disrupting Enterprise Software Maintenance Markets

As we know, the 1990s were a chaotic time for Russia as the Soviet Union's centralized, defense-heavy infrastructure was gradually torn down and replaced by decentralized, commercial enterprises. Seth Ravin describes his work there blandly as "defense conversion," but it was dangerous work where he faced kidnapping and death threats.

He is now into another type of conversion—going against what some would call today's "evil empires":

> *Did you hear what Safra Catz [Oracle copresident] told her investors last year? She said something on the lines of customers send them money for something they would be doing anyway, bragging to her investors about Oracle's 90%-plus gross margins, at the same time telling Oracle's customers how much value they are delivering to them.*
>
> *We deliver a better support value to Oracle's customers.*

Many of the customers that came to Oracle from its spree of acquisitions of PeopleSoft, Siebel, and others firms have decided that it does not make sense to continue paying that much for routine maintenance. They calculated Oracle would not deliver compelling future releases anytime soon. And if they chose to buy a future release, doing so would cost less than paying maintenance at 22 percent of the software value a year in the interim. However, these clients still need to get regulatory updates and break/fix support for the software they are currently using.

Enter Rimini Street, a pioneer in what is called third-party maintenance (often shortened to 3PM). It offers three significant advantages:

1. *It is priced based on likely level of support effort.* Oracle charges maintenance based on value of licenses, whether they are being used or not. So Rimini can reduce the cost by 50 percent or more.
2. *It lets customer stay on their current releases.* Most software vendors push their customer bases to upgrade regularly. Upgrades are cynically called "forced marches" because they are disruptive to customer operations and usually deliver little incremental value given that the applications are functionally very mature.
3. *It supports all application code, including any customizations, at no additional cost.* It also has a more responsive customer service model with a guaranteed 30-minute response time.

Of course, what Ravin has witnessed in software in the last few years makes his Russian experience look like a great training opportunity. SAP bought a third-party maintenance company that Ravin had previously cofounded, called TomorrowNow. SAP wanted to needle Oracle and cut into that 90-percent-plus-margin oxygen by offering Oracle customers cut-rate support. That led to a bruising catfight between Oracle and SAP in the form of a long-running lawsuit and an eventual decision by SAP to shutter the TomorrowNow unit. In the meantime, Ravin had left SAP in early 2005, shortly after selling TomorrowNow, and he had started Rimini Street as his next-generation offering in the emerging 3PM space. Rimini Street aimed to provide even more value and innovative service offerings for the same 50 percent annual savings goal. Since starting in late 2005, Rimini Street has continued to grow like kudzu as customers eagerly convert.

And here's the ironic twist: Rimini has started to also offer SAP customers a similar service. SAP naively thought it would offer Oracle customers cut-rate support but that its own customers were too happy to demand something similar. Ravin says:

> *Plenty of its customers are not impressed by what SAP is delivering in the way of value or innovation. And by trying to increase maintenance in the middle of a deep recession [SAP tried to increase maintenance costs from 17% to 22%], they have really shown how disconnected they are from their customers. Our depth and years of experience in the Oracle customer base and our growing footprint of customers around the world gives SAP customers the confidence and proof we can support them today.*

Following Rimini Street's 2009 results that include a strong 270 percent year-over-year revenue growth, Oracle declared war on Rimini Street and Seth Ravin personally by filing a complaint in U.S. federal court alleging copyright infringement, unfair competition, and other transgressions. In what may end up becoming marketing fodder for Rimini Street, the legal language claimed Rimini Street is selling its services for too low a price.

Reflecting on the battle ahead, Seth says, "Oracle started this war. I intend to finish it with a clearly free and open market for enterprise support providers."

The "converter" continues to do his thing.

ZDNet Blogs: Disrupting the Technology "Influencer" Market

"We are like a cat. We have used up many of our nine lives."

Larry Dignan, editor in chief of ZDNet, explains the twists and turns that the publishing industry and his entity has been through over the last decade. During two stints with ZDNet, Dignan has seen the company owned by Ziff Davis, and then spun off as a separate tracking stock, and next acquired by CNET and by CBS. If you go through the CBS Interactive list of properties, you see ZDNet last—one of the only sites focused on reporting about enterprise technologies in a menu of news, sports, and financial market sites. If there was any doubt about consumerization of technology, a trend we covered in Chapter 4, this should be a resounding reminder.

Resources came and went along with the string of owners until Dan Farber, the previous ZDNet Editor in Chief, built a network of bloggers. In a publishing market where big media brands are shutting down or being sold for a song, CBS paid $1.4 billion for CNET, parent of ZDNet, in 2008 partially because of assets like this blogger community Dignan now manages.

Today ZDNet's 50-plus bloggers write about specific technology markets like storage or open source. Some are vendor-centric: Microsoft, Google, Apple. Others are industry-focused: government, health care. Most are ex-journalists, whereas some are ex-practitioners from vendors such as IBM and Accenture.

Dignan explains, "We are a collection of individual brands—very different than the analyst firms like Gartner, which subsume the individual brand."

The brands include Mary Jo Foley, one of the most respected followers of Microsoft, and Dennis Howlett and Oliver Marks, covered in Chapter 17. Dignan comments: "They are part industry analyst, part journalist, part entrepreneur, part circus monkey. Entrepreneur is a key trait. Part of the reason the publishing industry is in bad shape is the reporter was never aware of the economics."

What's that bit about circus monkey? Dignan replies, "Oh, we also have a very lively reader community and have to be entertaining."

That community challenges the bloggers. Members of the community challenge each other—sometime in rude terms. Here's an example of a member comment to another with the Web moniker of Zealot: "Now go upstairs Zealot and take the trash out for your momma. . . . Sheesh, you would think a grown man living in mommy's basement could earn his keep by doing a few simple chores now and again."

Dignan shrugs his shoulders and says, "Most of our conversations are pretty incisive. Go be a fly on the wall in any IT buyer-vendor negotiation, or debate around private or public clouds, and you see fur fly. We are just bringing those conversations that happen every day in every company into the sunlight."

Unlike traditional media or industry analysts, where the conversation flows one way, this forum actively involves technology crowds. That, in turn, attracts advertisers like IBM, even if the etiquette would not pass

IBM's own internal guidelines, which say, "It is fine for IBMers to disagree, but please don't use your external blog or other online social media to air your differences in an inappropriate manner."[6]

Dignan continues: "There are few industry forums with this much transparency and debate. And let's face it—technology is a full-contact sport."

There you go—it fits with other sports properties. That's the real reason CBS bought ZDNet!

Agresso: Easing Disruptions at Its Customers

While the general perception is technology moves at a fast pace, Ton Dobbe, VP of product marketing for Agresso, a European enterprise resource planning (ERP) software vendor, argues that, in fact, many technologies hold enterprises back. Their rate of business disruption exceeds the rate at which their technology allows them to react. Dobbe explains:

> *We have noticed a certain type of customer was repeatedly attracted to us: one that lived in a constant state of turmoil. The reasons were varied—restructuring/reorganizations, new government compliance requirements, ongoing M&A [merger and acquisition] activities, etc.— but these types of "hyperactivity" companies kept selecting us. It was such a constant in our customer base that we trademarked that characteristic: Businesses Living IN Change (BLINC for short).*

In a survey the research firm IDC conducted for Agresso, respondents said the inability to easily modify their ERP system delays product launches, slows decision making, and delays acquisitions and other activities that ultimately cost them between $10 million and $500 million in lost opportunities.

"Change to ERP paralyzes the entire organization in moving forward in other areas that can bring more value," said one survey respondent. Another added, "Capital expenditure priorities are shifted into IT from other high payback projects" just to keep the ERP system in line with business. The impact is significant: Some 20.9 percent average declines in stock price, 14.3 percent revenue losses tied to delayed product launches, and 16.6 percent declines in customer satisfaction.

Dobbe explains how his software allows his customers the flexibility:

> *The VITA™ architecture underlying our software is an intertwined grouping of business data, business processes and reporting/analytics that move in lockstep. Role-based changes can be made via easy drag-and-drop actions. Departmental managers can bypass the need for IT*

intervention to create new divisions; collapse, expand, or append activi-
ties or workgroups; analyze and experiment with outcomes.

Another study, by *CFO Magazine*, showed that the average midmarket
company is struggling under a recurring annual spend for ERP system
change at $1.2 million a year.[7]

Dobbe concludes: "There are almost limitless variations of changes that
should be accomplished by non-IT people. It saves companies that useless
investment the *CFO Magazine* article discusses."

Of course, it's not just young companies that disrupt. Larger technology
vendors, when it suits them, provide disruption of their own. Next, let's
look at how HP and Cisco are going after each other's turf; how traditional
pharmaceuticals, generic manufacturers, and newer biotechs are disrupting
each other; how SAP is going after Oracle, IBM, and other database
markets; and how Verizon is going after cable companies and other telcos,
such as AT&T.

HP and Cisco: Disrupting Each Other's Markets

Although HP is the market leader ripe to be disrupted when it comes to
printer ink, it is trying to disrupt Cisco, the market leader in routers and
other networking gear. Cisco, for its part, is going after HP's dominant
position in the data center server market.

Why would Cisco move down market into servers where margins
average 25 percent when its networking business has yielded 65 percent?
That is the question many asked as Cisco announced its Unified Computing
System in early 2009. Its marketing said it "represents a radical simplification
of traditional architectures, dramatically reducing the number of devices
that must be purchased, cabled, configured, powered, cooled, and secured."

Some would argue that a new class of infrastructure software—
virtualization—had broken down traditional boundaries between computers, storage, and networking, and that Cisco was merely reacting to
that trend.

Others would argue that HP, in particular, pushed Cisco to do so.
Before Mark Hurd arrived as CEO at HP, there was a strong partnership
between the two companies, with HP selling hardware and Cisco selling
networking gear. Indeed, HP's previous CEO, Carly Fiorina, was on Cisco's
board. After Hurd arrived, HP started to promote its own ProCurve networking brand while continuing the partnership with Cisco. HP storage
networking solutions were positioned with Cisco high-end switching directors by both of their sales forces.

Grumbling started when HP introduced its Virtual Connect product in
2006. The industry had been moving to blade servers, which are easy to

expand by plugging new blades in or out of the chassis. While blades made life easy for the server administrator, they created problems for network and storage administration. With Virtual Connect, various network addresses were virtualized inside the module, as were the links back to the server blades on the other side. Changes in server configuration did not affect network or storage administrators, nor did changes in network or storage affect the server administrator. HP claimed that Virtual Connect could increase administrators' productivity by a factor of three because of this flexibility. The foundation for next-generation network virtualization was laid. Rumors started floating that HP saw an opportunity and Cisco saw the threat in the network sector.

As it introduced its Virtual Connect Flex-10 Ethernet module in 2008, HP changed its message from administrator efficiency to network economics, saying it could "cut network hardware costs up to 75%." Flex-10 distributed the capacity of a 10-gigabyte Ethernet port into four connections to dramatically lower the cost and complexity of network connectivity.

By late 2009, the split was confirmed as HP announced its Converged Infrastructure Architecture and started aggressively promoting its ProCurve networking gear. Cisco, in turn, set up a joint venture to tighten relations with EMC around storage. Then came HP's $2.7 billion acquisition of 3Com, and it was all-out war.

HP was going after Cisco's more profitable network business, and Cisco was going after servers to keep customers from adopting the complete HP "stack." There was competition at each level. If HP can be accused of milking its dominant position in printers and related consumables, it should be given credit for taking on Cisco, as the latter milked its dominant position in network switches and routers.

When Disruptors Get Disrupted: The Pharmaceuticals Example

Few industries depend more on new products than the pharmaceutical industry. Given aging populations and growing world markets, the demand for their products would seem endless. With grand challenges such as cancer and periodic threats of pandemics still waiting to be tackled, there would seem to be all kinds of innovation opportunities. Instead, the industry seems to be, in some ways, worse off than it was a decade ago, and now financial pressures in most countries are turning up the heat on pharmaceutical pricing and margins.

A decade ago, things appeared to settle down. Big pharmaceutical companies such as Roche and Merck focused on traditionally formulated and validated drugs—or, as the industry called them, "small molecule" drugs. Start-up biotech firms, such as Genentech and Amgen, focused more on proteins and on a new generation of bioengineered drugs. Generic makers, such as Teva from Israel and Ranbaxy from India, waited for pharma patents to expire and introduced cheaper alternatives.

Then lines started blurring. Big pharma has been on a relentless quest to consolidate to squeeze costs and spread risks of large R&D investments. The term "biotech" has been bastardized to cover all start-ups even if they are chemical based. Generics have thrived; IMS Health, a health care market intelligence company, says generics saved the U.S. health care system more than $734 billion in the decade from 1999 to 2008.

Now big pharma is big into biotech—Eli Lilly has been partnering or acquiring a number of smaller biotech firms. Genentech is now part of Roche. Generic manufacturers now want to focus on biotech by introducing what are called "biosimilars." Biotech firms, in return, object to the term "similar"—their molecules are far more complex and much more dependent on access to the original clone.

Big pharma is also finding that it can continue to sell its brands even after patent expiry because their brand equity is so strong that consumers continue to pay a premium over competing generics. It also has learned to do much more consumer marketing. Commercials for Viagra, Lipitor, and other brands are as common as those for beer and toothpaste.

In reverse, some of the generic manufacturers are also doing original-product development and learning to be wary of newer generic makers. A phenomenon has arisen called "reverse settlement payments" in which big pharma sues a generic manufacturer for patent infringement, and then settles the case. The two parties agree to a "pay-for-delay" agreement, whereby the generic accepts a payment to stay out of the marketplace for a certain period of time. Obviously, governments are investigating such behavior, but the games go on, each side disrupting the other.

SAP: Trying to Disrupt the Database Market

Although Larry Ellison, CEO of Oracle, likes to mock his competitors in public, Dr. Hasso Plattner, one of the founders of SAP, does it in small groups. Ellison is a frequent target of Plattner's barbs. Plattner has been known to describe how he mooned Ellison's tender vessel when it refused to help his yacht when it was in distress with a broken mast. Or how Scott McNealy supposedly approached Plattner at a Sharks game (both are investors in the San Jose hockey team) about buying Sun Microsystems (the company McNealy cofounded) before he called Ellison at Oracle. Oracle ended up acquiring Sun.

Beating Ellison in a sailboat would bring extreme satisfaction. Nothing, however, would please Plattner more than to replace Ellison as the "Duke of Data Management" (as we discuss in Chapter 15). He is doing it gradually via SAP's acquisition of Business Objects and its business intelligence and analytical tools.

Plattner has also reached into academia. The Hasso Plattner Institute (HPI), funded by his foundation, has been investing research in a number of technology areas at Potsdam, Germany, and at Palo Alto in the United States. One of his pet projects involves in-memory computing and the possibility of using columnar databases rather than the row-based ones prevalent today.[8]

Memory is increasingly ubiquitous and affordable. Blades with 8 CPUs, and CPUs with 16 cores, allow enterprises to leverage 500 gigabytes of main memory. If your database can fit in that, you would be far less dependent on slow access to data on storage. Some of SAP's customers, however, have more than 30 terabytes of transaction data, and that database is growing at explosive rates.

Plattner's radical concept is to get a 100× compression by rethinking traditional data and storage optimization. The research at HPI shows that columnar databases can yield a 10× space advantage compared to row-based ones. With increased processing power available today, we can also compute on-demand aggregate data, which historically was more efficient to store in databases. That provides another 2× advantage. Finally, Plattner would tier data based on currency—storing only recent (and more likely to be accessed) data on the memory on the blade server, which could provide another 5× compression. 10 × 2 × 5 would get the 100× compression he seeks.

You can argue about the merits of columnar databases or the potentially wishful counting in his estimates, but it is good to see Plattner challenge status quo thinking. If he can get even a fraction of the efficiency he seeks, it would spur Oracle to even better performance—or to much lower economics.

For now, it has only led to another Ellison public mocking: "In-memory databases? Yes, SAP is going after this. We [Oracle] missed it and IBM missed it, and it's good that SAP CEO Hasso [Plattner] and his five guys in a garage got it. It's wacko."

Verizon: Disrupting Cable and Other Telcos

Verizon is not a vendor you expect to deliver 80 percent for 20 percent—that is, unless it chooses to go after a competitor that is ahead in a segment. Then things can get feisty.

Throughout 2009, Verizon ran commercials mocking the bearded cable guy, as its high-speed FiOS fiber-optic broadband service started to become more widely available. In earlier years, Verizon was inconsistently available around the country, so it did not go after cable companies aggressively. But beyond the humorous commercials, its pricing is helping cannibalize its own landline and long-distance rates while significantly increasing the speeds of its broadband service. Its customers are getting close to the 80 percent for 20 percent for their phone, Web, and TV service.

In 2009, it also started to attack AT&T Wireless in commercials comparing both networks' wireless 3G coverage. Verizon did so as it was introducing the Motorola Droid phone. That allowed it to mock the very successful Apple iPhone (which has an exclusive contract with AT&T in the United States) as a "clueless beauty pageant queen." Its commercials ended with the phrase "The Droid trades a hairdo for can-do."

In 2008, Verizon had packaged an unlimited-voice plan that AT&T and the rest of the wireless industry were forced to react to. For heavy cell phone users, it represented an 80 percent for 20 percent solution.

Customers have learned to become wary of telco versions of 80 percent for 20 percent. Termination fees, shortfall fees, late fees, and number of other charges show up with regularity, as we saw in Chapter 7. The world continues to need smaller vendors like MAXroam to keep telcos like Verizon honest.

Recap

Why do the Pat Phelans and Seth Ravins of the world carry their slingshots around looking for Goliaths like Verizon and Oracle? Whatever their personal drivers, they represent one-hand clapping. Until customers step up and take advantage of their flame throwing, magic cannot happen.

Edwin Land, founder of Polaroid, is supposed to have said, "Innovation is sudden cessation of stupidity." There is plenty of stupidity in technology spend, as we saw in Chapter 2. We need to take advantage of the arsonists to innovate around our technology economics. Our own low margins are screaming for that innovation. Polymath enterprises do not just focus on innovation—they deliver that innovation at efficient economics, often by working with such arsonists. Let's now hear from Bill Hambrecht, the dean of the school of 80 percent value for 20 percent.

CHAPTER 10

Polymath Profile #4:
W. R. Hambrecht

"How do you deliver 80% of the value at 20% of the price?" asks Bill Hambrecht tantalizingly. He is channeling an advisor of his, Clayton Christensen, the Harvard Business School professor and author of *The Innovator's Dilemma.*[1]

Hambrecht has the answer. But the forum isn't appropriate for a long business conversation. Almost to make that point, George Zimmer, the chief executive and TV pitchman for the Men's Wearhouse, is there. The man who made famous the phrase "I guarantee it" is always in a suit on television but is not wearing one on this evening.

Hambrecht and his wife, Sally, are playing host to their grandchildren and some of their friends from school. And then there is Nancy Pelosi, the Speaker of the U.S. House of Representatives. "Besides, those gentlemen deserve all the credit. They can explain the 80 percent for 20 percent magic." Hambrecht points to David Marcus and Jim Donohue in one corner and Michael Huyghue and Clinton Wu in another. More about them and the Speaker in a moment

The guests come and go from the fourth-floor suite at AT&T Park, home of the San Francisco Giants baseball team.

AT&T Park, which opened in 2000, is symbolic of neighboring high-tech Silicon Valley. The fourth floor is called the Oracle level, as in the software company. The giant TV screen was one of the first in the country to show high-definition images on its three million LEDs. The entire park is Wi-Fi enabled, so local geeks can play hooky at the game and nobody would know. It was the first major league baseball stadium to have solar panels that feed the local electricity grid. The stadium has one deficiency in spite of AT&T's sponsorship: Mobile service at the stadium is patchy, as it is throughout the city—a sore subject for many locals. But we digress.

It is a crisp Thursday evening in November. No kayaks are waiting for home run balls in McCovey Cove adjoining the stadium as they do during baseball season, which is now a distant memory. The crowd that has gathered at AT&T Park tonight is there for a football game.

Dennis Green and Jim Haslett are coaching the two teams on the field. The men have long been fixtures on the National Football League scene, bringing teams to the playoffs and winning various coaching accolades. But at tonight's game, something feels very different. The referees on the field are wearing red, not zebra, jerseys. Doug Flutie is not throwing miracle "Hail Mary" passes but is providing the color commentary. Officiating decisions are being made in the replay booth, not by the referees on the field. And the teams are named the California Redwoods and the Florida Tuskers.

Tuskers?

United Football League

Yes, welcome to the United Football League (UFL), a new professional league Hambrecht founded with plenty of technological pedigree. Hambrecht's first firm, Hambrecht & Quist, took many a tech company public since it was founded in 1968. He is a legend in Silicon Valley. Tim Armstrong, ex-Google and now CEO of AOL, is another founder of the league. Mark Cuban, another technology billionaire, broadcasts UFL games on his network, HDNet.

From game one, the new league has technology the NFL took decades to introduce. The UFL has instant replay in its games, the first-down yellow line on TV, and skycams that show the game from different angles. It has video on demand and other ancillary content on its Web site. It blogs and is on Twitter and Facebook. The games are broadcast in high-definition on Versus (a sports network) and HDNet networks.

Today, we take some of this football technology—like the yellow line—for granted. That feature, by itself, takes plenty of computing power to adjust the camera's constant movements as it zooms and tilts. The computers must be able to distinguish between grass, on which the line should be painted, and everything else (players, referees, the ball), on which it should not. The UFL offered the yellow line feature from its beginning last year. Part of the 80 percent value to consumers.

Michael Huyghue is commissioner of the new league. This evening he is rooting for the Redwoods.

Wait—as the commissioner, isn't he supposed to be neutral?

"Always root for the home team," he says with a wink as Paul Pelosi walks in. Pelosi owns the Redwoods and, yes, he's the Speaker's husband—which is why she is also cheering for that team.

Why start a new league when the NFL is dominant and so many others before have failed?

Huyghue responds:

The appetite for football in this country is insatiable. But you cannot change the format too much. The [now-defunct] Arena League reduced the number of players to 8 and had other significant differences crowds did not care for. Our approach is to go into cities the NFL is not physically in. The NFL is much more focused on TV revenues and does fine by not being physically in about half of the metro markets in the U.S. We are happy to go to cities like Orlando and Las Vegas where they are not.

As a Las Vegas Locos fan told UFL Access (a Web site aimed at UFL fans), "Look, I've been to NFL games before—but only two, or three, in my entire life. I've gone to every Locos game this year, and I can keep on going because it is affordable."[2]

Indeed, as NFL teams such as the Dallas Cowboys build billion-dollar stadiums, ticket prices get out of reach. The average ticket to a Cowboys game cost $160 in 2009. The rest of the NFL averaged $75. And that's just the ticket price. The parking, the food, and the paraphernalia add another two to three times the cost; it's the "charge what the market will bear" phenomenon. This situation makes it hard for a middle-class family to justify a trip to a game more than once every few years. Or it just attracts the corporate suits on expense accounts.

The UFL model sounds eerily similar to the one Southwest Airlines adopted more than three decades ago. Southwest used to fly into secondary cities and didn't worry about competition with the larger airlines. Its competition was car travel. That sharpened Southwest's focus and, as it turns out, that allowed the airline later to compete with the bigger airlines with 80 percent for 20 percent.

Marcus and Donohue leave the suite and go mingle in the stands. They are not with the league. They are bankers who run WR Hambrecht + Co.'s Equities business and pitch the OpenIPO auction method that the firm has pioneered. It's their version of 80 percent for 20 percent in taking companies public compared to the traditional model used by much larger Wall Street firms, such as Goldman Sachs and Morgan Stanley.

Marcus and Donohue find that the mood in the stands is electric. The fans are average Joes, not corporate types, who enjoy football. They sway with the stadium's Shure UHF-R sound system and sway even more as players celebrate in the end zone—something the players likely would get penalized for in the NFL. The new league has changed rules thought to be not fan-friendly, such as sudden death in overtime, or those that were confusing to fans, such as the "tuck rule."

The quality of play on the field is excellent. The local team is keeping up with the Tuskers, who have an unbeaten season record so far. The fans this evening certainly think this game is 80 percent for 20 percent. Huyghue continues: "The Tuskers [based in Orlando] could beat their neighbors, the NFL Tampa Bay Buccaneers."

That's not saying much, since the Buccaneers have been on a downward spiral, but the quality of UFL players would meet the 80 percent threshold even at stronger NFL teams. Most players either came from the NFL or are knocking on the door. The UFL season is timed to take in players who have been cut from NFL teams after training camp. The end of the season is timed to allow NFL teams to sign UFL players as they beef up for their playoff runs. Indeed, at the end of the past season, the Redwoods quarterback was picked up by the NFL Indianapolis Colts, home to one the best quarterbacks ever: Peyton Manning. Another 15 UFL players made the jump to NFL teams over the next couple of weeks. Huyghue emphasizes: "We are going to be complementary to the NFL. Our teams have been using systems the NFL uses to break down film and to evaluate scouting videos on prospective players."

Complementary but not the same—and they may offer more fan-focused technology. Huyghue explains:

> *The UFL grants access for their broadcast partners inside the locker rooms for pregame and postgame speeches by the head coaches. The league also allows for in-game sideline interviews and microphones inside the huddle. The league is also a beta testing ground for in-stadium first down lasers and mobile signage that displays video advertisements and digital graphics on the sidelines.*

Clinton Wu is the assistant to the commissioner. He played football at Princeton, but it is clear he did not skip his computer science classes. Wu describes some of the technology the UFL is tinkering with:

- *A GPS chip inside the football.* Fans would enjoy tracking the velocity and trajectory of the thrown ball. Referees would get more precise measurements for first downs and ball spotting.
- *Impact sensors in helmets and shoulder pads.* Fans could see an impact meter on the broadcasts that would measure the forces of each hit. Also, on the medical side, concussive hits could be cataloged and studied further.
- *Brain-computer-interface technology* from NeuroSky to measure brain wave activity. Fans would enjoy seeing a meter on the big screen showing the "nerves" of a kicker as he anxiously sets up for a game-winning field goal as the clock counts down.
- *LCD wristband.* Instead of the traditional wristband quarterbacks wear with plays written on a white card, introduce a wristband from ID Coach with a thin, almost unbreakable, LCD screen. A coach could

send a play in wirelessly that shows on the quarterback's screen, with each position's assignment indicated. This method could also revolutionize how new players learn a team's playbook.

Other ideas include fantasy football scenarios, iPhone applications, and possibly even player reality shows incorporating Flip cameras.

In the meantime, Donohue and Marcus are on the sidelines of the field, a few feet from the Redwoods' kicker practicing field goals. Yes, it would be interesting to watch the kicker's anxiety waves on the big screen.

It would be also interesting to see a map of the bankers' own anxiety as one of their equity auctions winds down. The conversation drifts back to their own 80 percent for 20 percent value proposition—on Wall Street.

The Hambrecht OpenIPO Process

The OpenIPO process idea had been brewing for years in Hambrecht's head, and it was clearly reinforced when Hambrecht & Quist went public in 1998. The general perception is that an IPO is successful if the first-day stock gain is significant—40, 70, or 150 percent. That is money, however, the stock issuer left at the table. When an issue is that underpriced, the underwriter is really taking care of its buy-side customers instead of the issuer. In a traditional IPO, underwriters allocate stock to their best clients: mutual funds and hedge funds. The bankers typically underprice the stock. When it pops the day after pricing, the windfall goes to those lucky clients. An unwritten rule is that a third of that pop gets funneled back to the bank in trading commissions. With the traditional IPO investment, banks can often make more from trading commissions than from underwriting fees. To remind the issuer whose side they represent, the legal documents can contain language such as "The Underwriters owe no fiduciary duties to the [Issuing] Company" and "The Issuer waives any rights it may have against the Underwriters in connection with the offering."

Already in his sixties, Hambrecht could easily have just gone along with the system. Instead its unfairness gnawed at him. So he started the OpenIPO Dutch auction process whose mission statement says, "Bring transparency, fairness and efficiency to the capital formation process by leveling the playing field for issuers and investors."

An example of the model's integrity came when a large institution called on the last day of the auction bidding window and basically said, "Tell your client if they want us in the deal, this is the price they have to agree to," says Marcus. He continues:

We took their bid—it was a large volume—and stacked it with the others. Their price did not meet the clearing price. The next day they

were shocked they did not qualify for a single share. Were they upset?
Absolutely. Did it show our strict adherence to the process? Absolutely.
Though they were initially upset, they have since bid in all our deals!

Enter Christensen, who knows a thing or two about disruptive business models. The *New York Times* summarizes:

As soon as Mr. Hambrecht began describing his method of taking companies public, Mr. Christensen said to himself "This is one of those. When conventional investment banks disparaged Bill, I said, 'Of course. It is very predictable. This is the classic pattern.'" Wall Street was pooh-poohing auctions because they were such a threat.[3]

Soon twenty-three companies had chosen to go public via Hambrecht's auction process. But then came the Great IPO Shutdown in 2007 and 2008. And while Wall Street has gone through plenty of review and cleanup since, things do not appear to have not changed much in the IPO process. Marcus explains:

As the IPO market opened up again in the second quarter of 2009, the online restaurant-reservations system OpenTable popped 60% the first day. That was $40 million in cash they could have used towards their own expansion plans. Rosetta Stone, the guys who do language CDs, likely left over $50 million. It's still difficult to argue that it's better that the bank and its clients got this money rather than the issuer.

Donohue makes his case:

The numbers tell our story convincingly. On day one, our IPOs went up on average 3% compared to 14% for a traditional deal. While the traditional deals are considered more "successful," our issuers, from Morningstar to NetSuite, got more of the IPO money. But here is what is really interesting. Two quarters out from the IPO date, the performance of our deals and those of the broader market are, on average, equal. Once the company is in the public arena, it will trade based on the performance of the company, not the manner in which it went public. But even better, when you compare from IPO date to December 2009, our companies had gone up 40% and the conventional model portfolio actually went down 8%!

Marcus continues:

That is an indicator that the method of IPO, traditional or auction, does not determine the long-term performance of the company. We are also finding the funds that participate in our deals are longer-term investors. The ones that want to flip in the first couple of days don't show up. Six of top 10 buyers in the Morningstar IPO held stock for over two years despite the 230% stock gain.

Because anybody who bids at or above the clearing price (or offer price) receives stock on a uniform pro rata basis, the auction provides access to deals for midsized institutions and retail investors, constituencies often passed over in a traditional IPO where the underwriter has discretion over who receives stock. As an example, we received 647 bids from 298 unique institutional accounts for the Interactive Brokerage Group IPO.

Investors have also learned to "tier" their bids at multiple price points—so they can have a basket of bids in the auction. It is much more realistic market pricing.

The bigger underwriters are just not interested in small IPOs. Their scale does not allow it. And with recent mergers, they are even bigger. We have a far lower threshold, which is so much more relevant for infotech, biotech and cleantech. And there are plenty of funds that are interested. The myth is only the big hedge funds are the investors.

There are other ways in which Hambrecht is innovating—with technology. The typical IPO road show is a brutal two-week process with plenty of plane flights, presentations, lunches, and the like. Says Donohue, "It is increasingly clear these road shows aren't efficient in bringing in new investors—they are more of an industry tradition."

Hambrecht is experimenting with doing first-level pitches via Web conferencing. Then, if serious investors ask to meet the issuer management team, the team flies out. With telepresence, even that reduced travel may become less necessary.

Donohue elaborates about other technology investments: "We have also helped issuers develop a targeted, SEC [Securities and Exchange Commission]-compliant affinity marketing campaign via e-mails and placement on selected Web sites. With CRM [customer relationship management] technologies evolving rapidly, Wall Street can become so much better with such campaigns."

Add to those growing efficiencies the fact that Hambrecht's fees cost the issuer 4 percent of the higher proceeds versus the 7 percent that large firms charge for the lower proceeds, and Hambrecht gets issuers a more diversified, longer-term investor base.

You see that, pretty soon, the 80 percent for 20 percent statement is not far off.

But why does Hambrecht do it? He is revered in Silicon Valley, and as was clear at the game that evening, he is adored by family and friends, many of whom are very powerful. He is 72 years old—he has nothing left to prove. The UFL lost $30 million it its first year and could likely lose more over the next few years. Likewise, the OpenIPO model, attractive as it is, has to continue to fight the brand and market power of the bigger banks.

Huyghue could have continued in a role somewhere in the NFL. Wu could be a savvy marketing guy at any technology company. Marcus and Donohue could be making plenty with traditional Wall Street firms. Why do they need to tilt at giant windmills like Wall Street and the NFL? As Hambrecht says, "I like to stay in the game." An appropriate pun, given the UFL focus.

Whatever the personal drivers of these men, they represent one-hand clapping. Innovators take their chances on these rebels and the ones we described in Chapter 9. Their 80 percent for 20 percent calculus is just too compelling.

Recap

Bill Hambrecht could have easily retired from a very successful firm, Hambrecht & Quist. Yet, after having taken so many disruptors public in that firm, it is not much of a surprise that he continues to look for disruptive models. Although his targets—Wall Street and the National Football League—are formidable, his mantra of "80% of value at 20% of the price" should be a rallying cry for rebels and disruptors everywhere.

For their ability to apply their concepts to a wide range of industries, Hambrecht and his team have earned the right to be called polymaths when it comes to disruptive business models.

CHAPTER 11

Interfaces:
For All Our Senses

The QWERTY keyboard was originally designed in the 1860s for type-writers we don't use anymore. It was a clever design to prevent jamming from common combinations of alphabets. You would think that, long ago, someone would have solved the jamming problems rather than persist with the dysfunctional layout. Nope, QWERTY lived on.

In the 1940s, the lore goes that the U.S. Navy experimented with an alternate, "simplified" Dvorak keyboard. They found it much more productive for workers, only to have the Treasury Department veto plans to adopt it en masse. QWERTY survived again. As we moved to word processors and computers, where the jamming issue is less relevant, surely we would have moved away from that layout. No such luck.

There was a quantum leap forward when the mouse arrived with the Apple Mac in 1984. That transition to point-and-click solidified even more the role for QWERTY. More recently, we made the keyboard smaller to fit on our BlackBerries and other PDAs, thus buying QWERTY another lease on life.

And so the majority of the world still interacts with computers with technology that annoys our eyes, tires our hands, and mostly ignores our other senses. Particularly gnawing is that software vendors go through waves of "next-generation" user interface projects but keep wasting billions because they don't seriously question the role of QWERTY.

Well, this is a book celebrating disruptors, so let's highlight even small ways in which progress is being made around tired old QWERTY: via voice, brain-machine, surface, and several other interfaces that we can increasingly leverage.

Let's start with the way we communicate with autos.

The BMW iDrive

"TechnoThrill"—that's what *Motor Trend* magazine called the 2009 BMW 7 Series. The car's 281-page press kit (which probably weighs more than the new, light aluminum fenders the automaker introduced) covered some of ways the car communicates with the driver and passengers.[1]

The nerve center is the iDrive system, which has four direct-entry buttons that provide the tactile interface to the driver. The car's steering wheel has a vibration device to alert the driver. The 10.25-inch, high-resolution display provides the visual interface. Its rear screens provide passengers with a vibration-resistant visual interface. The sophisticated Logic7 speaker system and Bluetooth-enabled microphone provide the audio interface.

Here are some of the features these systems facilitate:

- Lane Departure Warning, which vibrates the steering wheel if you change lanes without using the turn signals
- Navigation with all the usual features, plus a 3-D map view that enhances guidance through mountainous or hilly country
- Music via a 40-GB hard drive that can be accessed by compact discs, MP3 players, or USB sticks. The system is also iPod and iPhone compatible if you do not want to use the car storage.
- Hands-free calling with speech recognition via the Bluetooth microphone
- Active Blind Spot Detection, which senses vehicles up to 200 feet behind and flashes on the screen and vibrates the steering wheel if you put the turn signal on
- Rear-passenger entertainment system that allows Internet access

Most BMW customers disliked the iDrive when it first came out in 2001, and critics were even less generous. BMW persisted, however, and today it is impressive how much communication, navigation, and entertainment functionality it is bringing to drivers, with few demands on their hands or eyes.

But even BMW had to compromise: Originally the iDrive controller went in one of four cardinal compass directions; the BMW 7 series added four ordinal compass directions for a total of eight. Soon, we may end up with the QWERTY keyboard again!

Mercedes has its COMAND, GM offers features via On-Star, Ford via Sync (in collaboration with Microsoft)—so it's not just BMW but most of the auto industry has been doing its share to work around QWERTY. Let's now look at another area where Microsoft is innovating.

Microsoft Surface Computer

Walk into an AT&T retail store and you may see people hovering around a 30-inch-display table. They see features of a particular mobile device by simply placing it on the display. If they place two devices side by side on the unit, the display allows them to compare features. They can see AT&T 3G coverage maps at the national, state, local, or street level. Using simple touch and hand movements, they can scale and move the maps, determining their coverage area. In the future, they will be able to drag and drop ring tones, graphics, and video by "grabbing" content with their hands from a menu on the display and "dropping" it into the phone.

This magical confluence of physical and virtual objects is made possible by Microsoft's Surface Computing. Surface has four unique features:

1. *Direct interaction by touch and gesture.* No mouse or keyboard is necessary.
2. *Multiuser.* The large, horizontal, 30-inch display makes it easy for several people to have a collaborative, face-to-face computing experience.
3. *Multitouch.* The screen responds to many points of contact simultaneously—not just from one finger, but from dozens of contact points at once.
4. *Object recognition.* You can place physical objects on the screen to trigger different types of digital responses.

Although you can use gestures and fingers with Surface, Microsoft has also been researching four new types of mice designed for multitouch environments: FTIR (Frustrated Total Internal Reflection) Mouse, Orb Mouse, Side Mouse, and Arty Mouse. Each explores a different touch-sensing strategy, which leads to differing form factors and interactive possibilities.[2]

The Sonos Controller

"The best interfaces are 'invisible.' If you have to think about the interface, it has failed."

Doug Stoakley should know—he has spent a lifetime with interfaces of different kinds. Currently, he is with NVIDIA which makes graphics cards that are used many games and powerful workstations with demanding visual requirements. Previously, he was with Logitech, which makes a wide range of keyboards, mice, Web cams, and speakers.

What is Stoakley's favorite interface example?

He raves about the Sonos controller (or its free app available for the iPhone, whose interface in itself wins his thumbs-up), which helps him run his sound system at home. Change the song in the kitchen from the den. Play the same song all over the house, or mix and match across rooms.

That already sounds complicated—but you have to take Stoakley's word, given that he knows a bad interface when he sees one. Here are some interface failure points that he highlights:

- Some just try to "show off" all aspects of the technology/device and end up overwhelming users.

  Good interfaces are like onions—the user can peel the layers to get deeper and deeper if he/she chooses to.

- Some try to do too much.

  Too many buttons, too many menus, too many icons. They overstimulate the user. It's particularly true of those that combine tactile and visual.

- Some are just plain boring.

  Interfaces must integrate touch, sound, and sight into their solution to keep users engaged.

- Some are doomed from the start since they magically try to improve a so-so product.

  Think of the multifunction machines when they first came out and tried to print, fax, scan, etc., but did none very well.

Asked for examples of interfaces that he did not think much of, Stoakley responds:

Previous-generation Motorola phones had confusing menus. On some sets, the music player was hidden in the "Games & Apps" category.

Personally I am a not a fan of the remote control of some Denon A/V [audio-visual] systems. Some of the settings require pressing of the "<" button instead of the "ENTER" button. They were often difficult to read in daylight, and had tiny signs on some of the buttons.

Stoakley concludes: "While I learned plenty from the amazing product designers and engineers at the companies (like Logitech) I have worked at, frankly it is even more fascinating to spend time with our customers and understand what they are planning with these tools."

Did one of his customers design the remote control that had an attitude and overrode what Adam Sandler wanted in the movie *Click?*

Suddenly, the music gets too loud and Doug cannot be heard. The Sonos obviously has one more useful application.

The Tablet PC

John Dean has an eye for office ergonomics and etiquette. He spent years as CIO at Steelcase, the company that has innovated much in office furniture, including the recent award-winning Cobi chair, which flexes and adjusts to your body.

He invested in campus Wi-Fi ahead of most other companies, so employees would be constantly connected and have easy access to "institutional knowledge." "Of course, everyone would come to meetings with their laptops. Have you observed how, in a group setting, laptops look like personal shields? They are barriers. And how disruptive keyboard chatter is? Not very conducive to creativity."

So he led by example and used tablet PCs. "The keyboard can be unplugged, making the tablet a slate, and you can hold it in your lap like a pad of paper. The entry of content and navigation is a whisper."

Starting with the HP Compaq TC1000 in 2003, Dean has been a proud user of several models since:

If I was in the driver's seat in a meeting, I would have a blank PowerPoint presentation ready for incorporating into the session through a projector or display. The combination tablet and display became the digital ink whiteboard we would use in the session to co-create. When we were done with the session, everyone would get a copy immediately via email or Sharepoint.

I would do the same if I was a participant. I would quickly duplicate what was put on the whiteboard. People get visual when they have a whiteboard. You can sketch out a presentation so fast with a tablet ... both the text and the diagrams. I would then pass it on to a PowerPoint wizard after others have reviewed my drafts.

If I could get 15 minutes to spend with anyone, I could convert them to using a tablet. But I would only target those that were doing things where a tablet offered a better way. Digital ink isn't for everyone.

When you mess with the physical interaction aspect of a technology, the change can be traumatic. We are stuck in a keyboard/text/formal content world with fingers (or thumbs) as the means of interaction. Tablets are capable of making us so much more creative, but you better be really good at writing cursive in digital ink. The interaction with the "tablet" computer is going to have to evolve to the paradigm of the Wii before broad adoption occurs.

Or the iPad, which Apple introduced in 2010 to accolades like "magical" and "revolutionary." Consumers seemed curious enough in the iPad— particularly as something that could out-Kindle the Amazon Kindle.

For broader business adoption of tablets, John thinks it will need significant organizational mindset changes:

Organizations need to redefine what is a "good-enough" deliverable. I wish I could just share what I sketch out on my tablet. But today I have to translate it into language of the Word and PowerPoint world. Ideally, those tools should be used for a limited number of formal documents and external presentations.

Adobe Flash

Dan McWeeney, computer scientist at Adobe Systems, is describing his work in the Flash developer community and his transition there from a Fortune 500 company with a heavy investment in SAP:

Talk about UI [user interface] heaven. 3D rendering, there's a project for that: Papervision3D. Simulated physics, there's a project for that: WOW Physics. Custom animation: there are dozens of projects for that.

This sort of UI innovation is driven from Adobe's core makeup. The company services design and artistic professionals, and those style sensibilities permeate the company. We worked closely with multiple UI designers on every facet of the system, from icon designs, to colors, to the most sensible user gestures.

In contrast, McWeeney describes a SAP procurement project at his previous company that "pulled defeat out of the jaws of victory":

The project was implemented on time and to spec—and yet was a staggering failure at the end of the first quarter. The projected savings are *nowhere to be found—the system was so hard to use, so impenetrable that most everyone gave up before they ordered anything. So much for the projected savings. The $20 million project was essentially a write-off.*

Everyone had gotten so good at modeling complex processes and so focused on getting the process right that they had all forgotten about the start and end of the process, the user.

McWeeney also did a tour of duty at SAP Labs and describes that experience:

At the 2007 SAP TechEd Demo Jam we showed off Majority Desk [yes, a take-off on the interface in the Tom Cruise movie]. It was a thought experiment in 3-D software UIs. The basic premise was that people manage all sorts of tasks using stacks and piles on their physical desks, so why shouldn't the software they organize their work that more accurately resembles such a setup?

The interface consisted of a pair of WiiMotes (the remote controller for the Nintendo console) that were used to move two "hands" on the screen. With these "hands," a user, with haptic feedback, could pick up "widgets" and interact with them, tossing them around the environment or making them small or larger.

My team ... received great feedback from a major aerospace firm about using a 3-D desktop we had created for navigating complex CAD [computer-aided design] drawings. But it did not seem to "fit" anywhere in SAP's portfolio or product strategy.

Part of the issue was tooling and design freedom. In the SAP developer world, there were few ways to specialize an interface that would still be "supported." The out-of-the-box components were good for doing obvious things, like tables of numbers and forms to enter data, but when using them to make a richer experience, they became weak and fragile.

Adobe's openness as a platform, their developer communities, and their design heritage allows the company to be more concerned about how something looks or how easy it is to use rather than complying with the Brazilian tax code or German payroll laws.

McWeeney summarizes the state of interfaces on most business applications:

When I arrived at Adobe, I was part of a seed project focused on business technology users. Not just picking on SAP—our going-in assumption was [that] most companies have stable, well-implemented ERP [enterprise resource planning] systems—which no one uses.

There are plenty of "let's put lipstick on this pig" projects at any given time in many a company.

I wish they would adopt our Flex framework—a UI description language based on our Flash player. The player allows for complete control over the user interface, from animations, to complex user gestures. This expressiveness allows for rapid innovation—anything the Flash player can do, we can build some UI control around that concept.

In other words, even if you are stuck with QWERTY, at least make it easier on your eyes.

Scanners and Bar Codes

"The best user interface is no user interface."

This quote is a corollary from a business process engineering design principle: "Capture information once at source and in a digital format." Too many processes try to pretty up the interface when they should not require human interaction. They could use bar codes and scanners as an alternative.

The grocery industry has never been the same since June 26, 1974, when a cashier at a Marsh Supermarkets store in Troy, Ohio, scanned a 10-pack of Wrigley's gum. GS1, the standards body, says there are more than 10 billion scans a day for the 59 machine-readable black-and-white bars on the Universal Product Code (UPC).[3]

Think how much effort it would take at checkout, no matter how intuitive the user interface, if employees had to QWERTY those bar codes. And how many errors we would have. GS1 estimates bar codes save the grocery industry more than $17 billion a year. And that amount is about to increase as the new DataBar gets rolled out for coupons and loose produce, such as fruits and vegetables. The DataBar can be configured to fit a smaller space or carry additional information, such as "best before" or expiration dates or lot numbers.

Of course, code variations have gone way beyond groceries. Cars have them for their vehicle identification numbers (VINs). The bar code is the lifeblood of the logistics industry. All kinds of assets are tagged with barcodes. Driver's licenses use the two-dimensional PDF417 bar code format.

Along the way there have been innovations in bar code scanners and printers. They come in many varieties: laser, LED, thermal. All this proves a point: Some things are better not done by humans, so let's not just pretty up a user interface for their benefit.

Digitized Information at Source

While scanners at least reduce some of the human error normal in the reading-then-typing process, even better would be to not have to read any paper. The Swedish government has been on a crusade over the last few years to go paperless.

Itella, a leading international logistics company, and Agresso, an ERP software company, provided the solution in a shared company called Offentliga Dokument to enable the electronic invoicing process across the state-run agencies. Thirty percent of their suppliers accounted for 75 percent of the monetary volume, so once they were accounted for, the paper invoices came primarily from smaller or more casual suppliers.

The obstacles were many, says Christopher Lovén, the project manager and managing director of Offentliga Dokument:

> *It was not easy getting 260 state agencies to agree on a common standard—and to get them to agree to a common rollout schedule. We had to get legal approvals to archive electronically and get agreements signed with all the suppliers. This required coordination with 85,000 suppliers and working with different IT maturity standards in the supplier base. The EDI value-added networks [VANs] had to scale to handle over 12 million incoming supplier invoices and 4 million outgoing invoices.*

In the end, the payback will be worth it. It is estimated that the large implementation completed in 2008 will save the agencies 500 million euros in just four years. The postage/print savings for the suppliers are expected to be 1 euro per invoice.

As important, not printing invoices helps the environment. It is estimated that each invoice not printed saves as much energy as boiling an egg or running a 40-watt lamp for a month. Besides, it obviates the need for archived boxes and paper. That reduces real estate costs; only electronic versions are now archived for a decade.

And, of course, electronic invoicing bypasses QWERTY.

Wearable Computers

In 2007, Star Simpson, a student at MIT was arrested at gunpoint because Boston Logan Airport security thought she was wearing a suicide bomb. In fact it was her version of wearable electronic art: a circuit board with wires, LED lights, and a battery.[4]

No such risks at the wearIT@work project, financed by the European Union, which is piloting wearable technology for aircraft maintenance among other applications. A vest allows maintenance engineers on aircraft to have hands-free access (via a head-mounted display) to data from onboard systems, repair manuals, spare parts availability, and communication with other colleagues.[5]

Another application is aimed at firefighters. The wearable computer is rugged enough to cope with the harsh environments they work in and helps them navigate under reduced visibility. It improves communication with colleagues, and helps them better assess danger levels. The application aimed at medical staff makes electronic patient data available on ward rounds and provides easy-to-use devices for staff to enter observations.

Wearable computing is designed to provide workers with critical information with a minimum amount of human-machine interaction so they can stay focused on the work environment.

As you can imagine, trying to focus your hands and eyes on QWERTY is not practical in any of the previous scenarios.

The CNN "Magic Wall"

"John was very skeptical of the wall, but it just became an extension of his brain."

That is how David Bohrman, senior vice president and Washington bureau chief for CNN, describes correspondent John King and the multitouch "Magic Wall" he used to slice and dice results throughout the U.S. state primaries and national elections in 2008.[6]

Skeptical? Although King may have been skeptical, the Magic Wall had most of the United States, and the world, riveted throughout the race. Indeed, it earned King the moniker of "Chairman of the Board."

Bohrman had seen the multitouch screen at a military trade show. Jeff Han of Perceptive Pixel, the screen's maker, explains why such walls were interesting in defense applications where video from drones and pictures from satellites are streaming with overwhelming volume: "So having maps that are very easy to use and that you can lay side by side and show how a terrain changes over time. . . . Rather than a computer expert using it, this is something that a high-ranking commander can use."[7]

Not just military; it sounds like something executives at any company swimming in lots of information could use to visualize their complex data sets.

"SixthSense"

No, we are not referring to M. Night Shyamalan's haunting movie but what Pranav Mistry, an MIT grad student, calls on his Web site "wearable gestural interface that augments the physical world around us with digital information and lets us use natural hand gestures to interact with that information."[8]

Don't let that long description scare you off. In fact it is fairly intuitive. It needs no large wall or long display table. It relies on touch and gestures, but it allows the display to be anywhere—on your hands, your newspaper, wherever.

Mistry tore down two computer mice, took out their trackballs, and used the four tracks to do his initial experimentation. He has replaced them with four finger-worn sensors and a lanyard-mounted camera and projector. The camera can track gestures made by the sensors, and the projector can display anywhere.

With SixthSense, you can take pictures simply by framing an image with your hands, check e-mail by making an "@" symbol with your finger, watch a video displayed on a regular piece of paper, and make phone calls. You don't need a keyboard or a mouse or a display.

And here is the real disruption: Mistry says it costs about $350 to put together. Call it the poor man's Surface Computing (the Microsoft offering described earlier). Or perhaps, we will soon call Surface Computing the rich man's SixthSense.

Voice Recognition

Go to www.gethuman.com and you see which buttons you need to push to bypass the Interactive Voice Response (IVR) choices and get to a live human at the call centers of hundreds of companies. It is a testimony to the fact that most people do not really like talking to machines—and that machines are still not able to catch accents and other variations in our voices consistently.

That is a shame because better voice interaction would revolutionize the human–machine interface. Most people speak more than 120 words per minute but type fewer than 40 words per minute. They can also be doing other things with their hands and eyes while talking or dictating.

The absence of reliable voice recognition systems has led to a cottage industry of transcription services around the world. Medical transcription, by itself, is supposed to generate over $200 million a year for Indian services firms. Caregivers dictate into recording devices, and employees at the other end turn around a written text document.

Nuance Communications of Burlington, Massachusetts, wants to change that with its voice recognition software. It converts text to Microsoft Word and other formats. Nuance is also working with AT&T to turn voice mail messages into text or e-mail messages.

Voice recognition, like artificial intelligence, seems like technology that has been around the corner for years. Previous versions had so many errors that the edits negated the automation advantage. Now Nuance claims accuracy is up to 99 percent.

We are starting to see some of these applications, such as voice dialing on various mobile devices. On the Google/HTC NexusOne phone introduced early in 2010, each field accepts voice input, so you can dictate your e-mail if you want. And as Martin Geddes points out, in Chapter 7, telcos have many other opportunities to innovate their voice-based services.

Digital Smelling and Tasting

Okay, so we have covered how computers help us see, feel, and hear. Surely computers have little to do with smelling and tasting?

Welcome to the e-nose of NASA , which was brought to the International Space Station in 2008. Gases that light and cool the station, such as ammonia, can also be harmful to the astronauts, so NASA wants to monitor for leaks. The e-nose has 32 sensors that can detect a wide variety of chemicals and gases and provide early warnings.

NEC System Technologies of Japan announced, in 2005, a robot capable of "tasting" foods. The food is exposed to infrared light of varying wavelengths, which bounce back to the robot, which analyzes the spectrum of the bounced-back infrared light and can interpret which molecules are inside the food.

The Brain–Machine Interface

In the movie *Avatar*, the paralyzed Marine, Jack Scully, is able to telepathically manipulate his humanoid clone on the planet Pandora. The film is set in the next century and draws on Hollywood's vivid imagination. But here, today, there is already fascinating work in what is called the Brain-Machine Interface (BMI).

Honda Research Institute, Advanced Telecommunications Research Institute International (ATR), and Shimadzu Corporation have collaboratively developed BMI technology that uses electroencephalography (EEG) (measurement of electrical activity in the brain) and near-infrared spectroscopy (NIRS) to enable control of a robot by human thought. It does not require any physical movement such as pressing buttons.

Toyota and the Japanese research foundation RIKEN have similarly demonstrated a wheelchair steered by mind control.

Obviously, these technologies have exciting implications in health care for disabled people. They may also allow more of us to perform Jedi mind tricks with a wave of our hands!

Unicode and Exotic Scripts

Go to the Google home page and navigate via the "Other" menu option to the Translate page. Now play around with different languages. Google currently supports more than 50 languages, from Afrikaans to Yiddish.

Arabic reads from right to left. Russia, Yugoslavia, Ukraine, and several other countries use the Cyrillic script, which has 21 consonants and 10 vowels. Hindi, spoken in India, is written in the Devanagari script; in it, if a vowel follows a consonant, the two characters are merged into one.

Anne Katherine Petterøe is a keen linguist and has experienced many of these scripts firsthand in her travels around the world. The Norwegian consultant could write a book on "lost in translation":

When I studied Russian I brought along a Russian keyboard, but neglected to check it had both Cyrillic and Latin letters. Couldn't find anything the first few days.

I have dealt with projects in China, where you have to adjust to double-byte characters. Made Cyrillic look easy!

When I lived in India I taught myself Hindi and a bit of Urdu. Hindi was sort of easy to learn writing because it is left-right, but Urdu, which like Arabic is written right-left, turned out to be a bigger struggle. I am right-handed and it felt like writing with the left hand to begin with.

Her last name has caused her endless questioning at airline check-in:

My last name is spelled with a Norwegian letter "ø," which only exists (in that form) in Norway and Denmark. Some airlines will transcribe "ø" as "o," while others write "oe." You can imagine how much grief I get since the name on the ticket and the passport isn't identical.

We have not been nice to QWERTY through this chapter. Now let's give it some credit. The keyboard and its cousins around the world are allowing for electronic scripting of all kinds of modern and ancient languages.

The scripting is facilitated by a standard called Unicode. When it was first adopted in 1991, it supported 7,161 characters. In version 5.2, which came out in 2009, it supported 107,361 characters. That's amazing progress in the last two decades. Unicode covers 90 scripts; the latest release supports 1,071 Egyptian hieroglyphs.[9]

Now it's time to acknowledge that a keyboard has an advantage over a voice-based interface when you are trying to use the two "soundless" characters in Cyrillic. Similarly, it would not be smart to have a haptic device vibrate and scare the living daylights when you are looking for the ark somewhere in the dark of an Egyptian tomb. There, we found another lease on life for QWERTY!

Recap

The last several years have seen the introduction of a mind-boggling array of user interfaces on mobile devices, games, tabletops, and walls. Yet the majority of the business world toils with keyboard-driven and unexciting interfaces.

Many of those interfaces may be retired as scanners replace user input. Many may be moved to alternative voice, haptic, and other types of interfaces. Finally, even those that stay with the keyboard/mouse form/factor can have far more pleasing Flash and other interfaces. QWERTY may continue to live on, but polymath enterprises will do their best to trivialize its role as they design interfaces for various technology applications.

CHAPTER 12

Sustainability: Delivering to Both the Green and Gold Agendas

They say never discuss religion or politics in polite company. We should add sustainability to that list. The much-anticipated Copenhagen conference on climate change in 2009 was to many a disappointment leading them to call it "Nopenhagen." The topic of sustainability has torn apart the U.S. Chamber of Commerce; several Chamber members have resigned over its position questioning whether global warming is man-made. Even Osama Bin Laden, in one of the periodic messages attributed to him, has chided the West for not worrying about climate change!

Vinod Khosla, founder of Khosla Ventures, which has been an aggressive investor in cleantech, argues we need even more massive disruption: "Even with the successful solar and wind companies, the scale will not be a large enough dent in power generation carbon emissions to be material." He goes on to say, "We're in a crisis, and there is an opportunity to reinvent our energy infrastructure; it would be a folly to waste it."[1]

While the world continues to argue, sustainability is leading to a massive amount of investment and innovation. In the Kleiner Perkins profile in Chapter 13, we will see the breadth of investments it has made in cleantech. The choices it made were tricky—it passed on 5,000 investment opportunities in deciding on its cleantech portfolio. The bounty Kleiner explored is a sign there is plenty of innovation occurring in the sustainability sector.

In this chapter, we look at how nations and cities are approaching sustainability and cleantech; how supply chains and lifestyles are being affected; how sustainability is driving a new type of accounting and other scorekeeping; and how sustainability is morphing education and industry events.

Sustainability and Innovation in Public Policy

Here we look at how the nations of China and Germany, the City of San Francisco, and the new planned city of Masdar in the United Arab Emirates are approaching the sustainability opportunity.

China and Cleantech

In November 2009, China announced a $10 billion aid package for Africa. That package cemented a relationship China has aggressively fostered with the continent for a few years now. In the process, it has locked up supplies of oil and other strategic materials.

Buried in the announcement was a statement that China was also committed to "100 clean energy projects" in Africa.

That is in sharp contrast to China's images of smog around its showpiece 2008 Olympics. China has also been the target of accusations around contaminated milk and lead-tinged products. As *Forbes* magazine pointed out: "In addition to its cheap labor costs, China has another comparative advantage as the world's factory: Companies often pay almost nothing to pollute China's air, water and soil and to poison its people."[2]

At the Copenhagen summit in December 2009, ABC News reported that "China, the world's top polluter, doggedly resisted pressure for outside scrutiny of its emissions."[3]

But it is the other China that John Podesta, President and CEO of the Center for American Progress Action Fund (and former Chief of Staff for President Bill Clinton), asked Congress not to underestimate. In Senate testimony on October 29, 2009, after a visit to China with a U.S. trade delegation, Podesta stated:

> *China fully grasps the strategic economic opportunity that the clean-energy sector represents. As Li Keqiang, first vice premier of China and Premier Wen Jiabao's deputy, has publicly said on various occasions, the development of new energy sources represents an opportunity to stimulate consumption, increase investments, achieve stable export opportunities, and adjust China's energy structure, all while enhancing its international economic competitiveness.*
>
> *According to a recent report, the clean-tech market in China alone has a potential to develop into a $500 billion to $1 trillion per year market by 2013.*[4]

China is investing $300 billion in a bullet train system that will connect most of the country and cut travel time between its two major cities, Beijing and Shanghai, down to five hours, at speeds of up to 220 miles an hour.

And, of course, it would be much cleaner than comparable traffic on highways or by air.

Gansu Province in northwest China is planning a wind farm by 2020 that will have energy capacity similar to the gigantic Three Gorges Dam—in itself an engineering marvel. By then, the province will have an installed capacity wind power base capacity of 20 gigawatts, more than 10 times the current capacity. China projects that by 2020, the rest of the country will be accessing another 100 gigawatts from wind power.

Podesta continues:

> *China's emerging leadership in electric vehicles is based on its innovation in energy storage technology. The world's first mass-produced, plug-in hybrid is the F3DM, launched by China's BYD Auto last December. Just six years ago BYD Auto was only in the business of making batteries for mobile phones. The F3DM sells in China for approximately $22,000, and the founder of BYD, Wang Chuanfu, is now China's richest person.*

And, of course, all these investments are positioning China to become a major exporter to the world: "Where some five years ago there were virtually no domestic manufacturers of wind components, now there are as many as 70 to 100 companies, with Sinovel now the seventh-largest in the world" and "[China] accounts for nearly 40 percent of the global production of solar photovoltaic panels."

Other Chinese manufacturers are also starting to emphasize energy efficiency. Huawei, the telecommunications equipment manufacturer, cites the example of the southern Pakistan village of Theri Mirwah. The cost of maintaining traditional wireless base stations in the region using diesel was prohibitively high. Leveraging the area's abundant sunlight, Huawei tailored a solution using solar base stations in harsh conditions where daytime temperatures can exceed 130 degrees.

Let's now look at Germany.

Germany and Cleantech

New Braunfels, Texas, with its beer gardens and sausage dinners, has been described as "old Germany in the middle of Texas Hill Country." But it has something the "New Germany" would die for: plenty of sunshine. BBC Weather charts show that Houston, 175 miles due east of New Braunfels, gets on average two and a half hours more sunlight each day than does Munich in Germany—about 50 percent more. And Munich is in southern Germany; as you go north toward Hamburg, the sun shines even less. Yet Germany has the largest installed capacity of solar photovoltaic panels in the world—which, of course, would yield even more energy if the country could reposition itself a few degrees south.

In 2007 and 2009, "Team Germany" won the top place in the Solar Decathlon. This bi-annual event is hosted by the U.S. Department of Energy and described further below. A major reason for German team's victory was that the team scored the maximum number of points in the "Net Metering" phase of the competition. Each house in the decathlon was connected to a power grid and equipped with a meter that measured both its consumption and production of energy. Team Germany's meter showed a negative number, which means it had generated surplus energy.

Germany has a "feed law" that permits homeowners and farmers to connect their solar power systems to the grid and sell excess energy. The price they get for renewable energy (solar or wind) is considerably above market rates. With solar panel costs declining, for many families, an investment in panels has been a much better vehicle than the stock market, especially as they realize that above-market price compensation will not last forever.

If its solar industry is impressive, Germany's wind energy sector is even more so. Germany has more than a third of the world's installed capacity, and no other country has more wind turbines. Wind provides 5 percent of Germany's total electricity consumption and ranks even higher than hydro-electric power, a traditional source of renewable energy.

Germany also has one of the most aggressive greenhouse gas (like carbon dioxide, methane, etc.) emissions reduction targets under the 1997 Kyoto Protocol it signed with several other countries. In 2008, its greenhouse gas emissions were recorded at the lowest levels since 1990.

Given Germany's leadership in so many sustainable initiatives, it is not surprising that its own companies do well on various "most sustainable" lists. But the real excitement lies in Germany's "Solar Valley" with companies like Q-Cells, now one of the largest manufacturers of solar cells in the world, and Enercon, which has installed 15,000 wind turbines around the world.

These companies and several other start-ups have revitalized portions of what was East Germany, which had languished for years after the reunification. The solar and wind sectors employ about 125,000 people, according to the German Federal Ministry of Economics and Technology, so sustainable energy clearly is attractive from an economic perspective.[5]

Now let's look at the City of San Francisco and its sustainability efforts.

City of San Francisco

Sometimes when all the action is swirling around you, you don't feel the need to step up. The City of San Francisco could just wait for its neighbors in Silicon Valley to innovate, but instead it is blazing a trail.

Travel and Leisure magazine looked at sustainability in the city from the tourist point of view and cataloged, among other things:[6]

- No plastic shopping bags and no plastic water bottles are allowed at civic events.
- San Francisco boasts the nation's first LEED-certified hotel. (The Leadership in Energy and Environmental Design rating system was designed by the U.S. Green Building Council, a voluntary body that sets "green" standards for office and other buildings.)
- A farmers' market is open twice a week at the Ferry Building.
- There is a new Federal Building that is impressive both in architecture and in green features.
- The recycling dump proudly offers tours and art exhibitions.

Fortune ran a picture gallery that looked at other aspects of San Francisco's green activities from a citizen's point of view:[7]

- Low-carbon-emission buses stop at solar-powered bus stops, which also double as Wi-Fi hotspots.
- There is a planned program in collaboration with MIT Technology Labs for electric vehicles to get citizens from homes to bus stops and train stations.
- A pilot hybrid car rental program has begun.
- An iPhone app gives users information on the nearest recycling and trash disposal facilities.

In the meantime, Mayor Gavin Newsom has been leading San Francisco with innovative composting, toxic waste management, a green business program, and plans to plant 25,000 new trees over the next few years. The city has a map of the solar potential of every building to help citizens adopt that renewable energy. It is home to Pacific Gas & Electric, which, as mentioned earlier, is considered one of the most innovative electric utilities in the world. Even more ambitious, the mayor has talked about tidal power and turning Treasure Island, a now-defunct naval base, into the "Super-Green" city of the future.

Finally, let's look at Masdar.

Planned City of Masdar

It seems odd given its location in oil-rich the United Arab Emirates (UAE), but Masdar is a 2.5-square-mile planned city with very lofty green goals. It will be carbon neutral and will recycle all its waste. No gas-powered vehicles will be allowed. Small, driverless electric vehicles will provide local transit. Tall buildings will shade most of the city to reduce the need for air-conditioning. Wind turbines, solar arrays, and plenty of trees will keep this city of the future self-sustaining.

Norman Foster of the architecture firm Foster and Partners explains the plans on its Web site: "The environmental ambitions of the Masdar Initiative—zero carbon and waste free—are a world first. They have provided us with a challenging design brief that promises to question conventional urban wisdom at a fundamental level. Masdar promises to set new benchmarks for the sustainable city of the future."[8]

Sustainability and Energy Frugality

In this section we look at emerging efficiencies in the car and at home:

- Some drivers squeeze every last drop of efficiency from their tank of gas. *USA Today* describes them as

    a loose-knit legion of commuters who've made racking up seemingly unattainable mpg (often 100 mpg) an art. . . . Hypermilers practice such unorthodox techniques as coasting for blocks with their car's engine turned off, driving far below speed limits on the freeway ... pumping up tire pressure.[9]

- Then there are those who vie to be on reality TV shows, such as the Discovery Channel's *World's Greenest Homes.* Each episode highlights two stand-out residences that show off these homes' style and decor, architectural boldness, and other green features.
- The *Wall Street Journal* asked four architects: What will the energy-efficient house of the future look like? The answer: "It could have gardens on its walls or a pond stocked with fish for dinner. It might mimic a tree, turning sunlight into energy and carbon dioxide into oxygen. Or perhaps it will be more like a lizard, changing its color to suit the weather and healing itself when it gets damaged."[10]
- A bit more down to earth, every couple of years, the U.S. Department of Energy hosts a decathlon where it invites teams from selected universities to design, build, and operate the most attractive and energy-efficient solar-powered house. Twenty teams took over on the National Mall in Washington, D.C., for five days in October 2009 and were judged on architecture, market viability, engineering, lighting design, communications, comfort zone, hot water, appliances, home entertainment, and net metering. The German team won in 2007 and 2009, as we described earlier.[11]
- Chapter 3 showcased General Electric's Net Zero Home Project, which will bring together by 2015 a variety of technologies, such as small wind

turbines, home energy manager, next-gen battery cells, and more. GE believes a Net Zero energy home will cost about 10 percent more than the conventional kind but will help homeowners save money in the long run as well as make the electricity grid more efficient.

Sustainability and Innovation in Supply Chains

"Meet the farmer who grew your wheat today," says the Stone-Buhr Web site. The company sells sustainable flour products. If you enter the lot number on one of its packages, it links you back to the farmer's profile and video clip.

Traceability

There is growing consumer interest in "traceability," especially as every year seems to bring more news of contaminated milk, E. coli, mad cow disease, and bioterrorism. Bad peanut butter was responsible for the recall of close to 4,000 consumer products. Indeed, you cannot discuss sustainability today without showcasing traceability through your supply chain.

Although automobiles, aeronautics, electronics, and pharmaceuticals have long had traceability at various levels—vehicle identification numbers and lot numbers, for example—it has been tougher to provide such transparency in the food supply chain. It is changing gradually with industry initiative and legal mandates.

Here are some food supply chain traceability solutions:

- Given the number of points between the farm and the store, a company called TraceGains, in Longmont, Colorado, has developed recall traceback and track-forward technologies. A recall alert can be initiated within minutes, reducing potential exposure to only a segment of the supply chain—and reducing damage to brands. Other TraceGains functionality helps monitor temperature for perishable items through the supply chain and signals likely contamination risks.
- YottaMark, a Redwood City, California, company provides unit-level tracing, marketing, and mass-serialization solutions for a variety of markets, including fresh foods, pharmaceuticals, consumer goods, and even inks and toner.
- TraceTracker, a Norwegian software company, is working with Intel to build a halal meat traceability solution in Malaysia—something that should have applicability to the Muslim population around the world.

Walmart's Supplier Scorecard

Walmart, the giant retailer, announced the "mother of all traceability efforts" in July 2009. It asked its suppliers 15 questions in four major categories:[12]

1. Energy and Climate: Reducing Energy Costs and Greenhouse Gas Emissions
   - Have you measured your corporate greenhouse gas emissions?
   - Have you opted to report your greenhouse gas emissions to the Carbon Disclosure Project (CDP)?
   - What is your total annual greenhouse gas emissions reported in the most recent year measured?
   - Have you set publicly available greenhouse gas reduction targets? If yes, what are those targets?
2. Material Efficiency: Reducing Waste and Enhancing Quality
   - If measured, please report the total amount of solid waste generated from the facilities that produce your product(s) for Walmart for the most recent year measured.
   - Have you set publicly available solid waste reduction targets? If yes, what are those targets?
   - If measured, please report total water use from facilities that produce your product(s) for Walmart for the most recent year measured.
   - Have you set publicly available water use reduction targets? If yes, what are those targets?
3. Natural Resources: Producing High-Quality, Responsibly Sourced Raw Materials
   - Have you established publicly available sustainability purchasing guidelines for your direct
   - Suppliers that address issues such as environmental compliance, employment practices and product/ingredient safety?
   - Have you obtained third-party certifications for any of the products that you sell to Walmart?
4. People and Community: Ensuring Responsible and Ethical Production
   - Do you know the location of 100 percent of the facilities that produce your product(s)?
   - Before beginning a business relationship with a manufacturing facility, do you evaluate the quality of, and capacity for, production?
   - Do you have a process for managing social compliance at the manufacturing level?
   - Do you work with your supply base to resolve issues found during social compliance evaluations and also document specific corrections and improvements?
   - Do you invest in community development activities in the markets you source from and/or operate within?

Smaller companies, such as Patagonia, were already rating supplier products for sustainability in their Footprint Chronicles Web site. That allows consumers to trace the supply chain path each product has taken. What is staggering is it is being attempted at Walmart's scale—the company has revenues of $400 billion and 100,000 suppliers around the globe.

The questions are fairly basic—certainly they are not product specific—so don't expect to see a green score on boxes of cereal at Walmart any time soon (the company projects that that will happen by 2013), but it is the start of a large effort to make sustainability a major consideration when Walmart evaluates suppliers and products.

Three statements in the frequently asked questions (FAQ) section that Walmart shares with suppliers show the company's attitude and approach:

You will not be penalized for not participating. However, we want to stress our commitment to delivering great products that help our customers save money so they can live better. Sustainability is an important factor we will use to determine which products fit this profile, and answering these questions will help us evaluate suppliers' progress fairly.

Responses to this questionnaire will be accepted in good faith, relying on the integrity of the supplier. Violation of that good faith will be considered very serious by Walmart.

In order to keep this process from becoming onerous for our suppliers, the first phase of information gathering is focused largely on our suppliers' measurement and goal setting for key factors around sustainability. Eventually, we intend to ask other questions about suppliers and products.[13]

Think of all of Walmart's suppliers and the company's expectations of those suppliers, and you can see how a relatively low-tech survey form will have a ripple effect on technology needed around such areas as supply chain visibility, product and packaging design, and carbon accounting.

Sustainability and Innovation in Keeping Score

Sustainability is driving a new language when it comes to benchmarks and metrics:

- Professors at the Gund Institute for Ecological Economics at the University of Vermont suggest that our current economic frameworks and measurements, such as gross domestic product (GDP), are sending us the wrong signals. In a paper, Professor Robert Costanza of the institute says that two major components are missing in today's economic data: Natural Capital, which ". . . includes the world's ecosystems and all the services they provide," and Social Capital, which "includes all the formal and informal networks among people: family, friends, and neighbors, as well as social institutions."[14] If we were to compare GDP instead to an index he calls Genuine Progress Index (GPI) we would see GDP has steadily increased since 1950, with the occasional recession, but GPI peaked in about 1975 and has been gradually declining ever since. The results vary widely, however. The institute calculated that the GPI of every person in the State of Vermont had increased over the entire 1950 to 2000 period and is now more than double the national average.

We recently estimated the GPI of the State of Vermont and of Burlington, the state's largest city, and found that this was due to Vermont's attention to protecting and enhancing natural, human, and social capital in balance with gains in built capital—accomplished through the application of strong, local democratic principles and processes still actively at work in Vermont.

- Increasingly, a goal for a number of companies is for their buildings to reach the new LEED Platinum status. To do so, you have to get at least 80 out of a score of 100 based on factors such as public transportation access, innovative wastewater technologies, refrigerant management, use of salvaged or refurbished materials, and access to natural lighting.[15]
- "In the time it takes to do a Google search, your own personal computer will likely use more energy than we will use to answer your query." claims Google.[16] Not just Google—data centers at Amazon, Yahoo!, eBay, and the ones Mike Manos describes at Microsoft in Chapter 18 are rewriting benchmarks for data center efficiency. That quest is also driving data center proximity to cheaper fuel sources. Even with its seismic risks, Iceland touts cooler weather and abundant geothermal power to attract data centers. Yahoo! chose to locate one of its data centers in Quincy, Washington, to take advantage of nearby hydroelectric power. It is leading to a radical rethink of data center energy needs and a focus on acronyms like CFD and PUE. CFD refers to computational fluid dynamics using specialized software to look at airflow and temperature patterns in data centers. As servers and other equipment in data centers get denser and generate more heat by the day, their need for cooling has grown tremendously. PUE stands for power usage effectiveness—the ratio of power entering a data center divided by the power used to run the computer infrastructure within

it. The Yahoo! center at Quincy is at 1.21, which is a very efficient benchmark. In many data centers, the PUE is as high as 2 because much of the energy goes toward cooling and lighting, not toward processing. Utilities are starting to do their part. Duke Energy, for example, gives rebates to companies that can demonstrate investment in energy-efficient servers.

- Some software, such as Hara in Kleiner's portfolio discussed in Chapter 13, helps companies account for their energy, water, waste, carbon, and other resource use. SAP has developed a "sustainability map" (see Figure 12.1) to let its customers start to plan for a world with a different set of operational metrics.

- Trucost has not been waiting for companies to implement Hara or SAP. Since 2000, the environmental benchmarking firm has been populating a data model that accounts for more than 450 industries and tracks more than 700 environmental impacts from carbon and other greenhouse gases to water, waste, metals, and chemicals.[17] It uses reported data and its own algorithms to make estimates. *Newsweek* used Trucost data to derive its green rankings of the largest companies in the United States.[18]

- Hara and Trucost are providing better estimates of an enterprise's environmental impact costs. A growing body of knowledge now focuses on estimating the "cost of nature." A recent United Nations–backed the Economics of Ecosystems and Biodiversity (TEEB) study estimated loss of natural capital due to deforestation and degradation at between $2 trillion and $4.5 trillion every year.[19] A follow-up TEEB study will focus on ways to put an economic value on biodiversity and ecosystem services.

SUSTAINABILITY PERFORMANCE MANAGEMENT	Assured Reporting	Benchmarks & Analytics	Strategy & Risk	Financial Performance		
ENERGY & CARBON	Energy-Efficient Assets	Energy Management	Carbon Management	Smart Grids		
PRODUCT SAFETY & STEWARDSHIP	Product Compliance	Material & Product Safety	Recycling & Reuse	Recall Management	Product Footprint	Sustainable Design
SUSTAINABLE SUPPLY CHAIN	Procurement	Traceability	Commodity Trade & Risk Management	Resource Optimization	Supply Chain Optimization	
ENVIRONMENT, HEALTH & SAFETY	Environment Compliance	Occupational Health	Industrial Hygiene & Safety	Emergency Management		
SUSTAINABLE WORKFORCE	Labor Compliance & Rights	Diversity		Talent Management		
IT INFRASTRUCTURE	Availability, Security, Accessibility & Privacy			Green IT		

FIGURE 12.1 SAP's Sustainability Map
Source: SAP, http://sapsustainabilityreport.com/solutions/.

■ Finally, there is old-fashioned questioning about the cost and payback from these "green" investments. If you look at the German success story described earlier, there are plenty of subsidies in the form of above-market pricing for surplus energy from residential solar adoption. If you look at Germany's Solar Valley, plenty of incentives went into creating the area in what was previously East Germany. If you look at China, the state is investing in wind farms and bullet trains on a massive scale. Will Walmart's "value" shoppers accept higher prices if the company's supplier sustainability efforts increase costs? Are SAP's customers ready to pay another round of investments after their massive ERP investments over the last two decades? The debate and scrutiny is healthy. It is said that real sustainability occurs where environmental, societal, and economic interests converge. Unless we go through such analysis at every level—consumer, enterprise, and nation—we will be "guilted" and "greenwashed" into a number of expensive cleantech decisions.

Sustainability and Innovation in Education

His transformation is impressive.

In 2007, M. R. Rangaswami was "Mr. Rolodex" when it came to the enterprise software industry. After a career at major software companies, Rangaswami turned investor and event organizer. His Sand Hill Group conferences reflected his wide range of connections in the venture capital, vendor executive, and CIO communities. Then he sold the event business and began a new life in cleantech. "I wanted to do something new and also be a good role model for my young kids. Many of my smart friends were getting into clean and green. I decided to pursue this space and utilize my skill set as a conference producer and organizer. This lets me accomplish both my goals."

Rangaswami now runs the Corporate Eco Forum, a peer networking and benchmarking group for sustainability-focused executives at several large companies. Although he is discreet about what that closed group discusses, he coauthored an article in the *Harvard Business Review* that describes what Unilever and Staples are doing in their sustainability efforts.[20]

While it is impressive to see how Rangaswami has changed careers, the way his events have morphed in the last three years is even more remarkable. It's not just that the agenda now reflects sustainability rather than software topics. As Christine Virsunen, who has been Rangaswami's event organizer for years now, points out:

■ *Energy and water conservation track records are as important now as location in our picking the event hotel.*

- *We are printing as little as possible. Agendas and presentations are on Web sites and little USB sticks.*
- *We recycle signs, lanyards for badges, everything.*
- *We are using much more LED lighting on stage.*
- *We look for biodiesel buses to shuttle our attendees around.*
- *The limo companies we recommend to and from the airport have largely hybrid fleets.*
- *No more bottled water. Attendee hydration has gone retro.*

The main dinner during the last Eco Forum gathering reflected the sustainability theme. It was held at the California Academy of Sciences in Golden Gate Park in San Francisco. In Virsunen's words, the building "is a 400,000-square-foot structure that houses an aquarium, a planetarium, a natural history museum, and a four-story rainforest all under one roof—which adds to its extensive science library with over 26 million specimens and artifacts." Virsunen next elaborates on the catering:

My challenge as a planner was to ensure local ingredients for the menu—little of which had hopefully seen the inside of a fridge. So to the north, we used Cowgirl Creamery, which began in a barn in the grassy hills of the northern Marin County coast. Despite its small production, Cowgirl has quickly assumed a reputation for superb artisan cheeses made from neighboring Straus Family Creamery's organic milk. Farther north at Sonoma County Poultry, "Liberty Ducks" are raised by a fourth-generation duck farmer. [The ducks are] reared in an open environment without antibiotics or hormones and regarded by today's chefs as more flavorful and meaty than other ducks. To the northeast, the Beaulieu Gardens grows organic zucchini and wax beans in the verdant Napa Valley. Continuing northeast, Riverdog Farms is a family-owned, California Certified Organic Farm in the Capay Valley. The area's intense summer heat and winter frost enables the farm to grow a variety of vegetables, including the dinner's Little Gem lettuce and cauliflower. To the south, Driscoll's has been growing strawberries in the Pajaro Valley for more than 100 years. These fresh, organic berries have not been irradiated or genetically modified. Coke Farm, grower of the organic beets we served, is a proud year-round employer in the San Benito County community, where the farm's vegetables and fruits thrive in the area's four distinct microclimates.

San Francisco is blessed with all this abundance. But as I talk to my peer event planners everywhere, they are all looking for local and organic ingredients.

Now let's look at how sustainability is helping train the next generation of workers:

- The students of MIT professor Timothy Gutowski conducted detailed interviews and estimated the energy usage of 18 lifestyles, including that of a vegetarian college student, a five-year-old and the "ultrarich": Oprah Winfrey and Bill Gates. The team derived a system for making such comparisons that they call ELSA—environmental lifestyle analysis.[21]
- FastCompany identified six academic programs, each with its own environmental twist:[22]
  1. The University of Pennsylvania's dual-degree program allows students to earn an MBA and a master's in environmental studies in about three years.
  2. The College of the Atlantic has only one major: human ecology.
  3. Rocky Mountain College of Art + Design offers a degree in green interior design.
  4. The London College of Fashion has a specialization in sustainable fashion.
  5. The University of New Hampshire has an offering in "ecogastronomy."
  6. East Carolina University has an offering in sustainable tourism.

Recap

In spite of the hand wringing about the failure at Copenhagen and the climate change doomsday scenarios, there is plenty of innovation around sustainability. Some of it is at the personal level: in our cars and at home. Some is at the office building and data center level. Beyond energy frugality, though, sustainability is also redefining our expectations of traceability of the food we eat, and of our education.

What is remarkable in all of this is how much politics and rancor differentiate cleantech. The exciting technologies and innovations that a polymath like Kleiner Perkins (profiled in the next chapter) is investing in, are often lost in the other noise about sustainability.

CHAPTER 13

Polymath Profile #5:
Kleiner Perkins Cleantech

"The radar showed a perfect storm developing. But it took a persuasive hand-waver to make us even notice the weather map," says Ray Lane.

Lane is describing the "aha" moment his venture capital firm, Kleiner Perkins, faced in 2003. "Some trends are murky and meandering. This one showed a triangulation of weather systems: economics—the hope of cheaper energy; environment—the promise of a cleaner future for our children; strategic interest—less hostile, more reliable sources of energy."

Adds Bill Joy, Lane's partner at Kleiner Perkins: "If you cannot solve the problem, make the problem bigger. If you draw a bigger circle, you start to see several systems you can work on." It was as if the firm had not bitten off enough already merely by thinking of entering the emerging "clean" technology sector.

Actually, in 2003, the firm had a couple of investments in cleantech: Bloom Energy, which is focused on fuel cells, and the Segway, the personal transporter you see on city tours and civil services. These companies were clean, but not mainstream for the storied firm with whopper successes in Amazon and Google, among others. The Kleiner comfort zone, with exceptions such as Genentech in biotech, was in information technology.

The hand-waver Lane refers to above is Dr. K. R. Sridhar, the founder of Bloom Energy. It took persistence on Sridhar's part, but once he got Kleiner's attention, the company assembled a dream team focused on cleantech.

The team included John Doerr, the legendary investor who is as comfortable in world capitals as he is on Sand Hill Road; Joy, the "engineer's engineer" who was cofounder of Sun Microsystems and has influenced countless technologies since; and Lane, who led Oracle through its remarkable growth in the 1990s. In the early years, the team also included Vinod Khosla, who has since started his own fund but coinvests with Kleiner in a number of deals.

There was also a supporting role for Al Gore, the former U.S. Vice President and star of the Oscar-winning documentary on the fragile state of the world's ecology, *An Inconvenient Truth*. And it included Sridhar's own not-too-shabby qualifications. Prior to this entrepreneurial stint, he had done research at the University of Arizona as part of a NASA program creating a technology that could sustain life on Mars.

Talk about a polymath team.

The Cleantech Market Opportunity

Figure 13.1 is taken from the Annual Energy Review done by the Energy Information Administration, the statistics wing of the U.S. Department of Energy.[1]

It gives a nice bird's-eye view of the major energy supply and demand drivers in the United States. (With some exceptions, the patterns also apply to other developed countries. France, for example, is a more aggressive user of nuclear energy, which has been almost impossible to sell in the United States since the incident at Three Mile Island.)

It is a bit of a misnomer to call electric power a demand sector—it is more of a pass-through since the electricity is consumed by residences and businesses. But doing so highlights how dependent utilities are on coal and also how much transportation is dependent on oil. Lane explains: "The negatives around coal are about emissions. Coal is the most abundant fossil

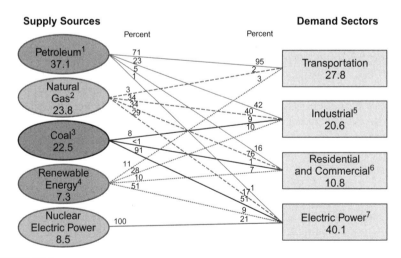

FIGURE 13.1 Primary Energy Consumption by Source and Sector in 2008
Source: Energy Information Administration.

fuel around the world, but it is also the dirtiest with almost twice the greenhouse gas emissions (for the same yield) as natural gas. With countries imposing carbon caps, there is a huge incentive to make coal cleaner. The negatives around oil are because so much of it is in volatile parts of the world."

In a presentation Joy made at his alma mater, the University of Michigan, he presented the factors in what is called the Kaya calculator: Carbon dioxide emission = Population × Gross domestic product per person × Energy intensity × Carbon efficiency.[2] The first two components keep going up as world population and affluence levels continue to grow. The third and fourth components have to improve dramatically if we are to offset some of the dependence on fossil fuels and related emissions of the last few decades. Joy elaborates: "Through compounding, if we could create energy with half the impact, deliver with 20% less loss, use it three times as efficiently, recycle 20% of that, we can get a 10 times improvement. In fact, we need to aim higher in each of the create, deliver, use, and recycle phases to offset any shortfalls we may have in the others."

Those "stretch goals" helped the Kleiner team spell out some grand challenges across the energy landscape. Some of the areas of focus were:

- *Electric generation.* Solar photovoltaic, energy storage, and wind, particularly on a small scale
- *Electric efficiency.* More efficient lighting, heating/ cooling, pumping, and the like
- *Transportation fuels.* Electric, cellulosic (derived from cell walls of plants) fuels
- *Transportation efficiency.* Lightweight vehicles, lower electric battery costs
- *Building efficiency.* Better insulation, heating/cooling
- *Resource efficiency.* Around production of cement, steel, and other infrastructure components

In each area, the team evaluated current art, any underexploited areas (e.g., relatively cheap oil may have encouraged certain types of behavior), the practical best, and the theoretical scientific limits.

Since 2003, Kleiner has evaluated more than 5,000 investment opportunities and has invested more than $1 billion in cleantech companies.

Joy says, only half jokingly, "I have an associate who knows how to game Google. He knows the right keywords to enter, and we find the world's expert on the topic somewhere on a campus in Lithuania. We had to kiss a number of frogs as part of the discovery process."

The discovery process has made Lane a walking encyclopedia on fuels. He can rattle off ethanol yield from sugarcane versus that from corn and other biofuels. He can compare fuel technology innovations in Germany, Brazil, and Israel. It's a far cry from the cash flow metrics and global operations he managed at Oracle. Lane elaborates: "Cleantech investments are far more influenced by global economic and political vagaries than information technology ever was. Of course, it means Kleiner's traditional ability to help entrepreneurs morph business models and aggressively manage cash flow is even more critical."

Sridhar explains further: "In information technology (IT), VCs [venture capitalists] thought in terms of six to eight quarters to a liquidity event; now it is six to eight *years*. The funding needs to factor what used to often come from mezzanine-level investors in IT. Also, IT pilot projects were mostly funded at customer sites. In cleantech, they are calling for a new variety of project financing." Bloom Energy's own journey fits that pattern, as we describe in detail below.

Some of Kleiner's cleantech investments include:

- Luca Technologies (described in detail in the next section), which helps turn coal into much cleaner methane
- GloriOil, which uses "microbial-enhanced oil recovery" to coax more yield out of mature oil fields
- GreatPoint Energy, which uses a catalytic process, known as hydro-methanation, by which coal, petroleum coke, and biomass are converted directly to pipeline-quality natural gas

But here come the complications. Natural gas used to be twice as pricey as coal. The price gap, however, is shrinking as huge new gas reserves are being located in the United States and elsewhere. The value Luca, GreatPoint, and GloriOil deliver has to be measured against changing gas prices.

Cheaper gas or more oil, of course, will not help utilities as governments around the world emulate California's Renewables Portfolio Standard (RPS) which calls for utilities to get 20 percent of their energy from renewable sources in 2010. "Renewable" energy is generally defined as coming from solar, wind-driven, tidal, and geothermal sources. California has since put out a secondary, longer-term goal of 33 percent by 2020.

That likely demand from utilities for renewables provided Kleiner its justification for investing in Ausra and in Miasole. Ausra's Compact Linear Fresnel Reflector (CLFR) concentrates sunlight to boil tanks of water. The resulting high-pressure steam is then used for power generation.

Miasole makes thin solar film out of copper, indium, gallium, and selenium. Film technology promises to be cheaper than traditional solar technology because it uses little or no silicon, the most expensive component in today's solar cells.

These investments are focused on making the fodder for power utilities cleaner and renewable. Another Kleiner company, Silver Spring Networks (also described in detail later in the chapter), focuses on the downstream, customer-facing operations of a utility. It is one of the more successful Kleiner cleantech companies to date, with utilities in Florida, California, and several other states deploying its networking technology as part of their smart grids.

Kleiner's investments in Fisker Automotive and V-Vehicle Company (where Lane became interim CEO in April 2010) are aimed squarely at the transportation demand sector, the biggest consumer of oil, as shown in Figure 13.1.

Fisker's first model, the Karma, burns no fuel for the first 50 miles. For daily commutes, which are generally under 50 miles round trip, all you need to do is plug the vehicle in at night to charge from the electric grid. For longer trips, the gasoline engine turns a generator which charges its lithium-ion battery. Fisker also plans to offer a solar roof that will help charge the car while it is parked and provide cooling for the interior cabin. At $89,000 per vehicle, the Karma is meant to appeal to the "eco-chic." A projected model, the Mina, will be aimed at the mainstream market and is expected to be priced around $40,000.

Kleiner's investment in the software company Hara is more about the new "accounting" that is emerging around sustainability. Hara's solution helps companies with what it calls "auditable transparency" around resources consumed and expended by an organization—energy, water, waste, carbon, and so on.

Portfolio Company: Luca Technologies

"Think of it as a cocktail of nutrients."

Luca Technologies is based in Golden, Colorado, where Coors Brewing is headquartered, and you wonder what exotic concoction Robert Pfeiffer is offering. But he is into something far more exotic.

Pfeiffer explains: "Check out the microbes on our Web site. Tiny ones, magnified up to 10,000 times in the pictures. They are anaerobic organisms [those that are buried deep and can survive without oxygen] in coal beds, shale, and older oil fields. Our nutrients coax them to release methane."

Pfeiffer is CEO of Luca Technologies, and the company has several patents to document what he is talking about. The venture arm of BASF is also an investor in Luca. BASF has been expanding its traditional chemical roots into enzymes and ferments. In Chapter 1, we described a BASF bioengineering initiative around rice seedlings:

Methane [natural gas] is the cleanest burning hydrocarbon fuel. Histor-
ically, we have had to drill for it where we discover promising gas fields.
We are showing you can harvest the hydrogen and leave the carbon in
the coal in situ. Burning Lucagas generates only half the CO_2 if we had
extracted the coal and burnt it. In contrast, "clean coal" technologies
have as their basis the burning of coal, the recapture of CO_2 and the
sequestration of that CO_2 back into the ground. We pre-sequester the CO_2.

During 2006 and 2007, Luca experimented on more than 100 wells in
the Powder River Basin in Wyoming. The results were promising even
though they started influencing the microbial population and dynamics with
only modest volumes of water and nutrients. To date, Luca has produced
and sold more than 1 billion cubic feet of methane—that according to the
American Gas Association's estimates of average gas consumption would
provide energy to about 14,000 homes for one year.[3]

But it is still fossil fuel—that can't be good. Pfeiffer explains:

The reality is for the next 5 to 10 years, even if my fellow solar, wind,
and fuel cell entrepreneurs are wildly successful, we will be dependent
on coal and oil. Why not get something with less carbon and right here
at home? Just the Powder River Basin coals represent the equivalency of
over 8,000 trillion cubic feet of methane—an enormous resource. If just
1% of this coal can be converted to Lucagas, it would total almost four
years of current United States domestic consumption.

Portfolio Company: Silver Spring Networks

"In Florida, they had to prove the equipment could stand up to high
winds and electric storms. In California, to mountainous terrain and
high-population-density issues."

Scott Lang, chairman, president, and CEO of Silver Spring Networks,
is describing the "torture" two of his earliest and biggest customers, Florida
Power & Light (FPL) and Pacific Gas and Electric (PG&E), put his equipment through as part of their initial deployments. These utilities and several
others are investing in making their grids much "smarter" by allowing two-
way communication between all devices on the grid. Silver Spring's mission
is to create a platform for utilities to connect any device that generates,
distributes, or uses energy.

Silver Spring's solution facilitates communication between home and
utilities. It warns of outages and sends energy usage information among
other messages. Beyond the hardware, Silver Spring also provides software
and services to connect every device on the grid, creating the platform for
the smart grid. The solutions is built on IPv6—the next-generation Internet

Protocol (the standard is not new, but few companies have deployed it)—so the company is "future proofing" its clients and providing a platform for innovation:

> *FPL and PG&E are planning to roll out their smart grids to nearly 10 million homes and businesses by 2011. Add to that buildings, distribution automation points, and the coming wave of electric vehicle charging stations—our networks will help link all these nodes, enabling transparency across the grid and empowering consumers to manage their energy use. Since our Smart Energy Platform is designed for two-way traffic, we will also be able to support "feed laws" similar to those in Germany, where homeowners can sell excess solar energy back to the grid.*
>
> *This is the kind of infrastructure UPS and Walmart built decades ago to give themselves supply chain visibility and ruthless efficiency. Think what utilities will be able to do with usage information every 15 minutes versus waiting for manual meter inspections once a month. Think what customers will do when incented to move demand away from peak hours—do your laundry at 9:30 P.M., for example, at much lower rates than at 1 P.M. The potential savings are huge.*
>
> *Some of my utility clients call it their "virtual power plant." They should be able to postpone investment in new physical plants from the energy savings. Our Outage Detection Software will allow them to send out their repair trucks even before the first customer calls in to report a downed line.*

Silver Spring's technology and growing operational experience with some of the largest utilities in North America and abroad puts the company in a pole position, pun intended. Says Lang:

> *In some cases, utilities are asking us to be the prime contractor, which is a huge vote of confidence in us.*
>
> *Also, while other countries may lead us in alternative energy generation, as I travel around the world, I am hearing [that] U.S. utilities lead in smart grid innovation and deployment. As a result, we are seeing interest in our solutions from utilities around the world.*

So, what's a gating factor?

> *The back office in the utilities will need a significant investment. Batch programs will need to be updated to handle the impact of interval data and real-time control. The data stores will explode with that much information flowing in.*

Portfolio Company: Bloom Energy

"Oh, I wasn't at all sure it could be done."

Doerr is telling the CBS show "60 Minutes" his initial reaction to Sridhar when he came looking for an investment in 2001. And Sridhar asked for at least four times the investment Kleiner had made in Google![4]

Clearly, Kleiner saw potential in the work performed by Sridhar and his team as part of the Mars space project described earlier. They had built a device capable of producing air and fuel from electricity and/or electricity from air and fuel.

In 2002, Kleiner Perkins made its investment in Bloom. With financing in place, the Bloom team headed to NASA Ames Research Center in Silicon Valley to set up shop. In early 2006, Bloom shipped its first 5kW field trial unit and conducted two years of field trials to validate its technology. The first commercial (100kW) products were shipped to Google in July 2008. The company shipped other "Bloom Boxes" to companies like Fedex, eBay, and Staples but continued in stealth mode for another 20 months, till early 2010.

The Bloom Energy Server converts air and nearly any fuel source—ranging from natural gas to a wide range of biogases—into electricity via a clean electrochemical process, rather than dirty combustion. Even running on a fossil fuel, the systems are approximately 67 percent cleaner than a typical coal-fired power plant. When powered by a renewable fuel, they can be 100 percent cleaner. Each Energy Server consists of thousands of Bloom's fuel cells—flat, solid ceramic squares made from a common sand-like "powder."

While the initial focus is on commercial use, the vision over the next few years is to deliver smaller versions for a home backyard. The idea is to one day replace the big power plants and transmission line grid. Says Sridhar: "We believe that we can have the same kind of impact on energy that the mobile phone had on communications. Just as cell phones circumvented landlines to proliferate telephony, Bloom Energy will enable the adoption of distributed power as a smarter, localized energy source."

With that home energy focus, you can see how Kleiner's portfolio fills another major niche in the supply/demand map shown in Figure 13.1 and in the grand challenges the company focused on internally.

The Shifting Sands

For eight years, Bloom Energy's one-page Web site provided little details on its product. Sridhar used to be coy about details till the "blowout" coming-out party in March 2010 (which Doerr gushed was "Like the Google

IPO"). So was Lane when you asked him about Bloom and several of Kleiner's other investments in cleantech.

Their stealth goes back to the comment about economic and global vagaries. Two years ago, dependence on the Middle East and Russia for oil challenged the West's strategic interests. That dependence is still a problem, but just as worrisome today is the rapid ascendancy of the Chinese as potential cleantech competitors (as described in Chapter 12). The West has watched warily as China sealed up oil and other energy contracts in Africa, South America, and elsewhere. The concern now is that China could become to green technology what the United States is to global information technology: the dominant player.

It's not just China; Germany, Japan, and a slew of other countries are competitors. In a survey Kleiner commissioned, only six U.S. companies were listed among the top 30 global green technology vendors. Lane explains: "The United States is clearly the biggest market for green technology. But there is a scenario in which the other countries become our largest suppliers. And of course, that means they would also be the suppliers to the rest of the world."

Or they could end up as investors in promising cleantech companies. Sridhar says Germany and China are often interesting sources for project financing. That situation brings its own set of issues: How do you protect your intellectual property across borders? Are you compromising national interests?

"The good news is it is generating more urgency in Washington about incentives and financing," says Lane. Sridhar, a bit more cautious, explains: "The will is certainly there but [it has] to be filtered against budget deficits . . . now, if we could have had the same willingness in 2004!"

Lang is more bullish. The Department of Energy has funded more than $3 billion for smart grids, and it has helped his customers justify their investments.

Washington may be more aware of the strategic importance of cleantech, but there has been an interesting reversal in California. During Meg Whitman's campaign for the office of governor of California, she pushed for a moratorium on the state's RPS. Who would have thought the former CEO of eBay—a refugee from information technology like Lane—would not be an enthusiastic cleantech supporter?

More twists and turns.

Or who would have guessed that a utility like PG&E, instead of lobbying against the RPS requirements, would quit the U.S. Chamber of Commerce in protest? Its resignation letter said: "We find it dismaying that the Chamber neglects the indisputable fact that a decisive majority of experts have said the data on global warming is compelling and point to a threat that cannot be ignored."[5]

Or as Sridhar points out: "There is a reason we call them fossil fuels—they are inherently limited. As global economies pick up again, the focus on energy as a national priority will peak again."

Even more twists and turns.

Kleiner's journey since 2003 shows the wide expanse of the opportunity in cleantech. After all, after looking at 5,000 opportunities, Kleiner has invested in only 1 percent of them.

It also shows the tricky board game the firm is navigating. There exist so many conflicting vested and emerging interests that often have little to do with technology. Lane summarizes:

> *But that's what we do: invest where we can deliver breakthroughs, not just step change. At 62, I have little left to prove. But it has been enormously fulfilling to work with this group—differently than in information technology, these entrepreneurs have the bit extra—they firmly believe they are changing the world.*

The grand challenges they are tackling needs that breakthrough mindset. As Joy says, "keep making the problem bigger." And keep scouring Lithuania and every other corner of the world for solutions.

Recap

Little in Kleiner's background, impressive as it was around infotech investments, suggested that the firm could make a transition to the world of methane and selenium.

By bringing in plenty of new talent and a disciplined sourcing process where it invests in only 1 of 100 companies it evaluates, it has developed a wide portfolio that covers most niches in the cleantech market—from making carbon fuels cleaner to developing renewable fuels more efficiently to next-generation batteries to enabling utility smart grids.

Kleiner's broad vision and investment portfolio easily qualify it as a cleantech polymath. Its success will be a barometer of how well the United States catches up to Germany and competes more effectively against China and others in the fast-growing cleantech industry.

CHAPTER 14

Singularity: Human–Machine Convergence

Scenario 1: 2023

We have the technological means to create superhuman intelligence—which could take five forms:

1. *AI scenario.* We create superhuman artificial intelligence (AI) in computers.
2. *IA scenario.* We enhance human intelligence through human-to-computer interfaces—that is, we achieve intelligence amplification (IA).
3. *Biomedical scenario.* We directly increase our intelligence by improving the neurological operation of our brains.
4. *Internet scenario.* Humanity and its networks, computers, and databases become sufficiently effective to be considered a superhuman being.
5. *Digital Gaia scenario.* The network of embedded microprocessors becomes sufficiently effective to be considered a superhuman being.

Scenario 2: 2045

Human Body 2.0 is here. Nanobots travel our bloodstreams destroying pathogens and reversing aging processes. Our nonbiological intelligence will be billions of times more capable than our biological one. It will self-heal and improve.

Scenario 3: Sometime in the Twenty-Second Century

A paralyzed Marine is drafted to go on a distant mining mission. Humans cannot breathe the air on that moon, but the indigenous humanoid race can. Genetic and telepathic technologies have evolved where we can clone such a humanoid and allow the human who donated the DNA to mentally control the clone. On that beautiful planet, the solider is not paraplegic and wheelchair bound—he has incredible dexterity and strength.

Scenario 1 is from Vernon Vinge, the computer scientist and sci-fi author. In 1993, he wrote his version of Singularity and said it would happen in 30 years. At the midpoint of his projection, in 2008, he wrote an article for the *IEEE Spectrum* where he said we are on track and laid out his five forms of "superhuman intelligence."[1]

Scenario 2 is from Ray Kurzweil, author of *The Singularity Is Near*. He is not from Hollywood; he is a technologist who has developed optical-character recognition and speech-recognition software. He presented his thoughts on 2045 in a 2005 issue of *New Scientist* magazine.[2]

Scenario 3 is from the movie *Avatar,* James Cameron's 2009 epic. Jake Sully, the paralyzed Marine, his cloned Na'vi humanoid, and the planet Pandora in its spectacular beauty and intrigue are brought out in vivid 3-D.

There is also Scenario 4 which extrapolates today's realities with some countries with a life expectancy of less than 40 years and where tens of millions of people have no health insurance. How on earth can we pay for the nanobots, humanoids and nonbiological intelligence? And given the waves of swine and other flu and nonstop wars that ravage the world, how realistic is it to talk about quantum improvements in health?

Though the first three scenarios might be considered Hollywood's imagination run amok or the ideas of kooks delusional about their mortality, the reality is that genetics, nanotechnology, and computing power continue to evolve rapidly.

Additionally, health care has received wide attention in U.S. politics over the last year—something previous presidents have tried and failed to get a mandate around for six decades. While "mandate" may be a stretch given the bitter disagreements the health care debate brought out, it should result in an era of innovation in many aspects of healthtech.

Coming from the other side—the machine side—it is impressive how devices and sensors and motes and robots are doing many human functions—in many cases, better than humans can.

Let's look at the state of the art—both in how humans and machines are evolving and in how they are converging. First, we get a tour of the current state of medical technology from an industry insider. Then we look at five areas where medicine and machines are evolving:

1. The Internet of humans and things
2. Medical cities and high-tech villages
3. Heartwarming robots and heartbreaking autism

4. Personalized medicine and personalized doses
5. The tiny and the giant: nanotech and giant sensory networks

State of Medical Technology

"It facilitates three-way matching."

Dave Watson is playing tour guide and showcasing things he considers innovative at a health care technology show. The former CTO of Kaiser Permanente has spent a lifetime in the pharmaceutical and health care industries. Now, as COO of MedeAnalytics, he is helping an industry-focused performance management vendor develop better products for this market.

But his companion is puzzled. Why is Watson talking about an age-old accounts payable/accounting concept of matching invoice with purchase order and receiving report?

> *Because the concept has been adapted in health care to reduce medication error with technology. The three-way match here is across patient, prescription, and caregiver (whether certified to administer the medication) information. And it involves RFID [radio-frequency identification] and other sensors, bar codes and software to check on and prevent conflicts, and drug dispensers with their own controls built in.*
>
> *It's actually more about the "five rights": right patient receiving the right dose of the right medication at the right time via the right route.*

Medication error is a serious problem in health care. The U.S. Food and Drug Administration (FDA) estimates that four million visits to hospitals, doctor offices, and health care clinics each year stem from misuse—both intentional and unintentional—or overdose, with more than 100,000 resulting hospitalizations. Once you get to the hospital, the problem can be just as bad. A study in 2008 showed 1 in every 10 patients admitted to six Massachusetts community hospitals suffered serious and avoidable medication mistakes.[3]

So you can see the need for three-way matching and the five rights. But it's not just for error avoidance. Watson continues:

> *Device manufacturers have also woken up to the potential of feeding clinical telemetry from the device level to the electronic medical record. Players such as Siemens, Phillips, and others are enabling their endpoints with network connectivity. The connected devices significantly increase the richness of the data available for clinical decision making, but they also create new headaches for IT [information technology] because of the massive data stores they create.*

As the tour moves to a software booth, Watson points out some health care software vendors:

Vendors like Cerner and Epic are expanding their data models to handle additional types of data such as that from the telemetry we just saw. There is a similar progression to that experienced by the ERP [enterprise resource planning] vendors in the 1990s in the manufacturing sector, as they started expanding into supply chain management, customer relationship management, and other functional areas.

The accumulated data allows for much better disease management. Watson explains:

The ability to ratchet up the precision and to identify and deploy fact-based clinical best practices is immense. Systems such as Kaiser (which are incented by their business model to practice wellness) and others such as the NHS [National Health Service] in Britain are beginning to push the boundaries and deliver significant improvements in wellness outcomes with reductions in medical treatment costs across a range of diseases, including heart attacks, diabetes, and others.

The next stop on the tour is a Johnson & Johnson booth. Its Animas division is demoing its OneTouch Ping glucose meter. It is meant for diabetes patients to transmit data wirelessly to the insulin pump at the patient's belt level. It is discreet—you think a person is checking a text message on a PDA. Watson is excited about such devices:

The industry talks predominantly about health care in the home, but I find that too limiting. People with chronic diseases don't want to stay home; they want to live their lives! The availability of fairly ubiquitous and high capacity wireless coverage combined with a hip-mounted computing device enables a "health care wherever you are" model.

The conversation then drifts to progress in genomics: "It is exciting to see companies like Genomic Health, which allow for commercialization of tests for identified markers, say for breast cancer, that let oncologists better target their treatments—saving money and improving outcomes."

Over coffee, Watson gets more circumspect:

I have this two-stage notion of innovation—Stage One is when somebody perfects a piece of knowledge: a process, a medical procedure, an invention of a device or technology; Stage Two is the innovation of adoption, which is when somebody figures out how to get mainstream adoption for a discovery.

The issue with clinical innovation is often the pace of adoption. There are many studies that show normal clinical adoption of a new technique or innovation can take 15 to 20 years to go mainstream. This is the conundrum of health care—significant innovation with snail's pace adoption. There are a variety of causal factors, including regulatory overhead and the method of dissemination of knowledge—master to apprentice, for example— and others.

We could really use more much innovation in the adoption, in Stage Two.

Let's now drill into some of the areas Watson covered.

Internet of Humans and Things

In 2005, IBM ran a humorous commercial where a truck comes to a screeching halt to avoid hitting a woman and her help desk in the middle of the highway. The woman tells the truckers they are lost. How does she know?

"The boxes told me."

This commercial highlighted the growing use of RFID and sensors in so many aspects of life—what is being called the "Internet of Things." In the BP profile in Chapter 21, for example, we cite several examples in its "game changer," called sensory networks, which utilize many of those RFID chips and sensors.

In 2009, the European Union Commission sent a paper to its Parliament titled "The Internet of Things—An Action Plan for Europe":

IoT [Internet of Things] should not be considered as a utopian concept; in fact, several early-bird components of IoT are already being deployed as illustrated hereafter:

- *Consumers are increasingly using Web-enabled mobile phones equipped with cameras and/or employing Near-Field Communication. These phones allow users to access additional information regarding products such as allergen information.*
- *Member States are increasingly using unique serial numbers on pharmaceutical products (supported by bar-codes), enabling the verification of each product before it reaches the patient. This reduces counterfeiting, reimbursement fraud and dispensing errors. A similar approach taken on the traceability of consumer products in general would improve Europe's ability to tackle counterfeiting and to take measures against unsafe products.*

- *Several utility companies in the energy sector have started deploying smart electrical metering systems which provide consumption information to consumers in real time and allow electricity providers to monitor electrical appliances remotely.*
- *Within traditional industries, such as logistics (eFreight), manufacturing and retail, 'intelligent objects' facilitate the exchange of information and increase the effectiveness of the production cycle.[4]*

Now let's contrast this "Internet of Things" to how the human-oriented Internet is evolving to support health care. In particular, let's look at Google's efforts around tracking the spread of the flu virus and vaccine availability.

The Google's Flu Trends Web page is based on the finding that there is a close relationship between how many people search for flu-related topics and how many people actually have flu symptoms:

Of course, not every person who searches for "flu" is actually sick, but a pattern emerges when all the flu-related search queries are added together. We compared our query counts with traditional flu surveillance systems and found that many search queries tend to be popular exactly when flu season is happening. By counting how often we see these search queries, we can estimate how much flu is circulating in different countries and regions around the world.[5]

Can you imagine if anything close had been available during the Black Death (the plague in Europe in the fourteenth century)? That disease is estimated to have spread at the rate of a few miles a day. The plague wiped out a third to half of the population of many towns on the continent and is called the first recorded pandemic in history.

Google also set up a Flu Shot Locator Web page to show where vaccines were available:

We've been working with HHS [Department of Health and Human Services], the Centers for Disease Control and Prevention [CDC] and state and local health agencies to gather information on flu vaccine locations across the country, particularly for the H1N1 flu vaccine (both the nasal-spray vaccine and the shot). At the moment we have data for locations of flu vaccine directly from 20 states and counting. We are also continuing to add information from chain pharmacies and other providers in all 50 states.

Medical Cities and High-Tech Villages

An electrophysiology lab is treating more than 50 patients a month. The proton beam, which cost over $100 million, is helping target cancer tumors. Leonardo Da Vinci, the robot is helping perform surgery. Bariatric surgery, with new techniques such as sleeve gastrectomy, is available to the clinically obese.

All this advanced health care is available within a few square miles—in Jacksonville, Florida.

Jacksonville, Florida? It's not exactly top of list if you were asked to name advanced medical cities. But that technology and care is available at the Mayo Clinic (at a local branch of that famous institution), the Shands Center, Baptist Health, and Memorial Hospital, among several other local hospitals.

The city has a thriving biotechnology industry. It has research and residency collaboration with a number of local and state educational institutions.

It is not just Jacksonville; cities around the world are marketing to non-locals—in a trend called medical tourism.

India has become known for heart surgery, hip resurfacing, and alternative and traditional local medicine. Thailand is known for eye surgery and kidney dialysis. Argentina sells its prowess in cosmetic surgery, and Hungary, dental procedures. Some of these countries target rich neighbors. Korea, for example, attracts Japanese citizens; Dubai attracts medical visitors from around the Middle East. South Africa pitches its weak rand—favorable to visitors—as an advantage. Michael Moore, as controversial as he can be, did open eyes in his movie *Sicko* to the cheap but potentially high-quality medical services available in Cuba.

Telling patients to fly thousands of miles for a medical procedure is not that easy a sell. There are questions about the quality of care, certification, and malpractice protection. But as U.S. employers and insurance companies look for cost savings, they are bringing a level of due diligence to such locations. WellPoint, for example, has a pilot program with Serigraph, a Wisconsin-based company, to let members opt for procedures in India. Also, some of the West's best medical facilities are helping set up foreign collaborations. Johns Hopkins, for example, has a branch in Singapore, and Harvard Medical School has a center in Dubai.

While cities like Jacksonville are seeing an influx of medical tourists, in contrast farms and villages are trying to make do with fewer and fewer people.

Tony McCormack is nodding vigorously as a visitor shows him his house on Google Maps on a PDA. When he is impressed, a distinctive nod accompanies a smile. The roads leading to his house in Longford, Ireland, though, are mostly unnamed on the map. "We are low tech here in rural Ireland," he says with a shrug.

But once you get McCormack talking, he catalogs how technology has changed his dairy farm. A decade ago, calving season meant interrupted sleep as he woke in middle of night to check on his cows. Now he can monitor them via Web cam from the warmth of his home office.

His cows have transponders that help him customize the quantity and composition of feed for each one. Try doing that manually, when cows eat on average eight times a day. On large farms, farmers use GPS to apply fertilizers more precisely. McCormack gets animated when he describes how he had heard GPS tracking had helped track down stolen tractors being shipped to Poland.

Dairy farmers must be the hardest-working people in the world. In a world of massively industrialized agricultural farms, dairy farming is mostly still a labor intensive industry (even in the United States, the average dairy farmer has a herd of only 100 cows). So technology is challenged to deliver productivity: Larger herds for every labor hour and more milk yield from each cow. And in recent years, dairy farmers have had to worry about the safety and security of the milk supply chain (felt more acutely with the increase in biohazard threats), environmental issues (the impact of cow-emitted methane on global warming), and more. So automated milking, nutrition optimization, biogas generation, and lot traceability are several areas where technology is helping the dairy farmer.

As for unnamed roads—that's still the beauty of Ireland. You get to stop and ask neighbors for directions. And those conversations meander into so many other topics that keep "social networks" going as they have for centuries.

Heartwarming Robots and Heartbreaking Autism

In 1981, the band Styx famously sang "Domo Arigato, Mr. Roboto"—that's "thank you" in Japanese. They were prescient. Japan is the world's largest robotics supplier, but most of the robots have been for industrial uses. Japan has more recently been focusing on "service robots," particularly for care for the aging population. The robot market is expected to total around ¥6.2 trillion in 2025, of which ¥4.2 trillion will likely be linked to day care and nursing.[6]

On YouTube, you can see a video where the employees at a Zappos warehouse based in Kentucky actually had a derby for their robots. The winner, not too surprisingly, was a robot named Robotariat, as in Secretariat, the thoroughbred legend who won the Kentucky Derby and the Triple Crown in 1973.

People are warming up to robots, even at companies with stand-out human customer service like Zappos, which Amazon acquired last year.

The core competence of Zappos is not as much the shoes and other merchandise it sold; it is its highly regarded customer service. The service was respected enough that it started to offer it as an outsourced offering to other companies.

What does not get as much focus is that Zappos uses another innovative technology in that warehouse in Kentucky—robots made by Kiva. Instead of having people walking around and looking for ordered items, the robots do the running around and bring the items to the workers, who check the orders and seal them in shipping boxes.

Servers wirelessly route orders to robots in the warehouse, which then route appropriate pods to workers. The robots use cameras to read bar code stickers on the floor tracks to route them around the warehouse.

Workers appreciate not having to walk around large warehouses, but the journal *Supply and Demand Chain Executive* reported some other surprise feedback on the robots:

> *Unlike the airport runway levels of noise in a warehouse outfitted with conventional automation, the noise level in a robot-equipped warehouse is low enough to allow conversation at ordinary voice loudness.*
>
> *The work autonomy afforded by a mobile robot system gives associates another reason to seek out these workplaces: a sense of personal accomplishment. Because the robots enable each worker to independently complete each order he or she works on, associates report an increased sense of ownership of the result—ownership of the order quality as well as the speed with which they fill the orders.*
>
> *Worker independence also lets associates take breaks at will rather than having to schedule breaks so that other workers are not affected. In a robotic automation environment, the work automatically migrates to other team members when an associate is on break, so high-priority orders stay on track.*[7]

Robotics show promise in helping us take care of aging parents and, of course, assisting our employees. In contrast, two mothers are highlighting how little technology has been applied in the care of autistic children.

Electronic medical records (EMRs) have been getting plenty of interest and investment in recent times. President Obama is spending $20 billion to induce care providers to maintain patient records electronically. United States private health care networks have invested billions in going paperless. Likewise, the United Kingdom has spent billions on its National Programme for IT Health. Because most such projects are still works in progress, many constituents have not seen the benefits so far.

One group, in particular, would likely have not seen any benefits irrespective of the progress of these initiatives: parents of children with autism. They keep hearing that autism is not a disease or there is no cure. So there has been little in the way of electronic records or systematic tracking of data related to autism.

Elizabeth Horn, mother of Sophia, a child with autism, says, "The Centers for Disease Control and Prevention [CDC] calls autism an epidemic. The newest statistics are shocking: 1 out of every 100 children in the United States has an autism spectrum disorder. Even with that remarkable prevalence, there is little cause/effect data compared to other diseases."

Horn has teamed up with Pramila Srinivasan, also mother of a child with autism, Siddharth. Srinivasan founded MedicalMine, which developed ChARM (Children's Autism Recovery Map).

ChARMtracker is treatment management software created for the 1,600-plus parents who have signed up since it was launched in May 2009.

Says Elisabeth Einaudi, one of these parents, "With a few easy keystrokes, I enter basic treatment info once and daily observations, and then ChARM converts it into information that I can use."

Although today parents need Web access to enter the data, there is no reason why they could not use text or Twitter messages with short hash tags to make such notations directly from their mobile phones.

The ability to post observations about their children is a very promising feature of the tracker. Parents can document an unusual word or gesture and their thoughts on what may have caused it. The hope is that this growing database will help to identify biomarkers that may help guide treatments in the future.

ChARM Physician, the physician portal, allows the same data to be viewed by medical practitioners. Physicians can communicate, visualize, and analyze patient data from any Web browser. Researchers might one day be able to use sophisticated tools to analyze the data in this longitudinal tracking system. So, in many ways, it is an EMR for the physician as well as a treatment management and a social networking site.

Granted, Horn and Srinivasan are no ordinary mothers. They are tech savvy and live in Silicon Valley. Their husbands are chief executives of software companies. (Zach Nelson is profiled in Chapter 18; Sridhar Vembu in Chapter 9.) Horn spent the early part of her career making movies for technology companies. In her doctoral research at Purdue, Srinivasan focused on problems in data processing algorithms for analysis and classification. She has helped with algorithms in several engineering start-ups in the valley.

Beyond ChARM, Horn and Srinivasan are exploiting other technologies to bring more attention to autism. For the last decade, Horn has worked on the production and marketing of a film about children recovering from autism, entitled *Finding the Words*. The documentary has been seen by more than a million people around the world. Its YouTube preview has also been seen by thousands. Horn is currently editing a new version for American television, entitled *The Fight for Children with Autism*. Horn says:

> *Traditional views of autism are being challenged now by new research and new ways of thinking about this disease. It's no longer "incurable" or "untreatable," and the children in this film prove that. If just one child who was given no hope of ever having a normal life can get dramatically better, that child changes the paradigm for all of us. And once you have hope, you can change things for your child. And ChARM will help you do that.*

ChARM is a harbinger of similar social networks of patients with other afflictions. While governments around the world try multiyear, multibillion-dollar health care initiatives, affordable Web services, video, and other technology can provide hope and help in the interim. It just needs passionate, driven sponsors like Horn and Srinivasan.

Personalized Medicine and Personalized Doses

The cancer Biomedical Informatics Grid® (caBIG) is a network to connect researchers around the world and enable them to share information, helping to unravel the complexities of cancer genetics.[8] These researchers speak a new language: "One marker, rs6983267 on chromosome 8q24, has been linked to both colon and prostate cancer, and could be a susceptibility marker."[9]

ViiV Health care is GlaxoSmithKline and Pfizer's joint spin-off venture to market HIV treatments. One of the drugs that came to it from Pfizer was Selzentry, which is indicated for CCR5-tropic HIV-1 patients. It is marketed with a diagnostic test Trofile, which is designed to establish a patient's tropism status prior to administering the drug.

This genetic profiling is becoming possible as a result of the Human Genome Project, the massive effort to sequence human DNA that was completed in 2003. While interest in the topic should have stayed primarily in medical journals, it has gone mainstream quickly with 23andMe and other "retail genetics" sites, such as Navigenics and Pathway Genomics, which offer personal genome analysis.

Initially, it was believed that consumers would be more interested in the ancestral tracing potential of genome scans, but today many see genetic information as a way to inform health decisions. For this reason, they are pressuring caregivers and pharmaceutical companies to "personalize medicine."

This is yet another example of the consumerization of technology that we discussed in Chapter 4, with all its opportunities and risks.

Let's now turn to how technology is helping avoid some of the medication errors that Watson talked about earlier, by personalizing our doses. Let's look at the growing sophistication of the humble infusion pump.

Dr. Philip Settimi of Hospira is describing his company's Symbiq Infusion System. Software, communication technology, and usability influenced the design that won the 2007 Medical Design Excellence Award:

> *We set out to reinvent the infusion pump. Customers don't buy pumps and sets—they buy patient safety solutions.*
>
> *Symbiq works with our MedNet safety software, which allows companies to customize drug libraries and dosing limits. Its platform can support embedded advanced decision support applications, such as EndoTool for intelligent glycemic control.*

The bidirectional wireless data communication can match patient, order, and pump data (which a nurse would scan using bar codes). If correct, the order is checked against the drug library and dosing guidelines. Once verified, the pump can be automatically programmed and the infusion can begin.

Watson's concepts of three-way matching and five rights are being automated. Settimi continues:

> *There are other safety features. An automated medication "cassette" protects against the accidental free flow of medication.*
>
> *Symbiq is capable of becoming a true computer at the hospital bedside. Decision support will be the next wave, helping to guide clinicians at the bedside administer higher-risk but medically necessary therapy such as insulin and heparin.*
>
> *Symbiq's large touch screen—8.3 inches—ensures ease of use. We looked at optimal font sizes and brightness during deep clinical user assessments in the development process. The display is legible from across a room—even 12 feet away. We tested various auditory and visual alarms. We created unique melodies to distinguish them from sounds from other devices like vital signs monitors.*
>
> *Every feature and specification was developed to enhance caregiver productivity, clinical outcomes and a safe patient experience.*

For the focus on usability, the Human Factors and Ergonomics Society awarded the product its 2006 User-Centered Product Design Award.

In the next form/function, Symbiq should feature more input from other devices—so, as an example, feedback from a patient monitoring device may trigger a slowdown in the infusion flow. Or embedded RFID tags could program the pump automatically.

The Tiny and the Giant: Nanotech and Sensory Databases

Cris Orfescu was born in Romania and has a strong science background common for so many from the former Eastern Bloc. But he is also a self-taught artist and that part of him has blossomed since he immigrated to Los Angeles, California. He blends science and art in what he calls nanoart.[10] Orfescu provides high-resolution electron scans of nanosculptures, man-made and occurring naturally, and encourages artists to alter the images and create even more new nanoart.

Nano, as in nanometer which is one billionth of a meter (a printed page is roughly 100,000 nanometers thick), must rank high as candidate for the innovation word of the decade. There is the iPod Nano and the Tata Nano, the under-$3,000 car from India. And, of course there is plenty going on in nanotechnology.

Nanotechnology is showing up in decay-fighting microbes, asthma sensors, and contact lenses for patients that can monitor their eye pressure for glaucoma. At nano levels, however, materials behave differently than at larger scales. Some change their conductive capabilities, others become much stronger. Consider "buckypaper," which is 500 times stronger and 10 times lighter than steel and is made from carbon molecules 50,000 times thinner than a human hair.

And therein lies some of the risks with nanotechnology: While the products may be fine for industrial applications (and for new forms of art), how will items made with nanomaterials affect our bodies? The Project on Emerging Nanotechnologies lists more than 1,000 consumer products, including toothpaste, sunscreens, wound dressings, cooking oil, and pet sprays that have some nanomaterials.[11]

K. Eric Drexler, a pioneer in the field with his book *The Engines of Creation,* coined the term "molecular manufacturing," but he is also on record as talking about the risks of nanotechnology: "Advanced lethal and non-lethal weapons, deployed quickly and cheaply, could make the world a more dangerous place. The list of potential consequences is long, and as with all powerful technologies, the results will depend on the intent of the users."[12]

While nanotechnology is taking us into minute form/factors, the growing proliferation of sensors is creating massive databases of the messages they can deliver.

Daniel Gabriel Fahrenheit would be fascinated. He invented the mercury thermometer, a type of temperature sensor still in use, and worked with a number of liquid-in-glass barometers.

Today, if you call a home security company, it will be happy to install motion and smoke detection sensors. And don't be surprised if the company also offers sensors to monitor for carbon monoxide, freezing temperatures (to watch for impact on water pipes), and moisture (to watch for basement flooding) among other applications.

Take a look at your car. You may have a vibration-triggered car alarm sensor. You may have a tire pressure monitoring sensor and a sensor to turn on your lights automatically at night. You may have another to turn on your wipers as it senses moisture. Of course, cars contain other sensors you may not even know exist—such as oxygen sensors, which measure air to fuel mix and impact on engine performance.

Cities around the world have been enthusiastic sensor adopters. The city of San Francisco, for example, uses sensors to alert citizens about open parking spots via displays on street signs, or on screens of their smartphones. Stockholm uses sensors to monitor peak-hour traffic. York, Pennsylvania, has sensors that monitor for gunshot sounds to alert emergency services. Cambridge, Massachusetts, has sensors to monitor air quality. Under its BioWatch program, the U.S. Homeland Security Department has been deploying air sensors in several cities to detect the presence of potential biological weapons.

GE's Sensing division offers several categories of sensors: pressure, humidity, flow, temperature, gas, moisture, and electrical. But there are many more. At the 2009 Sensors Expo in Chicago, exhibits included products with sensors that measured piezoelectricity (measure pressure or acceleration by converting into an electrical signal), radiation, and vibrations.

One of the more interesting sessions in that conference focused on energy harvesting, discussing solar, vibration, and other energy to fuel the sensors beyond the batteries and capacitors that run them today.[13]

Of course, the data from these billions of sensors is leading to opportunities for data mining. Sun Microsystems has developed its Yggdrasil (as in the mythical Norse ash tree whose branches extend to the heavens) framework for use with sensors and other small, wireless, embedded devices. It factors their unique characteristics: limited power, need to operate unattended under harsh environmental conditions, the fact that many devices "sleep" often to conserve energy and wake up periodically for a short time to record and/or transmit sample readings.[14] The Yggdrasil framework is designed to make it easier for field researchers to create applications that collect sensor data over long periods of time—small bursts of data, but voluminous in aggregate.

Recap

Humans and machines are surely converging, but the advantage seems to be to the machines. After all, Kurzweil's vision of singularity seems centuries away when we cannot get basic health care coverage issues resolved, when cancer continues to be a major killer, and when the risks of pandemics seem to be accelerating around the globe. Or when, Watson points out, that adoption always takes much longer than innovation in health care technology. Or when pharmaceutical companies seem more interested in merging with each other and in marketing than in R&D as we saw in Chapter 9.

Nevertheless, plenty of innovation is going on in health care. Technology is becoming more ubiquitous, as Horn and Srinivasan point out. Quality of care is improving worldwide as cities vie for medical tourism. In the United States, national health care has risen to the highest level of policy attention. That could lead to a new wave of innovation.

More steady is the flow of innovations in the Internet of Things. Armies of sensors, devices, robots, and tags are being deployed worldwide. We are seeing a wide range of applications for workers in every field and an explosion of nonhuman messaging traffic that makes our cities smarter and homes safer.

Progress on both fronts will ebb and flow, but the opportunities for a polymath enterprise to innovate based on the convergence of technology advances around humans and machines are impressive.

CHAPTER 15

Analytics: Spreadsheets, Search, and Semantics

The year 2008 was a wake-up call for most enterprises. At that time, the realization sank in that after investing tens of billions in analytical tools, their business forecasts were not just off, they were off spectacularly.

Against that backdrop, the National Hurricane Center profile we present in Chapter 16 is even more impressive. The center gathers primary data in hostile circumstances, uses massive processing power to crunch that data, then considers and cautiously blends multiple forecasting models and probabilities. In the end, it delivers impressive savings in lives and avoided evacuation costs.

Of course, storm track forecasting is just one analytical application. And it pales compared to the data defense agencies are collecting—most of it "unstructured." Says *National Defense Magazine* in an article appropriately titled "Swimming in Sensors and Drowning in Data": "Unpiloted aircraft in the skies over Iraq and Afghanistan collect full-motion video. Satellites—belonging to both the National Reconnaissance Office and commercial operators—take images from space. Signals intelligence experts eavesdrop on the chatter of insurgents who may be planning to bomb civilian targets."[1]

Analyze all that!

Like the multidimensional cubes and 3-D charts most companies are used to seeing from their analysts, the subject of analytics itself is being viewed from many perspectives: competitive intelligence, risk management, pattern recognition, and customer profitability analysis, among others. And it is being viewed against the backdrop of how poorly most companies did with their business forecasting in the recent economic slowdown.

We turned to three practitioners who have watched and influenced the evolution of business analytics—and who each wrote a book on the topic recently—to get their multidimensional view on innovations in the area.

- Howard Dresner coined the term "Business Intelligence" (BI) in 1989. Then, for over a decade, he was an influential Gartner analyst on the BI market sector. He left to become chief strategy officer for Hyperion (now part of Oracle) and now runs his own advisory firm. He recently authored *Profiles in Performance.*[2]
- David Axson cofounded The Hackett Group, which many a Fortune 500 company has used as a gold standard for business process benchmarks. He then did a stint as head of corporate planning at Bank of America and now runs an advisory firm, The Sonax Group, specializing in strategy and performance management. He is author of *The Management Mythbuster.*[3]
- Nenshad Bardoliwalla spent a decade with analytic technologies at large software companies such as Siebel, Hyperion, and SAP, and has a wide perspective on what enterprises expect from their analytical tools and teams. He is currently in "stealth mode" in a start-up and is coauthor of *Driven to Perform.*[4]

If you tally the key trends for the analytics market from these three thought leaders, you end up with several hundreds. The nine key themes can be summarized as:

- "The Black Swan is not that rare." Says Dresner:

Nassim Nicholas Taleb of The Black Swan *book fame talks about "highly improbable" events and how historical data simply cannot help us fully anticipate them. Armed with our BI-derived assumptions, we must go out into the real world and test them—to develop a more complete perspective. Failing this, organizations will make decisions—perhaps ruinous ones—based on a flawed view of the world.*

- "It's the age of Big Data." Says Bardoliwalla:

To tackle today's truly massive databases of the kind for meteorological forecasting and genomic sequencing we will have to leverage innovations in parallelism, in-memory processing and columnar storage.

- "Deemphasize slice and dice, reemphasize decisions." Says Axson:

There's an old adage that says, "You can't manage what you can't measure"; however, in today's digitized world, it would be more accurate to say "You can't manage what you can measure." We need to get back to decision-, not data-, centricity.

- "We still have plenty of small data." Says Dresner:

  Enterprise tools can be inflexible and oftentimes don't reach all users or meet all needs. It's easy to use desktop tools like Excel to import data and begin analyzing it. Multiply that across all of the users in an enterprise, the problem becomes clear. We need a happy medium.

- "Don't ignore unstructured data." Says Axson:

  Most data today is organized around transactions (e.g., orders, sales, payments), subject areas (e.g., marketing, production, human resources), or time periods (e.g., monthly, quarterly, annually).

- "And then there is Web and social data." Says Bardoliwalla:

  A new breed of Web analytics players is fusing traditional page view algorithms with social media assets, looking for key influencers, recommendations among peers, etc., and this will only continue to grow.

- "This much data equals better visualization tools." Says Bardoliwalla:

  With consumers aware of the power of capabilities like Google Maps or the tactile manipulations possible on the iPhone, richer visuals will find their way into enterprise analytics at a rapid speed.

- "This much data equals massive storage requirements." Says Dresner:

  The rich video and graphics files, the attachments we e-mail everyone, new compliance requirements on data retention—all this has led to an explosion in storage needs. Not only have we stretched our mental boundaries to analyze data, we are stretching the physical limits of storage management and the financial limits of our infrastructure budgets.

- "This much data equals predictive powers." Says Bardoliwalla:

  The race is on for technology to predict future outcomes by sensing and responding, with literally no latency between event and decision point.

Let's look at an example of innovative thinking or application in each area.

The Black Swan Is Not That Rare

Paul Kedrosky is explaining how most enterprises approach analytics: "Why does the drunk look for lost keys under the lamp post even though the keys were dropped far away? Because that's where the light is. They are looking for confirmation when they should be looking for falsification, as the philosopher, Karl Popper would argue."

Dr. Kedrosky is an investor, writer, entrepreneur, and analyst for CNBC. On his blog Infectious Greed and in presentations at various industry events, he has repeatedly unearthed a surprising data point or analytical conclusion. Example: When the Bernie Madoff fraud scandal broke in late 2008, Kedrosky argued it was not an unsophisticated scam, as many other analysts were suggesting.

> *I took Madoff's monthly returns from December of 1990 to May of 2005, as contained in a Fairfield Sentry performance data document. There were 196 months in total, more than enough to credibly expect the distribution of the numbers 1 through 9 in the most significant digits of the performance numbers to track fairly closely log10 ((d + 1)/d). . . . It almost certainly means Madoff's numbers would have been generated algorithmically. He didn't pluck them from air at the end of each month.*

When prodded to disclose the whiz-bang analytical technology he has access to, he struggles. He says he relies primarily on Excel and tools like the OutWit plug-in to his Web browser (which helps him with pattern recognition in his Web searches) and the 10Kwizard (which allows him to compare company filings with the Securities and Exchange Commission and draw out subtle changes company management may be reporting from one period to another). He elaborates:

> *My biggest tool is my curiosity. Too many enterprises have outsourced primary research to the Gartners and the sell-side investment analysts and so tend to get data which has been filtered and summarized and deprived of the original nutritional value.*
>
> *The other mistake many enterprises have made is to build models that were anchored around a couple of long-unquestioned assumptions. The real estate econometric model had historical data which did not show any declines for eight decades. To paraphrase Charles Perrow's classic* Normal Accidents, *we need to be careful and not build complex models with too tight a coupling.*[5]

Howard Dresner adds a pilot's perspective:

Even with the amount of instrumentation at the disposal of pilots, it's always a good idea to occasionally look out of the window. And, even when flying in the clouds and in IFR [instrument flying rules] conditions, the point of the instrumentation and associated flight planning is to get you to where you once again have visual references in order to land.

More optimistically, Kedrosky says, "There is so much data and so many analytical tools available for so cheap. I see a new generation of artists—not just data jocks, but those with the appreciation of the aesthetics of data. A Renaissance is coming to analytics."

It's the Age of "Big Data"

Bob Evans at *InformationWeek* is commenting on Larry Ellison's presentation at his annual customer gathering, Oracle Open World, in October 2009. Oracle was waiting for regulatory approval to acquire Sun Microsystems, but that did not stop Ellison from proudly showing off his new database engine, Exadata, on Sun gear.[6] "He's never run a hardware business but he's calling out the company that invented it [IBM]."

In the background, the engine purrs softly while carrying a big stick. It is twice as fast (as version 1, which used HP hardware, now a fading memory, given the Sun acquisition) for data warehousing, and it also runs applications. Traditionally, specialized hardware has done better at analytics versus transaction processing (OLAP versus OLTP, to use industry acronyms), but this version adds Sun's caching technology to converge the two.

Ellison's slides accentuate his mocking:

5X faster than Teradata and Neteeza [specialized solution providers for crunching large data sets].

20X faster than IBM's fastest computers.

Of course, Exadata is modular to scale—a full rack (8 database servers and 14 storage servers) down to a basic system (1 database server and 1 storage server).

Now Ellison's on a roll:

IBM's fastest computer is 4X more expensive for OLTP than Exadata.

Then comes the coup de grace: Ellison offers a $10 million prize to anyone who can show an application that does not run at least twice as fast on Sun servers as it does on IBM's:

IBM, you are more than welcome to enter. If you'd like to take us on, make our day.

As the über-machine gulps at its master's chutzpah, Evans summarizes: "Larry Ellison surely makes this business more interesting, but more importantly, he makes it a whole lot more valuable."

Yes, he does—Ellison may be brash, but he is definitely the Duke of Data Management. And the avid sailor is only too happy to offer customers rescue as they try to stay afloat in an ocean of data.

Of course, it's not just Oracle or IBM or Teradata or Neteeza, as Bardoliwalla points out:

Let's not forget large Web players like Google, Yahoo, Amazon, and Facebook have built their own solutions to handle their own incredible data volumes, with the open source Hadoop ecosystem and commercial offerings like CloudEra leading the charge in massive scale data management.

Deemphasize Slice and Dice, Reemphasize Decisions

Axson talks about decision-centric analysis: "Instead of starting with the data and thinking about the types of analysis that could be performed, start with the decision and organize the data and analytics around it."

Stephen Baker would say that is a good start—but you need to add some of the "global math elite" to lead the analysis. In his 2008 book *Numerati,* Baker identified a wide range of analytical applications in use by the elite.[7] He mentioned how:

- Dating sites, such as Chemistry.com, were creating algorithmic profiles of people and lining up mathematical correlations with potentially compatible mates.
- Pollsters were categorizing voters into fine segments and customizing messages to them.
- Surveillance methods used in Las Vegas to identify cheats and card counters were being adapted for other types of fraud detection.
- Algorithms originally used to combat e-mail spam by predicting its mutations were being repurposed to predict the mutations of the HIV virus.

Talking about the global math elite, Hal Varian, chief economist at Google, has been quoted as saying, "I keep saying that the sexy job in the next 10 years will be statisticians." He goes on to explain: "The rising stature of statisticians, who can earn $125,000 at top companies in their first year after getting a doctorate, is a byproduct of the recent explosion of digital data."[8]

We Still Have Plenty of Small Data

"He's been where no man had ever been before. To IV65536."

Chad LaCrosse is not talking about Trekkies and obscure planets. He is talking about a colleague who ran out of cells in his Excel spreadsheet. Until the 2007 version of the Microsoft spreadsheet increased the dimensions, the bottom-right cell of the spreadsheet defined the boundary. That, by the way, represents 256 columns and 65,536 rows—so over 16 million cells with generous width and height dimensions.

LaCrosse and his colleague showcase the breathtaking analytical power available to today's knowledge worker. At his current company, the medical device company Hospira, he has built an estimating model that uses up to seven variables to approximate the effort and cost of small/medium-size information technology (IT) application development projects. He calculates the cost by incorporating a multidimensional rate matrix based on Hospira's wide range of internal and external resources. Other spreadsheets that LaCrosse has built allow users to select a resource loading pattern, such as front-loaded, back-loaded, flat, or hyperbolic.

His models allow Hospira IT to be extremely responsive to its CFO. It also gives the department a leg up on its vendors, who have multiple LaCrosses of their own and whose spreadsheets approach 1 gigabyte each with pivot tables and complex formulas that go across multiple workbooks.

This is modern weaponry in use in most negotiations, budget cycles, and expense reporting. A generation earlier, an analyst like LaCrosse would have drooled over Lotus 1-2-3, one of the first PC-based spreadsheets—with its 30 times fewer cells.

Microsoft, looking ahead to the next generation of LaCrosses, delivered 1,000 times more cells in the 2007 version.

The bottom-right cell to aspire for now is XFD1048576. And we call spreadsheets "small" data?

Don't Ignore Unstructured Data

"Beyond search entrepreneur."

That's how Ramana Rao describes himself. "Because of the roaring success of Google, people have until recently focused too much on the magic in responding to the query in the search box and not enough on the results as a canvas for ongoing dialog."

Before launching his current venture, iCurrent, which is focused on personalized news delivery, Rao spent his career at Xerox PARC, the birthplace of such innovations as laser printing, the Ethernet, and the PC graphical user interface. From PARC, Rao spun out Inxight, a pioneering company focused on text analytics and information visualization. Inxight got some of its funding from In-Q-Tel, which is focused on emerging commercial technologies that the Central Intelligence Agency and broader U.S. intelligence community can leverage. It was acquired by SAP's Business Objects division in 2007.

Rao explains his mission:

I have lived my life trying to help people get value from the huge wealth of information, particularly what gets called unstructured data in the industry. My new venture is a continuation of that vector into building a product for the mainstream consumer audience. We are pursuing the functionality to simplicity ratio of the Great American Newspaper in the digital world. We marvel at the nice simple package that robustly fit in our lives as they once were.

To some people, *The New York Times* is "the book of record." To others, it is pages and pages of stock quotes in *The Wall Street Journal.* To still others, the newspaper invoked the expression "easy like Sunday morning." Rao continues:

Now as we move to truly personalized papers—each with a circulation of one—we still want those older values preserved. We're adding requirements, not subtracting. We now want a greater degree of personal relevance and help in serving an ever-broadening set of interests that the Internet is fueling.

Of course, there is no way to give somebody what he/she wants without the person being meaningfully involved. Personalization requires the person not just to "consume" the product but to participate in its very production. One way to think of this is Pandora for content. In the Pandora music streaming service, you start with stations based on genres or artists but then you "thumbs up" or "thumbs down" songs and, over time, it become uniquely tuned to your tastes.

In their [Pandora's] case, they use the musicologist armed with power tools to tags songs with hundreds of features like "Varying Rhythmic Feels," or "Gravelly Female Vocalist." And these features are used to build a model of your preference based on the songs you vote on. This works really well, and it's even fun and engaging to many people to see why songs were picked.

It has been fun to create the simple driving experience akin to Pandora's music listening experience while providing more direct control for different "channels of information" across a really wide range of interest. This requires the sophisticated semantic extraction technologies that we used in the enterprise intelligence apps we built at Inxight.

It's also been fun to focus on a consumer audience using the newspaper framework. As you can imagine, there are so many other business applications which could use similar solutions around unstructured enterprise data. Ironically, it may just turn out easier to work outside the firewall to create a model of how to apply text analytics technology and then come back into the enterprise in the platform shift to the cloud.

And Then There Is Web and Social Data

Ask many salespeople about working in a retail setting, such as Best Buy, and they will turn up their nose and say, "You have no control over when the interaction with the customer may take place." You could argue, though, that once a customer shows up, salespeople are trained to read body language and build a rapport with the customer.

You would think that a digital store would combine the two negatives—difficult-to-predict customer timing and, of course, the impossibility of "reading the room."

Steven Wood disagrees. The author of *Digital Body Language* says customers give you plenty of clues online via:

- Web visits to company blogs and landing pages
- Their response to marketing: e-mail, direct mail, or offline (e.g., from trade shows)
- Customer entry of any Web forms related to the company or its products
- Search terms and queries used on major search engines
- Many other digital paths[9]

Wood gets to see plenty of companies that mine data well—and others that do not—through the software company he cofounded, eloqua.

Wood likes to cite the example of Forex Capital Markets (FXCM), a long-time eloqua customer. FXCM brought back in house an outsourced e-mail model and saw e-mail volumes along with customer "e-mail open rates" jump dramatically. That is a common occurrence with many customers.

Wood explains: "As data flows into your marketing database from various online and offline sources, be ruthless about standardizing and 'deduplicating.' Without that, even simple personalization, segmentation, or scoring of leads becomes difficult."

FXCM's has several automated e-mail cycles in response to prospect e-mail activity, Web visit, or predetermined "drip marketing" schedule. As an example, prospects signing up for a trial account would trigger a succession of six unique e-mail messages over the course of several weeks. These e-mails point to product demonstrations, trading resources, and educational offers.

Wood offers a caution about data collection: "Don't be greedy about collecting customer-related data all at once. Ask only two or three incremental questions at a time (but never ask the same question twice), and you can progressively profile your audience with each interaction in a long-term campaign."

The sales team at FXCM can immediately see the effects of many demand-generation programs through eloqua's integration with salesforce.com. When prospects demonstrate a pattern of activity signaling their potential to be ready to do business, a salesperson makes the call.

Wood explains:

> Salespeople generally have a good understanding of the dynamics of an account, its key people, and its culture. By feeding key interaction data directly in their CRM [customer relationship management] systems or through e-mailed notifications when interesting account activity occurs, you are giving them just-in-time input on steps to take in the account. It allows them to respond to customer clues, not just push.

Bardoliwalla comments: "Web analytics is increasingly being combined with content creation, whereby companies are seeking to explicitly instrument every portion of their Web presence, not just the more explicit monetization channels such as shopping carts."

This Much Data Equals Better Visualization Tools

"Many Eyes," a site that IBM's Collaborative User Experience research group launched in 2007, allows anyone on the Web to use data visualization tools and then share summary results with others.[10]

The Many Eyes site says:

> It is that magical moment we live for: an unwieldy, unyielding data set is transformed into an image on the screen, and suddenly the user can

perceive an unexpected pattern. As visualization designers, we have witnessed and experienced many of those wondrous sparks. But in recent years, we have become acutely aware that the visualizations and the sparks they generate take on new value in a social setting. Visualization is a catalyst for discussion and collective insight about data.

Some of the artistic expressions allow users to:

- See relationships among data points in a scatter plot or network diagram
- Compare a set of values in a bar chart or a histogram
- Track rises and falls over time via a line or stack graph
- See the parts of a whole via a pie chart or a tree map
- Analyze text using a word tree or a tag cloud
- See the world using various maps

Bardoliwalla says Many Eyes is bringing capabilities to the masses that "vendors like Tableau, QlikTech, and Spotfire [now Tibco] have been offering for a while to enterprises to spice up their analytical graphics."

This Much Data Equals Massive Storage Requirements

You cannot talk about analytics and data management without thinking about the explosion in storage needs. The research firm IDC estimates that enterprises double their storage needs every 18 months. E-mail, video, and other rich media files are, of course, growing rapidly. Adding to that are multiple backups to meet a growing set of compliance requirements.

So why was Enrique Salem, the chief executive of Symantec, which sells storage, telling customers to stop buying storage? At a conference, he told the audience to focus instead on "storage resource management, thin provisioning, data deduplication, and intelligent archiving."[11]

One of the hottest areas in storage is "deduplication." Take e-mail— large attachments are stored in each recipient's mail box and archived. Deduplication technology can reduce the attachments to one instance stored. The technology is compelling to buyers; with that level of compression, not only can they reduce their storage needs but they also can move away from older tape archiving to disk storage. The market was compelling enough to EMC that it started, and won, a bidding war with NetApp for deduplication vendor Data Domain in 2009.

"Thin provisioning" is a concept from manufacturing markets; it refers to a just-in-time supply of storage to ensure that it is being utilized efficiently before more is ordered. Thin provisioning applies to internal storage, but another hot area is use of cloud-based storage (see more on clouds in Chapter 18)—which allows for just-in-time and pay-per-use storage. The economics of many cloud storage providers, such as Amazon and Nirvanix, are also extremely competitive—often many times cheaper than the total cost of storage from traditional outsourcers, such as IBM and HP.

There is also growing market appreciation about how much data is truly static. Although the number varies from site to site, some estimates say that 80 percent of data on high-speed drives is almost never accessed and could be moved to less-expensive storage tiers. Likewise, plenty of data does not change after minutes of its creation. This is leading to backup strategies to focus primarily on the data that changes. It is also opening up tiering opportunities to store much of the static data in cheaper formats.

This Much Data Equals Predictive Powers

We see in Chapter 21 how BP is using predictive analytics in its refinery asset management and maintenance. FICO, previously known as Fair Isaac Corporation, has helped hundreds of customers in the financial services industry make practical use of predictive analytics. Perhaps most famously, it provides the FICO score, whose algorithms help companies manage risk by predicting consumers' likelihood of repaying debt.

Says Dr. Mark Greene, chief executive of FICO: "Banks and insurance companies use our tools to identify fraud and other patterns. That use of analytics technology saves them hundreds of millions of dollars. But just as exciting is when marketing professionals in consumer industries use our tools to make money by modeling likely customer behavior."

Best Buy, the electronics retailer, is one example. The company has made an art form out of customer segmentation. It talks in terms of "Buzz" customers—young gadget enthusiasts—and "Jill" stores aimed at suburban moms.

Beyond this high-level segmentation, Best Buy has 15-plus terabytes of data on over 75 million customers: products they have bought; neighborhoods they live in from shipping addresses and rebate checks; often credit and employment histories. Its sophisticated analytics has allowed it to identify that a sliver—just 7 percent of its customers—drive 43 percent of the company's overall sales volume. So valuable to the company are these individuals that it would take approximately 39 "Uncommitted Customers," (which account for approximately 12 percent of all customers), to replace the lost lifetime value of just one of the best customers.

FICO has allowed Best Buy to take that sophistication further. According to Greene, "Best Buy has built thousands of customer-product correlations. As an example, the Buzz customer is five times more likely to buy a digital camera 30 days after he buys an MP3 player."

Best Buy has also used FICO models to build a sophisticated lifetime value model that factors in a host of customer behaviors.

Besides customer value, Best Buy analyzes factors such as:

- *Promotional sensitivity.* Which customers are price conscious and promotion driven?
- *Channel preferences.* Which customers prefer to interact online versus in-store?
- *Ability to buy.* Which customers have disposable income?
- *Technology adoption.* Which customers are likely to buy new technology ahead of the mainstream?

Says Greene, "Finding the patterns around 75 million customers and tens of thousands of products and likely reaction to thousands of promotions—like a 15 percent off coupon or free shipping—is what we help Best Buy model."

One area FICO has not been able to help Best Buy predict is when a customer is likely to walk into one of its stores. Most retail marketers are extremely envious of airline and other travel companies that actually know when the customer is likely to arrive. If we could set aside the privacy issues, it would be a great opportunity for FICO to discuss with BP its "people tracker" capability showcased in Chapter 21.

Recap

A wide range of analytical tools and technologies is available to enterprises today. Particularly encouraging is the progress around unstructured analytics, predictive analytics, and data visualization.

Of course, recent misses in economic forecasting have reemphasized the need for "human intelligence." For that reason, it is nice to see a new generation of analytical "artists" like Paul Kedrosky emerge and the general move to a decision-, not data-centric, analytical framework.

In the next chapter, we see how the National Hurricane Center, a polymath when it comes to the use of analytics, gathers data it needs for its forecasting, crunches the data through multiple, often conflicting models, and does an impressive job of improving its forecasts year on year.

CHAPTER 16

Polymath Profile #6:
National Hurricane Center

James Franklin has science, not finance, degrees from MIT. He is much more comfortable talking in engineering and military terms than about dollars and cents. His language includes "platforms," and acronyms such as AMSU, which he kindly expands for the uninitiated as "Advanced Microwave Sounding Unit."

Franklin is the branch chief at the National Hurricane Center (NHC) in Miami, Florida, part of the National Oceanic and Atmospheric Administration (NOAA). "We are forecasters, of course—but not the financial kind," he explains. Nonetheless, he should be a role model to every financial analyst because his forecasts keep improving year on year, while the recent economic "hurricane" caught most business forecasters off by miles.

Another reason that he should be emulated is because his team's forecasts provide significant return on investment. Although most of the attention goes to hurricanes when they make landfall and cause chaos, his team's contribution is even more valuable: They help reduce the "false positives," so that at-risk areas do not have to be evacuated unless absolutely necessary.

The NHC updates on its Web site every six hours a "cone of uncertainty" for every major storm it is tracking. The narrow end of the cone shows where the storm is now; the wide end of the cone shows where it will likely be in five days. The track is created based on the past five years of forecast data and error rates.

And most years, the track path accuracy improves. The track forecast error in the 1980s, 48 hours out, was 225 nautical miles. Today, that error is a little less than 100 nautical miles. The track forecast is used by the NHC to declare hurricane watches and warnings depending on likely time and location of landfall. Those guidelines are interpreted by state and local authorities to announce evacuations, and that triggers a series of emergency civic and security services. Low-lying areas and those expected to get dangerous storm surges usually receive mandatory evacuation notices. If evacuations can be minimized, so can emergency services, not to mention panic shopping, and other community disruption. Over the years, the improvements in track forecasts have amounted to hundreds of miles of coastline not evacuated and millions of dollars saved in emergency services.

Of course, the savings to local communities vary dramatically depending on location. Compare an evacuation of a neighborhood in Miami with one in a less populated area, for example, in rural Texas. Franklin would rather accountants worry about those financial numbers around savings in emergency services; he focuses more on human numbers and their safety. Better forecasts translate to earlier warnings so that people have more time to respond or evacuate.

Data Sources and Models

To deliver those forecasts, the NHC team takes an invasive approach to collecting a wide variety of external, real-time data. Too much business forecasting today is based on internal and historical data or looks at Google or external sources, such as Bloomberg and Gartner for its primary data.

Franklin's team, however, goes to the source and utilizes several platforms:

- *Satellites.* Geostationary satellites that are always in the same position with respect to the rotating Earth give a big-picture view of storms. The team supplements this information with data from lower polar-orbiting satellites
- *Data buoys.* Buoys in waters around the world collect data on wind speed and direction, wave information, air/water temperature, and sea-level pressure. They communicate the collected data via the geostationary satellites. The NHC uses information from the buoys throughout the year; individual sailors access the buoys to ascertain local conditions.
- *Dropsondes.* Dropsondes are weather reconnaissance devices that are parachuted from planes. They have a short life as they descend at 2,500 feet a minute through a storm. But at $750 each, they are a bargain; their sensors transmit pressure, temperature, and humidity data. As the storm batters them mercilessly in their downward paths, the data relayed by their GPS chips also allows for calculation of wind information.
- *"Hurricane Hunters."* Brave men and women fly the "Hunters" into storms to collect data. The U.S. Air Force maintains a fleet of 10 WC-130

planes—modified and fortified cargo planes, which account for the bulk of the sorties. NOAA's P-3 Orions and Gulfstream IV are used mostly for research but also help on forecasting as storms threaten to make landfall. These planes carry Doppler radars to provide a three-dimensional description of a storm, from sea level to the storm's top.

The air pressure, humidity, temperature, wind, and other data collected from each platform needs to be scrubbed for historical error rates. Then the information is processed using multiple forecast models, both for redundancy and for validation.

Some of the models are three-dimensional. Since storms change course by the minute, the higher resolution the grids on the models, the better the accuracy. Like high-resolution TV screens, high-resolution grids require more computing power. And that is *super*computing power based on IBM Power 575 Systems, rated at 69.7 trillion calculations per second. These computers are 30 times as fast as those available just a decade ago. And yet the accuracy could be even better.[1]

Data Products

The NHC next synthesizes the conflicting and complex data from its models into usable data for average citizens. It packages its reports (in Franklin's words, its "products") in the 11 text and 7 graphical formats shown in Table 16.1.

These reports have a wide range of users. The text-based ones are handy for reporters to read on radio and TV weather bulletins. Citizens in the likely path of the storms avidly follow the graphic products on the NHC Web site. In addition, Web sites such as Stormpulse.com and TV meteorologists take raw data from the NHC and present it with their own layer of visualization, some of which makes for stunning graphics.

Take the Public Advisory text product shown in Figure 16.1. Issued every six hours for active cyclones (intense storm systems), it gives the cyclone position in latitude and longitude coordinates, its distance from a well-known reference point, and its current direction and speed of motion. Each advisory includes the maximum sustained winds and the estimated or measured minimum central pressure. It also provides a general description of the predicted track and intensity of the cyclone over the next 24 to 48 hours. When warnings are in effect, the advisory also includes information on potential storm tides, rainfall or tornadoes associated with the cyclone, and any pertinent weather observations.

The bulletin in Figure 16.1 was advisory 19 for a September 2009 system named Fred, which reached hurricane speeds at sea, then

TABLE 16.1 August 2009 National Hurricane Center Product Description

Text Products

a	Tropical Cyclone Public Advisory
b	Tropical Cyclone Forecast Advisory
c	Tropical Cyclone Discussion
d	Tropical Cyclone Surface Wind Speed Probabilities
e	Tropical Cyclone Update
f	Tropical Cyclone Position Estimate
g	Tropical Cyclone Watch Warning Product
h	Aviation Tropical Cyclone Advisory
i	Tropical Weather Outlook
j	Special Tropical Weather Outlook
k	Monthly Weather Summary

Graphical Products

a	Tropical Cyclone Track Forecast Cone and Watch/Warning Graphic
b	Tropical Cyclone Surface Wind Speed Probabilities
c	Cumulative Wind History
d	Maximum 1-minute Wind Speed Probability Table
e	Tropical Cyclone Wind Field Graphic
f	Tropical Cyclone Storm Surge Probabilities
g	Experimental Graphical Tropical Weather Outlook

Source: National Hurricane Center.

progressively weakened and never threatened land. Hurricanes are assigned short, distinctive, human names like Fred. The World Meteorological Organization maintains pre-assigned names for each hurricane season for 10 global zones—the Atlantic Region being one zone. The names start with A, B, C, etc. and they are assigned to storms in that zone in the order of their first reaching hurricane speeds. There are regional sensitivities—in the Atlantic, there are several Hispanic names. Also names which start with Q, U, X, Y, Z are avoided in the Atlantic. Until 1978, all names were female. The names are rotated every six years unless a named hurricane was devastating in which case the name is retired.

The corresponding product called Track Forecast Cone and Watch/ Warning in Figure 16.2 shows advisory 19 in graphic detail. The cone represents the probable track of the center of a tropical cyclone over the next five days and is formed by enclosing the area swept out by a set of

```
ZCZC MIATCPAT2 ALL
TTAA00    KNHC    DDHHMM
BULLETIN
TROPICAL STORM FRED ADVISORY NUMBER 19
NWS TPC/NATIONAL HURRICANE CENTER MIAMI FL    AL072009

...FRED MOVING LITTLE AND WEAKENING...

AT 500 AM AST...0900 UTC...THE CENTER OF TROPICAL STORM FRED WAS
LOCATED NEAR LATITUDE 17.8 NORTH...LONGITUDE 33.6 WEST OR ABOUT
645 MILES...1040 KM...WEST-NORTHWEST OF THE CAPE VERDE ISLANDS.

FRED IS NEARLY STATIONARY. A TURN AROUND THE NORTH AND THEN THE
NORTH-NORTHWEST WITH A CONTINUED SLOW MOTION IS EXPECTED LATER
TODAY...FOLLOWED BY A TURN TOWARD THE NORTHWEST WITH AN INCREASE
IN FORWARD SPEED ON SUNDAY.

MAXIMUM SUSTAINED WINDS HAVE DECREASED TO NEAR 45 MPH...75
KM/HR...WITH HIGHER GUSTS. ADDITIONAL WEAKENING IS FORECAST
DURING THE NEXT 48 HOURS AND FRED COULD DEGENERATE INTO A REMNANT
LOW BY SUNDAY NIGHT.

TROPICAL STORM FORCE WINDS EXTEND OUTWARD UP TO 105 MILES...165
KM FROM THE CENTER.

THE ESTIMATED MINIMUM CENTRAL PRESSURE IS 1002 MB...29.59 INCHES.

...SUMMARY OF 500 AM AST INFORMATION...
LOCATION...17.9N   33.6W
MAXIMUM SUSTAINED WINDS...45 MPH
PRESENT MOVEMENT...STATIONARY
MINIMUM CENTRAL PRESSURE...1002 MB

THE NEXT ADVISORY WILL BE ISSUED BY THE NATIONAL HURRICANE CENTER
AT 1100 AM AST.

$$
FORECASTER BLAKE

NNNN
```

FIGURE 16.1 Hurricane Advisory
Source: National Hurricane Center.

circles (not shown) along the forecast track (at 12, 24, 36 hours, etc.). The size of each circle is defined to include two-thirds of historical official forecast errors over a five-year sample.

If Fred had been close to land (and the graph was in color), the associated coastal areas on the map would show color bands: red for hurricane warning, pink for hurricane watch, blue for tropical storm warning, and yellow for tropical storm watch. The black dots show the NHC forecast

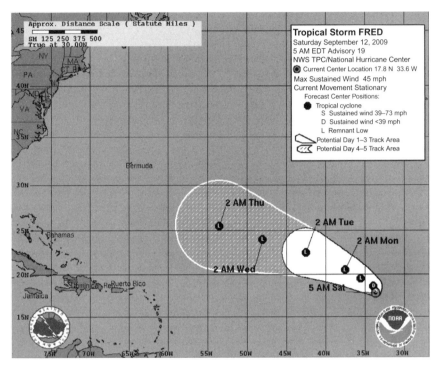

FIGURE 16.2 Tropical Storm Fred
Source: National Hurricane Center.

position of the center at the times indicated. The letter inside the dot indicates the forecast strength of the cyclone category: *D* for depression; *S* for storm; *H* for hurricane; *M* for major hurricane; or remnant *L* for low.

Continuous Improvement

Even as storm tracking and reporting have become better, the ability to predict storm intensity (using what is called the Saffir-Simpson Scale, with its 1 to 5 categorization based on the hurricane's intensity. Category 5 is the most intense, with sustained winds greater than 155 mph) has not improved as quickly. Since wind speed can vary by tens of miles and storm surges by several feet depending on storm intensity, that information would allow even more-accurate evacuation guidance.

This is where Franklin invokes the AMSU acronym. Microwaves are promising to help in that forecasting since they can penetrate clouds that infrared satellites cannot. They can provide a picture of the structure of the hurricane: more detail on the eyewall and rain bands. Forecasters can use knowledge of this structure to make better intensity forecasts.

How about using unmanned aircraft? Someday, says Franklin. Now it is still more efficient to have manned flights. Aren't those flights hairy? Earlier in his career, Franklin flew on close to 100 hurricane-penetrating missions. On the way to the hurricanes, most flights are calm and boring. However, once you approach them, Franklin can tell stories that would make most of us cancel our next commercial flight and the one after that. As the crews who fly the "Hunters" like to say in understated fashion: "Air sickness is just part of flying."

Although most businesses cannot afford the supercomputers and the satellites Franklin's team has access to, they can increasingly leverage powerful enough analytical computing resources, such as Oracle's Exadata, discussed in Chapter 15.

And how the hurricane team works provides lessons for every business forecaster: they relentlessly (and bravely) pursue primary, external data; they drive to measure and improve on errors in forecasting and they build plenty of redundancy into models in their estimating process.

Recap

The NHC reaches out to a wide range of data sources in hostile circumstances. It apples multiple, conflicting models to interpret the data. The data is presented in multiple formats, depending on audience sophistication. The forecasts keep improving year after year.

For all these reasons, Franklin and his team at the NHC have earned the right to be called polymaths around analytics.

CHAPTER 17

Networks Again: Communities, Crowds, Contracts, and Collaboration

When Charles Handy, the management philosopher, wrote his seminal book *The Age of Unreason* in 1990, he envisaged enterprises moving to the "shamrock organization." The three leaves of the shamrock represent core management, a long-term but contractual talent pool, and a transient, flexible workforce.[1]

Handy was prescient, but in his wildest dreams he could not have envisaged that the third leaf of the flexible workforce would have several branches of its own: communities, crowds, and contractors. He also could not have forecast a whole generation of collaboration technologies to "coordinate the shamrock" that Professor Andrew McAfee at Harvard Business School calls Enterprise 2.0.

Let's look at how communities and crowds are evolving, how outsourcing is morphing, and how good old-fashioned employees continue to be a major part of what Cisco appropriately calls the Human Network. First, we look at the customer angle of the human network, and then we turn to the talent part.

Aren't Communities a Relic from Communism?

"Don't forget your day job," advises IBM's internal employee guidelines on social computing.[2] Most companies are even more restrictive—they do not even allow access to social networks from work.

Avon is bucking the trend. As it grows its *mark* brand aimed at Gen Y women, it is making Facebook an integral part of the day job of its reps. Starbucks' community site MyStarbucksIdea garnered 65,000 ideas from its social network—in its first year. More about both Avon and Starbucks in a bit.

Many CIOs roll their eyes when they hear anything that starts with "social." But surely "thar's gold in them thar hills." As of April 2010, the Facebook community had over 400 million registered users—fairly active ones with 35 million updating their status on a daily basis. Twitter had more than 100 million registered users who broadcasted an estimated 10 billion tweets in 2009. In both cases, the numbers are outdated by the minute—Twitter is estimated to add 300,000 new users a day.

Here are the typical objections from many corporate executives:

Facebook and Twitter have no business model—if there was value in these communities surely they themselves would be swimming in money.

And:

Whatever payback there is from social applications would be small compared to the time employees would waste on social networks.

Ashton Kutcher is out to prove them wrong. The actor with the most followers on Twitter—four million plus—could bask in the ego trip that such large a following could encourage. He could continue to focus on his acting career. But he is also on a mission to monetize the following for clients such as Pepsi. Kutcher's company, Katalyst, is helping Pepsi with a "DEWmocracy" campaign around its Mountain Dew brand. It lets Facebook members pick not only the flavor, name, color, and label of new sodas but eventually the in-store merchandising and the ad agency, in an online bake-off. Fans can also submit their own ads.

Kutcher tells FastCompany: "My theory is, you have to engage the constituency and let them be the voice of the brand ... I help connect people to the Mountain Dew brand so they can be creative with it."[3]

Frank Cooper, chief marketing officer for beverages for Pepsi North America, while delighted with the campaign, provides more fodder for the cynics. "A lot of senior managers at consumer brands feel like their role is to control the communications around a brand. They are uncomfortable with the transparency of social media because people will say negative things about you," he says.

The objections continue:

Look, you have to admire the technical architecture to support scale that Facebook and Twitter are building. How do you roll out new features to 400 million users and not bring the site down? However, with little revenue, with disgruntled customers, and with time-wasting employees— tell us again why we should be thinking about communities and crowds?

They should talk to Paul Greenberg, the bestselling CRM author who has recently written about the emerging social customer:

The pivotal year was 2004—that was the year in which the Edelman Trust Barometer showed skyrocketing trust in "people like me"—and dropping trust in various institutions. In 2003, "people like me" was 22%. In 2004, it was 51%, and those trusted peers have never looked back since. By 2009, that number was 58%.

Enter Social Customer Relationship Management

The first edition of Greenberg's book *CRM—At the Speed of Light*[4] came out in 2001; the fourth came out in 2009. He consults, blogs, and is in continuous touch with trends around customer-facing technologies:

People could now communicate with those trusted peers in real time through text messaging, social networks like Facebook, channels like Twitter, using Skype or just via an old-fashioned phone call. How we communicate has gone real time, free of location and via multiple channels.

We can communicate with "people like me" who we knew were similar in nature to us—by how they congregated on the Web—which communities, etc. They were invisible to us before."

The expectation was raised that institutions—be they social, business, political—would be responsive in the same way our newly minted friends were. They would respond in real time, they would be transparent and honest, like our friends—known or not—were. That they would be authentic.

Another pivotal point came in 2007 with the MyBarackObama.com site a.k.a. MyBo, which became a hub for volunteer activity ranging from fundraising, to getting out the vote, to issues-oriented meet-ups and digital petition signings. Obama's team understood the nature of these new peer relationships driven by the Web.

In one month they raised $55 million online! And people say there is no money in these social networks?

Enter the dawn of social CRM, which is the subtitle for the fourth edition of his book:

Some businesses have started to recognize that this social customer needs to be treated differently than customers have been treated in the past. So, Twitter is being used as a customer service channel by companies like Comcast. Facebook was used to build the 3.5-million-strong Coca-Cola fan page. Procter & Gamble began to tap into its 600,000-mother Vocalpoint network. They recognized that this kind of access for the customers was not only invaluable to P&G for the knowledge they gained but also helped the customers feel like they had a say in what the company was doing—the kind of transparency that the social customer is looking for.

Social CRM is evolving from this acknowledgment that the customer is increasingly controlling the conversation. Where it differs from traditional CRM is pretty simple. "Classic" CRM was operational—it was based on improving the internal workings of a company, i.e., the processes and even the culture, so they could work on managing the customer's relationships with the company. It was transactional—companies pretty much focused on the purchasing history with the company. For example, an optimal customer was a loyal one—one who had a high customer lifetime value (CLV).

Social CRM is not operational—it's collaborative more often than not. It is based on the company and customer's interplay. It's no longer how do you manage a customer but how you engage that customer. What do you do to elevate the experience of that customer? It captures and acts on not just the transactions but the interactions between the customer and the company. It measures not just customer lifetime value (CLV) but customer referral value (CRV). In other words, the social CRM-savvy company understands the social customer as someone with a network that he or she influences. It then invests in trying to provide their customers with what they need to become not just loyal but advocates—social customers who will evangelize on the company's behalf with their peers."

You have to be careful not to go overboard. The social customer is typically a small percentage—today—of the bell curve of customers. And this customer is not easy to deal with—they bristle at corporate spin. But increasingly, the social customer is the trend setter. And it leads to areas where there are few answers. Do you utilize social channels to communicate directly with your customer and to provide access "pipes" to your customers so that they can communicate and collaborate in return? Do you capture the data—structured and unstructured—that is so important to aiding (not substituting for) insight into those customers so that they can enhance the experience?

Now let's look at the Avon experience.

"Ding-Dong, It's the Avon Lady"

How do you reinvent for Gen Y women a 100-year-old model of direct selling? Avon is moving from door to door to Facebook friend to friend with its *mark* brand, targeting Gen Y women.

Annemarie Frank, who leads eCommerce activities for Avon's *mark* division, says, "My challenge is to go where my target market is hanging out. And guess what? They aren't on e-mail, they're on Facebook."

So *mark* developed a social CRM Facebook application to help its reps engage with their friends. It's was only a matter of time before somebody took advantage of that vibrant 400-million-plus-strong community.

Frank explains how it works:

> *Our reps have a **mark** Facebook application added to their profile. That shows them **mark** promotions and a list of their friends who might be interested in this content—the app makes suggestions based on location, demographics, interests, activities ... anything on someone's Facebook profile. That makes it really easy to make a word-of-mouth referral.*
>
> *The invitation brings the prospect to a microsite created for this event. It brings together the who, what, when, where for this event, and gives her an opportunity to respond or even add it to her own profile to share with her friends. Or she can check out **mark**'s other offers ... even signing up to become a rep herself.*

Whenever a friend expresses interest in this event, her information is recorded in salesforce.com who referred her and which keywords were used to drive the referral. The *mark* team can automatically generate e-mails, kick off workflow, and run reports on exactly what's working and what's not in a social marketing campaign:

> *The best part is the analytics. We can see which reps have been most active at generating word-of-mouth referrals. We can see which campaigns are getting traction—a mix of product promotions and general interest items seems to work best for **mark**'s community. And we can see what keywords are matching in Facebook, so we can refine how we target. And we're encouraged by the results—we're seeing a much higher response rate and double our average order size.*

A cloud solution provider called Appirio (described more in Chapter 18) helped Avon build an application that links the salesforce.com platform with Facebook and Avon's back-end provisioning system. Ryan Nichols, VP of cloud strategy at Appirio says, "Every brand is thinking about how to use social media to engage their community. It's exciting to help companies like Avon use cloud platforms like Facebook and Force.com, salesforce.com's platform (explained more in Chapter 19) to make this happen faster and cheaper than ever before possible."

Now let's look at Starbucks' experience.

Starbucks' Pledge 5

Walk in with an "I voted" sticker and Starbucks gave you a free cup of brewed coffee on U.S. Election Day in 2008. In fact, if you walked in that day, voter or not, U.S. citizen or not, you got a free cup just for standing in line at a store.

The idea to celebrate voting had come from the company's community site MyStarbucksIdea. The company turned it into a nice slogan: "You vote and good things happen. Sounds like democracy to me!" on its blog— referring to the fact that members of the community propose ideas and the community also votes. Each idea averages 10 votes from others in the community.

Chris Bruzzo, VP of brand, content, and online, then realized that Inauguration Day in January was going to be another day to bring out the community spirit. Feeding off President-elect Obama's call for national service, an idea was born: Pledge five hours of community service, and celebrate that over a free cup of coffee. The free promotion would run for five days around the inauguration. HandsOn Network supplied a nation-wide list of thousands of local volunteer opportunities.

This time Starbucks wanted not just people walking into stores and pledging but also its million-person Facebook community to participate. Of course, there were a few more viewers once Oprah Winfrey talked about it on her show.

Three weeks later, Starbucks was live with the Pledge 5 site. Narinder Singh, cofounder of Appirio that also helped on this project says, "When Chris first called, my reaction was—is it not too early to do this for the 2012 election? Then it sunk in we had three weeks to get it done!"

Three weeks to provision infrastructure, develop a commerce site, test it, and unleash it to potentially millions of viewers? In a company as big as Starbucks?

Starbucks also went with the Force.com platform the team did not have to worry about infrastructure. Says Bruzzo: "We knew that would build quickly and scale infinitely." The team from Appirio architected the solution, while Bruzzo's team designed the user interface elements and assisted with coding.

Communities are not born overnight. But once they scale, they can be turned into idea machines. MyStarbucksIdea garnered 65,000 ideas in its first year—from complete strangers who scored each idea based on its merits and gave Starbucks not just the ideas but also the customer feedback loop.

First Generation of "True Customer Interaction" Applications

Of course, the objections to the Avon and Starbucks applications are likely to be that they are "light" applications. Readers may wonder when the last time a really important system was built in three weeks.

They would be missing Paul Greenberg's point. Traditional information technology systems, even first-generation CRM systems, never really interacted with customers. And if they did, it was often through the lens of a call center experience, usually a negative one. Light as it may be, social CRM is the first generation of true customer interaction applications.

There is, of course, the reverse—the impact of upsetting a social customer. The adage used to be "An unhappy customer tells 10 others about his/her bad experience." Now it can be far worse.

Greenberg, again:

Social customers know that they have access to the ears of potentially millions of peers like them and they know that those peers are going to be responsive to their anger if it's justified. For example, Canadian country musician Dave Carroll had his guitar smashed by United Airlines baggage handlers on a flight through Chicago. He tried for over a year to get United to make restitution, around $1,200, but United ignored his pleas.

That is, until he wrote a rather catchy tune now immortalized as "United Breaks Guitars" and posted it on YouTube. It became an overnight sensation with, as of late 2009, over 6 million views. It was a major embarrassment for United, which finally mea culpaed ... and then promptly lost his baggage again on his way to a RightNow User conference. Ironically, this is a vendor focused on customer relationship management and he was presenting on how United failed at customer service!

It's not just United Airlines. Bank of America, Southwest Airlines (their experience with Kevin Smith is described in Chapter 4) and others are finding social customers can be passionate advocates—or just as easily the exact opposite.

You Call This a Light Application?

Almost to mock the fact that communities focus on light topics, a *New York Times* article describes how two different groups are trying to share intellectual property. Eco-Patent Commons is supported by IBM, Nokia, Pitney Bowes, and Sony, among others. Green Xchange was started by the Creative Commons, a nonprofit organization, in collaboration with Nike and Best Buy. With slight differences, both groups allow companies to contribute intellectual property for communal use.

Green Xchange plans to allow contributors to charge users a fixed annual licensing fee; contributors also can restrict any licensing by rivals or for competitive use. In addition, even if no annual fee is charged, patent users must register so there is a record of who is using what technology.

The efforts are bringing to light thorny conflicts between which intellectual property brings competitive advantage and which would be better from collaborative advantage. The article quotes Andrew King, a professor at the Tuck School of Business at Dartmouth: "Deciding which patents to pledge or license to a commons requires that the legal counsel, R.&D. staff, business unit, and corporate sustainability groups all work together, and most organizations just aren't set up for that."[5]

Nobody Ever Accused SAP of Being a Light Application

SAP has been cultivating and growing three communities around its enterprise application products—with more than two million members. The SAP Developer Network (SDN) focuses on technical content; the Business Process Expert (BPX) focuses on process, implementation, and solution issues; and the Business Objects Community (BOC) focuses on business intelligence and information-management topics—more around its acquisition of the analytics vendor, Business Objects.

The communities have evolved differently but broadly offer members moderated forums, blogs, software downloads, and wikis to allow for open communication.

Jim Spath at Black & Decker (since merged with the Stanley Works) says: "SAP has built out an amazingly lively space for all manner of dialog to commence, not simply questions and answers. SDN has expanded my network of contacts beyond an existing peer circle in the Americas SAP Users Group (ASUG)."

Unlike the GE community Support Central described in Chapter 3 and Cognizant 2.0 described in Chapter 6, which are focused primarily on internal users, SAP's communities bring together users, consultants, and other SAP partners. The variation in skills and, particularly, interests in such a wide group is significant.

Spath says, "Many of us who tackled basic SAP problems a decade ago find our current needs are typically too complex to just list on forums."

He's not interested in SDN or ASUG forum replies that say "Call us, we can help you," as he believes in expanding community-based knowledge. So he leverages the network and communicates with a growing global peer community on Web casts, chat streams like Twitter, and face-to-face events.

To improve the richness of the conversation, SAP rewards members for contributions. Well-written blogs can earn up to 120 points (which are used for staff recognition). Video blogs earn up to 300. SAP also encourages members to pose technical questions, and it rewards answers: 10 points for "resolved my problems," 6 for "very helpful," and so on. It then honors the top contributors by showcasing them live. Many work for SAP, but most work for its partners and customers.

One SAP executive was quoted as saying, "Average time from question to answer is less than 30 minutes. I wish our own customer support channels were that effective."

So why not move more or even all support effort to the community?

In effect, it has already been happening. The top 10 contributors to SDN are employees of Infosys (which led with a total of 110,786 points between August 2008 and July 2009) and other outsourcing firms, such as Wipro, IBM, and Accenture. These firms are working on SAP projects and SAP application management contracts—customers are paying billions for these services. So, in effect, customers are funding the SDN and other SAP communities.

This leads to two questions:

1. Are the employees of firms like Wipro sharing client-specific intellectual property proprietary with the community?
2. If the community is moving effort from SAP's support channels, shouldn't SAP be reducing its own maintenance charges to customers?

SAP's community guidelines clearly state that "You must have copyright ownership of all material that you post on our forums" and "You take responsibility for your own postings and use the information provided on this site at your own risk."

Spath points out: "Users typically take on system abusers, by nominating themselves as moderators and then doing required housekeeping and host work. SAP rewards such pro-community efforts."

But on the question of reducing maintenance charges, SAP deflects the issue. As communities mature, questions of who funds them, what to do about shared intellectual property, and other issues will need better resolution.

Let's now hear from Thomas Malone at MIT, who has been studying the "genetics" of these new human networks.

"Genomes" of Communities and Crowds

Ask MIT Professor Malone what has changed most since he wrote his 2004 book *The Future of Work* and you expect him to say "more mobile workers, more telepresence or shifting talent pools around the world."[6] But he responds with "crowdsourcing."

During his work at MIT's Center for Collective Intelligence, the professor and his colleagues have gathered 250 examples of Web-enabled "collective intelligence," including Google, Wikipedia, eBay, Linux, and the Netflix Prize project. After analyzing these examples, they have identified building blocks ("the genes of collective intelligence," Malone calls them) that are combined and recombined in various ways in different collective intelligence systems.

Figure 17.1 is adapted from a white paper he coauthored and shows how the genes are sequenced for Innocentive, which throws out "challenges" to a scientific community, and for Threadless, which invites its audience to design T-shirts. Malone explains: "These two genomes are nearly identical. The only difference is the addition of the intermediate Decide by the Crowd in Threadless. For InnoCentive, such a step probably would not make sense, because the company with the problem that needs solving typically would not want the crowd to see all the entries."[7]

Question	Gene
Who	Crowd
	Hierarchy
Why	Money
	Love
	Glory
How—Create	Collections
	Contest
	Collaboration
How—Decide	Group Decision
	Voting
	Averaging
	Consensus
	Prediction market
	Individual decision
	Market
	Social network

Example	What		Who	Why	How
InnoCentive	Create	Scientific solutions	Crowd	Money	Contest
	Decide	Who gets rewards	Management	Money	Hierarchy
Threadless	Create	T-shirt designs	Crowd	Money Love	Contest
	Decide	Which designs are best	Crowd	Love	Averaging
	Decide	Which designs to use	Management	Money	Hierarchy

FIGURE 17.1 Genetics of Communities
Source: © 2009 Thomas W. Malone, Robert Laubacher, and Chrysanthos Dellarocas. Malone, T. W., Laubacher, R., & Dellarocas, C. "The Collective Intelligence Genome," Sloan Management Review, Spring 2010, 51, 3, 21–31 (Reprint No. 51303. Also available at: http://sloanreview.mit.edu/the-magazine/articles/2010/spring/51303/the-collective-intelligence-genome/#1.)

What's noticeable about the "how" genes are how recent technologies, such as prediction markets and social networks, are facilitating certain responses we could not have attempted in 2004. Malone says: "As computing and communication capabilities continue to improve, we will have plenty of other new tools."

What's also interesting around the "why" genes are answers like love and glory. Clearly, those are important in why people work for a living but they appear higher than money in many crowd models.

Malone says: "There is still much work to be done to identify the conditions under which of these genes are useful—but our base of 250 'genomes' gives other companies a framework to start evaluating their own crowd strategies."

Love and glory are some of the reasons why people participate in communities? Hmm . . . and businesses are supposed to rely on such talent?

We Are Supposed to Rely on Love and Glory in Our Talent?

Many enterprises are rightly wary of communities. They may be noble, but what do they have to do with business and technology? And, surely, people who are active in communities and crowds must have too much time on their hands? They are either unemployed or neglecting the jobs they are getting paid to do. Remember the IBM guideline about not neglecting your day job?

Now let's meet a living, breathing, very active community member: Dennis Howlett.

"What lifestyle is he talking about?" would be the reaction of the tens of thousands who know Dennis Howlett when he says, "We moved to the mountains of Andalucía in southern Spain for the lifestyle."

They know him as the man who never sleeps.

Although physically located a three-hour drive and at least two flights from most major international cities, Howlett is remarkably influential in several communities around the world:

- He writes a well-read blog on enterprise software for ZDNet (the community discussed in Chapter 9). It is not unusual for some of his posts to get 20,000 views over a couple of days.
- He is a founding member (along with the author of this book) of two blogging groups called Enterprise Irregulars and Enterprise Advocates, which attracted other software bloggers. He set up the blogging platform for both groups. They, in turn, get their own thousands of followers.

- He is part of the SAP Mentor program—a respected group of practitioners and influencers SAP polls to get industry perspectives.

Spath, introduced above, describes his interaction with Howlett:

I've dealt with Dennis on multiple projects in and out of the SAP Mentor program. He leverages his access to the highest management levels at SAP to forward his agenda, which I happen to agree with for the most part. He also works with the user community down to simple tribe building exercises like the SAP Community Network video competition we ran.

In a prior career, Howlett was a practicing accountant in the United Kingdom. He has followers in that community with his Accman blog and as content advisor to the IT Faculty of the Institute of Chartered Accountants in the United Kingdom and Wales, which has more than 8,000 registered members.

Howlett is constantly conducting Webinars and talking to someone or another in one of those communities or at his consulting clients on Skype video conference. When he travels to industry conferences, he takes plenty of photos and videos and posts them on Flickr and YouTube. One of his quick-and-dirty user videos shot outside a café on a rainy Amsterdam afternoon attracted more than 1,500 views over three days. He has 5,000 followers on Twitter, and he tweets at all hours.

Most of his tools are free—YouTube, Twitter, video editing in iMovie, LiveStream for live broadcasting—or near free: He pays $20 a month for Skype, $25 a year for the "pro" version of Flickr, and $75 a year for the blogging software WordPress, which he has helped many a blogger migrate to.

Video equipment is one area Howlett has invested in. He started out using his Smartphone, so again arguably free, graduated to the $150 Flip, and then to the $500 Canon Vixia HF10. He finally invested $4,500 in a Canon XL2, Sennheiser wireless microphones, and other broadcast-quality paraphernalia but explains that it "allows me to compete with the $100,000 and up equipment used by CNN and other networks."

It's fair to say that he has a bigger following than individual analysts at research firms like Gartner or Forrester.

Says Simon Griffiths, who works for the ERP vendor Syspro 5,000 miles due south:

Dennis's comments and analysis are applicable in many contexts. From a South African perspective, his articles provide a "third-party insight" that is relevant and applicable, and not "too far out." The knowledge

*and understanding I get from his unique blend of accounting, journal-
ism and programming have been applied in my ERP consulting engagements and in formulating plans for the businesses where I work; most
currently in terms of Software-as-a-Service [SaaS] opportunities.*

And, yes, what about the lifestyle he moved for? Howlett elaborates:

*Food and drink with a dozen or so friends is deeply ingrained into the
Andalucían lifestyle, influenced by ancient Phoenician, Arabic, and
Roman culture. It's about deep, rich riojas, rougher vinos de casa,
pungent olive oils, salt baked sea bass, a thousand kinds of air cured
ham, and the ubiquitous gazpacho.*
     And yes, siestas—contrary to myth, I do sleep.

Then There Are Contracted Crowds, Better Known as Outsourcing

Things were simpler when Charles Handy wrote about the shamrock organization. Outsourced talent used to come in a couple of flavors: contractors
hired on a one-off basis and project teams typically on fixed-price contracts
from consulting firms.

Now you hear of "build-operate-transfer"—where an outsourcer builds
a capability, matures it over a couple of years, and then hands it over to
the client. You hear of "rebadging"—where, in reverse, outsourcers take
over some of the client's employees in a transfer. In SaaS, which we discuss
in Chapter 18, software and hosting and application services are bundled
together. In business process outsourcing, entire processes are outsourced
and priced per check or invoice processed. Dell and others offer multiyear
desk-side support contracts to companies, while Best Buy's Geek Squad
offer one-time support visits.

There are projects with bonuses and penalties based on timeliness,
budget compliance, customer satisfaction, and even business results. For
legal reasons, to keep them separate from employees, few companies ever
hire a contractor directly. That has led to the emergence of staffing firms
and professional employment organizations (PEO) to manage administration of contractors. Outsourced talent comes from everywhere, as Francisco
D'Souza described in Chapter 6. Even within a country, it is not unusual
for consulting projects to have 20 percent additional costs in consultant
travel expenses.

Of course, there is technology to keep all this straight. Fieldglass, based
in Chicago, Illinois, offers a unified technology platform to "acquire all types
of human capital, including contingent workers, service providers and direct

hires." Tools like those from Concur, based in Redmond, Washington, help make consultant expense tracking easier. BMC, based in Houston, Texas, offers service-level management software. Deltek, based in Herndon, Virginia, has verticalized ERP solutions to help outsourcers and service providers run their own operations.

The outsourcing vendor landscape itself is morphing significantly with the emergence of newer players, causing established players to rethink their business models. Let's look at one of these newcomers: Corefino.

It's a Plane, It's a Bird . . . It's an Outsourcer?

Karen Watts is describing the epiphany that led her to start Corefino, which she describes as a "twenty-first-century accounting solution":

> *CFOs have long nudged, even pushed their peers in manufacturing, HR, IT and other domains to outsource but have tended to keep their own operations in house. I grew up in that financial world where we worked our way up the management chain to controller and CFO. We drew comfort from cube after cube of head-down workers tirelessly crunching numbers, rechecking compliances, and performing "routine financials."*

Watt's wants to replace "the toxic combination of wasteful ERP installations matched with internal accounting staffs" with Corefino's three-part solution:

1. *Technology.* Incorporates more economical and flexible SaaS financial solutions (like FinancialForce.com and Intacct). This removes the technology headache of performing routine financial processes on-site.
2. *People.* Utilizes a scalable team of off-site Corefino accounting experts, each selected for their skill in a particular area, with each process passing from one expert to the next.
3. *Process.* Leverages Corefino's Triple-C Platform™, which is a Web-based database of more than 500 best practices and workflows across connect-correct-comply processes.

Dave Morrison, chief financial officer of Shop.com, a Corefino customer, says, "Corefino's about taking away that sinking feeling you have when lying in bed at night when you ask yourself, 'Are the auditors going to find something? Is everything in order?' A CFO should be looking for revenue flow, not worrying about the numbers."

Like Appirio, which is described in Chapter 18, Corefino is a new breed of service provider—wait, is it a service provider? Increasingly, the lines between software, services, and networks are blurring—it's about results.

What's Accenture Doing with Lego?

Over the years, Accenture's model of large teams of young staff members has been the butt of many jokes about school buses and snot faces. But their initiative with Bug Labs has nothing to do with young staff even though Bug's product could be called "Lego for the Geek."

Bug's product is an electric base to which you can literally snap in or snap out a touch-sensitive LCD screen, speaker, GPS unit, motion detector, and several other additions. As the company says, there is no need to "solder, learn solid state electronics, or go to China."

So what is Accenture, which thrives on complex systems development and outsourcing, doing with something that "uncomplex"? And what is a company that typically avoids much to do with hardware doing with this device?

Accenture is hoping its corporate clients use the device with its new Accenture Mobility Operated Services (AMOS) to track fleets and other logistics applications. And, in another departure, Accenture's fees will be transaction based, not based on its traditional billable hours model.

In fairness, Accenture will continue to get most of its $25-billion-plus revenue stream from complex ERP, business process outsourcing, and other revenue sources.

But then again, maybe it will not. Players like Cognizant are delivering application services with more economical talent pools around the world as we described in Chapter 6. Players like Amazon and Microsoft will be using the scale and efficiency of their massive cloud data centers (described in the next chapter) to change the economics of infrastructure outsourcing. And players like Appirio are trailblazing new paths with their services in the SaaS market.

So it is good Accenture is looking at different business models and products; that is its version of change and innovation.

Employees Are *Still* a Major Talent Category

In all this excitement—and fear—about communities and crowds and outsourcing, it is easy to forget that employees—remember them?—are still the biggest talent source for most companies and, of course, their outsourcers.

Is the human resources (HR) function innovating? Is HR technology morphing? Let's listen to two professionals who have spent their lives in HR World.

Bill Kutik has been a fixture in HR technology for decades now. He runs conferences, writes articles, and knows most senior HR vendor executives by their first name.

He is interviewing Arie Ball, VP of sourcing and talent acquisition at Sodexo, the large food service and facilities management company, on *The Bill Kutik Radio Show®*. Ball proceeds to talk about the role blogs, virtual worlds, and social networks play in her team's recruiting efforts:

> *On the Second Life career fair, we were targeting Gen Y candidates, and we thought we would get mostly technology candidates. Lo and behold, we attracted several hospitality candidates: all generations, experienced candidates. In the end, we hired a chef whose avatar was Chef Bellagio into one of our health care divisions.*

What a contrast to places where you still fill out paper employment applications!

Kutik wishes other companies leveraged as Ball is doing what Prof. Malone of MIT described earlier as "collective intelligence":

> *At the last HR technology conference I ran, someone in the audience asked in response to companies blocking network access for employees, "Twenty years ago, would you have asked employees to leave their Rolodex at home because they might call a friend? Now you're asking some employees to leave half their brains at home by cutting them off from their network."*
>
> *But HR is usually a laggard along with the legal department. Remember the corporate terror that ensued when employees first got access to the Internet. The market boomed in spyware, so HR could make sure employees weren't "wasting time" surfing the Internet. Or when e-mail first arrived in offices, HR fretted that some employee might write something inappropriate to the CEO. That usually wasn't a problem in those early days, since most CEOs had their administrative assistants screen and print out incoming e-mails!*
>
> *I saw recently a telling stat in a survey of companies which have established a "social media" policy. HR and marketing were involved in roughly the same proportion in defining the policy. But HR was 10 times more involved when there were violations of the policy. Which is understandable, but instead of just focusing on compliance, shouldn't HR, like marketing, use it to meet business goals?*

But there is a tidal wave of change coming. LinkedIn is replacing the old resume for both employers and employees. Tools like JobVite are letting employers create invitations to apply for jobs that employees, colleagues, etc., can publish to social networks like Facebook.

One area where Kutik has seen the HR market evolve nicely is around talent management:

I actually did some archaeological work and discovered the term "talent management" was first used by a vendor in 1998. But a decade later, it is now real. At the annual HR technology conference, our signature event is a "vendor shoot-out" where four vendors demo their software to a script and the audience votes. Last couple of years we have focused on talent management. This year two ERP vendors, Lawson and SAP, competed against two talent management specialists—Plateau and Salary.com. That is a sure sign of market maturation when the bigger vendors focus on a category.

Yes, you do to groom and grow a new breed of avatar talent like Chef Bellagio.

Jason Corsello is the vice president of the Center of Excellence at Knowledge Infusion, a specialty HR consulting firm. The firm helps clients develop talent management strategies. In his position, Corsello gets to see plenty of HR innovation at clients and at vendors:

Would you believe Utah as a hotbed of HR innovation?

Some of the most progressive HR technology innovation is happening well beyond Silicon Valley. Take HireVue based in Salt Lake City, Utah. They are bringing TiVo to HR. It's ideal for first-round interviews. (HireVue was described in detail in Chapter 5.)

Or just down the road in Provo, Utah, Entice Labs is transforming the way companies find skilled talent. Instead of waiting for employees to find the job opportunities at your company by sifting through job boards and career sites, Entice Labs uses job advertising technology to target the skilled talent for your company. Say you need to find a shoe designer for an upcoming new product. Entice Labs' TalentSeekr product will precision target sites such as industry blogs, social networks, or relevant sites where that talent hangs out. Passive sourcing [an industry term for finding candidates who may not be actively looking for another job], long foreseen as the holy grail of recruiting, is becoming reality.

Or Rypple, based in Toronto, Canada, which puts performance management in the hands of the employee, not the employer, by leveraging social networks and real-time interaction so individuals can

*immediately access performance feedback and opportunities to collabo-
rate and track personal and career development. So different from the
demeaning paperwork most companies make employees go through to
justify a 2.7% merit increase.*

Innovation is found not just in the vendor world. Corsello points to
examples in the corporate world:

*Many companies are experimenting in the use of mobile applications
for better workforce communication. Disney is using it to adjust its
hourly workforce. If one ride is experiencing heavier traffic than normal,
"associates" will communicate via Yammer and their mobile device for
additional support from other ride associates. Other staffers will also use
Yammer to communicate the operational health and even cleanliness
of the park.*

*We are seeing innovative HR groups involved in telepresence deci-
sions to reduce employee wear and tear from travel, data mining to
better analyze employee base patterns, in technology decisions around
work-at-home employees.*

*The days of HR buying technology to merely facilitate and automate
HR functions is over. HR-influenced technology, with SaaS as a key
delivery model, is extensible to all employees to drive more efficient and
effective people decisions.*

How Do All These Talent Pools Collaborate?

Oliver Marks, who writes the Collaboration 2.0 blog on ZDNet, is focused
on the challenge of integrating myriad sources of talent—some employees,
some at contracted outsourcers, and some in communities—and the wide
range of technologies they communicate with. "It is a jarring contrast,"
Marks explains. "Today's office is more likely to be mobile technology from
a car, or a VoIP call from a home office, but with the continued popularity
of Dilbert comics and the TV hit *The Office*, the old world of cubicles,
monitors, fax machines, and water coolers seems to be frozen in time."

Ross Mayfield has seen that transition from cubicle to car at SocialText,
the company he cofounded in 2001. In the decade since, his product has
become a polymath when it comes to collaboration software. Its platform
includes "Social networking, microblogging, wiki workspaces with integrated blogs, distributed spreadsheets, and a personal home page for every
user. Connectors to Microsoft SharePoint and Lotus Connections (from
Lotus) are also available."[8]

In homage to the PCs that became indistinguishable with cubicles in
the 1980s, Mayfield's spreadsheet was developed in collaboration with Dan

Bricklin. Bricklin is famous for having codeveloped VisiCalc, the first electronic spreadsheet, while he was a student at the Harvard Business School in the late 1970s.

One of the hottest places to collaborate these days is likely to be a Cisco telepresence room. Six people interact with six others thousands of miles away with life-size images on three 65-inch, 1080p resolution plasma screens. You can get really fancy with participants from other locations in a multipoint session with voice-activated switching of participants on the screens. This product is starting to make a dent in international travel.

Various Web conferencing tools allow for even larger virtual meetings. Tools such as Adobe Connect, Cisco's Webex, Citrix's GotoMeeting, IBM's Sametime, and Microsoft's Live Meeting offer facilities to allow hundreds of participants to collaborate

Of course, there are times when you want telepresence from the shop floor or you want to "virtually" walk over to someone in one of those dreaded cubicles who ignored the request to dial into the conference call. HeadThere, a start-up, has developed a videoconferencing robot called the Giraffe that can take you to those elusive destinations.

With giants like Cisco, IBM, Microsoft, and Adobe focused on the collaboration market, you would think it is a mature one. Professor Andrew McAfee at Harvard Business School disagrees. McAfee coined the term "Enterprise 2.0" in 2006 to describe the new world of collaboration. His recent book with the same title provides plenty of case studies on how the concept of collaboration is evolving in enterprises.[9]

On his blog, McAfee cites feedback he has received from several members of the U.S. intelligence community, including this: "Before Intellipedia, contacting other agencies was done cautiously, and only through official channels. There was no casual contact, and little opportunity to develop professional acquaintances—outside of rare [temporary duty] opportunities, or large conferences on broad topics." If the ultra-secretive, compartmentalized intelligence world can benefit from these tools, more mainstream enterprise functions surely can.[10]

But . . . Collaboration Is Mostly Unstructured!

Sig Rinde chuckles at enterprise software vendors jumping on the collaboration bandwagon. The founder of Thingamy says they don't understand "barely repeatable processes" (BRPs):

> *Only a third of the world's GDP [gross domestic product] is run by our structured ERP, CRM processes for production, procurement, HR, distribution and sales and marketing. The rest are BRP: support, health,*

education, and other "people" processes, which are supported by to-do lists, fax-mail-phone, meetings, and management involvement.
    The bigger vendors—salesforce.com with their Chatter, SAP with StreamWork, Google with Wave, etc.—are all trying to stitch collaboration tools together hoping for some process structure to ensue.

Rinde's firm helps companies create "ultralight" applications for BRP— you don't want to burden those processes with large, complex enterprise software.

He calls his tool the "Work Processor," and you start it with an issue, an idea, or a request: "A customer calling, an idea that hits you in the shower, a patient with a broken leg, perhaps some observations in the field or a sudden drop in sales figures. Register that, and you have the start of a value creating workflow."

And who knows, you may just about deliver on Rinde's challenge: "Here's 30 megs; now plonk it on your laptop and run Germany with it!"

Recap

Enterprises are slowly and warily starting to understand that they should be leveraging social media communities such as Facebook and Twitter as customer channels. Early success at Avon, Starbucks, P&G, and Pepsi are helping reduce concerns of social networks as time-wasters.

Other companies are using internal communities to harvest and manage internal knowledge stores. Some, such as SAP, have been pioneering communities that involve customers, vendors, and partners and learning what customers will share in such blended communities. Still others are becoming comfortable with more amorphous "crowds" as talent and idea sources.

Someday, communities and crowds will seriously challenge outsourcers and internal employees as talent sources. But for now, next-gen outsourcers like Appirio are emerging. And it is also good to see innovation in the way enterprises hire and manage internal employees.

The old adage "People are our most important asset" still applies. The talent just comes in many different formats, as Charles Handy's shamrock model predicted and polymath enterprises have learned to manage. And increasingly that talent is also part of the new generation of Paul Greenberg's social customers. Learn to do social right—or wrong—and you influence two important stakeholders: your customers and your talent.

CHAPTER 18

Clouds: Technology-as-a-Service

Most companies have spent billions on ERP and other enterprise software. While that was sold as "integrated" from a business process and data perspective, the deployment turned out to be anything but integrated. The software may have come from SAP, but customers likely bought the hosting from IBM, the systems integration from Accenture, the application management from TCS, and periodic upgrade services from boutique consulting firms.

Sounds like a perfect opportunity for a polymath to step in. Vendors such as NetSuite and salesforce.com (profiled in Chapter 19) saw an opportunity to amalgamate these offerings and offer them under a single contract. To be able to do so they had to learn about cooling efficiencies, storage economics, and 24x7 operations that software vendors traditionally outsourced to myriad partners.

After a decade of pioneering, they are now getting rewarded as their offerings are part of the hot new trend of Cloud Computing. Want proof? There are thousands of YouTube videos on the topic! This new religion has a wide following of believers and detractors.

Broadly, cloud computing can be defined as hosted services delivered over the Internet. And those services can be categorized into three broad groups, as Bessemer Venture Partners does in Figure 18.1.

The graph showcases the major cloud components—Software-as-a-Service (better known as SaaS—to cover business applications from accounting to sales pipeline management); Platform-as-a-Service (to allow for new development and extensions to applications), which vendors like salesforce.com have pioneered; and Infrastructure-as-a-Service (to cover data center tasks such as processing and storage), which Amazon, Microsoft, and others have invested in. Each layer is expected to grow at healthy 20 to 70 percent rates over the next few years.

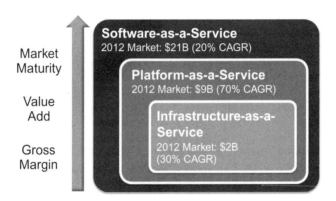

FIGURE 18.1 Cloud Computing Ecosystem
Source: Bessemer Venture Partners. Data taken from AMR, Gartner, and IDC.

We will come back to Bessemer later in the chapter. For now, let's look at the huge investment Microsoft has made in the cloud as it catches up to Google, Yahoo!, and others who made similar cloud investments a few years prior.

Microsoft's Cloud Infrastructure

"Follow the moon."

Mike Manos talks a different language from Francisco D'Souza of Cognizant, who talks about following the sun in Chapter 6.

D'Souza is talking about talent pools to develop and maintain applications 24/7 across the world. Manos is talking about the "pyramids of the twenty-first century": massive data centers that drive the new world of cloud computing. He is talking about energy efficiency: moving the most power-hungry applications to data centers where temperatures are lower at night and where utilities charge less as their citizens sleep. That explains the moon worship.

Manos spent the last several years building Microsoft's cloud computing infrastructure. He is now VP of service operations at Nokia, helping the company build and run its global infrastructure around mobile cloud applications.

He describes the scale of the "pyramids":

The definition of data server computing scale has changed dramatically in the last few years. The discrete unit of provisioning used to be a single server. Then we moved to racks of servers—between 40 and 80 servers. Then we started thinking about containers—2,500 servers worth. When you are deploying data centers with 200,000 servers, you have to think about the efficiencies of shipping, setup, reconfiguration, etc.

Yes, containers as in 40-foot ones you can easily load on a railcar and haul in and out of buildings, which in turn do not need the raised floors traditional data centers were famous for. Microsoft calls them "C-Blox" containers. Even though they may weigh 30 to 60 tons, they can be moved easily into "parking spaces." The buildings are designed to be energy efficient and rely on air-side economizers (which use cool outside air, particularly during certain seasons, to cool the indoor space), not water, as was traditionally used for cooling. Air-conditioning can account for 25 to 40 percent of the power used in a data center.

The location decision starts with site analysis—where to build these monsters. Manos says: "Thirty-five to 70 individual factors, like proximity to power, local talent pool, are considered for most centers. But three factors typically dominate: energy, telecommunications, and taxes. In the past, cost of the physical location was a primary consideration in data center design."

Like Las Vegas, which owes its existence to cheap and plentiful power from the Hoover Dam, modern data centers are leveraging proximity to hydroelectric power. Google does that with a center in The Dalles, Oregon, and Microsoft does it with a center in Quincy, Washington. Iceland is attracting data centers that use its plentiful geothermal fuel. When you are sucking thirty megawatts an hour, you can see how cheap power drives your decisions.

The next location factor usually is driven by telecom latency and costs: "It's amazing how quickly the user experience deteriorates with even sub-second delays," Manos explains: "So distributing data centers around the world becomes a design principle. And often a deployment nightmare."

"Maps of fiber are surprisingly primitive in the telecom industry. There are lots of turf battles—who owns what in each territory." And that is even in developed markets; now think about rural markets close to the more efficient energy sources.

The third factor is taxes. Tax incentives are negotiated up front as states and countries try to attract jobs to their markets. But just as important are ongoing taxes on revenues from cloud services that will flow from these centers. Remember the mobile containers—they could be gone overnight if regulators get greedy about taxes. Microsoft moved some of its planned cloud services from its Quincy center to its San Antonio, Texas, center to arbitrage tax differences.

Microsoft did not need to move any of its servers physically, even though the container design makes doing so a lot easier. It did so with software—a sophisticated new breed of software to manage these data centers. The software allows for customer-specific reporting and analytical tools that run real time to track energy consumption. "We had to custom-build this software—we could not repurpose existing data center management applications in the market. But this type of software is going to push even more enterprises and vendors running their own data centers to the cloud. For example, how many of them will be able to rewrite their data center tools to report carbon data?" Manos says.

If proximity to energy sources and low taxes are important, how can we explain Microsoft's decision to locate a $500 million data center in Northlake, Illinois, in the suburbs of Chicago? Recall the 70 site decision factors Manos mentioned earlier. Some of those factors came into play. Chicago is a major rail hub, so movement of containers was a lot easier. It has a well-established labor pool of longshoremen—again important for the container logistics. And there is plenty of fiber in the I-294 corridor, and Microsoft negotiated good power rates.

What were some of the challenges in getting Microsoft to invest in the cloud? Manos provides details:

> *The capex [capital expenditure] commitment of $300 to $500 million for each of these data centers was culturally a tough sell. It was a significant mind-set change at Microsoft, where the biggest capital investment some of their software executives had ever made was in their office building.*
>
> *Also, there is the need to move to an "excellence in operations" mind-set. The industry model has been software publishers develop code, and systems integrators and hosting firms implement and operate them. Now the software vendor has to learn to do all that—and do that very well.*
>
> *This is about industrialization of technology. Remember the central telecom switches which occupied hundreds of operators. Or the electric substations which similarly needed many engineers, repairmen, etc. Those tasks have been largely automated. Something similar is happening in data centers. Microsoft can run these massive centers with a staff of just 30 to 40.*
>
> *How can traditional data centers ever expect to compete with the people, power, and processing efficiencies of these new cloud centers? And even SaaS and outsourcing vendors which are building more efficient data centers will eventually find it more economical to buy wholesale capacity from these megacenters.*

The convergence of Marc Benioff's "democratization of technology" and Mike Manos's "industrialization of technology" is causing seismic shifts in the world of enterprise computing.

But shouldn't enterprises be worried about security and data ownership in that massively shared services concept? Let's hear from a CIO who has made the transition.

DeVry in the Cloud

"My epiphany about cloud computing came in 2002. For years I had been the victim of countless business rants that IT is 'not nimble enough.' When I stopped trying to defend IT, I realized they were correct."

Eric Dirst is CIO at DeVry, one of the largest degree-granting higher education systems in North America. In 2002, he was at SIRVA, a moving company that specializes in relocations. He continues:

> *In IT we spend a ridiculous amount of time, money, and effort on our IT Infrastructure, or what we refer to as the "plumbing." Unfortunately, the business finds zero incremental value—upgrading software releases; testing and deploying upgraded hardware; testing and applying security patches or changes to comply with the latest vulnerabilities or changing audit landscape (SOX, PCI, HIPAA, etc.); etc. etc.*

Since his "wake-up call," Dirst has made up for lost time and deployed a wide range of business processes to the cloud: sales force automation, CRM, payroll, compensation planning, talent reviews, 401(k) management, travel booking, expense reporting, purchasing, training, knowledge management, security penetration testing, and firewall management.

But what about the worries about security and other areas in the cloud? Dirst's response:

> *Many of my peer CIOs will cite risk areas like security, service-level agreements, data ownership, recovery point objectives, and vendor longevity. These are valid concerns, but I've found that proper due diligence and well-written contracts can minimize these issues to manageable risks.*
>
> *The dirty little secret in our industry is how much downtime there is and how poorly tested are the disaster recovery plans for the data centers we run or outsourcers run for us. The better cloud vendors actually offer a step-up in availability, security, and failover support.*

Prior to SIRVA, Eric was CTO at a start-up developing a hosted solution (before the terms "cloud computing" and "SaaS" had been invented) and was keenly aware of the big checks he wrote for Sun, Oracle, and other "branded" infrastructure. So he pushes his cloud vendors to optimize their own processing, networks, and storage. He elaborates:

> *Even though clouds are allowing us to buy IT on a much more variable basis, there is too much history in our industry of costs getting calcified. Too many cloud vendors give you flexibility to grow but want to lock you in to prevent shrinking your commitment to them. This can be overcome, but it takes plenty of negotiating.*
>
> *Cloud vendors also need to step up in business functionality. It is still uneven when it comes to areas such as finance (AP, AR, GL), billing, pricing configuration, imaging, and customer/partner portals.*

At 42 years old, Dirst is one of the most seasoned CIOs when it comes to cloud computing. He builds 10-year models of his company's future growth—organic or by acquisition—or retraction and then embeds those scenarios into his cloud computing contracts. The way DeVry has been growing, he does not need to worry about shrinking his cloud footprint, but he is savvy enough to plan for any contingency.

He is using the cloud experience to help guide DeVry's own education delivery. DeVry is a leader in online education and extensively uses internal clouds in its "iLabs." That platform gives students access to the software tools they need for such topics as varied as chemistry and game design delivered over the Internet. DeVry has leveraged a cloud vendor, eCollege, to help them deliver their online courses for years.

Why not develop that technology themselves? Dirst explains:

> *Online learning environments have become a commoditized product, much like e-commerce, collaboration, or document management platforms. The differentiation comes in the quality of the course content, the pedagogy employed to deliver the content, and the experience and passion of the faculty teaching the class. The old saying is true—it's what you do with the product.*

DeVry has also seen that the cloud can enhance onsite learning in the traditional classroom. This blended model mirrors most employer workplaces as they blend office, online, and "private cloud" technologies—creating a work environment DeVry students will be well prepared to thrive in.

The next big effort for Dirst is to work with the Dean of the College of Engineering & Information Sciences to update DeVry's technology curriculum to keep pace with the fast changing cloud computing landscape.

Says Dirst:

We will incorporate PaaS concepts and tools into our computer science track. We plan to leverage the platforms of leading vendors to teach our students the latest methodologies, like Agile, SCRUM, and others, that are natively supported via PaaS environments. Giving our students real-world hands-on experience with the tools they'll be using in the workforce is a key tenet of our educational methodology.

I want our students to get their "epiphany" about clouds much earlier in their careers than I did. It's the future of our industry.

Much of the discussion so far has focused on leveraging shared infrastructure in the clouds; now let's hear about some business benefits.

NetSuite's Macro View from the Clouds

"We have some of the best leading indicators on the economy. We can aggregate order value, cash flow, and several other metrics instantly in our base of over 6,000 customers and watch trends," gushes Zach Nelson, CEO of NetSuite. "We can do so because we designed our solution to run a business, not just a department."

Nelson offers more details:

I monitor NetSuite's own key performance indicators [KPIs] constantly using our software. One day, I noticed our customer leads were down significantly—specifically those originating from Google. A couple of phone calls later, we found we had not paid our AdWords bill. What could have taken weeks to diagnose and fix was repaired in a few hours.

My customers similarly monitor their KPIs on a real-time basis—even on an iPhone. It is a capability still rare in the SaaS world where most solutions are typically departmental—CRM or HR focused—in reach. And we deliver them at price points customers of larger vendors like SAP and Oracle can only drool about.

Soon, those customers will be able to benchmark themselves against aggregated data of their peers. That would obviate the need for mailed-in surveys. That capability has been the domain of benchmarking firms like Hackett, not of the software industry, so that is another innovation NetSuite is working to deliver. Nelson explains: "Take those benchmarks and some of the creative BPO [business process outsourcing] partnerships we are exploring (such as one announced in April 2010 with Genpact, the spinoff from GE described in Chapter 3), and the industry could see SLAs [service-level agreements] that don't just monitor technical metrics like systems availability but business process metrics that have been elusive to codify."

His fellow SaaS pioneer Marc Benioff shows his passion in public, as we show in Chapter 19. Nelson's passion is much more visible in smaller settings, such as the company's infrastructure, another differentiator Nelson calls "small iron." NetSuite built its infrastructure on a mesh of cheap HP Proliant servers. In fact, since NetSuite was born in 1997, like Google, you could argue that it deserves as much credit as Google gets for a fault-tolerant and commoditized architecture where loads are spread across a wide range of easy-to-replace and easy-to-scale assets.

Ironically, the "small iron" thinking came from NetSuite's largest investor, Larry Ellison, who as CEO of Oracle sells companies "big iron"— Oracle's Exadata solution on high-end Sun hardware, described in Chapter 15. Ellison has publicly mocked cloud computing. Nelson says, "Larry is one of the most creative and flexible technology architects there is. He can embrace contradictory trends, even while dissing them in public."

The NetSuite solution is also "green." Nelson points out that by reducing the need for servers and support equipment, such as server room air-conditioning, an independent study by Greenspace found that the average NetSuite customer can cut its electricity bill by more than $10,000 per year.[1]

Now let's look at clouds from an investor's point of view.

Bessemer's Investments in the Cloud

"Less is more! Leverage the cloud everywhere you practically can."

This is the first of 10 laws Byron Deeter and his colleagues at Bessemer Venture Partners have put together for the SaaS market. Deeter's battle cry is aimed as much at customers as it is his portfolio companies:

> *The SaaS companies we have funded recently have required more up-front capital than the on-premise software vendors we funded in the '90s and early part of this decade. I would say 25 to 35% more. That's partly because all your costs are front-loaded as in a traditional software company, but the revenues are stretched monthly instead of front-loaded in the perpetual model. And partly because you are investing in data centers and infrastructure traditional software companies did not.*
>
> *However, in the next several years that infrastructure capex should decline nicely as the "public cloud" infrastructure from vendors like Microsoft [as Mike Manos described earlier], Amazon, and others mature. Our entrepreneurs should be able to apply the "less is more" law when it comes to their own infrastructure.*

Bessemer is the oldest venture capital firm, with roots going back over a century. Cloud computing and SaaS make up the single biggest category of investment for his firm, says Deeter. They currently have two dozen SaaS/subscription investments, including eloqua, the marketing automation SaaS vendor (profiled in Chapter 15) and LinkedIn, the professional networking site with more than 50 million members worldwide.

Previous successful investments in the category include Postini (e-mail filtering), which was acquired by Google, and Trigo Technologies (product information management), which was acquired by IBM.

Bessemer's SaaS investments are increasingly verticalized. Deeter says: "We have a lot of interest in health care IT, and the financial services vertical has always been a nice early adopter for our companies."

The 10 laws Bessemer has put together reflect the growing body of cloud experiences. Law 4, for example, says, "Forget everything you learned about software channels. The Internet is your new channel—it makes distribution far more efficient especially in the small to mid-size customer market."

Probably the most critical one is Law 2, which calls for measuring six key financial metrics:

1. Committed monthly recurring revenue (CMRR)
2. Cash flow
3. CMRR pipeline
4. Customer churn
5. Customer acquisition cost
6. Customer lifetime value

Deeter summarizes: "In our analysis of more than a hundred cloud businesses, we encountered several successful companies that were on the borderline with one or two of our 10 laws, but none that challenge several of them."

Yes, Deeter is helping write new rules for a new world. This new world, by the way, is allowing for a new set of consulting and outsourcing firms to emerge.

Let's look at one of them: Appirio.

Appirio: Clouds for Clients and for Itself

Appirio was mentioned in Chapter 17 and elsewhere in this book. The company is just three years old, but already it has helped more than 150 enterprises—including much bigger, much more experienced companies, such as Japan Post Network, Ltd., Pfizer, and Qualcomm—with their baby steps in the move to cloud computing. The Appirio Web site invites you to follow the company on Facebook and Twitter. It is part of a new generation of outsourcers—part systems integrator/part software company—that has emerged with the "as-a-Service" model.

"Our raison d'être is cloud computing," says Chris Barbin, CEO of Appirio. Most of his team comes from old-world computing, with experience at SAP, Borland, and Accenture. And like most converts, they are passionate—and impatient.

"We want to accelerate those baby steps into long-distance runs. We would love to get our clients to be 100% in the cloud."

And he wants to do it by example. Appirio itself runs 100 percent in the cloud. Continues Barbin:

> We spend less than 2% of our revenues on IT, compared to benchmarks of about 7% for companies our size. Because we run our business on platforms like salesforce.com and Google, we did not have to do a single thing as we scaled from less than 10 employees three years ago to a global team of over 200 today. No upgrades, no new servers or routers, nothing!
>
> Besides, the benefits go far beyond cost and scalability. salesforce.com enables us to seamlessly tie our sales processes into our project management/planning application, something we've struggled to do in our much bigger, previous firms. With Google, our employees get instant access to the latest collaboration technology, such as the voice chat and video conferencing features of Gmail. Can you imagine how big an IT group I would need to get the same pace of innovation if we were using traditional on-premises applications?

The cloud platform benefits not only Appirio's internal operations but also its client engagements and products.

> Since development is on top of platforms like Force.com and Google's AppEngine that abstract away the infrastructure, applications can be built in weeks instead of months. (As happened with Appirio's work for Starbucks described in Chapter 17.) These apps benefit automatically from innovative new features like salesforce.com's Chatter. Appirio was the first partner to demo the Chatter capability at Dreamforce [the salesforce.com conference] where the feature was first announced. They truly give teeth to the concept of agile development—a huge advantage as we deliver projects and develop products.

In a market exploding with new cloud services each day, Appirio took the initiative to create an "ecosystem map"—something industry analysts typically deliver in their "magic quadrants" and "waves," says Ryan Nichols, head of cloud strategy for the firm. He elaborates:

> *The cloud ecosystem map breaks out 70 different layers of technology across applications, platforms, and infrastructure. We had started the ecosystem map to track for ourselves the rapid evolution of the market. We then decided to publish it to help others assess the lay of the land. With broader community involvement, we can create a living, breathing map where anyone can access, drill down, and interact with dynamic information.*
>
> *The day we announced availability, the Appirio site saw its highest single-day traffic—a clear validation of market interest.*

Given the benefits they have experienced in their own services organization, Appirio also saw an opportunity to package the features in a solution it branded the Professional Services Cloud. It is aimed at larger services firms that are running their shops using legacy and custom-built solutions, with plenty of painful spreadsheet workarounds.

That turns the Software-as-a-Service model on its head—it's service-as-software. Most outsourcers invest in people training, not software; this is another way that Appirio is a new breed of outsourcer.

Now let's now take a look at PaaS.

PaaS, as in Leapfrog

In 2008, the product strategy leadership at salesforce.com conducted an exercise to identify which software vendors would be good candidates to recruit to its Force.com platform to build their next-generation cloud computing applications. Conventional wisdom pointed to the emerging and new vendors, but Anshu Sharma, VP of product management, worked with an intern, Shai Alfandary, from U.C. Berkeley's Haas School of Business, to identify key criteria that would drive such platform adoption.

Says Sharma: "Somewhat surprisingly, our analysis came back showing that it was existing software companies that had been around for a while with little to no cloud expertise and penetration and were on mature platforms for their on-premise solutions that would be most likely to derive greatest benefit by essentially leapfrogging using Force.com."

This resulted in a top-100 vendor target list. A year later, the prediction came true as CA (formerly Computer Associates) and BMC Software, which have been around since 1976 and 1980, respectively, announced new product offerings based on Force.com. CA plans an agile development tool and BMC plans one that enables IT staff to identify and track server connection problems for PC users.

John Swainson, then CEO of CA, said, "There will be a pre-cloud era and a post-cloud era just as there was a pre-mainframe era and a post-mainframe era. This is the most profound change I've seen in IT in 30 years."[2]

In retrospect, it makes sense: Established companies like BMC and CA have the most to gain by quickly leveraging an already developed cloud computing platform, minimizing upfront costs while allowing them to bring new products to market at a much faster pace. Sharma confirms several more from the Top 100 list are in the active pipeline.

Schumacher Group and the Network Effect

Schumacher Group manages emergency department physician staffing across 150 hospitals. The providers at Schumacher Group treat three million patients across 19 states annually. Hurricanes Katrina and Rita accelerated Schumacher Group's move away from on-premise computing—headquartered in Lafayette, Louisiana, which is the bull's eye for many an intense storm. Another accelerator was the high-speed network in that town (described further in Chapter 7).

CIO Douglas Menefee explains:

The Lafayette Utilities System has been building out a Fiber-to-the Premise (FTTP) network in the Lafayette community for the past five years. Every business and house in Lafayette will have direct access to fiber connectivity. This initiative has made bandwidth a moot issue in the Lafayette community.

Schumacher Group has multiple fiber connections from competing vendors at a fraction of the cost we pay for telecom services in metropolitan areas such as Dallas, Atlanta, Houston, and Orlando.

Interestingly, Schumacher Group has never developed a formal strategy to migrate to the cloud. As a business requirement presents itself, the group evaluates on-premises versus cloud solutions.

Menefee says: "It's an interesting contrast. Typically, our Web services team will bring me a prototype of the solution while our on-premises team will bring a project plan. Our final decision is based on time of delivery, cost, HIPAA compliance, and project prioritization."

As a testament to the attractiveness of cloud computing versus on-premises computing, Menefee estimates at the end of 2009, 70 percent of Schumacher Group's processes were in the cloud.

The cloud computing landscape at Schumacher covers many complex workflows for physician recruiting, credentials management, enrollment process with insurance payers, e-commerce with patients, and patient issue resolution.

The organization is leveraging several cloud solutions:

- Tangier from Peake Software helps schedule physicians and other emergency staff for the hospitals Schumacher Group manages. It also facilitates physician personal scheduling via their personal digital assistants.
- salesforce.com helps the company keep track of individual contracts, pay rates, and the hospitals where each doctor can work.
- Workday helps with HR management needs as the employee base goes global.
- Eloqua helps the company with lead management and other marketing automation.
- Apttus helps manage thousands of contracts.
- Docusign and Echosign provide Schumacher with electronic signature solutions.
- Conga has worked with Schumacher to automate the process of loading data into hundreds of various applications required by insurance companies to enroll providers for reimbursement purposes.

The Force.com platform from salesforce.com is the glue that holds the cloud architecture together. Schumacher Group has leveraged the Force.com application programming interfaces and integration software from Cast Iron Systems to integrate with on-premises solutions as well as other cloud services.

Speed of cloud deployment has been another boon. Says Menefee about the Workday project:

In less than six months we had the core HR processes loaded and deployed. Immediately thereafter we began benefits integration and transitioning payroll onto Workday—that was done in three months. That's impressive for a service-, people-intense business. Next, the integration to salesforce.com took less than two weeks.

Having to worry less about managing infrastructure and its related impact on business continuity has allowed us to focus more on innovation and faster delivery of solutions to enable a positive impact on the delivery of health care.

Such an endorsement from Menefee, who has twice been recognized as innovator of the year by the governor of Louisiana, is telling.

Looking ahead, Menefee says, "We need a bandwidth revolution. Our next big effort will be around migration of terabytes of data associated with patient charts and data warehousing. There is no foreseeable plan to migrate these services out of the existing data centers—however, it does remain a topic in our enterprise architecture conversations."

Private versus Public Clouds

Put aside DeVry's and Schumacher Group's enthusiasm for clouds. Many CIOs raise three major issues:

1. With virtualization, can't we get many of the cloud benefits ourselves?
2. We hear of cloud security and outage issues all the time. Shouldn't we be concerned?
3. What do I tell my CFO: Write off the existing data center? Pay a hefty early-termination fee on our outsourced data center contracts?

Incumbent hardware and outsourcing vendors are only too glad to point out that external clouds have security, availability, and other issues. Instead, they are pushing their own "private clouds."

Timothy Chou, who started Oracle's internal online unit over a decade ago and now runs the *Cloudbook* resource on everything related to cloud computing, explains the whopping economic advantages the public cloud model promises:

> *The average enterprise application costs over $1,000 a user a month. Most company's IT budgets are now fully allocated to managing the software they bought over the past twenty years.*
>
> *Now if you take that same software and standardize the delivery, you can get the cost to under $100 a user a month. And furthermore if like salesforce.com, Concur, Taleo, Successfactors, or NetSuite you engineer applications for even higher degrees of standardization, then the cost (not price) goes to $10 per user per month. But that's not the end of the story—back of the envelope; Google's cost to deliver is less than $1 per user per month.[3]*

In other words, try competing with public cloud economics with those at private clouds.

Laef Olson, CIO at RightNow, a cloud CRM company, shakes his head about security concerns and says:

> *RightNow has been doing business with the U.S. federal government for more than 10 years and has over 160 public sector clients, including*

every U.S. cabinet-level agency and major military commands. Our solution has achieved the certification and accreditation required at the federal level—bringing the highest level of government into the commercial cloud for the first time. If we can do this for the Air Force and Army, we can do it for your company.

Dan Druker, senior vice president at Intacct, a cloud accounting vendor, also shakes his head when he hears about scalability and high availability:

We have a partnership with the American Institute of Certified Public Accountants [AICPA], the national professional association for CPAs. The endorsement of cloud computing for core financial applications by the largest professional organization in North America is a milestone in itself. An inherently conservative organization like the AICPA does not make a move like this lightly. Over time, literally millions of small and midsized businesses across America will be touched by accounting in the cloud.

And so the arguments rage. But if you are lucky to not have any infrastructure to worry about writing off, the choice is pretty simple, as the Altimeter Group illustrates.

Altimeter Group: Born in the Cloud

Charlene Li was interviewed on the influential CBS *60 Minutes* show about Facebook and CEO Mark Zuckerberg. She coauthored the bestselling *Groundswell* about a hot technology area: social networking. With such a personal launch platform, it was easy for Li to leave the analyst firm Forrester Research in Cambridge, Massachusetts, and start her own firm, Altimeter Group.[4]

A year later, other Forrester analysts joined her, including Ray Wang, who analyzes enterprise software, and Jeremiah Owyang, who also follows social platforms. Li also brought in Deb Schultz, who had put together the Social Media Lab at Procter & Gamble. Several others have joined since.

Although still a small firm by number of employees, Altimeter has plenty of computing, collaboration, and communication needs. When it announced its expansion with the partners above, given their savviness about social media, it drummed up 800 participants to join a virtual "open house."

Plenty of analysis could be done on how firms like Altimeter are disrupting the technology industry influencer model that analyst firms and media have dominated for years. But just as fascinating is the technology Altimeter is using to run operations.

Ray Wang, who consults with clients on SaaS decisions, is also acting CIO. He marvels at the SaaS tools his firm leverages at little or no cost to run the operation including:

- *Blogs*—Wordpress
- *Project management*—Basecamp
- *Wikis*—Socialtext
- *Office productivity*—Google Docs
- *Communications*—Google Voice, Skype
- *E-mail*—Google Mail
- *Finance*—Quickbooks Hosted
- *Webinars/Telecon*—Go-To-Meeting
- *CRM*—High Rise
- *File management/storage*—Box.net
- *Microblogging*—Twitter
- *Distribution*—Scribd, Slideshare

Looking ahead, Wang is evaluating these and other SaaS products:

- Tenrox or OpenAir for project management
- salesforce.com for sales lead management and platform
- Intacct for financials

Jeff Kaplan, who runs the SaaS Showplace, an online gallery of SaaS vendors, can tell you about each of these vendors and thousands more. He has been watching the landscape since 2006 and has seen it get crowded as he sorts vendors into 80 application, industry, and enabling technology categories.

And if you add the vendors that Chou's CloudBook and Nichols's ecosystem map show, you can see that there are plenty of cloud choices both for small, ambitious firms like Altimeter and for larger enterprises. Indeed, Google, with its recently announced Apps Marketplace, is recruiting many of these application vendors to provide extended functionality around its own e-mail, calendaring, word processing, spreadsheet, and other SaaS applications. As more of their applications integrate with each other, they will make life even easier for people like Wang. He will need less time for IT and have more for his clients.

Recap

Cloud computing in its various manifestations—applications, platforms, infrastructure services—is one of the most disruptive technology trends enterprises have to reckon with.

Pioneers like Benioff of salesforce.com and Nelson of NetSuite have been talking about it passionately for a decade now. Their delivery track record and those of other cloud pioneers has gradually minimized concerns about downtime, data access, security, and vendor viability.

Traditional, on-premise computing is not giving up without a fight, but whether it is a small firm like Altimeter, a larger one like DeVry and even larger ones, clouds are factoring in most IT budgets and decisions. Now, let's take a look at a polymath when it comes to clouds—salesforce.com.

CHAPTER 19

Polymath Profile #7: salesforce.com

Centralized power and power to the people don't usually mix. To contradict that truism, Marc Benioff, CEO of salesforce.com, tells his audience, "We are democratizing technology."

Benioff has just heard Michael Dell (CEO of Dell Computer), who has joined him onstage, say, "Physics does not stop for economic slowdowns. We plan to help run massive data centers similar to those at Lawrence Livermore Labs where they can process a quadrillion floating operations a second."

Benioff explains how centralized investments are helping bring technology to the masses: "The infrastructure we have in our three data centers— can you imagine how much our 68,000 customers would have to invest in servers, routers, databases, monitoring tools, the ability to provision more capacity in minutes and so much more if they did it themselves?"

His company, salesforce.com is a polymath organization that has converged multiple products and service that enterprises get today from a combination of software vendors, hosting providers, offshore application management vendors, and internal IT staff. As Benioff told *The New York Times*, "Every time someone buys a server, a switch, or a data center, I have failed."[1]

Democracy in Action

During a customer panel at salesforce.com's Dreamforce conference in November 2009, at one end of the table sat a ball of color—D.A., of the indie band Chester French, with his bob of red hair and purple trousers. At the other end was Joe Drouin, CIO of Kelly Services, which places 650,000 contract staff around the world, in a dark suit and white shirt. Quite a contrast in size of customer and dress code.

That's Benioff's democracy in action.

In a keynote presentation, Benioff plays master of ceremonies and gives equal time to Appirio, a next-generation systems integrator we describe in Chapter 18, and to Accenture, which is 1,000 times bigger. He gives time to Vetrazzo, a start-up that makes countertops from recycled glass, and to Lawson, the second-largest convenience store chain in Japan (behind 7-Eleven). He gives bloggers front-row seats during his keynote speech ahead of industry analysts and technology media. He high-fives onstage with left-leaning San Francisco mayor Gavin Newsom and hugs General Colin Powell, the former U.S. Secretary of State.

The democracy talk has actually toned down over the last decade. Says Benioff:

When we started the company, unlike the rest of the industry, we charged the same per seat, whether someone wanted two licenses or two hundred. It was the most democratic way. Why should someone pay less just because his or her company was bigger? I was unyielding on this. I heard the jokes behind my back that I wouldn't give even my grandmother a discount. It's true; I couldn't—that would ruin the democratic model on which salesforce.com was built.

Enterprise technology realities made him change his pricing model—the software industry has conditioned its enterprise customers to get volume discounts of up to 90 percent of list price. But it did not stop Benioff from harping on the "It is the end of software as we know it" message.

In an enterprise industry filled with conservative executives, Benioff stands out. It partly flows from the fact that Benioff (along with Steve Jobs of Apple) was one of the few industry executives who could see the powerful trend that is consumerization of technology (as we discussed in Chapter 4).

And he is not afraid to praise the consumer-centric technology executives he admires, saying, "We stand on the shoulders of giants like Jerry Yang [founder of Yahoo!], Pierre Omidyar [of eBay], Jeff Bezos [of Amazon], and Biz Stone [of Twitter]."

And Benioff markets his company as if he were selling to consumers, not enterprises. The giant screen behind him makes George C. Scott's flag at the beginning of the movie *Patton* look puny. He uses mood lighting to accent his talks. His oratory has been well trained by the likes of Tony Robbins, the motivational coach. He even has a mascot in the form of a button with a red line through the word "software." The mascot SaaSy is a fan favorite at his conferences—plays a mean air guitar and never tires of a photo op.

"SaaSy" is derived from SaaS (Software-as-a-Service)—the company's initial solution to facilitate sales pipeline management. It has since grown to support various forms of customer service and collaboration that mimic Facebook- and Twitter-like capabilities (but behind the firewall). The company calls it "Chatter": "The applications actually do talk to me," Benioff jests. As a partner, the U.K.-based accounting vendor FinancialForce.com demonstrates the chatter is not just chit-chat but useful business information. It could be warning you when the company bank balance falls below a certain threshold or a when departmental budget is exceeded.

Benioff plays stand-up comedian at his conferences with good quips and lame ones. He asks the Avon lady why the company misspelled his name in its new *mark* product line aimed at younger consumers. When he hears that someone's name is Luke, he asks: "Has the Force always been with you?"

Why not? It's another chance to plug his PaaS (Platform-as-a-Service), Force.com, on which his customers and partners are building new functionality. That includes FinancialForce.com, described above, which could have built its own SaaS the traditional way, by building the infrastructure (not just the data center but the entire software stack as well), spending upward of $20 million, and taken several years. Using the salesforce.com platform eliminated the need for servers, load balancers, and networking switches and for people to tune and maintain them, and it enabled FinancialForce.com to focus on exactly what it does best: accounting applications.

Between his growing flock of customers, prospects, and partners, Benioff has now a vibrant religion that routinely pulls thousands to his "cloud summits" held around the world.

The audiences hear Benioff talk about "multitenancy":

Think of it as an apartment building where the tenants of the building share common costs, such as building security or the laundry facilities, but they still have locks on their doors and the freedom to decorate their apartments as they wish. We saw how consumer Web services like Yahoo! Mail did not set up a new e-mail server for each consumer. And we asked why not the same model for business applications?

He is the real estate agent's worst nightmare: Don't buy, rent.

That gives his critics fodder. "Comingled data and security issues," they warn.

So Benioff's audiences hear him refute every objection thrown at the model. Less secure? Try selling 30,000 licenses to Citibank without having its due diligence teams crawl through your data center and network.

Less available? Try upgrading what you have today with a five-minute downtime window. And "we have an online set of SLA [service-level agreement] metrics which we dare any internal data center or outsourcer to consistently match."

Online and visible-to-all metrics surely sound like a suicidal move? They could very well have been so.

Transparency as Market Advantage

Benioff writes in his book *Behind the Cloud*:

In late 2005, our site went down. Customers quickly began to grumble that the service was unreliable. Making matters worse, a competitor signed up for a free trial as a way to ascertain when our service was down—and reported any problems to the press. Literally, within minutes, journalists would call seeking comment. Before long, salesforce.com's reliability issues were widely publicized, and we were in serious trouble. During the period we struggled with outages, we actually had an uptime rate of 99 percent, and our service was much better and much more reliable than on-premise software, but any disruption was understandably maddening for customers. We lost their faith.

We had to find a way to communicate quickly and candidly—even if going public with our problems felt like a defeat at the moment. Parker (Harris) [his cofounder] and Bruce (Francis) [vice president of corporate strategy] urged me to post our internal monitoring system, which we used to track our status (everything running perfectly appeared in green, performance issues were tagged in yellow, and service disruptions were marked in red). It was a bold move and a big leap of faith. We would be allowing the public—and the competition—to see exactly how our system was functioning every day. It meant that we would be sharing embarrassing details every time the system slowed or stopped working.

Ultimately, however, I let go of my fear and realized that complete transparency was what we needed if we were to restore trust in our company. In the middle of the disaster, we opened up our internal system for everyone to see. I called it the trust site. The site—located at trust.salesforce.com—offers real-time information on system performance. . . . It was liberating not to have to act defensively.[2]

This transparency is revolutionary in an enterprise world where project overruns and frequent downtime are normal—and mostly are hidden from public scrutiny.

But the nitpicking continues. "Oh, it is just a financing play," they object. To say that is to dismiss the innovations coming out of cloud computing vendors, such as the new data center designs Mike Manos describes in Chapter 18. It ignores Google's tax- and energy-efficiencies in its data centers. Compare those to the cold war bunkers many of today's internal and outsourced data centers represent. It undervalues the massive shared service efficiencies in application management NetSuite's Zach Nelson described in Chapter 18. It dismisses the payback from background upgrades vendors such as Workday (an HR vendor) are delivering compared to months of testing and other turmoil in current release cycles. It ignores the flexibility in licensing units and the speed in provisioning time vendors such as Zoho (which provides a Microsoft Office–type SaaS solution, described in Chapter 9) are delivering.

Benioff responds with economic sermons: Five times faster to implement. It is only half the cost. It is elastic—no more "shelfware" common in historical software purchases. Forget the decades where IT was the biggest capex line item. It has been hammered down to an affordable opex.

Religious Wars

What's not to like in cloud computing?

- Plenty, if you are an IT employee whose function gets moved to the cloud and you cling to the past rather than using the freedom to do more innovative things than managing infrastructure.
- Plenty, if you are a hardware vendor that has to now sell to Benioff a fraction of what you would directly sell to end customers: 15 units of salesforce.com customers run on one server. Smart hardware vendors like Dell realize that it is futile to fight the trend, so they join Benioff onstage to sing praises of the new religion.
- Plenty, if you are a software vendor used to selling to one customer at a time while leveraging the economies of servicing them all at once. The tide is turning, though—smart infrastructure software providers like BMC and CA are joining Benioff onstage and in the expo halls at his events. Bob Beauchamp, CEO of BMC, says about a CIO customer of his: "He tells me he has 30,000 servers and he hates them all. All he wants is the 100 or so services they provide."
- Plenty, if you are an outsourcer used to selling storage at $3 per gigabyte per month, when cloud vendors are coming in under 15 cents per gigabyte per month.

All of the above above give Benioff plenty of fodder to mock. Benioff on Microsoft:

I think Microsoft is still a dinosaur. More than ever, it tries to hold onto its monopolistic position around technology that they hold, whether it's SQL Server, whether it's NT, whether it's Windows, whether it's Office—these are their cash cows they don't want slaughtered.[3]

On SAP:

I have a hard time thinking about what SAP is going to be known for at the end of the day.[4]

Of course, Benioff's critics return fire. Larry Ellison, investor in Benioff's company and his former employer at Oracle, took shots on the company's rebranding away from SaaS to cloud computing:

Chanel last year had fuchsia; now it's called puce.[5]

Or Mark Hurd, CEO of HP who sounded a caution about clouds:

We have 1,000 hacks a day and I can't tell you why, but they keep showing up. We wouldn't put anything material in nature outside the firewall [in the cloud].[6]

It is a new religion, with all the pro and con passion that comes with young religions, often with surprising twists and turns. In April 2010, salesforce.com announced VMForce.com, a joint offering with VMWare aimed at the 6-million-plus Java development community. Said Phil Wainewright at ZDNet, "Little did I imagine that salesforce.com, creator of the archetypal proprietary cloud platform, would itself seize the initiative (with an open community)."[7]

It is part of what Benioff calls a move to "Cloud 2," the new world where YouTube, Twitter, and Facebook have opened our eyes to the power of communities, as we discussed in Chapter 17.

As you watch Benioff on stage sermonizing in booming voice, you cannot help but think about Neil Diamond and his Brother Love's Traveling Salvation Show. Yes, indeed, it is a new religion.

Recap

salesforce.com has gone from one success to the next. It started off showing that a single vendor could deliver software, data center, network, and other services in a single service-level agreement. It also demonstrated that enterprise technology need not be a fixed cost—it could be bought "by the drink." Then it raised the bar for the industry by showing off those service levels transparently for all to see. It has since positioned its development platform (and the cloud infrastructure it is built on) as the tool for others to build on rather than investing in their own.

Benioff and his team have earned the right to be called polymaths for bringing so many disparate technologies together and continuing to develop them in many new directions.

CHAPTER 20

Ethics:
In an Age of Cyberwar
and Cloning

Recently, the Google–China affair flared up over security breaches and Google's belated attempts to fight China's censorship of Web searches. Google's CEO Eric Schmidt was asked if his fiduciary responsibility to shareholders was not to maximize profits. His response was: "When we filed for our IPO [initial public offering], we attached to the document a statement about how we wanted to run our business. We said we were going to be different. We said that we were going to be motivated by concerns that were not always or strictly business ones."[1]

The Google moment of conscience came a decade after Bill Joy, cofounder of Sun Microsystems (now with Kleiner Perkins, as described in Chapter 13), asked some troubling questions in his essay in *Wired* magazine titled "Why the Future Doesn't Need Us": "Given the incredible power of these new technologies (robotics, genetic engineering, and nanotech), shouldn't we be asking how we can best coexist with them? And if our own extinction is a likely, or even possible, outcome of our technological development, shouldn't we proceed with great caution?"[2]

But what was remarkable was the fact that Schmidt's and Joy's comments were bookends. In the decade in between, few technology vendor executives felt comfortable discussing ethical issues. Indeed, for years Google itself had dodged questions about why it had agreed to China's censorship policies in the first place.

Sure, there exist bodies such as the Electronic Frontier Foundation, which is made up of "lawyers, policy analysts, activists, and technologists" and tackles issues around "free speech, privacy, innovation, and consumer rights." But for the most part, the discussions regarding technology and ethics have stayed in academia.

Google the term "ethical issues around technology" and you see these and other names:

- Lawrence Lessig, who runs Harvard's Edmond J. Safra Foundation Center for Ethics. Over his career, he has tackled many different kinds of legal issues around intellectual property (IP).
- Dr. James Moor, who wrote a seminal article "What Is Computer Ethics?" in 1985.[3] He is a professor at Dartmouth and he talked about "policy vacuums" and technology being different because it was "logically malleable."
- Deborah Johnson, a professor at the University of Virginia, and Donald Gotterbarn, at East Tennessee State University, among the coauthors of the code of ethics adopted in 1992 by the Association for Computer Machinery.[4]

But you do not see too many Joys or Schmidts.

Go to most hospitals and they can quickly convene an ethics committee, which often includes a doctor, nurse, social worker, attorney, chaplain, medical ethics professional, and a member of the community. The committee is available to a doctor or someone close to a patient to consult on an ever-evolving set of issues from genetic testing to euthanasia.

While individual technology vendors may not have enough ethical issues themselves, across the technology industry, should it consider establishing similar ethics committees?

There has arisen a growing body of cyberethical issues regarding privacy, God powers related to genetics and nanotechnology, the food/biofuel trade-off issues, crime in virtual worlds, and others. Legal constructs deal with product liability issues and how definitions evolve with new technologies.

You do not, however, see too many "innovators" tackling these ethical issues. So, this chapter presents instead a variety of perspectives: from academia, from law, from an author who has written several essays on technology's impact on society, and from a couple of practitioners who share their personal "compasses."

We also catalog a series of hypothetical scenarios, many of which use actual facts and people. But we put you, the reader, on the spot to ask what you would do in that situation. We hope you can recruit a colleague or a friend to debate different points of view of the scenarios.

There are no simple or correct or wrong answers. As we get into even thornier issues that technology is spawning, discussion and debate become even more important.

Discussion 1: Florida and Biofuels

Example

You are governor of Florida.

Brazil has been called the Saudi Arabia of biofuels. Over the last several decades, it has run much of its transportation on ethanol from its sugarcane crops. It has taken that experience and leveraged that to its vast soybean production. In contrast, Florida imports most of its fuel from other states and countries. Given its agricultural bounty, it could be as self-sufficient with biofuels as Brazil is.

At the annual state fair in Tampa, you are pleased to see children of all ages take a break from the rides and shows and walk through the "Farm to Fuel" exhibit, which shows the promise of orange peel as a biofuel. The state produces five million tons of orange peel each year, which could be converted into 60 million gallons of ethanol. In rural Highland County, there is excitement about exotic sounding plants such as jatropha and sorghum. They could be used to produce cellulosic ethanol and someday could make Florida a net exporter of fuel.

But as you travel the state:

- A livid lawn care operator accosts you at the fair. He has a very sore arm from having to repeatedly yank at his equipment. He is convinced ethanol in the blended gas has ruined many of his motors—and his shoulder. He has good company as boat owners around the state are filing lawsuits about ethanol corrosion and other damage to their fuel tanks and engines.
- A few miles farther east in the strawberry fields of Plant City, farmers tell you that their migrant workers worry whether, with the improving economy, tortilla prices will skyrocket back home in Mexico. The price of corn, a staple in the Mexican diet, doubled in 2008 after having already almost doubled in 2007.
- A few miles to the north, people joke that the movie should be called "Creature from the Green, not Blue Lagoon." Nitrate pollution from fertilizers in farms over the decades means the water at Silver Springs, where the movie was shot, is far from blue. If more crops are grown for fuels, the situation could worsen.

As governor, what position would you take on ethanol and other biofuels?

Herman Tavani: Ethical Computing

Professor Herman Tavani teaches computer ethics at Rivier College in Nashua, New Hampshire. He recently finished the third revision of his *Ethics and Technology: Controversies, Questions, and Strategies for Ethical Computing*.[5] His perspective:

> *There are purists who will argue the way we should look at ethical issues today has not changed since the days of Plato and his views in* The Republic *like those on censorship. On the other hand, some assume that every new technology introduces new ethical issues. For example, some suggest that recent encryption technologies generate brand-new ethical issues, such as new privacy issues that could not have existed before the introduction of encryption technology.*
>
> *I am somewhere in between. As existing technologies continue to mature and evolve, many of the ethical issues associated with them are basically variations of existing ethical problems that introduce themselves in new ways. At bottom, these issues are still about dignity, respect, fairness, obligations to assist others in need, and so forth. But the rate of change has increased significantly, as well as the scope and scale affecting these issues, so we cannot infer that cybertechnology has not raised some special issues for ethics.*

Tavani cites these examples as having occurred in just in the last couple of years, since the second edition of his book was published in 2007:

- Ethical and social aspects of blogging, including controversies involving personal and political blogs
- Controversies surrounding cyberbullying, including the Meier incident on MySpace
- "Sexting" incidents involving young teenagers and existing child pornography law
- Controversies involving "certified ethical hackers" (CEHs) who carry out preemptive counterhacking activities on the part of the organizations that hire them
- Counterhacking activities on the part of the organizations that hire them
- Global dimensions of the "digital divide" and whether affluent nations have a moral obligation to bridge the divide
- Ethical aspects of workplace surveillance and employee-monitoring practices
- Cybersecurity-related controversies affecting hacktivism, cyberterrorism, and information warfare

The dominant topics, though, based on interest in his classes and in discussion with peers, continue to be around privacy issues, followed by intellectual property issues and then security issues.

You would think Tavani gets frequent calls from technology vendors? He does not. Are business schools the most interested in his books? Most interest actually comes from computer science and philosophy classes. Clearly, this walking encyclopedia on cyberethics is not being leveraged enough by technology practitioners and future business leaders. (Professor James Moor at Dartmouth also confirmed he is not often consulted by technology vendors.)

In the meantime, the mutations of ethical issues keep getting more nuanced. Tavani explains:

Cybertechnology is converging with biotechnology and nanotechnology, generating new fields, such as bioinformatics and nanocomputing, as well as concerns affecting emerging technologies, such as ambient intelligence and ubiquitous computing in autonomous systems, and will likely continue to generate even more interesting ethical issues.

Discussion 2: GPS and Routing Traffic through Family Neighborhoods

Example

This time assume you are CEO of TomTom, the Dutch GPS company.

John Sanderson, chairman of the parish council in Wedmore, England, has sent you a letter requesting that his village be removed from your GPS navigation systems. *The New York Times* explains the source of his frustration: "Trucks and tractor-trailers come here all the time, as they do in similarly inappropriate spots across Britain, directed by GPS navigation devices, which fail to appreciate that the shortest route is not always the best route."[6]

In your own country, in The Hague, Stichting Onderzoek Navigatiesystemen, which conducts research on navigation systems, issued a press release in January 2008 that got worldwide attention as it called some of the GPS systems it evaluated "kid killers."

Motorists, it said, drive through "designated low-traffic residential areas and roads which are not designed for through-traffic. The navigation systems do not appear to be able to find ring roads."[7]

What would you do if you were CEO of TomTom?

Gregory Call: The Law and Technology Spawned Ethical Issues

Gregory Call, at the law firm of Crowell and Moring LLP, explains the legal point of view regarding product liability and how it evolves with new technologies:

> *Ignorance of current law is rarely a defense. But with new technology, especially disruptive technologies, companies need to not only understand existing law but anticipate how it might apply, how the law might be extended, and what new laws might be passed. The challenge is increased because many technologies impact people and economies across the world, bringing into play a wide range of unique, cultural, business practices and legal differences.*
>
> *In my experience, many companies developing new technology are aware of the need to understand how their technology will impact others and what rules might come into play. For United States–based companies, a starting point is to understand the basic rules regarding negligence, nuisance, product liability, and contract. For example, as Internet business activity with consumers took off, companies needed to understand how rules regarding contracts, privacy, and communications would impact their business. Likewise, as new energy technologies get developed, businesses need to understand existing rules regarding environmental impacts. Those rules include common law rules regarding nuisance and state and federal laws protecting the environment. Failure to think about these issues can create a legal and economic disaster for a new business.*

We then asked him to comment on the issues likely to come up in the hypothetical scenarios presented earlier in the chapter.

In the Florida example, he says:

> *There are existing rules requiring a business to control its emissions into the air, water, or onto land. If a company fails to do so it faces possible legal action by government agencies or private parties injured by release of waste. It would seem likely that a company in the biofuel business would consider the impact its operations would have and would internalize those costs into its operations by spending money to reduce the impacts and paying for the impacts that do occur. So, the cost of biofuel could include the costs of preventing or reducing such impacts and also the environmental impact on the waters and any corrosion impact on motors, fuel tanks, etc. The challenge in any legal action, of course, is*

proving the biofuel is responsible for the damage and allocating what is incrementally attributable to a new technology. But the process has been around for decades and has come into play regarding new products and technologies.

In the GPS example, he says:

It is not a new development that drivers use side streets to make their way to a destination in the least amount of time. When such use becomes a problem, local laws already allow neighborhoods to petition for speed bumps and road signs to limit or slow down traffic on certain streets. If the GPS devices are routing traffic through their streets, that would appear to be the ideal first resolution. Of course, if community after community reports this, you might see a government agency or an individual take legal action. Such a lawsuit might be based on common law theories of negligence or nuisance and would attempt to hold the GPS device manufacturers or the company providing routes responsible for local expenses to mitigate the risks or for any injuries that might have arisen from the increase in traffic. The risk of such action might cause GPS device manufacturers or route makers to limit routing onto certain major streets. And if they don't, you might see legislative solutions come into play.

He continues:

Most attorneys at technology vendors I know of [Call is based in San Francisco, and has a number of technology clients and peers at technology companies] are actively involved in new product introductions. They all counsel their companies on current interpretations of intellectual property, privacy, and other issues. And attorneys who work in the start-up community are particularly adept at that.

Discussion 3: Neelie Kroes, Former EU Commissioner for Competition

Example

Does technology need more regulators like Neelie Kroes, the European Union Commissioner for Competition, who finished her term in 2009?

The EU commissioner's brief was wider than just technology, but she brought high-profile cases against Microsoft, Intel, and Oracle (in its acquisition of Sun Microsystems). She also capped rates EU telecoms could charge for mobile roaming in her jurisdiction.

Technology vendors do well from regulation of their customers. Sarbanes-Oxley, the Health Insurance Portability and Accountability Act (HIPAA), the U.S. Food and Drug Administration (FDA) validation, standards from the Financial Accounting Standard Board (FASB), tax regimes, and compliance regulations have been good for technology vendors. And technology vendors certainly have their own regulations. Health technology has to go through its own validation. Hardware vendors have emission standards. Software vendors have specific revenue recognition policies. Telephone companies are regulated at local, state, and national levels. And various U.S. regulators have broken up AT&T and brought cases against IBM, Oracle, and Microsoft on grounds of competition.

But compared to other industries, you could argue the regulation of technology has been light. Software vendors often get away with poor quality and mostly limited product warranties. Systems integrators have few certification requirements and hardly ever get publicly scrutinized even after massive project overruns. The Indian government appears to have missed for years the scandal at one of its largest outsourcing firms, Satyam. The U.S. government has allowed significant reconsolidation in the telephone market back to a Verizon/AT&T duopoly.

So, more commissioners, or keep government out of technology?

Governments and Our "Wicked Problems"

As we discussed in Chapter 1, John Kao, former Harvard Business School professor and entrepreneur, has started the Institute of Large Scale Innovation, where he convenes key innovation-savvy officials from around the world to explore models for collaboration and stewardship. He says we need that collaboration to tackle "wicked problems" of global concern: climate, disease, financial meltdowns.[8]

It is a noble pursuit, especially since many of these countries represented in his gatherings are competing with each other for resources, ideas, and jobs as they seek innovation investments.

But these governments are also increasingly cyber-savvy and are themselves creating a new set of wicked problems.

In 2007, a cyberattack disabled much of the electronic infrastructure of Estonia—banks, media, and government services—affecting most of the country's population. It could have originated from a criminal gang or a hostile country. Either way, it woke us up to the fact that Web War I had broken out and that cyberwars would be increasingly more common.

Jeff Nolan's career in venture capital and technology operations has involved working with a number of international companies doing business in the United States. He worries about state-sponsored industrial espionage:

> *While we are familiar with stateless criminal gangs as it relates to identity theft, these same groups can be guns for hire for state- or industry-sponsored intellectual property theft and remain beyond the reach of all but the most determined law enforcement efforts.*
>
> *Clearly, they increasingly have manufacturing prowess, but what a number of countries like China need to advance their industrial programs is the computer technology that the U.S. and Europe have invested in disproportionately. Whether it is for defense technology or commercial applications, the core technology is increasingly the same, and the quickest route to acquiring it is to steal it. So industrial espionage attempts are getting more and more sophisticated.*

Although China also gets much negative press related to censorship, many Western economies lead in surveillance of their citizens. Some buses in London, England, have 16 Web cams on them, and as the BBC reported "Both the Shetland Islands Council and Corby Borough Council—among the smallest local authorities in the UK—have more CCTV cameras than the San Francisco Police Department." Yes, the Shetlands, known for wool, where sheep outnumber people 10 to 1.[9]

The Electric Frontier Foundation (EFF) says on its Web site: "EFF has prevailed in lawsuits against the federal government, the FCC, the world's largest entertainment companies, and major electronics companies, among others. EFF has also beaten bills in Congress and pressured companies to respect your rights."[10]

In their attempt to protect against counterfeiting and Internet-mediated piracy of music and movies, many Western governments are going to require Internet service providers to become "technological sleuths who monitor their customers' Web use."[11] In effect, they may be required to do "deep packet inspection" on Web traffic—the same type of inspection Iran and others have been accused of using to monitor their citizens.

Kao is right about bringing governments together to solve global, wicked problems—unfortunately, those very governments are also causing some new wicked problems.

Discussion 4: Google's Ethics

Example

It could be the words "Don't be Evil" on the Google Web site.[12] It could be that in Web world, we have increased expectations of transparency and accountability. But it appears that we hold Google to higher ethical standards than we do other companies.

Questions abound:

- Should Google be collecting so much of our personal data?
- Should it seek permission when it takes pictures of neighborhoods for its Street View?
- Should it delete links to, say, pornographic sites?
- Should it be filtering our personal mail to show targeted ads?

Nicholas Carr went much further and asked, "Is Google making us stupid?" in an article in the *Atlantic*.[13] He has since developed his thoughts further in a book titled *The Shallows*.[14] Carr may be best known—and maligned—for his asking "Does IT Matter?"[15] But he is an astute observer of macro trends in technology. In his last book *The Big Switch*, he predicted the rapid growth of cloud computing.[16]

In the *Atlantic* article, he was reacting to a comment by Sergey Brin, cofounder of Google.

"Certainly if you had all the world's information directly attached to your brain, or an artificial brain that was smarter than your brain, you'd be better off."

Carr's article ends darkly: "In the [Stanley Kubrick] world of 2001, people have become so machinelike that the most human character turns out to be a machine. That's the essence of Kubrick's dark prophecy: as we come to rely on computers to mediate our understanding of the world, it is our own intelligence that flattens into artificial intelligence."

And then came the spat with China early in 2010 and supporters and critics of Google came out in spades. Human rights advocates lauded. Critics said it would never have happened if Google were not a distant second to the local Chinese search engine Baidu. Nolan, introduced above, said that Google should never have agreed to China's censorship requirements when it started business in the country: "Google got beat by China and we are all worse off as a result. . . . You can't sleep with dogs and not expect to get some fleas as a result." Do we hold Google to a higher standard?

Professor Batya Friedman: Value Sensitive Design

"Value Sensitive Design (VSD) is a way of looking at systems that brings in human values—so informed consent, human dignity, physical and psychological well-being among others; designers can use VSD alongside their favorite design practices, doing their best technical and usability work," says Batya Friedman of the University of Washington who, along with a few colleagues, pioneered the approach.[17] The VSD Research Lab has done projects with industry partners, such as Intel and Microsoft, and worked with organizations such as the International Criminal Tribunal for Rwanda. Most of the lab's funding comes from the National Science Foundation.

Friedman explains: "VSD is about giving designers tools so they can tap into the values and priorities of the stakeholders who will be affected by the systems they design."

One of the researchers' projects, The Watcher and the Watched, investigated the effects of the people watching other people as they walked through a public area that was recorded by a Web cam. Friedman and her team studied not only the typical users of the system—the people watching the Web cam—but also the "indirect stakeholders"—the people who in the course of their regular business on the University of Washington campus passed through the scene and were filmed.

In another project, they compared the benefits of working in an office with a window view onto a beautiful nature scene versus an identical view shown on a large video-plasma display that covered the window in the same office. The goal was to compare a view of real nature through a window to an identical view (in real time) shown on a large video plasma display. To do so, they analyzed physiological data (via electrocardiogram), behavioral data (people's looking behavior out the window and elsewhere), and social-cognitive data (based on an interview at the conclusion of the experimental condition to get each person's perspective on the experience).

More recently, she and her colleagues have been developing "Envisioning Cards"—a deck of "design action" cards that help designers think through the potential longer-term impacts of their designs. Each card shows an evocative image related to a design concept on one side; the flip side describes a specific design action to support concrete forward thinking.[18]

Says Friedman:

One card challenges designers to consider the long-term impact and related trade-offs of their designs if they are successful—that is, if their product becomes pervasive. As an example, laptops typically use less energy than a desktop computer. But longer term, the proliferation of laptops leads to more toxic batteries in landfills. This card helps designers engage the value of sustainability. Another card invites designers to

think what will happen when their product crosses national borders and
is more or less dropped into a different culture.

We're well aware [that] most design teams—in fact, most people—
feel daunted thinking that far ahead, especially with fast-paced project
deadlines. The card set includes a three-minute sand timer, to make the
point that even in a short time frame, the cards can go some distance
in stimulating creative thinking.

Discussion 5: Environmental Trade-offs

Example

This time assume you are an environmental activist.

The Mountain Pass Mine in the Mojave Desert in California has plentiful deposits of bastanite, from which several rare earths are extracted. Rare earths provide minerals critical for hybrid cars, wind turbines, and other cleantech technology. Today, China is the major supplier of rare earths, but its own internal consumption has forced it to cut back on its exports. There are rumors of total Chinese bans on exports of certain of those minerals.

Mining operations ceased at Mountain Pass in 2002 amid environmental concerns, although processing of previously mined ore continues at the site. Mining is expected to restart in 2011.

As an environmentalist, debate the trade-off: minerals critical for new cleantech versus environmental risks for which the mine was closed in the first place.

And are we replacing one dwindling resource—fossil fuels—with another—rare earths? Is that really sustainability?

Erik Keller: Technology Can Learn from Horticulture

A few years ago, Erik Keller was an influential software industry analyst. His home office was chock full of the latest technological gadgets. Most of the time he was on planes and phones around the world.

Then he went back to school and received a certificate as a master gardener from the University of Connecticut. He now also has a certificate in horticultural therapy from the New York Botanical Garden. He elaborates on his changed lifestyle:

When you work in the garden, you get to see the consequences of your actions. If you don't manage your soil and crops properly, you will either have poor crops next year or be forced into an increasingly expensive cycle of fertilization and care. There are no shortcuts; you can't cheat the system.

In contrast, too often the software industry releases poorly functioning and performing software. Or Google and others introduce "beta" software to the market, which implies that it is not ready for prime time. Shortcuts in quality and functionality are often taken to get a product out on time.

Erik also traded his Type A technocrat clients for special-education children and cancer victims.

We make our kids understand that they are stewards of the environment and the success or failure of the garden is in large part due to how they take care of their plants and the soil. At the end of the season, you measure success by how much you have harvested and how well you have left the garden for next year's farmers.

In the technology business, we often don't think about tomorrow's impact of today's actions. The term "legacy" is considered a negative in technology whereas in farming it is a positive. Because the nature of technology is not to preserve the past, it often functions in a circular, self-destructive mode.

This is not to say that gardening and growing plants can't benefit from different types of technologies and innovation. The difference is that any new approach has to accept and build on the past rather than reject it.

Discussion 6: Isaac Asimov and Rules for Robots

Example

In 1942, Isaac Asimov, the famed science fiction writer, published his three laws for robots:

1. A robot may not injure a human being or, through inaction, allow a human being to come to harm.
2. A robot must obey any orders given to it by human beings, except where such orders would conflict with the First Law.

3. A robot must protect its own existence as long as such protection does not conflict with the First or Second Law.[19]

Are drones robots? Should we using them in the war in Afghanistan? Are they actually reducing casualties by being more precise in targeting military versus civilian targets than are bombs or missiles?

The television series *Frontline* had an episode on the pilots who navigate drones remotely from a base near Las Vegas. It discussed the scenario where, for the first time in history, a solider goes to war each day and then goes home to dinner at night. How should we be counseling the pilots about "detachment"?[20]

The Federal Aviation Administration (FAA) is being very cautious about drones for commercial use in the United States. As a society, should we be optimizing technology for positive use (as BP has tried as described in Chapter 21 for monitoring remote pipelines) before we use it for defensive purposes?

Troy Angrignon: Learning from Hari Seldon

Troy Angrignon calls himself an adventure capitalist. Unlike Jim Rogers, who wrote a book with that title after traveling the world on a motorcycle and again in a Mercedes, Angrignon navigates and draws elaborate maps of technology markets as a consultant and analyst. He recently helped build an elaborate map of the hundreds of cloud computing solutions coming to market.

Angrignon was interested in maps and complex technologies even as a young man. He explains how his interest in science fiction shaped his moral compass:

As far back as I can remember, I used to draw spaceships and space colonies. In grade four, I had written a paper on cryogenics. My teacher and librarian naturally didn't know what to make of this.

I created my first company when I was 12 and named it "Foundation Software" in honor of Isaac Asimov's epic science fiction series, in which the series' protagonist, Hari Seldon, predicts the decline and collapse of the Galactic Empire, followed by a 30,000-year dark age before the rise of the next civilization. In order to shorten the Dark Age, he builds two foundations, which act as knowledge stores in the hopes that their existence will ignite the rise of the second empire in 1,000 years instead of 30,000.

Like Hari Seldon, and also like my dear friend and mentor Peter Koestenbaum [the business philosopher], I believe we need to question our preconceived notions and then act ethically and courageously to move us towards that new future.

Let me tell you about my illusions. I registered in college in the environmental studies program. I was the only entrepreneur in a sea of militant eco-philosophers espousing Gaia theories and giving courses on how to spike trees and protest logging. I wrote a paper on nuclear power at the time, taking the position that nuclear power's risks were too great and that we should utterly relinquish all nuclear power. Like Stewart Brand, creator of the Whole Earth Catalog or Amory Lovins of the Rocky Mountain Institute, I no longer hold that position. I think that the short-term carbon issue overwhelms the long-term nuclear storage and proliferation issues.

We have so much already to build our modern-day version of Foundation—that includes social tools, nuclear power, and nanotechnology. With appropriate checks and balances, they all have a role to play in helping us solve the largest issues facing our species' survival.

Discussion 7: Genetic Markers and Prophylactic Treatments

Example

This time assume you are a hospital administrator.

Patient X has checked in for a double mastectomy. But it is prophylactic—she is doing it because her family medical history suggests a higher risk later in life. She has no insurance coverage since there is no cancer yet. There are no external support groups since she is technically not a "cancer survivor."

Should you convene your hospital's ethics committee?

Would you discount her fees to those negotiated with insurance companies? Would you actively discuss with insurance companies the likely spread of such procedures as more patients seek proactive treatments based on growing availability of genetic marker tests?

Technology and Work/Life Balance

Only 30 percent of Dutch working-age adults believe that new products or services will improve their lives in the next six months, compared with 60 percent of U.S. consumers and 80 percent in India and the United Arab

Emirates, according to a 2008 survey by the Institute for Innovation & Information Productivity.[21]

Are the Dutch on to something? Do they have a better grip on work/life balance? Have they, like the Amish discussed in Chapter 1, devised a way of selecting which technologies are "good" and which ones are better off left alone?

Of course, for every cautious adopter of technology, there are others who are going the other way, living in virtual worlds, sharing every moment of their life on streaming video, and boasting thousands of Twitter messages each week.

No wonder we keep having to come up with more nuanced definitions of "reality" such as "reality TV," "virtual reality," and "augmented reality."

Discussion 8: The "Patently Absurd" Patent System

Example

Take turns to debate the U.S. patent system as it currently stands. Alternate roles between representing Microsoft and i4i after considering the facts presented next.

Microsoft was sued by i4i for infringing its XML editor. "Merely one of thousands of features within [the product] Word," said Microsoft after losing an appeal.[22]

The Wall Street Journal in an editorial summarized the mess the patent system is in as it tries to support widely different industries and as the U.S. Patent Office struggles to keep up with the rate of new filings: "New drugs require great specificity to earn a patent, whereas patents are often granted to broad, thus vague, innovations in software, communications and other technologies. Ironically, the aggregate value of these technology patents is then wiped out through litigation costs."[23]

The Microsoft i4i case was litigated in Marshall, Texas, like many others involving intellectual property disputes, because "In the rough calculus of intellectual property litigation, [its] tough judges equate with speedy cases—and that's exactly what you want if you're a plaintiff with limited cash, but potentially big-time settlement payments or damages from a company you claim is infringing on your patent."[24]

So the town of 20,000 "with more pottery manufacturers than software companies" has become famous around the world. It comes complete with its folklore of a "rocket docket" for the speed of its cases

and of lawyers making "rattlesnake speeches" similar to the loud pos-
turing the venomous species does to warn of its presence.

The U.S. Congress has, in multiple sessions over the last decade,
tried to push through patent reform—but there are too many conflicting
parties. Congress is charged under Section 8 of Article 1 of the U.S.
Constitution: "To promote the progress of science and useful arts, by
securing for limited times to authors and inventors the exclusive right
to their respective writings and discoveries."

Also consider this: Ben Franklin, a founding father of the United
States and an inventor in his own right, disagreed on the need for
patents, saying, "As we enjoy great advantages from the inventions of
others, we should be glad of an opportunity to serve others by any
invention of ours; and this we should do freely and generously."[25]

Brian Sommer: Where Are the 10 Commandments of Technology?

Brian Sommer, a former Accenture partner and now a technology consultant at his firm TechVentive, describes his personal values: "Ray Lane,
former COO of Oracle [now at Kleiner Perkins as discussed in Chapter 13],
once told me that I was too squeaky clean for the software industry. I took
it as a compliment. I was raised in a family with strict values. I was even
an altar boy for more years than I care to remember. I am the eldest of
five children. I get values, ethics, and how to make good decisions."

His view of the challenge around cyberethics:

*Speed is omnipresent in our incredibly innovative and technical world.
In contrast, obsolescence reigns in how we apply ethics to these new
creations.*

*We've dissected the human genome but we still don't know whether
we should use it to determine which fetuses are carried to full term. We
can track all sorts of user Web surfing data and we don't know if companies should be accessing the data, let alone selling it. Companies right
now are selling your prescription drug information, but should they?
We don't have a way to make ethical decisions regarding the use of new
technologies, but we really need one. Worse, we have nontechnical
bureaucrats "studying" things for years and still incapable of providing
the guidance that society needs and wants.*

*I'm not sure what exactly the ethical answer should be, but my life
experience tells we need something to hang on to. I believe technologists
and innovators need something like the Hippocratic Oath. We need*

people to question whether their works "do no harm" or could potentially be used in harmful ways. While I'm not a religious person, I am amazed at the durability of the 10 Commandments. Here's a list of acceptable behaviors that's in three major religions and has survived thousands of years.

For ethical innovation and technology, we need to find a higher-level set of principles and we need them, like yesterday. If we don't, someone's going to invent something that's going to rob us of our privacy, our wealth, our livelihood, our relationships, and even our lives.

Recap

Innovation in technology is spawning a bewildering range of ethical issues. As infotech, biotech, nanotech, and cleantech morph and mash up with each other, the issues become even more nuanced.

But other than in hospitals, where there are ethics committees that can be convened at short notice, few other industries have mechanisms to effectively debate such issues around their technologies. Most technology innovators work within the current legal framework to avoid product liability issues and leave most of the ethical discussions to academic settings, and there in philosophy and arts, more than business and technology curricula.

The general school of thought is that it would be speculative even to imagine what issues would come up with a new technology. Let us react once the issues come up. Then we can handle them, or laws will change and we will comply. In many cases, regulators themselves are the cause of new ethical issues as they increasingly put their growing technology savviness to aggressive use. Many polymaths of old were also respected philosophers. Today's polymath's similarly have to factor ethics as integral components of innovation processes.

PART III

Grooming Your Own New Polymath

This part provides some "how to" guidance to develop polymath enterprises:

- Chapter 21 presents the BP CTO profile. It showcases how a team with a set of well-defined tools and processes and access to a vast ecosystem of innovation ideas consistently delivers value way beyond its small size would suggest.
- Chapter 22 brings together the hundreds of innovation voices from all the preceding chapters and organizes them into ten grand challenges for readers as they groom their own new polymaths.

CHAPTER 21

Polymath Profile #8: BP CTO

"Baking doughnuts as an application."

John Baumgartner is describing how kitchen training has turned out to be a successful, but unexpected, application for 3DVE (3D Virtual Environments) technology at BP, the giant energy company. He is chief of staff with a charter for technology innovation in the office of Phiroz Darukhanavala, VP and CTO for IT, better known as "Daru."

You would expect 3DVE applications in the far more complex exploration, refining, and engineering areas of BP, but sugary doughnuts? Baumgartner explains:

> *Our gas stations, like much of retail, tend to have plenty of employee turnover. Also the language skills of employees are pretty varied, so training manuals have historically yielded inconsistent results. On the other hand, a flight simulator–like capability showing employees how to bake doughnuts in the store kitchen . . .*

As Louis Pasteur, the famous French microbiologist, once said, "In the field of observation, chance favors only the prepared minds." *Prepared* is a good description for Darukhanavala's group at BP. It has had an impressive track record over the last decade of asking the offbeat questions, identifying appropriate emerging technologies, seeing them adopted in the field, and, even more important, delivering business value.

Baumgartner is full of episodes of such serendipity. Example: In a eureka moment, CTO Technology Director Curt Smith asked: "Could radio-frequency identification [RFID] chips be used to track people in industrial facilities like a refinery or chemical plant? There are hospital examples, but we have more complex needs." RFID chips are meant to track physical items: pallets being delivered to Walmart, expensive equipment, and so on. If the chips could also track people, they would be invaluable in a search-and-rescue operation to see if everyone had evacuated to safe locations. "Has anyone else done it? Could we make it work?"

Another example: In seeking a solution on how best to connect with offshore platforms in a country without adequate telecommunications, the CTO team considered tethered balloons, microwave towers, and even a communication line over a series of connected buoys. It turned out the solutions were not feasible for this location, but some are being tried out at other locations around the world. Baumgartner says: "Some of the solutions we get to see are so memorable in their creativity, I have no doubt we will find other uses for them in the future."

BP's wide presence around the world in exploration, refining, shipping and other transport, retail, and increasingly alternative fuels on a 2008 revenue base of $360 billion provides a wide palette for testing a variety of technologies—and for honing its "serendipity sensors."

In case of RFID usage to locate people, plenty of issues had to be resolved before the idea could be implemented. Could the chips fit on an employee badge? What networking technology would be needed in a refinery setting? (Heavy metals cause multipath reflection and cause wireless technologies like Wi-Fi to give inaccurate results.) Were the chips safe for humans to wear on a continuous basis? Were the chips "intrinsically safe," meaning, they would not spark and potentially cause an explosion or fire in the presence of hydrocarbon fumes? Could they show location accurate to within a foot or two in real time and in 3-D—critical in a search-and-rescue mission? (Technologies such as Wi-Fi are two-dimensional and updates can be infrequent, some every five minutes. Ultra-wideband reports at six times per second.)

CTO had been working with BP's trading group in London, which wanted to track trading documents in an office environment. That project identified a company, Multispectral Solutions, that was tracking assets in Navy ships. From that discovery they got the idea of using the technology to track people (and assets) in the heavy-metal refinery environment.

After much tire-kicking and persistence, BP innovated the first people tracker, invaluable in accounting for personnel in emergency situations.

Let's explore how this organization grooms its promising innovations, such as the RFID people tracker and much less elaborate ones, such as teaching employees how to bake. It is an interesting combination of "pushing" emerging technologies to the business and responding to the "pull" of challenges from the business. The group also leverages a wide range of antennae to find and validate technologies and promising vendors, which the team of 12 is constantly scouring the world for and conducting elaborate due diligence on.

Only 12 people? Before you scoff, let's look at the massive leverage this small team brings to bear.

We look at four aspects of the CTO operation:

CTO Processes and Program

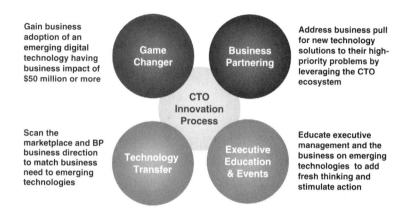

Gain business adoption of an emerging digital technology having business impact of $50 million or more

Game Changer

Business Partnering

Address business pull for new technology solutions to their high-priority problems by leveraging the CTO ecosystem

CTO Innovation Process

Scan the marketplace and BP business direction to match business need to emerging technologies

Technology Transfer

Executive Education & Events

Educate executive management and the business on emerging technologies to add fresh thinking and stimulate action

FIGURE 21.1 BP CTO Innovation Toolkit
Source: BP.

1. The "toolkit"—the techniques the team uses to identify innovative technologies and help their adoption
2. The philosophical principles behind the team
3. The composition and diversity of the team
4. The "ecosystem" the team leverages

CTO "Toolkit"

The CTO group identifies and matures innovation areas in four broad ways, as shown in Figure 21.1.

"Game Changer"

A source of many an innovation project the CTO team has facilitated comes from a concept it calls Game Changer. Broadly, the team, after much scrubbing and arguing in a process that lasts 9 to 12 months, agrees on a major theme each year. To qualify, the theme needs to have the potential to deliver at least $50 million to the bottom line.

Table 21.1 identifies the themes for the last nine years.

TABLE 21.1 Game Changer Themes

Years	Theme	Coverage
2002	Global Sourcing	Review of talent pools in India and other countries and of promising vendors
2003	Commodity Platforms	Linux- and Intel-based low-cost servers and other infrastructure
2004	Sensory Networks	Use of RFID, motes, and other sensors in a variety of field applications
2005	"Clipboard to Computer"	Field Force Automation—mobile and analytical capabilities to workers in plants and field
2006	Predictive Analytics	Pattern recognition in large data sets, particularly those being collected by various sensors
2007–8	Location Intelligence	Platform- and people-specific geographic information
2009	3-D Virtual Environments	Simulated environments for users to interact with using their avatars
2010	"Track and Trace"	Technologies to help with asset optimization, supply chain visibility, safety, and compliance

Source: BP.

Note that the themes are broad ranging—not vendor specific or even technology specific. The 2004 theme of sensory networks involved looking at how RFID, other sensors, mobile devices, Wi-Fi and other wireless networks, and event-driven and alert-triggering software could all be leveraged.

The projects under each theme are anything but rote. In the sensory network category, some of the projects included:

- *LPG cylinder tracking.* RFID tags were applied to more than 85,000 home-use LPG (liquefied petroleum gas) cylinders in Denmark. This allowed BP to create new filling plant efficiencies, support quality control, and reduce empty bottles in the supply chain. A profile record of each bottle was maintained to help improve filling accuracy and speed and to ensure the quality of the delivered bottle. At the retail location, a handheld scanner identified full bottles delivered and empties returned, and a wirelessly connected printer in the truck printed an accurate invoice or delivery note, saving time and eliminating paperwork for the driver.

- *Refinery safety and compliance.* BP worked with Emerson for wireless measurements in refineries to improve safety, environmental compliance, and process optimization. A trial of mote (a type of sensor) technology at the Cherry Point, Washington, refinery to capture "secondary readings" and environmental data provided results at 99.99 percent reliability on wide range of industrial measurements. Importantly, data could be monitored at a central location rather than by workers reading them at multiple, often hard-to-reach locations in the refinery.

- *Pipeline corrosion monitoring.* Previously, drivers manually read corrosion monitoring devices with a handheld data recorder at pipelines in Prudhoe Bay, Alaska. It could be done only once a week due to dangerous driving over remote Arctic roads. This project converted the manual system capturing the measurements to a wireless automated system that uses a mesh sensor network and enables readings to be analyzed every four hours rather than weekly.

- *Storage tank inventorying.* BP deployed a system for the real-time monitoring of LPG inventory levels in customer storage tanks in the United Kingdom. The system used highly accurate ultrasonic sensors attached unobtrusively to the outside of tanks and with a battery life of five years. Inventory levels were sent by radio to low-Earth-orbit satellites, which relayed the information to BP's ordering and delivery systems. This process allowed BP to schedule deliveries based on actual tank content, usage patterns, and other factors, thereby optimizing delivery patterns and effectively eliminating the risk of stock-outs.

Harry Cassar, one of the technology directors in the group, describes how "motes" were discovered and how they turned out be useful technology for the Sensory Network Game Changer. U.C. Berkeley had been experimenting in agricultural and vineyard settings with small plastic cylinders filled with a processor, a radio, some memory, an interface to sensors that collected temperature and humidity data, and a battery that could last for months. They were small enough to be placed on trees and, in concert, formed a sensory network.

Cassar says they "looked cute with the little wire antenna hanging out." In the trade, they are also called "smart dust" due to their tiny size. Although the size was attractive since the motes could be placed in tough-to-reach places, there were significant concerns about whether they could be made intrinsically safe for and robust enough for refinery environments and their harsh conditions for electronic transmissions. Also unknown was whether their battery life could sustain the much more frequent sensor transmissions BP required.

Cassar continues:

*Of course, we are a persistent lot and found an interim application. In the engine room of one of our large tankers, the **Loch Rannoch**, the environment is harsh from a radio transmission perspective and there is almost constant vibration but the solution does not need to be intrinsically safe as it would be in a refinery. We used the motes to automate the collection of vibration data from rotating machines to detect and predict the onset of mechanical problems. It was a previously boring, manual process, and the motes have taken [it] over. We used a solution set from Intel and Crossbow (which specializes in sensors and motes), and Rockwell helped in packaging the electronics for ship usage with their knowledge of collecting and analyzing vibration data.*

But when you are ahead of the curve, you learn through trial and error. The motes were originally designed for scalar measurements with transmission of data occurring from every second to once every 15 minutes or more. Vibration analysis calls for taking over 50,000 measurements a second from an accelerometer sensor. So, we had to make adjustments along the way, like move from an 8-bit to a 32-bit processor and make the battery easier to access and replace.

Of course, the world has moved on in the last five years since the Sensory Network Game Changer.

Smith explains:

We saw industry standards around RFID and tag technology beyond RFID had evolved nicely. Of course, portable and mobile devices had gone mainstream along with consumer/employee adoption. Location-based applications and mashups that take data from different sources had also evolved.

At the same time, we were getting inquiries from BP business groups which needed to track assets worth billions in offshore parts and spares for the Gulf of Mexico, lube bins in Australia, and vehicles and heavy construction equipment in Alaska.

All this provided Smith the fodder to propose what was adopted as the 2010 Game Changer, broadly called "Track and Trace." Smith himself prefers to call it a simpler "Keeping Track" and says the business value is expected to come from four broad areas:

1. *Better asset management.* In a massively capital-intensive company, there are plenty of opportunities to better track assets, to reduce rentals, to streamline spares, to optimize delivery queues at construction sites,

and so on. Just in the BP North Slope operations in Alaska, annual savings in the millions have been identified.

2. *Safety and compliance.* Example: In the San Juan field spread across New Mexico and Arizona, there are tens of thousands of pieces of equipment across thousands of wells that must be tracked for Sarbanes-Oxley and EPA [Environmental Protection Agency] compliance. Additionally in BP's offshore and remote locations around the world, there are opportunities to better track workers in emergencies and in lone-worker situations in remote areas of Canada and West Texas.

3. *Supply chain visibility.* Opportunities to manage assets in circulation, validate billing, improve forecasting, and proactively replenish customer stock. In the Gulf of Mexico, BP hopes to see a real-time view of all equipment and the ships, helicopters, and trucks that move it from onshore to offshore.

4. *Shrinkage management.* Opportunities to reduce lost or stolen equipment and inventory and to improve productivity by reducing manual searches.

Sometimes, one theme provides the impetus for the next one. As the team deployed sensory network projects, the theme of field force automation bubbled to the top and became the game changer for 2005.

Turnarounds (TARs in industry jargon) of chemical plants, refineries, and platforms present significant safety and cost challenges, as they typically involve 50,000 to 200,000 tasks, the use of large contractor staffs, and the shut-down and start-up of numerous pieces of equipment, all within strict time constraints due to the high opportunity cost of downtime. TAR task completions traditionally were tracked manually using clipboard-based systems involving thousands of signatures, which are prone to error and delay. BP worked with a vendor, Syclo, to develop a commercial-grade wireless system that allowed the capture and communication of completion sign-offs using handhelds at the point of activity. The system involved barcoding of equipment, provision of handheld devices for recording and communication of task completions at the site, and processes to monitor initiation and status of tasks. The system ensured that the right person signed off on the right job and checked that all critical tasks were completed at key milestones. The system also identified and optimized paths around bottleneck critical path completion activities. The project significantly improves turnaround safety and cycle times, with potential for dollar benefits in the hundreds of millions.

Each game changer theme has three stages, each lasting roughly a year. Stage 1 involves socializing the theme and identifying pilot projects. Stage 2 involves running pilots—10 to 20 for some themes, many more for others across various business units. Stage 3 involves transitioning to the business and being rolled out in many different projects. At any given time, three game changers run concurrently.

Paul Stone, another technology director in the group, summarizes how the predictive analytics adoption process worked for monitoring equipment health.

> *The CTO group started by funding small proof-of-concept projects with technology from a company called SmartSignal at a number of refineries and an offshore production platform. Often, monitoring equipment health relies on trending machine vibrations or utilizing complex first principle models to predict when there is an issue. SmartSignal, on the other hand, monitors a wide variety of sensors, which may include temperature, pressure as well as vibration, and correlates the relationships among them to spot the kinds of subtle differences that generally indicate a potential failure is likely at some future point.*
>
> *CTO worked closely with the "Refinery of the Future" group [an internal best-practices group looking at standards and improvements across all its refineries]. This team was impressed enough with the results of the proof of concept that they agreed to fund a series of pilots and to work with CTO to scale up the technology. The results from the pilots were again positive, leading to refinery implementations. There was some debate among the upstream engineers about the success of the trial on the production offshore platform. However, ultimately, this was recognized as a success since a predicted problem actually occurred. Other E&P [Exploration and Production] facilities followed. The central E&P technology group is now interested.*
>
> *It is a gradual rollout process; you have to show value at each stage and maintain confidence that value will be achieved.*

Technology Transfer

Like game changers, technology transfers originate from the CTO organization. But they are more ad hoc. Stone explains:

> *The group may hear of a promising technology from our ecosystem sources—like a VC [venture capitalist] or directly from a potential vendor and then present it to specific BP businesses who we believe will potentially benefit from that particular technology. The key is to be well connected, to be aware of what is happening external to BP and to be sure that the ecosystem knows where we are and are receptive to new possibilities.*

Smith provides a good example of a technology transfer:

We got a call from Intel—we have worked with them on a number of CTO projects [former Chief Executive Lord John Browne was also an Intel board member]—asking if there were potential applications for an industrialized ultra-mobile PC [UMPC]. They were looking to widen applications for their Atom chip devised for mobile devices. We asked around and provided feedback that a ruggedized UMPC, made "intrinsically safe," with features like GPS, RFID, 3G wireless, and camera, could make it possible to automate many field processes which we could not previously automate.

A year or so later, Panasonic (based on input from Intel) called us about their Toughbook U1. It is rugged—can handle a four-foot drop. It is all-weather. It is ultra-mobile—a little over two pounds. It has a camera, scanner, GPS, Bluetooth, 3G wireless, RFID scanner, 12-hour battery life, and runs Windows.

We had field employees who had jury-rigged docks for their laptops in their truck. They would lock the laptop in the truck and walk out to the pipeline with their cameras to take pictures and make manual notations about their observations. Now they can take the U1 out of their cars and take precise measurements. The GPS allows them to navigate to the site (and document better routes—say, on an unmarked road), photograph and geo-reference intrusions like fences and buildings or illegal digging so we can plan corrective action. They can take pictures with the device, make annotations with its stylus, and upload that on a 3G network. They can also scan asset bar codes.

The field productivity has improved dramatically. One pipeline right-of-way coordinator said the UMPC had changed his life and ordered one for every member of his team.

Could ultra-mobiles someday become part of a game changer? Potentially, but in the meantime, they are already delivering value to BP based on that phone call from Intel. That is why Stone calls the technology transfer technique "ad hoc."

Executive Events

Mention the words "Blue Chalk" within BP and you will either get an approving nod or a blank stare. The term comes from a meeting in the early days of the CTO group that Darukhanavala and the BP CIO had with Scott McNealy, then CEO of Sun Microsystems, at a namesake café in Palo Alto, California. They discussed various forums to showcase innovation and technologies to executives.

Over the next few years, CTO organized dozens of "Blue Chalk" events around specific themes, such as offshoring or social networks. The goal was to bring together BP executives, thought leaders, and selected technology vendors for an intense mind-meld.

Baumgartner says it takes an amazing amount of effort to organize such events. "Finding, vetting, choosing, and coaching the world's best thinkers [about BP], identifying the appropriate BP executives to attend, and the sheer logistics of it all are exhausting."

Although BP has moved away from the term "Blue Chalk," these executive events continue to provide a vigorous forum and have in many cases provided the fodder for a theme to be considered as a game changer.

Figure 21.2 provides the list of speakers for a two-day event focused on social networking tools. You can see the high-level BP executive sponsorship of the event along with thought leaders and university professors. After each speaker, the agenda leaves time for "table talk" to digest and react to the material and consider what it might suggest for BP. On the second day, most of the time is devoted to breakout sessions in which the speakers participate right along with the BP executives for open, constructive dialog addressing BP challenges.

Importantly, this team continually asks, Who else has done it before? They are unafraid to reach out—in this case to Raytheon and L'Oréal, among others, because they were considered market leaders.

Social tools are much more mainstream today; remember, this event was organized in 2005.

Social Tools Speaker Slate

BP Leadership
— CIO and GVP ; GVP Communications & External Affairs, and GVP, Group Marketing

Landscape
— James Surowiecki, Author, *The Wisdom of Crowds*

IBM—Blogs, Jams, and Collaboration
— Vice President, Strategic Communications

Landscape
— Clay Shirky, Professor, New York University

L'Oreal—Corporate Blogging
— Director, Internet and eBusiness Strategy

DreamWorks—Leading Edge Visualization
— CTO

InnoCentive
— Chairman

Raytheon—Social Networking
— Director of Enterprise Integration

FIGURE 21.2 Agenda to Discuss Social Networks
Source: BP.

Business Partnering

Business partnering is about helping a business unit with key challenges that it raises. Over time, CTO develops especially close and high-level relationships with particular business units, which become "business partners." (CTO may have four to six of these relationships at any one time.) Business partners share their key problems and opportunities with CTO—problems that might lend themselves to a technology-enabled solution not addressed by traditional transactional IT systems. CTO then exercises its vast ecosystem to break new ground for the business.

Here's one question a business partner posed to CTO: Can you help us more efficiently and more continuously monitor 10,000 miles of pipeline against leaks, sabotage, theft, urban sprawl, and vegetation encroachment?

Today, BP uses a fleet of Cessna 185s with pilots who fly by the pipelines, on average, once a week. They fly at a height of 400 feet and report trouble spots, such as erosion near stream crossings or digging equipment in the right-of-way. Field teams investigate these issues further.

CTO had evaluated unmanned aerial vehicles (UAVs) to augment the manned flights but met with regulatory concern about potential terrorist misuse and export restrictions regarding sensitive technology for overseas deployments.

But CTO wondered if the cameras and high-speed imaging systems on UAVs could be attached to manned aircraft to provide some immediate value. Smith reports his findings: "The problem we ran into is that most of the camera manufacturers provide solutions to the military. If the military is doing business with them, they are accustomed to those high price points. Sometimes that's many times the cost of the Cessna."

CTO found a good solution but could not justify the cost: $1.4 million for each plane. So CTO kept looking and found Cloudcap, a company B.F. Goodrich later acquired. Says Smith: "They were set up to sell camera systems for UAVs for commercial applications but ran into the same regulatory roadblocks that we did."

Cloudcap was excited with the idea of putting their cameras on the Cessnas, enhancing the information BP pilots collected—and also opening a new market for them. The digitized frames allow for better analysis of terrain changes as they are collected week after week, allowing long-term changes to be spotted. Combined with infrared technology, the detail they can show is impressive: vegetation dying from leaks, nighttime images of people tapping into pipes, and the like.

And they can allow pilots to fly higher than at 400 feet, which is a clear safety advantage.

So, yes, this should allow more efficient monitoring of pipelines. But it still leaves open the challenge of monitoring more frequently than once a week. Says Smith: "We have some ideas. . . . The business wants solutions—they did not constrain us to just look at aerial solutions."

In another example, the CTO group worked with the maintenance facility in Houma, Louisiana. With trucks and forklifts with heavy payloads coming and going all the time, it can be a dangerous place. Serious injuries and deaths have occurred from people straying. CTO helped develop a state-of-the-art safety system using RFID and ultra-wideband radio technologies. The refinery solution described at the beginning of the chapter showed people's location on a map; the Houma system took the solution a critical step further to identify authorized and unauthorized zones varying by job role and visitor status and to sound alarms when rules were breached.

Staff members and visitors wear badges that relay their locations to a computer system that checks positions against rules for authorized areas and sounds alerts if people enter restricted zones or visitors stray from escorts. Staff, escort, and visitor badges are distinct, with different rules, permissions, and interactions. If a trucker waiting in a safety zone while his truck is being unloaded decides to return to his truck, say, to retrieve his cell phone, as soon as he crosses the yellow line, he hears over a loudspeaker, "Please return to the waiting area; please return to the waiting area. . . ." As he sits down, a staff member arrives to go over facility safety rules again.

The system is also very flexible—new safe zones can be created on the fly, requiring a visitor to stay within 25 feet of a tagged cone. The system is also used for mustering and accounting for everyone at Houma. Evacuations can be played back later to review and improve the exercise.

CTO Philosophy

Darukhanavala likes to describe his team as a "captive VC." Venture capital firms are small but have wide networks and can quickly bring in nimble management teams and specialists to their portfolio companies. But Darukhanavala's is a knowledge capital, not a financial capital, VC. His team acts as a facilitator—sourcing knowledge from a number of areas, filtering and validating the opportunities, shepherding them through the due diligence and pilot stages, and, finally, as a VC would call it, "getting an exit" through successful transitioning to the broader business and IT groups.

One of the "design principles" in setting up his group was "small budget and no authority."

The smallness and the advisory role work well with BP's decentralized culture, which would rebel against a large, centralized, think-tank approach.

Stone elaborates:

Stage 3—broader rollout of a game changer—can be tricky in a decentralized organization like BP. In many other organizations, at that stage, a central group may be involved and aggressively roll it out under a mandate. They may even fund it, and then charge-back to the units. At BP, we are very sensitive to the fact that even though the technology shows huge promise to CTO, the business unit has its own portfolio of projects. It can often be frustrating, but we have to get to a point where we have demonstrated the value whilst working within the current business environment that exists at the time. Sometimes, the business may recognize the value but just not have the bandwidth to adopt it as timely as we'd like. More recently, BP has been looking at a number of changes that should make easier a common way of doing things across business units. The focus on ensuring business value will still remain.

Another area of humility—the team understands its limits in that it knows the energy business and related applications best. It does not know as much about raw, fundamental technology. That explains the attitude of the team: "We know what we know, and we don't know what we don't know and need to get from outside."

Says Stone: "It is easy in a large company to rationalize—we must be good, otherwise we would not be this big. And the oil patch has always thought itself unique. But at CTO, we are constantly looking outside BP and outside our industry for ideas and innovations."

There also is the opportunity to improve the CTO group itself on a continuous basis. Challenged in 2005 by an advisory team made up of executives and influencers external to BP to expand its horizons, the CTO group turned to its own ecosystem for input.

Says Baumgartner: "We brought together leading academic, research, and venture capital thought leaders, and conducted workshops around the world to explore the latest thinking on innovation processes and possible new directions for CTO. It led to our close partnering with businesses to understand their needs and an expansion of the 'ecosystem' the group used for its innovation ideas as we describe below."

Stone adds: "Over the years, we have also become better at measuring ourselves. It's not okay to just say game changers deliver tens of millions in business value. It is the business manager, not us, who determines the value, but we keep track and will jump in if necessary to help the technology director responsible for that year's theme to deliver to the business goals."

Smith adds his perspective: "Most of our focus has been on improving operational efficiency, improving safety, etc. I expect the business will someday call us to also help on revenue focused projects. That would challenge us in new dimensions."

Like VC firms, Darukhanavala's group finds that smaller, even obscure, start-ups are most promising sources for its innovations. Yes, even start-ups with cute names. In fact, Brian Ralphs, another technology director in the group, tells an amusing story. One of the start-ups he worked with was Qwaq. But as the small company started to target the pharmaceutical vertical, it realized that, in medical circles, its name had far worse connotations than duck sounds. It has quietly changed its name to its product name: a much blander Teleplace.

BP has relationships with many large technology vendors—IBM, SAP, AT&T, and HP among them—in Baumgartner's experience, they rarely show up as sources for early technology. There are exceptions—Intel worked with BP as it looked to transition to more commoditized computing platforms—but BP tends to use larger vendors more as it transitions technologies to the business and needs to scale their deployment.

An added advantage with this approach is that BP can negotiate volume-based contracts with demanding delivery metrics and service levels with larger vendors and not pay "innovation premiums." Of course, many start-ups that BP does projects with become attractive acquisition candidates for larger vendors; for example, one of the 3DVE start-ups BP worked with, 3Dsolve, was acquired by Lockheed Martin.

Unlike VC firms, though, this team has no external budget. This situation forces business unit commitment to provide the funding for the pilots after Darukhanavala's group has done the initial sourcing and due diligence. The end-result: It gets the business unit commitment, and also it acts as a brake against too academic a focus in the CTO group.

Darukhanavala cites the limited adoption his group saw as they initially tried to evangelize social tools such as blogs, wikis, and predictive markets. Gradually, the tools have become part of the BP fabric: But it was "when they, not we [in CTO], were ready for the technologies."

Also, unlike VC firms, this team gets nowhere near the personal financial rewards. It has done well in terms of recognition, though, winning several internal and external awards: the CIO 100 award in August 2009 for its 3DVE projects; the 2008 European Green IT award, the 2007 Product of the Year Award for its Turnaround Task Tracker; *Information Age*'s 2006 Effective IT Award for Best IT Team; *Wired* magazine's "Wired 40: Masters of Technology and Innovation in 2005"; and many more. And it has won the highly coveted, internal BP Helios Award for the technology deployed on the *Loch Rannoch*.

The group is also enshrined in a case study taught at the Kellogg School of Management at Northwestern University.[1]

But even there Darukhanavala deflects the commendations—the group is mature enough to give credit to the business. In fact, one of the other "design principles" for the group was "walk away from very successful projects—personally enjoyable as they might be and difficult as they may be to let go, the business needs to take them over."

Of course, there are exceptions. Cassar provides an example:

> *Intel, Crossbow, and Rockwell, the original partners on the mote project, were not positioned to take the kit through to commercial hardened devices due to an internal reorganization at Intel and changed business objectives. Now, Intel has been a very good partner to BP over the years so we understood their reasoning. But we wanted to make sure and transition it appropriately. I had to stay involved with the transition to a Honeywell-led solution, even though the CTO team had moved on to the next game changer themes.*

The small nature of the group and its humility have allowed it to play nice with operational IT and other technology groups and avoid the "you guys have all the fun, we get to do the dirty keep-the-lights-on stuff" syndrome. Although occasional skirmishes occur, the small group has so much on its plate that it typically walks away from any turf battles. The corollary to the design principle above is "Walk away from a project that is not working or where you are not cheerfully welcomed."

As the group's stature has grown within BP, many business unit leaders insist on its involvement in many innovation areas. Darukhanavala cites a recent example with a unit in Alaska. His team went up to discuss a previously identified set of projects. During that meeting, senior management pulled him aside and asked, "Why are we using you for such tactical projects? Let us show you far more complex challenges you can help us with."

CTO Team

Most of the technology directors profiled in this chapter are longtime BP employees. It certainly helps that they know the business, but they come from very varied backgrounds. Smith is American and a geologist by education. Cassar was born in Malta (he says wryly that he's "still not sure what the movie *The Maltese Falcon* had to do with that island-state") but has lived in the United Kingdom most of his life and has a degree in electrical and electronic engineering. Stone is British and has a PhD in chemistry from Oxford. Ralphs is originally from South Africa and has degrees in business and economics. So the team is pretty diverse—and of course, each brings his own Rolodex and perspective.

Some technology directors have come from the outside. One lives in France and was director of Accenture Labs in that country. Another came from an Internet start-up. Cassar did a stint at British Telecom before joining BP. This external blood brings unique technology perspectives to mesh with the business knowledge of the others who were raised within BP.

No wonder when asked what it takes to succeed in the team, Baumgartner hesitates, then says, "Oh, they are all unique."

Upon reflection, he lists a variety of traits: "Self-directed, fast learners, creative, persistent, entrepreneurial." He then invokes what they seek to emulate in Darukhanavala: "Well-connected internally and externally, humble. . . ."

Given the diversity of BP and the wide range of technologies the group evaluates, why only 12 professionals in the team? Darukhanavala says their initial size of six was too small, but when they grew to over 20, including contractors, they were too big and a touch bureaucratic. Twelve professionals plus administrative support has been optimal for the last few years.

He elaborates:

> *Parallel groups at BP—as in an Alternative Energy Group which helps identify promising technologies for BP product units to consider as they explore nonfossil solutions—have emulated our model. In fact, following CTO introduction they have been doing work with SmartSignal around wind energy. Our model could also work in other vertical businesses BP has—to me that is the better way to expand on what we have learned in the last few years.*

His team is concentrated in two major cities—London and Houston— and travels all the time either to BP businesses or to vendor sites. The "glue" is a weekly three-hour call everyone participates in.

When Darukhanavala does expand the CTO group or needs replacements, selection is a rigorous process. Every technology director interviews the candidate. That also helps the candidate get a good feel for the unstructured nature of the job: part technologist, part evangelist, part analyst, part traveling consultant.

The "Ecosystem"

Over the course of the decade, the group has tried, expanded, and abandoned a wide range of innovation sources. The sources reflect personal contacts and experiences of each of the team members.

Smith has found a steady source of ideas from the VC community. "We tour VCs on the West Coast every spring and those on the East Coast every fall." VCs line up relevant portfolio companies, which make 20- to 30-minute presentations to the CTO group. It mimics how VCs themselves decide whether to invest in a promising start-up. The decision making and feedback are rapid, and over time, the VCs get to understand BP's nuances better for showcasing future companies.

Smith continues:

> *We must have adopted technology from over 15 Kleiner Perkins, Sequoia, and Intel Capital portfolio start-ups as a result of this show-and-tell. The flow has slowed down somewhat in the last couple of years as West Coast VCs invest less in applications, and many of them have refocused to cleantech investments—which has turned their conversation to more of our alternative energy colleagues.*

They are exploring relationships with other VCs around the world. They are also using "virtual VC" models, such as ET Accelerator in Portland, Oregon, which facilitates discovery and conversation from its directory of thousands of start-ups. It also allows them to meet vendors virtually so the entire CTO team can potentially participate in the initial reviews.

As a multinational with presence in just about every country in the world, BP has long interfaced with regulatory bodies everywhere. But the CTO group increasingly gets new technology ideas from governments themselves as they become more "cyber-savvy" to service sophisticated citizens, tackle complex security issues, and handle gigantic masses of data.

BP selectively uses specialized research firms to understand high-level industry trends. Baumgartner cites the example of how they leveraged the "All that Data" conference hosted by the firm TTI Vanguard as they looked at trends in predictive analytics.

University research? BP has engaged with a number of the leading science and engineering schools around the world. Baumgartner's assessment is that this approach is very good in providing long-term trend analysis but usually not as useful in identifying currently deployable technologies and vendors. Stone has a slightly different perspective—and mentions his alma mater, Oxford. The U.K.-based CTO team has close links to the university's ISIS Innovation subsidiary, which is involved with commercialization of technology and much more focused on "currently deployable."

In recent years, the group has been encouraged by its advisory board to open up its ecosystem to more "crowdsourcing" and open innovation models. It has developed a "seeker" network of practitioners it can e-mail with specific challenges. Usually, the challenges BP throws out are truly "challenging"—one of a kind.

BP also has a relationship with NineSigma, which has facilitated more than 1,500 Open Innovation awards and more than $12 million in contract awards between clients like BP and solution providers. NineSigma, InnoCentive, and others formalize the crowdsourcing phenomenon with a prevetted group of scientists and other solution providers while handling the legal and administrative issues around intellectual property ownership.

With the wide net the group casts, it often sees unusual patterns. Ralphs saw many 3DVE start-ups in the Research Triangle Center in North Carolina (which has grown nicely as a technology talent hub beyond that of the larger companies like IBM and SAS which were early local technology employers). But sometimes they scour the world only to find a vendor locally. Baumgartner says it found SmartSignal in the backyard of a BP office in the Chicago suburbs after looking at predictive analytics vendors around the world.

Recap

The technologies BP CTO deploy, such as sensory networks and predictive analytics, are years ahead of mainstream market adoption, but it is their tools and methods that are truly impressive. That combined with a widespread innovation ecosystem and some bedrock guiding principles allows a group of 12 professionals to deliver tens of millions of dollars in payback to BP businesses around the world.

Darukhanavala's team does so year after year by nimbly transitioning technologies to business units and transitioning itself to the next game changer. It stays so while staying humble and accepting the constraints that a central resource often finds in a decentralized business environment. For the wide breath of its innovation toolbox, the wide geographic and vertical range of its customer base, and for the variety of solutions it facilitates, the BP CTO group definitely qualifies as a polymath for others to emulate.

CHAPTER 22

Moon Shots for Budding Polymaths

The conference location was set—Tuscany, the birthplace of the Italian Renaissance. The participants were the hundreds of innovators we have met in earlier chapters.

The agenda was in the spirit of "Moon Shots for Management"— where leading management thinkers such as Gary Hamel, C. K. Prahalad, Peter Senge, and Jeffrey Pfeffer and senior executives such as Whole Foods' John Mackey, W.L. Gore's Terri Kelly, and IDEO's Tim Brown came together to define "an agenda for management during the next 100 years."[1]

As we introduced in the prologue, the event went well till *they* arrived. *Field of Dreams* style, ten polymaths from history like Plato showed up to join the modern-day polymaths. So, the agenda had to be hurriedly redone and each of these guests was invited to lead a session track. Here is an unofficial transcript of the tracks and other activities at the event:

Michelangelo: Stretch the Stretch Goals

Michelangelo, the Italian Renaissance-era polymath famous for the Sistine Chapel in the Vatican and the sculpture of *David* in Florence, among many others, described his work and how he applied his personal attitude to stretch goals: "Lord, grant that I may always desire more than I can accomplish."

The GE (Chapter 3) water business explained that its "big market opportunity" is to go from "scarcity threatening" to "abundant and cleaner sources." Bill Joy of Kleiner Perkins (Chapter 13) suggested: "If you cannot solve the problem, make the problem bigger. If you draw a bigger circle, you start to see several systems you can work on."

But not all tried to "solve world hunger." Marc Benioff of salesforce. com (Chapter 19) explained his own stretch goal: "Every time someone buys a server, a switch or a data center, I have failed." The team from the Lafayette Utilities System (Chapter 7) encouraged other communities to set up their own broadband alternatives to the local telco and cable companies. Chris Barbin of Appirio (Chapter 18) exhorted other organizations to go 100 percent "in the cloud." Seth Ravin, Sridhar Vembu, Pat Phelan, and other rebels from Chapter 9 talked about dramatically reducing the cost of information technology. There was general agreement that corporate IT had become too risk-averse and dependent on larger vendors—and that a "stretch goal" for IT should be to encourage more of these "rebels."

Leonardo: Live by the Ethos of "And" Not "Or"

Being a polymath means bringing multiple technologies and solutions together, but Leonardo also challenged the audience to deliver that complexity in a form/factor that does not overwhelm. The ultimate polymath (discussed at length in Chapter 1) repeated one of his famous quotes: "Simplicity is the ultimate sophistication."

There was discussion on how specialized and siloed technology organizations had become and how that precluded what the GE team called "innovation at the intersection of disciplines." The GE team then talked about its Net Zero home project, which brings together appliances, solar, wind, battery, and energy management software. They also talked about their Trip Optimizer for locomotives, which brings combines sensors, GPS, and complex software. The BASF team (Chapter 1) explained about how it is putting robotics, radio-frequency identification, high-speed photography, and bio-informatics to develop strains of genetically modified rice. The BMW team (Chapter 11) discussed how many activities the iDrive interface facilitates and the challenges in keeping it user friendly.

The Hospira team (Chapter 14) described its Symbiq infusion system, which brings together scanners, wireless, large displays, auditory alarms, safety software, and library content to automate drug delivery in hospital settings. The folks at Plantronics (Chapter 8) talked about the Calisto Pro and how it supports landline, mobile, or VoIP calls in hand-held or earpiece format, and much more. They explained how with more of a focus on the consumer market, they had learned to deliver form/factors which delivered complex functionality but shielded users from the sophistication.

Plato: Think Big, Act Small

Plato, the Greek polymath, invoked his famous quote to discuss how constraints, even self-imposed, can help in innovation processes: "Necessity, who is the mother of invention."

Phiroz Darukhanavala, CTO at BP (Chapter 21), explained why he steadfastly keeps his team small—only 12 professionals—and his budget similarly small so his team stays focused on business units to fund their projects. His team discussed its better success with smaller technology vendors than with larger ones. Bill Hambrecht (Chapter 10) preached "80% of value for 20% of the price." The CIO of JetStar (Chapter 4) talked about the "good enough" 97.5 percent organization and how that last 2.5 percent is where the big dollars are. Karin Morton (Chapter 7) explained how her iPod Touch has freed her from the grip of big roaming charges when she travels.

The team from China would discuss its "instant cities" (Chapter 1) as it redefines time constraints, although Roland Sedziol at GE pointed to the risk of "the Valley of Death," where a good handoff has not happened between the lab and the business. Sig Rinde (Chapter 17) encouraged constraint-based thinking with "Here's 30 megs; now plonk it on your laptop and run Germany with it!"

Hypatia: Explore Exotic

Hypatia of Alexandria, the Egyptian polymath and one of the first notable women mathematicians, was well traveled for her time, having studied in Athens and Rome. She explained her guiding philosophy: "Life is an unfoldment, and the further we travel, the more truth we can comprehend."

Francisco D'Souza of Cognizant (Chapter 6) talked about scouring the world and finding talent in India, Argentina, Hungary, Egypt, and other "exotic" parts of the world. Mike Manos (Chapter 18) walked the audience through the 70 factors used to decide on location of data centers. Mary Hayes Weier and Kathy Brittain-White (Chapter 5) reminded the audience not to forget that women and rural communities are underleveraged in technology.

Paul Kedrosky (Chapter 10) pointed out that we need to seek falsification in data, not confirmation. Given the domination of QWERTY in so many of our interfaces, proponents of haptic, surface, brain-machine, and other "exotic" interfaces in Chapter 11 begged for some attention. The team at BP described all the elements of its wide innovation ecosystem from venture capitalists to NineSigma.

Shen Kuo: Exploit the Power of *N*

Shen Kuo, a polymath during the Song Dynasty in China and author of the encyclopedic *Dream Pool Essays*, described how he worked out likely permutations possible on a board of the game of Go. He was not intimidated just because words back then could not adequately describe the magnitude of choices: "The story is told that the Tang dynasty monk Yi Xing once calculated the total number of possible positions on a Go board and was able to discover all of them. I thought about this problem. It is easy but the numbers are large and cannot be expressed with the commonly used words for numbers."

Joy at Kleiner Perkins used a whiteboard to explain the effect of compounding on energy intensity and carbon efficiency: "If we could create energy with half the impact, deliver with 20% less loss, use it three times as efficiently, recycle 20% of that we can get a 10X improvement."

Dr. Hasso Platnner of SAP (Chapter 9) articulated, without using the whiteboard, his vision for 100 times compression to facilitate in-memory processing. The GE team explained product innovations via "adjacencies" and "global extensions." Several people from Chapter 14 talked about Singularity and the human–machine convergence and resulting synergies.

Thomas Jefferson: Hone Your Serendipity "Sensors"

Thomas Jefferson, an architect, horticulturist, mathematician, cryptographer, surveyor, paleontologist, author, lawyer, inventor, violinist, founder of a university, and the third President of the United States explained his philosophy on life: "I'm a great believer in luck, and I find the harder I work the more I have of it."

Even as enterprises try to formalize the innovation process, the smart ones try to build a culture where ideas feed off each other, go off in brand-new directions, and hit "fortunate accidents." The GE Global Research team talked about how the observation of the lotus leaf led to hydrophobic coatings and how composites used on planes have been adapted to wind turbines. The GE team also elaborated its philosophy about how "innovation occurs at the intersection of disciplines."

The BP CTO team talked about how 3-D virtual environments had unexpected applications such as helping train workers to bake doughnuts. Anshu Sharma at salesforce.com discussed the "aha" he saw when he explored business development opportunities around the company's Platform-as-a-Service offering. Martin Geddes (Chapter 7) described how he is exhorting telcos to learn from other industries—especially from the shipping industry.

Benjamin Franklin: Benchmark Often and Wide

Benjamin Franklin, one of the U.S. founding fathers, was also an inventor, diplomat, and plenty more. More important, he benchmarked himself regularly on 13 key virtues: temperance, silence, order, resolution, frugality, industry, sincerity, justice, moderation, cleanliness, tranquility, chastity, and humility. He exhorted today's polymaths to benchmark themselves similarly, but he sheepishly admitted he had personally not done too well on the chastity metric. He then led the tracks on metrics—innovative benchmarks, better ways to represent them, etc.

Benioff of salesforce.com recounted the gut-wrenching decision to showcase on his site key metrics on system performance for the whole world to see. The team from Emerson Electric explained its innovation measurement metrics discussed in Chapter 5. IBM showcased emerging visualization of data discussed in Chapter 15.

Professor Robert Costanza argued, as he does in Chapter 12, for measuring the Genuine Progress Index (GPI) as a better indicator of economies. The team from Walmart (Chapter 12) discussed its ambitious efforts to score its vast network of suppliers and products on sustainability metrics. The team from Best Buy talked about Buzz and Jill and its sophisticated customer analytics described in Chapter 15.

Franklin asked the group to benchmark their embedded technology against those of specialists. He pointed out how car dealers still expect to be paid plenty for embedded navigation and audio systems, when portable units are now at a fraction of the cost. Franklin also encouraged companies to evaluate their major technology suppliers and see if their products have delivered innovations in interfaces (in Chapter 11), analytics (Chapter 15), cloud computing (Chapter 18), and other areas. And if not, have the suppliers been delivering economics the disruptors in Chapter 9 are showcasing?

Isaac Newton: Leapfrog—Build on Baselines

Sir Isaac Newton, the English polymath famous for the Three Laws of Motion, among other things, invoked what he wrote to a contemporary, Robert Hooke, crediting predecessors such as Copernicus, Descartes, and Galileo, whose work they both carried forward: "If I have seen farther than others, it is because I was standing on the shoulders of giants."

The founders of the UFL described as they do in Chapter 10, how on Day 1 they managed to incorporate most of the technologies the NFL has taken years to build. The Plantronics team explained how it has gone from strength to strength by leveraging telco industry transitions to create products for call centers, small and home offices, mobile devices, and increasingly via software-based telephony.

Representatives from countries like South Korea and Estonia explained how they have leapfrogged richer countries when it comes to telecommunications infrastructure. The BP CTO team explained how one year's game changer theme has inspired others in later years. Elizabeth Horn and Pramila Srinivasan (Chapter 15) got a standing ovation as they explained how plenty of passion, combined with increasingly ubiquitous technology, allows for easy setup of sites like ChARM—their community for parents of autistic children. This contrasts with health care systems around the world, which are spending tens of billions developing electronic medical records.

Nasir al-Din al-Tusi: Stay Humble

Nasir al-Din al-Tusi, the Persian polymath, talked about humility: "Anyone who does not know and does not know that he does not know is stuck forever in double ignorance."

al-Tusi then led the audience through a vigorous debate on questions such as: Are innovators arrogant or just misunderstood because they march to their own tune? Are technology vendors respectful enough of their customers like GE, which are no slouches when it comes to product and process innovation? Is Silicon Valley arrogant? Is Bangalore arrogant compared to other Indian technology cities? Are Apple "fanboys" and those in social media too focused on their tools, and ignore innovations from other quarters?

The BP CTO team pointed out the biggest thing they admire in their leader, Darukhanavala, is his humility. Ray Lane at Kleiner Perkins explained why he continues to work so hard—for the chance to work with a new generation of cleantech entrepreneurs. James Franklin at the National Hurricane Center (Chapter 16) said his team's reward came from seeing how their forecasts help save lives, not from the estimates of financial savings from better forecasts obviating unnecessary evacuations.

Aristotle: Embed Ethics in Innovation Plans

Aristotle, the Greek polymath, expressed his philosophy in Socratic style, which he learned from Plato, who in turn learned it firsthand from Socrates himself: "It makes no difference whether a good man has defrauded a bad man, or a bad man defrauded a good man, or whether a good or bad man has committed adultery: the law can look only to the amount of damage done."

Having set an objective, lawyerly tone, he invited Plato to lead the group in debating the ethics scenarios presented in Chapter 20.

Professor Herman Tavani presented cyberethical scenarios from the long list he describes in Chapter 20 and foresees as arising as cybertechnology converges with biotechnology and nanotechnology. Professor Batya Friedman showed the audience the "Envisioning Cards" her team has developed, which help designers think through the potential longer-term impacts of their designs.

There was heated discussion on the need for governments to work together to solve the grand challenges of the world, particularly those around sustainability (Chapter 12) and health care (Chapter 14). There was wariness that those very governments are also causing some new wicked problems, such as cyberwars and intrusive surveillance, and they are putting enterprises in awkward positions, as Google has found with China. Brain Sommer made his case that technology markets should have their own version of the Ten Commandments (Chapter 20).

And the Sidebar Conversations

The ten polymaths from history mingled with and regaled the audience about the many disciplines they are good at—and in some cases, the disdain they had for each other. The old masters, in turn, were fascinated with today's technology. Plato was interested in technology in courtrooms. Al-Tusi could not get enough of Unicode and how it represented Farsi and other characters. Hypatia, a wide traveler for her time, was fascinated to see a modern lady like Esther Dyson prepare to be a space tourist.

There were jokes about Mr. Gorsky and penguins projecting. And Al Gore—until someone pointed out how few people are associated with the Internet *and* with climate change, two of the biggest drivers of technology innovation in the last couple of decades.

There were conversations about the shortage of polymaths today, given the explosion of disciplines and technologies. How specialization made us all "monomaths," as Edward Carr of *The Economist* calls them. The consensus that emerged was there is already a new generation of polymaths, such as Nathan Myhrvold and Steve Jobs. If we add up all the personal interests and skills that do not show up in formal resumes, there are plenty of other modern-day, mainstream polymaths. That crafting the right blend of monomaths leads to polymath enterprises, as in the eight ones that are profiled in the book. We need these polymaths to solve the world's wicked problems that Aristotle and al-Tusi and Jefferson never even imagined.

At the closing dinner amidst the breathtaking yellow mustard fields, Michelangelo had raised a toast to the *uomo universale*, the Italian term for polymath. He had invoked his Renaissance contemporary, Leon Battista Alberti:

"A man can do all things if he but wills them."

The Beginner's Mind

A few of them had stayed on for the postconference tour. Pisa had been kitschy, but as they sat in a café in Florence outside the Palazzo Vecchio admiring the copy of Michelangelo's *David*, the oohs and aahs about the conference flowed again.

Gretchen Lindquist had talked to Leonardo about the Renaissance-era bishop Marco Girolamo Vida, the focus of her master's thesis. Cris Orfescu explained how Michelangelo appeared fascinated with his nanoart—using naturally occurring and man-made nano structures.

Jim Spath described his favorite conference session—the one about *shoshin*. The session leader had described it as "Beginner's Mind"—a Zen Buddhist concept that refers to wide openness when studying a subject. He said it was associated with a martial arts *dojo*. That seeming oxymoron—openness and self-defense—struck him as a good way to look at the rapid way the world evolves.

The session leader had described several scenarios and asked the class for their "Beginner's Mind" reactions:

1. At the Copenhagen Climate Change summit, you could not have scripted a more unusual meeting as the Associated Press reported:

> *It was almost unthinkable. The President of the United States walked into a meeting of fellow world leaders and there wasn't a chair for him, a sure sign he was not expected, maybe not even wanted. . . . Along with India, South Africa and Brazil, the key member in the room was China, which recently surpassed the U.S. as the world's top emitter of heat-trapping gasses.*[1]

Political commentators were full of gossip. Why was the U.S. President doing a deal with the four growing powerhouses that likely will cause the most pollution in the next few decades? Why did China invite the other three to the meeting without telling the United States? Why were there no chairs ready for the U.S. delegation?

2. Biz Stone, cofounder of Twitter looked a bit startled when, at an industry event last summer, a woman representing Walmart stood up and posed a question that basically said:

I know you are searching for a business model. We may have one for you if you can help us analyze more finely Tweets that mention Walmart. Separate those that reflect customer sentiment from others triggered by a Walmart news item or other more casual mentions of our brand.

Two things were remarkable about that statement. Large enterprises are sold technology; they don't typically—certainly not in open forums—tell vendors that they are open to business. The other was a tacit statement that in the "freemium" model, firms like Twitter were experimenting with consumers may only go so far, but enterprises may be willing to pay for targeted access to those millions of users.

3. David Pogue, who covers mobile and other consumer tech for *The New York Times*, highlighted in a year-end post some of the best new features he saw in mobile devices and cameras in 2009:

- The dock designed for Motorola Droid can suction to the car windshield. Magnetic sensors help fill the screen with Google's GPS navigation application. Another dock for home turns it into a bedside alarm clock and provides weather updates while you charge it overnight.
- The MiFi is a "credit card-size, personal, portable, powerful, password-protected" Wi-Fi hot spot.
- The Nikon's Coolpix S1000pj introduces a built-in projector.
- Can't find your iPhone? On the me.com Web site, you can see where it is on a zoomable map.[2]

4. Richard Fisher of the National Aeronautics and Space Administration said after scientists discovered a mysterious ribbon of hydrogen around our solar system:

The physicists are going to have to go back and figure out what physical processes are being left out of these calculations, and my guess is that within a couple of years, we'll have a pretty good explanation.[3]

And:

We thought we knew everything about everything, and it turned out that there were unknown unknowns.[4]

Spath then walked the group through the instructor's own "Beginner Mind" reactions to each:

1. Why don't we talk much about South Africa as a potential powerhouse? What does Francisco D'Souza of Cognizant think of South Africa as a talent hub? Does that mean we need to get used to the term "BASIC countries"—the new acronym the media coined for the four emerging powers—Brazil, South Africa, India, and China?[5]
2. Is this the business model social computing firms like Twitter have been waiting for? Downplay consumer revenue and advertising models and switch to one that analyzes social media patterns for companies like Walmart?
3. How soon before the next "Jesus-phone" emerges that incorporates *all* these features? At the pace these innovations are coming out, how soon before David Pogue turns such a column into a weekly, not an annual, ritual?
4. Which businesses will benefit from a period of *increased* sunspot activity expected in 2012?

As the cappuccino flowed, the group provided their own *shoshin* reactions to each of the scenarios.

Spath continued: "The session got me thinking: Could we take the principles we have learned in the SAP SDN community and apply it to broader innovation? To me, that is my "Beginner's Mind" reaction to the conference. That form of Open Innovation"

Marilyn Pratt jumped in: "What a great idea! Let's discuss it on the next SAP Mentors call. By the way, my favorite session was that on cyber ethics. I had really enjoyed all the passion and debate around biofuels in Florida and about Google's ethics. I would like to take discussion of ethics scenarios also to a community format."

Craig Cmehil, who had joined them for the weekend, merely said, "Sweet!" as he thought about how his new leaders at SAP might use *shoshin* as they tried to reinvent the German software house.

In another realm, Michelangelo looked down and saw the Piazza della Signoria grow more crowded with tourists, and he turned his attention back to reinterpreting *David* in nanoart. Then he sighed that six centuries later he still had to worry about masterpieces Leonardo might create in this new art form.

Notes

Preface

1. New Florence. New Renaissance. Available at www.florence20.typepad. com.
2. Deal Architect. Available at www.dealarchitect.typepad.com.

Chapter 1

1. Dan Brown, *The Da Vinci Code* (New York: Doubleday, 2003).
2. Universal Leonardo. Available at www.universalleonardo.org.
3. LBNL Image Library. Available at http://imglib.lbl.gov/cgi-bin/ImgLib/ displaytag/BERKELEY-LAB/SEABORG-ARCHIVE/tags/96B05394?tag.
4. CNN Money. "On catching tech's next wave," March 7, 2008. Available at http://money.cnn.com/galleries/2008/fortune/0803/gallery.jobsqna .fortune/13.html.
5. Steve Lohr, "Can Governments Till the Fields of Innovation?" *The New York Times,* June 20, 2009. Available at www.nytimes.com/2009/06/21/ technology/21unboxed.html?_r=2&adxnnl=1&adxnnlx=1245582148 -7qf9w20+EO1BnTTPTIa1dw.
6. Rudiger Thiele, "Hilbert's Twenty-Fourth Problem," Mathematical Association of America. Available at www.maa.org/news/Thiele.pdf.
7. National Academy of Engineering. "Grand Challenges." Available at www.engineeringchallenges.org/cms/challenges.aspx.
8. United Nations Development Programme. "About the MDGs: Basics: What are the Millennium Development Goals?" Available at www.undp .org/mdg/basics.shtml.
9. Gartner. "Gartner Identifies Seven Grand Challenges Facing IT," April 9, 2008. Available at www.gartner.com/it/page.jsp?id=643117.
10. KurzweilAI.net. "The Law of Accelerating Returns," March 7, 2001. Available at www.kurzweilai.net/articles/art0134.html?printable=1.

11. Edward Carr, "The Last Days of the Polymath," *Intelligent Life* (Autumn 2009). Available at www.moreintelligentlife.com/content/edward-carr/last-days-polymath.

12. CNN. "Solving Global Warming with Nathan Myhrvold," December 20, 2009. Available at http://transcripts.cnn.com/TRANSCRIPTS/0912/20/fzgps .01.html.

13. Channel Web. "Bill Gates Joins Scientists to Take on Hurricanes," July 16, 2009. Available at www.crn.com/government/218500976;jsessionid =MZXLM2NDPVONRQE1GHRSKHWATMY32JVN.

14. Intellectual Ventures. "Our Inventions." Available at www. intellectualventures.com/inv_main.aspx.

15. Forbes. "Nathan Myhrvold: Inventions as an Asset Class," August 18, 2009. Available at www.forbes.com/2009/08/17/nathan-myhrvold -microsoft-leadership-clayton-christensen-intellectual-ventures.html.

16. Malcolm Gladwell, "In the Air," *The New Yorker*, May 12, 2008. Available at www.newyorker.com/reporting/2008/05/12/080512fa_fact_gladwell.

17. Steven D. Levitt and Stephen J. Dubner, *SuperFreakonomics: Global Cooling, Patriotic Prostitutes, and Why Suicide Bombers Should Buy Life Insurance* (New York: William Morrow, 2009).

18. Rafe Needleman, "Nathan Myhrvold at D6: Don't Call Me a Patent Troll," *CNET News*, May 28, 2008. Available at http://news.cnet .com/8301-17939_109-9954213-2.html.

19. "Patent Gridlock Suppresses Innovation," *The Wall Street Journal*, July 14, 2008. Available at http://online.wsj.com/article/SB121599469382949593 .html.

20. CNN Money. "Joy after Sun with his corporate ties cut, the 'Edison of the Net' speaks freely on the challenges facing Sun, the Net, and, of course, Microsoft," October 13, 2003. Available at http://money.cnn .com/magazines/fortune/fortune_archive/2003/10/13/350901/index .htm.

21. Baldesar Castiglione, *The Book of the Courtier*, trans. George Bull (New York: Penguin Classics, 1976).

22. Chris Murphy, "InformationWeek 500 No. 1 Company: CME Group," *InformationWeek*, September 15, 2009. Available at www.information-week.com/news/hardware/data_centers/showArticle.jhtml?articleID =219700577.

23. TechCrunch. "RedBeacon Wins The Top Prize At TechCrunch50 2009." Available at www.techcrunch.com/2009/09/15/redbeacon-wins-the-top -prize-at-techcrunch50-2009.

24. Peter Hessler, "China's Instant Cities," *National Geographic* (June 2007). Available at http://ngm.nationalgeographic.com/2007/06/instant-cities/ hessler-text.

25. The Seven Sins of GreenWashing. Available at http://sinsofgreenwashing .org/findings/greenwashing-report-2009.

26. UPS. "The UPS Delivery Information Acquisition Device (DIAD IV)." Available at www.pressroom.ups.com/Fact+Sheets/The+UPS+Delivery+ Information+Acquisition+Device+(DIAD+IV).

27. Elizabeth College. "Current Research: Professor Kraybill's current research involves several different projects related to Anabaptist communities."Available at http://users.etown.edu/k/kraybilld/current _research.htm.

Chapter 2

1. Based on an analysis of *Forbes*, "The Global 2000." April 8, 2009, available at http://www.forbes.com/lists/2009/18/global-09_The-Global-2000 _Company.html.

2. CIO. "State of the CIO 2010: Three Types of CIO Business Strategists Gain Ground," December 10, 2009. Available at https://www. cioexecutivecouncil.com/download.html?content_id=24.9ec.3605bd12.

3. Concurring Opinions. "American Law Institute Approves the Principles of the Law of Software Contracts," June 2, 2009. Available at www. concurringopinions.com/archives/2009/06/american-law-institute -approves-the-principles-of-the-law-of-software-contracts.html.

4. Marketwire. "Brightroam: Globetrotting Employees Inflate Corporate Cell Bills," Jan 23, 2008. Available at www.marketwire.com/press-release/Brightroam-813585.html.

5. Eatel. "Glossary of Applicable Fees, Charges and Taxes," May 12, 2008. Available at www.eatel.com/universal.cfm?pageid=225.

6. Jeff Bertolucci, "How Much Ink Is Left in That Dead Cartridge?" *PC World*, November 2, 2008. Available at www.pcworld.com/article/152953/ how_much_ink_is_left_in_that_dead_cartridge.html.

7. United Nations. "Report of the World Commission on Environment and Development," December 11, 1987. Available at www.un.org/documents/ ga/res/42/ares42-187.htm.

8. CBS News. "Climate Accord: Much Left to Do," December 18, 2009. Available at www.cbsnews.com/blogs/2009/12/18/world/worldwatch/ entry5997439.shtml.

9. U.S. Chamber of Commerce. "Your Feedback: Readers Debate Climate Change Bill," September 2009. Available at www.uschambermagazine. com/article/your-feedback-readers-debate-climate-change-bill.

10. Greentech Media. "Star Investor Vinod Khosla Responds: "We're in a crisis, and there is an opportunity to reinvent our energy infrastructure; it would be a folly to waste it," March 15, 2010. Available at www. greentechmedia.com/articles/read/star-investor-vinod-khosla-responds.

11. MSNBC. "U.S. Tops World in Health Spending, Results Lag." Available at www.msnbc.msn.com/id/34330376/ns/health-health_care.

12. U.S. Department of Health & Human Services. "The New Numbers (Health Insurance Reform Cannot Wait," September 16, 2009. Available at www.hhs.gov/news/press/2009pres/09/20090916b.html.

13. OregonLive.com. "On Health Care, America Looks Awfully Third-World," July 28, 2009. Available at www.oregonlive.com/opinion/index.ssf/2009/07/on_health_care_america_looks_a.html.

14. Grand Challenges in Global Health. Available at www.grandchallenges.org/Pages/BrowseByDisease.aspx#Other%20Infectious%20Diseases.

15. World Health Organization. "World Health Statistics, 2009." Available at www.who.int/whosis/whostat/EN_WHS09_Full.pdf.

Chapter 3

1. GE. "Opportunity to Reset," February 6, 2009. Available at www.ge.com/ar2008/letter_5.html.

2. David Kline, "Uncaptured Fortunes in Intellectual Capital," *Strategy+Business*, February 28, 2008. Available at www.strategy-business.com/article/08116?pg=1.

3. Justin Carretta, "GE: Beyond the Information Age," *Fleet Owner*, November 12, 2007. Available at http://fleetowner.com/information_technology/general_electric_high_tech_advances.

4. Reuters. "Globalization Is a Tough Sell, GE's Immelt says," July 7, 2007. Available at www.reuters.com/article/idUSN0620856720070708.

5. GE. Available at www.ge.com/files/usa/company/investor/downloads/webcast_05042006/webcast_presentation2_05042006_little.pdf.

6. "Manifesto for Agile Software Development." Available at http://agilemanifesto.org.

Chapter 4

1. Gartner. "Gartner Says Consumerization Will Be Most Significant Trend Affecting IT During Next 10 Years," October 20, 2005. Available at www.gartner.com/press_releases/asset_138285_11.html.

2. Josh Quittner, "Apple's New Core," *Time*, January 10, 2002. Available at www.time.com/time/magazine/article/0,9171,192601,00.html.

3. Richard Karlgaard, "Apple, the Outlier," Digital Rules Blog, October 21, 2009. Available at http://blogs.forbes.com/digitalrules/2009/10/apple-the-outlier.

4. The NV Flyer. "Southwest persuades court to shut down boarding pass company's operations," September 12, 2007. Available at http://nvflyer

.wordpress.com/2007/09/17/southwest-persuades-court-to-shut-down-boarding-pass-companys-operations.

5. Scott Watts, "Give Guests the In-Room Tech They Demand," *Hospitality Technology*, June 3, 2008. Available at www.htmagazine.com/ME2/dirmod.asp?sid=&nm=&type=MultiPublishing&mod=PublishingTitles&mid=3E19674330734FF1BBDA3D67B50C82F1&tier=4&id=3952307BDB A74D25863583EEC361DFF9.

6. Jeffrey O'Brien, "What's Your House Really Worth?" *Fortune*, February 15, 2007. Available at http://money.cnn.com/magazines/fortune/fortune _archive/2007/02/19/8400262/index.htm.

7. Lev Grossman, "*Time*'s Person of the Year: You," *Time*, December 13, 2006. Available at www.time.com/time/magazine/article/0,9171,1569514,00.html.

8. John Branch, "Promising Fans at Game a View From the Couch," *The New York Times*, January 29, 2009. Available at www.nytimes .com/2009/01/29/sports/football/29view.html.

9. Robert Capps, "The Good Enough Revolution: When Cheap and Simple Is Just Fine," *Wired*, August 24, 2009. Available at www.wired.com/gadgets/miscellaneous/magazine/17-09/ff_goodenough.

10. Brian Haverty, "Stephen Tame, CIO," ZDNet Australia, September 19, 2006. Available at www.zdnet.com.au/insight/business/soa/Jetstar -Stephen-Tame-CIO/0,139023749,339271110,00.htm.

11. Janet Kornblum, "No Cellphone? No BlackBerry? No E-mail? No Way? (It's True)," *USA Today*, January 11, 2007. Available at www.usatoday .com/tech/news/2007-01-11-tech-no_x.htm.

Chapter 5

1. Tom Peters, "Leading in Totally Screwed Up Times: The Leadership." Available at www.tompeters.com/slides/uploaded/ALA%2010-31-01.ppt.

2. WITI. Available at www.witi.com.

3. Technology Goddess. Available at www.technology-goddesses.org.

4. Global Women Investors & Innovators Network. Available at www.gwiin .com.

5. Penelope Green, "Home Crafts Get Wired," *The New York Times*, September 10, 2009. Available at www.nytimes.com/2009/09/10/garden/10led.html.

6. Rich Seely, "SOA Creates Order Out of Chaos @ Amazon," Searchsoa .com, June 23, 2006. Available at http://searchsoa.techtarget.com/news/article/0,289142,sid26_gci1195702,00.html#.

7. Jesse Schell, *The Art of Game Design: A Book of Lenses* (Burlington, MA: Morgan Kaufmann, 2008).

8. Brian Hindo, "Emerson Electric's Innovation Metrics," *BusinessWeek*, June 5, 2008. Available at www.businessweek.com/magazine/content/08_24/b4088046119515.htm?chan=search.

9. Newsweek. "Green Rankings: 2009 List." Available at http://greenrankings.newsweek.com/companies/view/pge.

10. Microsoft BizSpark. Available at www.microsoft.com/BizSpark.

11. Chris Anderson, "The Economics of Giving It Away," *The Wall Street Journal*, January 31, 2009. http://online.wsj.com/article/SB12333567842023 5003.html

12. Pilita Clark, "Lunch with the FT: Michael O'Leary," FT.com, December 18, 2009.

13. SageCircle. "NCVI are the four most important letters in the English alphabet for a Gartner sales rep," April 15, 2009. Available at http://sagecircle.wordpress.com/2009/04/15/ncvi-are-the-four-most-important-letters-in-the-english-alphabet-for-a-gartner-sales-rep.

14. André Andnian, Christoph Loos, and Luiz Pires, "Building an Innovation Nation," March 4, 2009. Available at http://whatmatters.mckinseydigital.com/innovation/building-an-innovation-nation.

15. Matt Richtel, "Tech Recruiting Clashes with Immigration Rules," *The New York Times*, April 11, 2009. Available at www.nytimes.com/2009/04/12/business/12immig.html.

16. Reena Jana, "Innovation Trickles in a New Direction," *BusinessWeek*, March 11, 2009. Available at www.businessweek.com/magazine/content/09_12/b4124038287365.htm.

17. Brett Forest, "The Next Silicon Valley: Siberia," *Fortune*, March 26 2007. Available at http://money.cnn.com/magazines/fortune/fortune_archive/2007/04/02/8403482/index.htm.

Chapter 6

1. Robert G. Eccles and Thomas H. Davenport, "Cognizant 2.0: Embedding Community and Knowledge into Work Processes," Harvard Business School case study, February 2010.

2. Mayur Sahni, "Cognizant 2.0: Leveraging Web 2.0 Technologies for Diving Innovation in Offshore Delivery," International Data Corp. (November 2009).

Chapter 7

1. Douglas MacMillan, Peter Burrows, and Spencer E. Ante, "Inside the App Economy," *BusinessWeek*, October 22, 2009. Available at www.businessweek.com/magazine/content/09_44/b4153044881892.htm.

2. Reputation Institute. "2009 Global Reputation Pulse." Available at www .reputationinstitute.com/advisory-services/global-pulse.

3. Carol Wilson, "Strigl: U.S. Telecom Industry Unfairly Maligned," *Telephony Online*, June 18, 2008. Available at http://telephonyonline .com/broadband/news/strigl-verizon-broadband-0618.

4. Cottonwood Communications. "Are you a Telecom/IT Master or Completely Lost?" September 4, 2009. Available at www.cottonwood-comm.com/2009/09/are-you-a-telecomit-master-or-completely-lost.

5. Verizon. "United States Securities and Exchange Commission, Washington, D.C. 20549, Form 10-K." Available at http://investor.verizon.com/sec/ sec_frame.aspx?FilingID=6435582.

6. Fake Steve Jobs. "A not-so-brief chat with Randall Stephenson of AT&T." Available at www.fakesteve.net/2009/12/a-not-so-brief-chat-with -randall-stephenson-of-att.html.

7. CFI Group. "iPhone, Android, and Pre Beat BlackBerry and Legacy Smart-phones in CFI Group Customer Satisfaction Study," September 30, 2009. Available at www.cfigroup.com/news/pressreleases/2009_Smartphone _pressrelease.doc.pdf.

8. Marguerite Reardon, "Lafayette, La., Finally Gets Its Fiber Network," *CNet.News*, February 6, 2009. Available at http://news.cnet.com/8301 -11386_3-10158583-76.html.

9. "UK Broadband 'Not Fit' for Future," *BBC News*, October 1, 2009. Available at http://news.bbc.co.uk/2/hi/technology/8282839.stm.

10. "Iran's Twitter Revolution," *Washington Times*, June 16, 2009. Available at www.washingtontimes.com/news/2009/jun/16/irans-twitter-revolution.

11. Nokia Siemens Network. Available at http://w3.nokiasiemensnetworks .com/NR/rdonlyres/467840D6-D8F8-497D-9094-3BC1E2084065/0/ ZCard_210907.pdf.

Chapter 8

1. World Intellectual Property Organization. "Movement Powered Headset." Available at www.wipo.int/pctdb/en/wo.jsp?WO=2008066685&IA =US2007023557&DISPLAY=DESC.

Chapter 9

1. Manek Dubash, "Moore's Law Is Dead, Says Gordon Moore," *TechWorld*, April 13, 2005. Available at http://news.techworld.com/operating-systems/ 3477/moores-law-is-dead-says-gordon-moore.

2. Ellen McGirt, "Intel Risks It All (Again)," *Fast Company*, December 1, 2009. Available at www.fastcompany.com/magazine/140/intel-risks-it-all -again.html.

3. Clayton M. Christensen, *When New Technologies Cause Great Firms to Fail* (Boston: Harvard Business Press, 1997).

4. "The 'Cloud Pioneers': Timothy Chou." Deal Architect Blog, April 7, 2009. Available at http://dealarchitect.typepad.com/deal_architect/2009/04/cloud-pioneers-timothy-chou.html.

5. Neil G. Chirico and Joanne Helperin, "Corner Garage vs. Dealer Service Department." Available at www.edmunds.com/ownership/maintenance/articles/43779/article.html.

6. IBM. "IBM Social Computing Guidelines: Blogs, wikis, social networks, virtual worlds and social media." Available at www.ibm.com/blogs/zz/en/guidelines.html.

7. CFO. "The High Cost of Change for ERP: What Does It Cost to Keep Up to Date?—A report prepared in collaboration with Agresso." Available at www.cfo.com/whitepapers/index.cfm/displaywhitepaper/13316056.

8. Hasso Platner Institute. Available at www.hpi.uni-potsdam.de/willkommen.html?L=1.

Chapter 10

1. Clayton M. Christensen, *The Innovator's Dilemma: The Revolutionary Book that Will Change the Way You Do Business* (Boston: Harvard Business Press, 1997).

2. UFL Access. "A Week in Vegas: The Guts and Glory of the United Football League," November 28, 2009. Available at http://uflaccess.com/uflaccess/a-week-in-vegas-the-guts-and-glory-of-the-united-football-league.

3. New York Times. "Open and Fair: Why Wall St. Hates Auctions," March 18, 2006. Available at www.wrhambrecht.com/about/media/20060318nyt.pdf.

Chapter 11

1. Angus MacKenzie, "TechnoThrill: 2009 BMW 750Li and 750i," *Motor Trend*, October 7, 2008. Available at www.motortrend.com/roadtests/sedans/112_0810_2009_bmw_7_series_technical_details/index.html.

2. Microsoft. "Works on virtually any surface. Better than optical. Better than laser. Period." Available at www.microsoft.com/hardware/mouseandkeyboard/tracklanding.mspx.

3. GS1. Available at www.gs1us.org/Default.aspx.

4. "MIT Student Arrested at Logan in Bomb Scare," *The Boston Globe*, September 21, 2007. Available at www.boston.com/news/globe/city_region/breaking_news/2007/09/mit_student_arr.html.

5. Wear It @ Work. Available at www.wearitatwork.com.

6. Alex Weprin, "NAB 2009: CNN's Bohrman Revisits Election Night Holograms, Magic Walls," *Broadcasting and Cable,* April 20, 2009. Available at www.broadcastingcable.com/article/209449-NAB_2009_CNN_s _Bohrman_Revisits_Election_Night_Holograms_Magic_Walls.php.

7. Kim Zetter, "TED: Jeff Han, A Year Later," *Wired,* July 3, 2007. Available at www.wired.com/techbiz/people/news/2007/03/72905.

8. SixthSense. About page. Available at www.pranavmistry.com/projects/ sixthsense.

9. The Unicode Consortium. Available at http://unicode.org.

Chapter 12

1. Greentech Media. "Star Investor Vinod Khosla Responds: "We're in a crisis, and there is an opportunity to reinvent our energy infrastructure; it would be a folly to waste it," March 15, 2010. Available at www.greentechmedia.com/articles/read/star-investor-vinod-khosla -responds.

2. Vivian Wai-yin Kwok, "China: Where Poisoning People Is Almost Free," Forbes.com, August 7, 2009. Available at www.forbes.com/2009/08/07/ china-pollution-riot-international-politics.html.

3. ABC. "Eyewitness: How China sabotaged climate talks," December 23, 2009. Available at www.abc.net.au/news/stories/2009/12/23/2779498 .htm.

4. Center for American Progress Action Fund. "Written testimony for the Senate Committee on Environment and Public Works, Legislative Hearing on Clean Energy Jobs and American Power Act, S. 1733." Available at www.americanprogressaction.org/issues/2009/10/pdf/podesta_epw .pdf.

5. Federal Ministry of Economics and Technology. About this Web site. Available at www.renewables-made-in-germany.com/index.php?id =50&u=570&L=1.

6. Karrie Jacobs, "San Francisco's Eco-Evolution," *Travel & Leisure* (April 2008). Available at www.travelandleisure.com/articles/san-franciscos -eco-evolution/1.

7. CNN Money. "San Francisco goes green: The city uses digital and green technology to increase urban efficiency," September 10 2009. Available at http://money.cnn.com/galleries/2009/fortune/0909/gallery.san _francisco_green_tech.fortune/index.html.

8. Foster + Parents. "World's first zero carbon, zero waste city in Abu Dhabi," 08/05/2007. Available at www.fosterandpartners.com/News/ 291/Default.aspx.

9. Chris Woodyard, "100 mpg? For 'Hypermilers,' that Sounds about Right," *USA Today*, June 27, 2008. Available at www.usatoday.com/money/autos/2008-06-23-hypermilers-saving-gas_N.htm?loc=interstitialskip.

10. Alex Frangos, "The Green House of the Future," *The Wall Street Journal*, April 27, 2009. Available at http://online.wsj.com/article/SB124050414436548553.html.

11. U.S. Department of Energy. Available at www.solardecathlon.org.

12. Walmart. "Supplier Sustainability Assessment: 15 Questions for Suppliers." Available at http://walmartstores.com/download/3863.pdf.

13. Walmart. "Sustainability Supplier Assessment FAQs." Available at http://walmartstores.com/download/4057.pdf.

14. Robert Costanza, "Toward Ecological Economy," *Chinese Journal of Population, Resources and Environment* 5(4), (2007). Available at www.cjpre.cn/Res/EnMagazine/344.pdf.

15. U.S. Green Building Council. "What LEED Is." Available at www.usgbc.org/DisplayPage.aspx?CMSPageID=1988.

16. Google. "Efficient Computer: Introduction." Available at www.google.com/corporate/green/datacenters.

17. Trucost. Available at www.trucost.com/newsweek/howTrucostWorks.php.

18. Newsweek. "Green Rankings: Our exclusive environmental ranking of America's 500 largest corporations." Available at http://greenrankings.newsweek.com.

19. UN News Center. "UN opens Biodiversity Year with plea to save world's ecosystems," January 1, 2010. Available at www.un.org/apps/news/story.asp?NewsID=33393&Cr=environment&Cr1=.

20. Ram Nidumolu, C. K. Prahalad, and M. R. Rangaswami, "Why Sustainability Is Now the Key Driver of Innovation," *Harvard Business Review*, September 1, 2009.

21. MIT. *Tech Talk*, 52(3). Available at http://web.mit.edu/newsoffice/2008/techtalk52-23.pdf.

22. Abha Bhattarai, "Six Degrees of Sustainability: The Hottest Schools for Environmental Studies," *FastCompany*. Available at www.fastcompany.com/blog/abha-bhattarai/abha-bhattarai/six-degrees-sustainability.

Chapter 13

1. Energy Information Administration. "Annual Energy Review: 2008." Available at www.eia.doe.gov/emeu/aer/pdf/aer.pdf.

2. "Kaya Identity Forecast of Future Carbon Emissions." Available at http://geoflop.uchicago.edu/forecast/docs/Projects/kaya_form_dw.html.

3. American Gas Association. "Average Residential Gas Consumption and Cost, 1996–2008." Available at www.aga.org/NR/rdonlyres/5778DC19 -E11C-4BB4-A121-F961A613B656/0/Table96.pdf.

4. CBS News. "The Bloom Box: An Energy Breakthrough?" February 18, 2010. Available at www.cbsnews.com/stories/2010/02/18/60minutes/ main6221135.shtml.

5. David Fahrenthold, "Utility Leaving U.S. Chamber Over Stance on Climate Change," *Washington Post*, September 22, 2009. Available at www.washingtonpost.com/wp-dyn/content/article/2009/09/22/ AR2009092203258.html.

Chapter 14

1. Vernon Vinge, "Signs of the Singularity," *IEEE Spectrum* (June 2008). Available at http://spectrum.ieee.org/biomedical/ethics/signs-of-the -singularity.

2. Ray Kurzweil, "Human Life: The Next Generation," *New Scientist*, September 24, 2005. Available at www.newscientist.com/article/ mg18725181.600.

3. Patricia Wen, "1 in 10 Patients Gets Drug Error," *The Boston Globe*, February 14, 2008. Available at www.boston.com/news/local/articles/ 2008/02/14/1_in_10_patients_gets_drug_error.

4. Commission of the European Communities, "Internet of Things—An Action Plan for Europe," June 18, 2009. Available at http://ec.europa .eu/information_society/policy/rfid/documents/commiot2009.pdf.

5. Google. "Flu Trends." Available at www.google.org/flutrends/about/ how.html.

6. "Robot Nurses Seen in Five Years," *Japan Times*, March 26, 2009. Available at http://search.japantimes.co.jp/cgi-bin/nb20090326a5.html.

7. Mitch Rosenberg, "The Surprising Benefits of Robots in the DC," *Supply and Demand Chain Executive* (June/July 2009). Available at www .sdcexec.com/print/Supply-and-Demand-Chain-Executive/The-Surprising -Benefits-of-Robots-in-the-DC/1$11521.

8. National Cancer Institute. Available at https://cabig.nci.nih.gov.

9. *Cancer Research* 68, 9982, December 1, 2008. doi: 10.1158/0008-5472 .CAN-08-1838. Available at http://cancerres.aacrjournals.org/cgi/content/ abstract/68/23/9982.

10. Nanoart. Available at http://nanoart.blogspot.com.

11. Project on Emerging Nanotechnologies. Available at www. nanotechproject.org.

12. K. Eric Drexler, "The Future of Nanotechnology," *Eurekalert* (2006). Available at www.eurekalert.org/context.php?context=nano&show =essays.

13. Available at http://sensorsexpo.adv100.com/sensorsexpo/v42/exhibitor _list/excatlist.cvn?id=4&p_navID=6.

14. Innovating@Sun. "Project Yggdrasil—Branching out with SunSPOTs," May 28, 2009. Available at http://blogs.sun.com/innovation/entry/ project_yggdrasil.

Chapter 15

1. Stew Magnuson, "Military Swimming in Sensors and Drowning in Data," *National Defense* (January 2010). Available at www .nationaldefensemagazine.org/archive/2010/January/Pages/Military%E2 %80%98SwimmingInSensorsandDrowninginData%E2%80%99.aspx.

2. Howard Dresner. *Profiles in Performance: Business Intelligence Journeys and the Roadmap for Change* (Hoboken, NJ: John Wiley & Sons, 2009).

3. David A.J. Axson, *The Management Mythbuster* (San Francisco: Jossey-Bass, 2010).

4. Nenshad Bardoliwalla, Stephanie Buscemi, and Denise Broady. *Driven to Perform: Risk-Averse Performance Management from Strategy through Execution should be in italics* in (Evolved Media, 2009).

5. Charles Perrow, *Normal Accidents: Living with High-Risk Technologies* (New York: Basic Books, 1984).

6. Bob Evans, "Oracle's Ellison Calls Out IBM: Why You Gotta Love the Guy," October 12, 2009. Retrieved from *Information Week*. Available at www.informationweek.com/blog/main/archives/2009/10/oracles _ellison_1.html;jsessionid=LAK3ZEKWVUKHXQE1GHOSKH4ATMY32 JVN.

7. Stephen Baker, *The Numerati* (New York: Houghton Mifflin Harcourt, 2008).

8. Steve Lohr, "For Today's Graduate, Just One Word: Statistics," *The New York Times*, August 5, 2009. Available at www.nytimes.com/2009/08/06/ technology/06stats.html?_r=1.

9. Stephen Woods, *Digital Body Language* (Danville, CA New Year Publishing LLC, 2009).

10. IBM Many Eyes. Available at http://manyeyes.alphaworks.ibm.com/ manyeyes.

11. Chris Preimesberger, "New Symantec CEO Tells Conference: 'Stop Buying Storage'," April 8, 2009. Retrieved from Eweek. Available at www.eweek.com/c/a/Data-Storage/New-Symantec-CEO-Tells -Conference-Stop-Buying-Storage-620161.

Chapter 16

1. gCaptain. "NOAA's Powerful New Supercomputers Boost U.S. Weather Forecasts," September 8, 2009. Available at http://gcaptain.com/maritime/blog/noaa%E2%80%99s-powerful-supercomputers.

Chapter 17

1. Charles Handy, *The Age of Unreason* (Boston: Harvard Business School Press, 1990).
2. IBM. "IBM Social Computing Guidelines: Blogs, wikis, social networks, virtual worlds and social media." Available at www.ibm.com/blogs/zz/en/guidelines.html.
3. Ellen McGirt, "Mr. Social: Ashton Kutcher Plans to Be the Next New-Media Mogul," *FastCompany*, December 1, 2009. Available at www.fastcompany.com/magazine/141/want-a-piece-of-this.html.
4. Paul Greenberg, *CRM at the Speed of Light: Social CRM 2.0 Strategies, Tools, and Techniques for Engaging Your Customers*, 4th ed. (New York: McGraw-Hill Osborne Media, 2009).
5. Mary Tripsas, "Everybody in the Pool of Green Innovation," *The New York Times*, October 31, 2009. Available at www.nytimes.com/2009/11/01/business/01proto.html.
6. Thomas W. Malone, *The Future of Work: How the New Order of Business Will Shape Your Organization, Your Management Style and Your Life* (Boston: Harvard Business Press, 2004).
7. Malone T. W., Laubacher R., and Dellarocas C, The Collective Intelligence Genome, Sloan Management Review, Spring 2010, 51, 3, 21-31 (Reprint No. 51303. Also available at: http://sloanreview.mit.edu/the-magazine/articles/2010/spring/51303/the-collective-intelligence-genome/#1.)
8. Socialtext. Available at www.socialtext.com.
9. Andrew McAfee, *Enterprise 2.0: New Collaborative Tools for Your Organization's Toughest Challenges* (Boston: Harvard Business School Press, 2009).
10. Andrew McAfee's Blog. Available at http://andrewmcafee.org/blog.

Chapter 18

1. Netsuite. "Research Shows Netsuite Cloud Computing Platform Saves the Equivalent of 423,000 Metric Tons of Carbon Dioxide per Year," July 15, 2009. Available at www.netsuite.com/portal/press/releases/nlpr07-15-09.shtml.

2. Mary Hayes Weier, "BMC, CA Join Salesforce.com Cloud," *Information-Week*, November 20, 2009. Available at www.informationweek.com/news/software/hosted/showArticle.jhtml?articleID=221900405&subSection=Hosted+Software.

3. Cloudbook. Available at www.cloudbook.net.

4. Charlene Li and Josh Bernoff, *Groundswell: Winning in a World Transformed by Social Technologies* (Boston: Harvard Business School Press, 2008).

Chapter 19

1. New York Times. "Salesforce.com Preaches Computing Power for Rent," March 22, 2009. Available at www.nytimes.com/2009/03/23/technology/companies/23benioff.html.

2. Marc Benioff and Caryle Adler, *Behind the Cloud: The Untold Story of How Salesforce.com Went from Idea to Billion-Dollar Company and Revolutionized an Industry* (San Francisco: Jossey-Bass, 2009).

3. CNET. "Marc Benioff taunts the awakened dinosaurs," March 17, 2008. Available at http://news.cnet.com/8301-13953_3-9895987-80.html.

4. Cloudbook. "Salesforce.com: SAP hasn't innovated," March 18 2008. Available at http://itknowledgeexchange.techtarget.com/sap-watch/salesforcecom-sap-hasnt-innovated.

5. Information Week. "CIOs are more receptive than ever to new software models—and not because they're trendy," October 10, 2009. Available at www.informationweek.com/news/software/hosted/showArticle.jhtml?articleID=220400019.

6. ZDNet. Between the Lines. "HP's Hurd: Cloud computing has its limits (especially when you face 1,000 attacks a day)," October 20, 2009. Available at http://blogs.zdnet.com/BTL/?p=26247.

7. ZDNet. "VMforce.com redefines the PaaS landscape," April 27, 2010. Available at http://blogs.zdnet.com/SAAS/?p=1071.

Chapter 20

1. Fareed Zakaria, "A Conversation with Google's Chairman and CEO," *Newsweek*, January 15, 2010. Available at www.newsweek.com/id/231117.

2. Bill Joy, "Why the Future Doesn't Need Us," *Wired* (April 2000). Available at www.wired.com/wired/archive/8.04/joy.html.

3. James H. Moor, "What Is Computer Ethics?" *Metaphilosophy* 16 (1985): 266–275.

4. Association for Computing Machinery. "ACM Code of Ethics and Professional Conduct," October 16, 1992. Available at www.acm.org/about/code-of-ethics.

5. Herman T. Tavani, *Ethics and Technology: Controversies, Questions, and Strategies for Ethical Computing* (Hoboken, NJ: John Wiley & Sons, 2010).

6. Sarah Lyall, "Turn Back. Exit Village. Truck Shortcut Hitting Barrier," *The New York Times*, December 4, 2007. Available at www.nytimes.com/2007/12/04/world/europe/04gps.html.

7. "Navigation Systems Seriously Undermine Road Safety," Research report, Stichting Onderzoek Navigatiesystemen, December 10, 2007 (English version). Available at www.stichtingonderzoeknavigatiesystemen.nl/_files/son_nav001_20071210_en_Navigation_systems_seriously_undermine_road_safety.pdf.

8. Steve Lohr, "Can Governments Till the Fields of Innovation?" *The New York Times*, June 20, 2009. Available at www.nytimes.com/2009/06/21/technology/21unboxed.html?_r=2&adxnnl=1&adxnnlx=1245582148-7qf9w20+EO1BnTTPTIa1dw.

9. "The Statistics of CCTV," *BBC News*, July 20, 2009. Available at http://news.bbc.co.uk/2/hi/uk_news/8159141.stm.

10. Electronic Frontier Foundation. Available at www.eff.org.

11. Paul Marks, "Net Piracy: The People vs the Entertainment Industry," *New Scientist*, December 3, 2009. Available at www.newscientist.com/article/mg20427375.200-net-piracy-the-people-vs-the-entertainment-industry.html.

12. Google. "Google Code of Conduct," April 08, 2009. Available at http://investor.google.com/conduct.html.

13. Nicholas Carr, "Is Google Making Us Stupid?" *The Atlantic* (July/August 2008). Available at www.theatlantic.com/doc/200807/google.

14. Nicholas Carr, *The Shallows* (New York: Norton, 2010).

15. Nicholas Carr, *Does IT Matter?* (Cambridge: Harvard Business Press, 2004).

16. Nicholas Carr, *The Big Switch* (New York: Norton, 2007).

17. B. Friedman, P. H. Kahn, Jr., J. Hagman, R. L. Severson, & B. Gill, "The Watcher and the Watched: Social Judgments about Privacy in a Public Place," *Human-Computer Interaction*, 21 (2006): 235–272.

18. P. H. Kahn, Jr., et al., "A Plasma Display Window? The Shifting Baseline Problem in a Technologically-Mediated Natural World," *Journal of Environmental Psychology* 28(2) (2008): 192–199. Available at http://mags.acm.org/interactions/20090708/?pg=8.

19. Isaac Asimov, "Runaround," *Astounding Science Fiction* (March 1942). Available at www.absoluteastronomy.com/topics/Runaround.

20. PBS. "War by remote: What do you think?" October 16, 2009. Available at www.pbs.org/wgbh/pages/frontline/digitalnation/blog/2009/10/new-video-fighting-from-afar.html.

21. Press Release, "'New' Does Not Mean 'Better' in All," Institute for Innovation and Information Productivity, January 22, 2008. Available at www.iii-p.org/news/iiip-080122.html.

22. Chloe Albanesius, "Microsoft Loses i4i Appeal, Will Alter Word Software," *PC Magazine*, December 22, 2009. Available at www.pcmag.com/article2/0,2817,2357496,00.asp.

23. "Patent Gridlock Suppresses Innovation," *The Wall Street Journal*, July 14, 2008. Available at http://online.wsj.com/article/SB121599469382949593.html.

24. Sam Williams, "A Haven for Patent Pirates," *MIT Technology Review*, February 3, 2006. Available at www.technologyreview.com/communications/16280/page1.

25. PBS. "The Autobiography of Benjamin Franklin." Available at www.earlyamerica.com/lives/franklin/chapt10.

Chapter 21

1. Kellogg School of Management, "BP's Office of the Chief Technology Officer: Driving Open Innovation through an Advocate Team," Case Number: 5-407-752, 2007.

Chapter 22

1. Gary Hamel, "Moon Shots for Management," *Harvard Business Review*, February 1, 2009. http://hbr.org/product/moon-shots-for-management/an/R0902H-PDF-ENG.

2. Mind Sports Worldwide. "Go and Mathematics," June 27 2000. Available at www.msoworld.com/mindzine/news/orient/go/special/gomath.html.

Epilogue

1. NPR. Available at www.npr.org/templates/story/story.php?storyId=121631491.

2. David Pogue, "The Pogie Awards for the Year's Best Tech Ideas," *The New York Times*, December 30, 2009. Available at www.nytimes.com/2009/12/31/technology/personaltech/31pogue.html?_r=1.

3. NPR. "NASA Discovers A Ring Around The Solar System," October 18, 2009. Available at www.npr.org/templates/story/story.php?storyId=113914677.

4. Jeff Houck, "50 Things We Know Now that We Didn't Know This Time Last Year," *Tampa Tribune*, December 28, 2009. www2.tbo.com/content /2009/dec/28/50-things-we-know-now-we-didnt-last-year.

5. Yahoo News. Available at http://in.news.yahoo.com/139/20091219/882/ twl-basic-countries-favours-kyoto-protoc.html.

About the Author

The wide coverage in the book reflects Vinnie Mirchandani's varied career as a technology advisor, industry analyst, entrepreneur, and implementation consultant.

He is president of Deal Architect Inc., a technology advisory firm that helps clients take advantage of disruptive trends such as cloud computing and business process outsourcing before they go mainstream. Between this firm and at a previous role at the technology research firm, Gartner, Inc. he has helped clients evaluate and negotiate more than $10 billion in technology contracts. *The Black Book of Outsourcing* has recognized his firm as one of its top advisory boutiques.

He also writes two well-read technology blogs. *New Florence. New Renaissance* has focused on innovation for more than five years and has cataloged more than 2,000 innovative technologies, companies, and projects. They cover more than 40 technology categories, from mobile computing to nanotechnology. His other blog, *Deal Architect*, focuses on waste in technology and was rated by *The Industry Standard* as one its favorites.

He spent five years as an analyst at Gartner assisting clients understand trends in enterprise software, systems integration, and outsourcing markets. He spent his early career at Price Waterhouse, first as an accountant and then as a technology consultant. (That division is now part of IBM.) Much of his work at Price Waterhouse was international. There and during his career since, he has traveled to nearly 50 countries.

Mirchandani has been quoted in most major technology and business publications and has presented at a wide range of industry events. He went to school at Texas Christian University, in Fort Worth, Texas, and qualified as a CPA in that state prior to his technology career. When he is not on a plane, Tampa, Florida, is now home. His wife, two teenage kids, and a beagle are frequent "sufferers" of his endless stories of technology innovation and waste.

Index

Accenture, 13, 20, 84, 115, 221, 227, 233, 252
Accman blog, 224
Adjacencies, 33, 35, 36
Adobe Connect, 231
Adobe Flash, 142–144, 150
Advanced Microwave Sounding Unit (AMSU), 205, 210, 211
Advanced Telecommunications Research Institute International (ATR), 148
Affinity Inc., 46
Agile, 239
Agile methodology, 46–49
Agresso, 116, 123, 124, 145
Agriculture, 182
Alberti, Leon Battista, 302
Alfandary, Shai, 243
Alhart, Todd, 39
Allen, Lily, 69
Altec Lansing, 109
Altimeter Group, 25, 247, 249
Amazon, 21–23, 69, 70, 160, 165, 182, 196, 202, 227, 233, 252
Amdahl, Gene, 116
American Law Institute, 21
Amgen, 125
Amish views on technology, 15
Analytics
  and black swans, 192, 194, 195
  data collection, 199, 200, 206, 207

and data management, 192, 195, 196, 201
data storage, 193, 201, 202
and data visualization tools, 193, 200, 201
decision-centric analysis, 192, 196, 197, 203
National Hurricane Center, 191, 205–211
overview, 191–193, 203
predictive, 193, 202, 203
social data, 193, 199, 200
spreadsheets, 197
unstructured data, 193, 197–199
Web data, 193, 199, 200
AND versus OR mind-set, 4, 10, 296, 297
Anderson, Chris, 74
Angrignon, Troy, 270, 271
Appirio, 217, 218, 227, 241–243, 252
Apple Inc., 4, 5, 11, 18, 53, 55, 56, 94, 100, 101, 105, 142
Apttus, 245
Argentina, 181, 297
Ariba, 19
Aristotle, 300, 302
Armstrong, Neil, 107
Armstrong, Tim, 130
Arrington, Mike, 11
Artificial intelligence (AI), 148, 175, 176, 266
As-a-Service, 117. *See also* Software-as-a-Service (SaaS)